Zephyrin Engelhardt

The Franciscans in California

Zephyrin Engelhardt

The Franciscans in California

ISBN/EAN: 9783742814647

Manufactured in Europe, USA, Canada, Australia, Japa

Cover: Foto ©Thomas Meinert / pixelio.de

Manufactured and distributed by brebook publishing software
(www.brebook.com)

Zephyrin Engelhardt

The Franciscans in California

THE

FRANCISCANS IN CALIFORNIA

BY

Fr. Zephyrin Engelhardt, O. S. F.

WITH A MAP AND NUMEROUS ILLUSTRATIONS.

CUM PERMISSU SUPERIORUM.

PRINTED AND PUBLISHED AT THE
HOLY CHILDHOOD INDIAN SCHOOL,
HARBOR SPRINGS, MICHIGAN.
1897.

To

*Father Junipero Serra and his Band of
Seraphic Laborers on the Pacific Coast
This Volume is Most Affectionately
Dedicated by their Brother in Christ—
The Author.*

Some hints concerning the pronunciation of Spanish
names and words occurring in this book.

A like *a* in *ab*.   E ike *e* in *they*.
I like the *i* in *bid*.   O like *o* in *so*.
       U like *oo* in *moon*.

C, (in America *generally*), before *i* and *e*
    has the sound of *s* in *so* or *must*, otherwise
    it has the sound of *c* in *cars*.
G, (before *e* and *i*), is sounded like *h* in *hill*;
    otherwise like *g* in *give*.
H is silent.
J is pronounced like *h* in *ball* or *hill*.
LL as in William.
ñ as *ni* opinion, or like *ny*.
Q like *k*.
X has the sound of *h* in *bat*.
Y, when it stands alone, has the sound of *ee*:
    otherwise as in English.
Z should be pronounced like *th* in *think*
    or *bath*; but it is frequently sounded as
    is English.
Ch is pronounced like *ch* in *charity*.

Other letters are sounded as in English.

PREFACE.

MUCH has been written about those noble pioneers that first introduced Christianity and civilization into California, but very little that is reliable. Ignorance and malice, through exaggeration and misstatements, have succeeded in making the old Fathers appear in so strange a light that even their friends fail to recognize them.

IT has long been the desire of their successors in the missionary field to possess accurate and more extensive information regarding the old missions and their founders. Unfortunately the Seraphic Pioneers of the West were more fond of work than of recording what they accomplished. Little they cared what later generations thought of their individual share in the wonders effected, provided the *Master* took notice of them, and marked them down in the "Book of His Remembrance".

HENCE comparatively little is on record, and much of this must be accepted upon the authority of writers not in sympathy with the aims of the missionaries.

THUS, for instance, the reader will find H. H. Bancroft frequently quoted in relating events that occurred after the year 1785; for nowhere else can the same facts and dates be found described so minutely. Bancroft, indeed, deserves well of the Franciscans, even though his bigotry and his ignorance of Catholic affairs at times make his statements extremely doubtful. However, as far as the author of this work has been able to discover, everything taken from this historian may be considered to be reliable, and all the more valuable for coming from a non-Catholic source. Where corrections were necessary the reader will find them pointed out.

Down to the year 1785 the writer has consulted the original Spanish works and compared the facts recorded with the statements of Bancroft, which were likewise borrowed from the same authors.

As to the statistics concerning the missions, the original reports of the Fathers from 1786 to 1831 were at hand. From 1831 down to about the year 1850, excepting Mission Santa Barbara, Bancroft was almost the only authority offering any accurate information.

THE author sincerely wishes that an abler pen had been selected to narrate the history of the Seraphic Pioneers of California. A more readable and entertaining work would have been the result.

VOLUMES might have been filled easily, but having in view only the rescue from oblivion of the names of the missionaries and their principal works, the author has excluded everything not bearing on the subject, even though he should appear dry and unentertaining.

HE was compelled to take this course not only because he was disinclined to write anecdotes, but also because his position at the head of a large missionary district and of an Indian industrial school made the labor of obedience and love a most arduous undertaking.

THE compiler of so important a work should have nothing else to distract his mind or to occupy his time. As the author did not enjoy this advantage it is with many misgivings he ventures to present his brethren and the lovers of history with the fruit of his research concerning the subject upon which he was directed to write.

THOUGH the spare time of four years was consumed in compiling this volume, and great pains were taken to have the figures and statements correct, under the circumstances errors were unavoidable. The reader will find a list of them at the end of the book.

As Catholic booksellers demand a heavy security, not within the reach of a poor missionary, for the publishing of a *historical* work, the author decided to utilize what facilities his school afforded and to have the volume brought out at this establishment. The printing done by unskilled, youthful hands, instructed for that purpose by himself, added immensely to the difficulties of his position, so that he feels greatly relieved to find his task at last finished. He hopes that, notwithstanding all its defects, the book may be of some value to his brethren and to historians in general.

At all events, the novelty of possessing a literary work treating about Indian missions and missionaries, written and printed at an Indian school, may reconcile the readers to the small investment which will be used for the benefit of the Indian School with whose management and maintenance the author is charged.

Even this volume will offer the readers a glimpse of what it is possible to accomplish with the 'wards' of the nation if left in charge of their natural guardian——*The Catholic Missionary.*

Contents.

PART I.

GENERAL HISTORY.

CHAPTER I.

CHAPTER II.

CHAPTER III.

CHAPTER IV.

CHAPTER V.

CHAPTER VI.

PART II.

LOCAL HISTORY.

CHAPTER I.

SAN DIEGO.

CHAPTER II.

SAN DIEGO (CONTINUED).

CHAPTER III.

SAN CARLOS.

CHAPTER IV.

SAN ANTONIO.

CHAPTER V.

SAN GABRIEL.

CHAPTER VI.

SAN GABRIEL (CONTINUED).

CHAPTER VII.

SAN LUIS OBISPO.

CHAPTER VIII.

SAN FRANCISCO.

CHAPTER IX.

SAN FRANCISCO (CONTINUED).

- xii -

CHAPTER XIX.
SAN JOSE.

CHAPTER XX.
SAN JUAN BAUTISTA.

CHAPTER XXI.
SAN MIGUEL.

CHAPTER XXII.
SAN FERNANDO.

CHAPTER XXIII.
SAN LUIS REY.

LIST OF ILLUSTRATIONS.

THE OLD
FRANCISCAN
MISSIONS
IN
CALIFORNIA.

PART I.

GENERAL HISTORY.

CHAPTER I.

THE FIRST MISSIONARIES—VARIOUS EXPEDITIONS—EXPULSION OF THE JESU-
ITS—FRANCISCANS IN CHARGE OF THE LOWER CALIFORNIA MISSIONS—
MISSIONS AND THEIR MISSIONARIES—MISSION TEMPORALITIES—DON
JOSÉ GALVEZ—DISHONESTY OF THE COMISIONADOS—PROCLAMATION OF
DON GALVEZ—PLANS FOR MISSIONS IN UPPER CALIFORNIA—DEPARTURE
OF THE VESSELS—THE LAND EXPEDITIONS—FR. JUNIPERO SERRA—SAN
FERNANDO DE VELICATA.

THE sons of St. Francis for the first time set foot
on California soil in 1596, just three hundred years
ago. In the year before, Viceroy Monterey of Mexico
ordered an expedition to set out for the purpose of
exploring the northwestern coast, and he requested a
number of Franciscans to accompany the fleet, in
order to spread the light of the Gospel in the regions that might be discovered. Five religious of the
Order were accordingly chosen for this work. These
seraphic pioneers were Fr. Francisco de Balda, as
commissary, Fathers Diego de Perdomo, Bernardino
de Zamudio, Antonio Tello, of the province of Xalisco, Nicolás de Arabia, or Sarabia, and the lay-
brother Cristóbal Lopez, (1)

---

(1) Zarate Salmeron, 'Relaciones,' no 12. Salmeron does not mention Father Antonio Tello; but the names as given above are found in the 'Intro-
duccion Bibliografica,' pag. XIX of the 'Cronica Miscelanea de la Santa
Provincia de Xalisco (Jalisco), libro II. Guadalajara 1891. Fr. Tello is the
author of the 'Historia de Xalisco y de la Nueva Vizcaya,' and of the
'Cron. Misc. de la S. Prov. de Xalisco,' publ. in 1653. Vide also 'Coleccion
de doc. para la Hist. de Mexico,' tom. 2.

UNDER the command of Sebastian Vizcaino the fleet sailed from Acapulco about the beginning of 1596. On reaching the port of Mazatlan the explorers landed to take in fresh water. Here, during the seven days that were passed in the neighborhood, forty of the soldiers seized the opportunity to desert their commander. The Indians were found to be very numerous, but entirely devoid of clothing. Father Balda meanwhile grew sick, causing him to remain behind when the fleet passed on to another port. Eight days were spent there among the natives who received the white stangers very hospitably. In one port the Fathers remained for fifteen days; and in the district of what is now La Paz the expedition continued for two months. The missionaries at this place asked the Indians to bring their children so that they might be taught the knowledge of God and His works. The request was readily granted. Unfortunately the work of the Fathers was interrupted by orders from the commander, who, seeing his provisions run low, and finding the country unequal to support his men, determined to abandon the undertaking. The Indians had meanwhile grown very much attached to the religious whom they earnestly entreated to remain with them, whereas the soldiers were as heartily disliked. The Fathers, however, had no choice in the matter, and reluctantly accompanied the fleet homeward. (2)

THUS ended the first attempt to Christianize the natives of Lower California. "Hence to the children of St. Francis," says Gleeson, "must be granted the honor of having first unfurled the banner of our holy religion on California soil." (3)

SIX years later, 1608, Vizcaino headed another expedition for a like object. He was this time accompanied by three Discalced Carmelites. After putting

(2) Salmeron, 'Relaciones,' 13-14.   (3) The Catholic Church in California by Rev. W. Gleeson, vol. I, p. 79.

into various ports along the coast, the fleet entered
San Miguel Bay on the tenth of November. On landing Vizcaino named the bay San Diego de Alcalá
(St. Didacus), doubtless with reference to his flagship,
and also to the day, November 12th, which is dedicated to San Diego. From here the expedition proceeded north to about the forty-third degree of latitude, and then returned to Mexico. (4)

In the year 1008, Francisco Luzivilla fitted out an
expedition at his own expense, with a view of forming a colony on the coast. Two Franciscan Fathers,
Juan Caranco and Juan Ramirez, accompanied him.
Whilst these religious exerted themselves in trying to
instruct the natives, Luzivilla organized a little colony
at Puerto de la Paz; but the difficulties proved so
great that he had to abandon the project. (5)

The last expedition undertaken at the expense of
the government set out in 1683. It was attended by
three Jesuit Fathers, Eusebio Kino (Kuehn), Juan
Bautista Copart, and Pedro Matias Goni. The expedition landed on the 2d of June, 1683, and remained
till September 1685. During this time four hundred
adults were prepared for baptism; but as the missionaries were unable to remain longer than the commander and his crew, none of the Indians, except
those in danger of death, were received into the
Church. Twelve years later, the country was entrusted to the same Fathers, and the missions were regularly established and continued until 1768, when an
ungreatful Masonic government expelled the devoted
missionaries. (6)

In June, 1767, on the enforcement of the decree of
expulsion against the Jesuits in Mexico, the California missions were offered to the apostolic college of
San Fernando, Mexico, of which Father José García

(4) Salmeron. 'Relaciones', 30-32.   (5) Glesson. I, 52-3.
(6) Ibid. I, 84.

was then guardian. The Sonora missions were transferred to the Franciscan colleges of Querétaro and Jalisco. The trust was accepted, and arrangements were made by the college to have seven Fathers set out from San Fernando who were to be joined by five others taken from the Sierra Gorda missions under Fr. Junípero Serra, then among the Indians in the Sierra Gorda district, However, nine religious were finally selected at the college, as it was not certain that five Fathers could be spared in the Sierra Gorda. The nine missionaries were: Father Junípero Serra, originally from the Franciscan province of Mallorca, doctor of theology, commissary of the Holy Office, and president or superior of the missions in California; Francisco Palou of the same province; Juan Moran of the province of the Immaculate Conception; Antonio Martínez of the province of Burgos; Juan Ignacio Gaston of the same province; Fernando Parron of the province of Estremadura; Juan Sancho de la Torre of the province of Mallorca; Francisco Gomez of the province of the Immaculate Conception; and Andrés Villumbrales of the same province. (7)

BEFORE taking leave the missionaries asked the Father Guardian's blessing. He gave it with fervor and said: "Go. Fathers, and dearly beloved Brethren, with the blessing of God and of our holy Father St. Francis, to labor in the mysterious vineyard of California which our Catholic sovereign has confided to our care. Go, with confidence along with your superior, the Fr. Lector Junípero, whom I appoint president of you all and of all the missions. I need not say anything more than that you should obey him as you obey me; and now farewell with God.' He could proceed no further. Fr. Junípero, too, was so affected that he could not utter a syllable. The little band of

(7) Palou, 'Noticias', I, 1-8; 'Vida del Padre Junípero Serra,' p. 52-55.

missionaries left the college of San Fernando, Mexico, for their new field of labor on the same day, July 14th, 1767. After a journey which lasted thirty-nine days, they reached Tepic on the 21st of August. They were we'come l by the Franciscans of the province of Jalisco, who possessed a hospice at this place. (8)

FINDING the newly appointed governor of California, Gaspar de Portolá, with fifty men ready to sail, Fathers Palou and Gaston, at the request of Fr. Junípero, set out with him on August 24th; but the ship was driven back to Matanchel on September 5th. Fr. Palou relates that when the tempest was at its height, and all expected to perish, Fr. Gaston cast some moss from the famous Cross of Tepic upon the raging billows, and Fr. Palou vowed to offer up a High Mass if they were saved, whereupon the storm instantly subsided. The vow was fervently fulfilled as soon as the hospice was reached, the entire crew of the ship assisting at the ceremonies. (9)

MEANWHILE the other Fathers from the Sierra Gorda had arrived. These five religious were José Murguía, Juan Ramos de Lora, Juan Crespi, Miguel Campa y Cos, and Fermin Francisco Lazuen. At the request of the missionaries the college sent two more Fathers, who reached Tepic on the last day of December. They were Dionisio Bastera and Juan de Medina Veytia. (10)

THERE were now sixteen religious ready to take charge of as many missions on the peninsula of California. During, their enforced stay at Tepic the Fathers did not remain idle, but conducted missions in the neighboring districts. At last, on the 14th of March, 1768, they were able to embark at San Blas, on the Concepcion, the same ship that had brought

(8) Vida, 55; Noticias, I, 3.   (9) Noticias, I, 4-6.
(10) Noticias, I, 7, 12.

the victims of Masonic hatred, the Jesuits, from
Lower California. The sixteen Franciscans reached
Loreto, the principal mission, on April 1st after
nightfall. On the following day, which was Holy Saturday, Fr. Junípero Serra and his companions for
the first time walked upon the soil of California.
They at once proceeded to the church of Our Lady
of Loreto, the Patroness of the peninsula, in order to
give thanks for their safe arrival. (11)

On Easter Sunday, and likewise on Monday and
Tuesday, High Mass was sung by Father Serra in
honor of Our Lady of Loreto in thanksgiving for
the safe arrival of the missionaries. After Mass the
Fr. President made an address to the assembled
multitude, in which he declared that the Franciscans
would, as far as possible, labor for the people in the
manner their predecessors had done. After the Mass
of Tuesday Fr. Junípero read his plan for the distribution of the Fathers as follows: San José del
Cabo, Father Juan Moran; Santiago de las Coras, Fr.
José Murguía; Nuestra Señora del Pilar (Todos Santos), Fr. Juan Ramos de Lora; Nuestra Señora de los
Dolores (La Pasion), Fr. Francisco Gomez; San Luis
Gonzaga; Fr. Andrés Villahumbrales (Villumbrales);
San Francisco Javier, Fr. Francisco Palou; San José

(11) Noticias, I, 8-17; Vida, 56; Banc., Hist. North M. S. Vol. I, p. 484.
The event is perpetuated in the "Libros de Mision," in the handwriting of
Father Junípero in the following words: "Dia dos de Abril, Sabado de
Gloria de este año 1708 entramos a esta Mission y Real Presidio de Loreto, cabezera de esta Peninsula de California diez y seis Religiosos sacerdo-
tes, predicatores, misioneros apostolicos del Colegio de Propaganda Fide
de Mexico, del orden serafico, enviados de nuestros Prelados padres Mini-
tros de todas las misiones de esta Provincia, que en nombre de su Magas-
tad Catolica, (q. Dios gñe), por decreto del Exemo Sr. Marques de Croix
Virrey y Capitan General de esta Nueva España. se pusieron a cargo del
dho apostolico colegio expelidos de este Peninsula y demas Dominios del
Catholico Monarca. pr motivos a su Magd reservados, los P. P. de la Sagrada Compañia de Jesus, y habiendo yo. el infra escripto Presidente de
dhos Religiosos, por el expresado Colegio resuelto quedarme a administrar
por mi mismo esta Mision y Real Presidio en compañia do P. Fr. Fernando Parson, uno de los de numo y colegio, asigné a las demas Misiones los
Ministros en esta forma." Then follow the names of the Fathers.

Comomdú, Fr. Antonio Martínez; Purisima Concepcion de Cadegomo, Fr. Juan Sancho de la Torre; Santa Rosalía de Mulegé, Fr. Juan Gaston; San Ignacio, Fr. Miguel de la Campa y Cos; Santa Gertrudis, Fr. Dionisio Basterra; San Francisco de Borja, Fr. Francisco Fermin Lazuen; Santa Maria de los Angeles, Fr. Juan Medina Veytia; Nuestra Señora de Loreto, Fathers Junípero Serra and Juan Fernando Parron. (12)

ALL the Fathers were pleased with the ordinances of their superior, and each one thanked God for the field assigned him. On the following day Fr. Serra once more fervently exhorted them to labor in the Lord's vineyard with credit to their apostolic college. Each Father then agreed to say twenty Holy Masses on hearing of the death of any one of their number, and nine Masses for the repose of the soul of any of the Fathers attached to the college of Querétaro.

LEAVING Fr. Serra and his companion, Fr. Juan Fernando Parron, at Loreto, the fourteen religious assigned to the other missions departed together for San Javier, where they were hospitably received by the chaplain of the royal troops, the Rev. Pedro Fernandez, on the evening of the eighth of April After resting a day the missionaries started for their respective stations on the tenth, five going south and eight travelling north, while Fr. Palou remained at San Javier. On reaching his mission each Father received from the military comisionado the church with its belongings, together with the dwelling and household furniture. An inventory was drawn up in duplicate of all the property so received, and signed by the missionary and comisionado. One of these certificates was preserved in the archives of each mission, the other was sent to the Fr. President, who forwarded all the documents to the college of San

Fernando, Mexico. At Loreto only the church and sacristy was turned over to the missionaries, but not the dwelling; for the latter, as well as all the temporal affairs, remained in charge of the governor with whom the two Fathers were obliged to board. The missionaries at all the other missions found themselves in a like predicament; they were furnished with board by the comisionados, and their functions did not extend beyond matters purely ecclesiatsical. (13)

"The evils of such a system," says the Protestant historian H. H. Bancroft, "had been clearly foreseen. The comisionados could not be expected to take a very deep interest in the welfare of the country, the prosperity of the missions, or the comfort of the natives. They lacked skill, interest, and conscience for an ecclesiastical administration of the temporalities. The Fathers could no longer attract the pagans by gifts or clothing; and their loss of power caused the neophytes to have less respect for them than for the Jesuits.....It has long since been demonstrated impossible to reach the heart of the savage through abstract ideas of morality and elevation of character. A religion, in order to find favor in his eyes, must first meet some of his material requirements. If it is good, it will clothe him better and feed him better, for this to him is the chief good in life.....The result of depriving the Franciscans of the temporal affairs of the missions justified the Fr. President's remonstrances. The missions rapidly declined under the new missionaries, and it soon became clear that, unless the spiritual and the temporal authority were reunited, a few years would suffice to undo all that the Jesuits had accomplished." (14)

The viceroy, to whom the whole matter had been referred, left it to the decision of Don José Galvez,

(13) Noticias. I, 21-24. (14) Banc., Hist, N. M. St., I, 455; Hist. Nat. Rac. I, 39.

who was on his way to the Jalisco coast to embark
for the peninsula. Galvez had come to Mexico in
1765 as visitador general of New Spain. He was invested by King Charles III, with almost absolute
powers to investigate and reform the administration
of the government in its different branches. Independent of the viceroy in many respects, only nominally
subordinate in others, he was to all intents the highest authority in New Spain. In addition to his power and independence, Galvez was also remarkable for
his practical good sense, business ability, untiring
energy, and disregard of all routine formalities that
stood in his way.

THE visitador general arrived at Cerralvo Island
the 6th of July, and proceeded to the mining districts of Santa Ana. The whole province was soon
in a flutter over the investigations and decrees of
the great man. He immediately called for exact reports from the missionary and comisionado of each
mission. Then he made a tour of investigation in the
south, beginning with San José del Cabo where he
ordered a church to be erected. Galvez soon detected
the evils and abuses of the existing system. The remedy was radical, and promptly applied. On August
12th he issued a decree ordering the comisionados
to turn over all mission property to the missionaries,
and at the same time to send in their accounts
through the Fathers, who were to examine and sign
them. Fr. Palou published two extracts of letters in
which the visitador general expressed his indignation
at the rascalities of the comisionados; yet it appears
that all escaped punishment at the intercession of
the missionaries. (15)

THE indefatigable visitador next turned his attention to the forming of settlements, and the improvement of the condition in which he found the In-

(15) Noticias. I, 24-29; Vida, 57; Banc., Hist. Cal. I, 115.

dians. If his reformatory measures were not always successful, it was not owing to any lack of energy or sagacity on the part of their author. Lands and natives were found to be very unequally divided among the missions, and many changes were made in order to remedy the disproportion. Dolores and San Luis, for want of sufficient land and water, were abandoned, and their neophytes transferred to Todos Santos, whose few people were sent to Santiago. Surplus families of San Javier were added to San José del Cabo, while the surplus of Guadalupe and Santa Gertrudis were transferred to San José Comundú and Purisima. Certain transfers of northern families, for the relief of poor missions like Borja and Santa Maria, were abandoned on account of the reluctance of the Indians to leave their homes. (16)

THERE was ample room, it appears, for the visitador's good offices. In a proclamation of November 28d, 1768, he expresses his surprise and disappointment at the state of affairs in which he found the peninsula establishments, after they had been in charge of the secular comisionados but a short while. After all the laws made and the moneys granted, he expected to find thriving settlements; but instead of these he finds mere haciendas de campo, or farms, with houses for the Fathers, soldiers, and servants only. The natives, having been withdrawn from the seashore, where they lived by fishing, go naked and are forced to wander in the mountains, living on roots and berries, often obliged to work without pay. Hence they look with dislike upon agriculture, and regard civilization as the greatest evil. Missions with fertile lands need laborers, while rancherías (17) are collected in sterile parts. No Indian is permitted to to own property. This system has reduced the population to 7,149 souls. In the proclamation, and

(16) Noticias, I, 30-33.   (17) A collection of native huts.

in a letter to Fr. Lasuen of the same date, the visitador general announces his determination to improve this state of things by settling the Indians in fixed domiciles, where they might till the soil and enjoy the fruits of their labor: and he appeals to the Fathers to help him. To prevent the missions from being overcrowded, he issued an order that no mission keep more Indians than it could feed and clothe; at the same time he sent supplies and clothing to the poorer missions in the north. Moreover Don Galvez, by employing surgeons, endeavored to check the progress of disease, especially of syphilis which was causing great havoc. Fr. Palou says that nearly all the natives at Santiago, and many at Todos Santos, were afflicted with this disease. (18)

THOUGH busy with so many different matters, the visitador did not neglect the project of extending Spanish dominion northward. After careful investigation he resolved to send four expeditions, two by land and two by water, which were to start separately, but all to unite at San Diego and then press on to Monterey. The proposed occupation of northern country was to be spiritual as well as military. The natives were to be converted, and not only presidios or garrisons, but missions also were to be established. The Fr. President was, therefore, invited to come down to Santa Ana for a personal interview with the visitador. Fr. Junípero gladly accepted the invitation and arrived at Santa Ana on October 31st, 1768. Here they agreed that three missionaries should go with the two packet-boats, and another follow in a third ship later on, whilst one Father accompanied the first land expedition, and Fr. Serra together with the governor lead the second expedition by land.

THE visitador decided to found three missions in Upper California: one at the port of San Diego, the

(18) Noticias, I, 27-28; Bancroft, Hist. N. M. States, I, 486-487.

second at Monterey, and a third, which should be
dedicated to St. Bonaventure, somewhere between
these two places. Another on the frontier of California was also decided upon, in order to facilitate
communication between the old and the new establishments. The vestments, altar vessels, ornaments,
and other church furniture for the new missions were
to be supplied by the old establishments; surplus
grain and other articles of food were to be taken as
gifts, while implements and live-stock were to be regarded as loans, and as such repaid in kind. Vestments, sacred vessels, and quantities of linen, laces,
silks, and other articles for church uses, taken from
the royal warehouse at Loreto, or collected at the
missions, were at once packed and for the most part
sent by water to the new establishments. Many of
the old vestments and church ornaments, some dating
back perhaps to this first invoice, are still preserved
in some of the missions of California. Galvez himself, from his headquarters at Santa Ana, superintended the collection at La Paz and Cape San Lucas
of everything that was to be forwarded by sea. Fr.
Fernando Parron was then sent to La Paz from Loreto to be ready to accompany the expedition by
water. (19)

BEFORE returning north, Fr. Serra visited the three
missions Todos Santos, Santiago, and San José del
Cabo. Finding that Santiago could be attended very
well by a secular priest, he turned the mission over
to Rev. Juan Antonio Baeza, who had been called
by the visitador to take charge of the place. Fr.
Junípero now returned to Loreto by land, and arrived there on the last day of January, 1769. (20)

ON the 21st of November the pious visitador general issued a proclamation naming St. Joseph pa-

(19) Vida, 58-60; Noticias, I, 83-87.   (20) Noticias, I, 88.

tron of the expeditions to Upper California. In it he referred to the driving away of the locusts from San José del Cabo in 1767, through the intercession of St. Joseph, as an additional reason for placing the Monterey expeditions under the saint's powerful protection. He moreover, requested the Fathers to celebrate Holy Mass in the saints honor on the 19th of every month, and to recite the litany of All Saints while the expeditions continued, in order to obtain divine protection through St. Joseph's intercession. To obtain the assistance of the Blessed Virgin, the protectress of all the California missions, the missionaries were to add regularly the Salve Regina in honor of the Queen of heaven. The loading of the ship San Cárlos was superintended by Don Galvez in person, the visitador often lending a hand in stowing away an unwieldy package, greatly to the encouragement and edification of his men and other witnesses. He was particularly zealous in packing for San Buenaventura, which he called *his* mission, and was delighted at having done his work more quickly than Fr. Junípero, who packed for Mission San Carlos. (21)

On the 9th of January, 1769, the San Carlos and her crew were ready. All who were to make the voyage north then confessed their sins, attended Holy Mass, received Holy Communion, and listened to a parting address of the visitador Don Galvez. He reminded them that theirs was a glorious mission, that they were going to plant the Cross among the heathens, and he charged them in the name of God, the king, and the viceroy to respect their priests, and to maintain peace and union among themselves. The Fr. President then solemnly blessed the vessel, the flag, the crew, and Fr. Parron, who was intrusted with the spiritual affairs of the com-

(21) Vide, 59-60; Banc., Hist. Cal. vol. I. 119.

pany. This ceremony over, the San Carlos put to
sea. The ship commanded by Vincente Vila had on
board sixty-two persons, including Fr. Parron, Lieutenant Pedro Fagés with twenty-five infantry men,
the engineer Miguel Constanso, and the surgeon Dr.
Prat.

WHILE the Fr. President returned to Loreto to
make preparations for the land expeditions, Don
Galvez gave his attention to the San Antonio, which
was to follow the San Carlos. After the usual cere-
monies and an exhortation by the visitador, the San
Antonio under Juan Perez sailed from Cabo de San
Lucas on the fifteenth of February, the feast of the
Translation of St. Anthony, patron of the vessel.
Besides the crew, she carried Fathers Vizcaino and
Gomez. (22)

ON March 24th the first land expedition commanded by Fernando Rivera, and composed of Fr. Crespi,
a company of twenty-five soldiers from Loreto, and a
band of forty-two native Californias, set out from
Velicatá on the northern frontier, (23)

MEANWHILE Fr. Junípero Serra was busy collecting
the necessary articles from the old missions. After
spending several days at San Javier with Fr. Palou
whom he appointed superior of the Lower California
houses, he slowly journeyed towards the north. Although suffering excruciating pains from a sore leg,
the Fr. President visited every missionary station except Santa Rosalía de Mulegó, which lay eighteen
leagues out of the road, and at last joined Governor
Portolá at Santa Maria on May fifth. Leaving this
place on the 11th, the expedition arrived at Velicatá,
where a mission was to be founded on Pentecost Sunday, May 14th. Fr. Serra at once blessed the great
cross, and named the new mission in honor of San
Fernando, the holy king of Castile and Leon. He then

(22) Vida, 60-61; Banc., Hist. Cal. 1, 130. (23) Vida, 68.

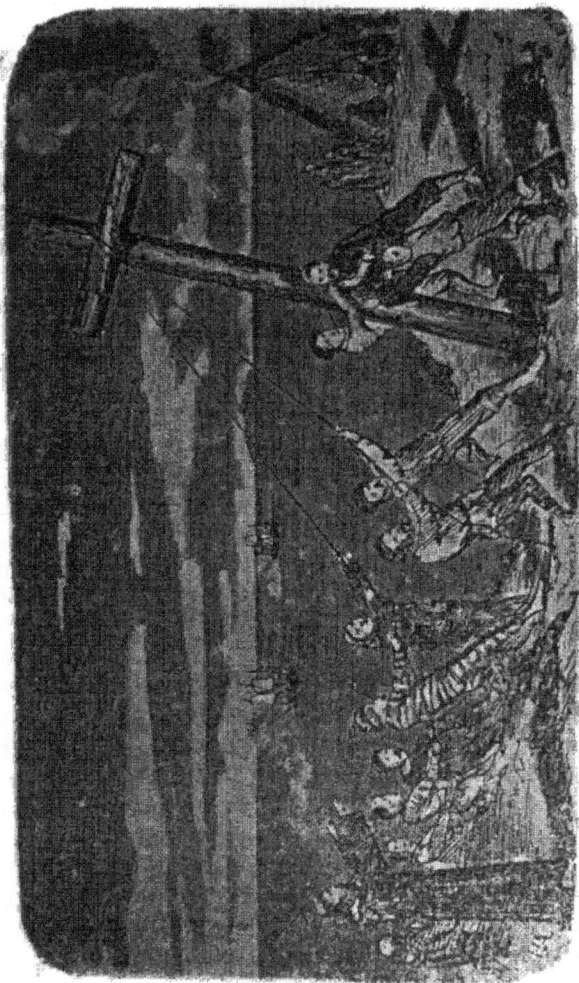

Founding A Franciscan Mission.

sang High Mass and preached on the feast of the day.
Thus Velicatá, the only mission founded by the Franciscans on the peninsula, came into existence. After
placing San Fernando in charge of Fr. Campa, Fr.
Junípero, on the next day, proceeded with the expedition on its way to Upper California.

To supply the northern missionary field with a
sufficient number of priests, at Fr. Serra's request,
the college had sent Fathers Juan Escudero, Juan
Vizcaino, and Benito Sierra to the peninsula early
in 1769. Santiago, San José del Cabo, and Loreto
were turned over to secular priests. By these arrangements six religious became available. One of
them, however, had to remain at Velicatá. (24)

WE now leave the expeditions on their way to the
north, in order to devote a few pages to the missions
and missionaries in Lower California.

CHAPTER II.

SOME CHANGES—EPIDEMICS—DEATH OF FR. MORAN—GOVERNMENT IN-
STRUCTIONS—FR. PALOU'S PROTEST—HIS PROPOSITIONS—MORE MISSION-
ARIES—GOVERNOR BARRI'S ANIMOSITY—THE FRANCISCANS CEDE LOWER
CALIFORNIA TO THE DOMINICANS—THEIR DEPARTURE—MISSION STATIS-
TICS.

AFTER concluding his labors in connection with the
expeditions to San Diego and Monterey, Don José
Galvez came to Loreto about the middle of April,
1769, accompaneid by the two Franciscan Fathers Juan Escudero and Juan Benito Sierra, who had lately
arrived from Mexico. On the 1st of May he sailed
over to Sonora, taking with him the Rev. Pedro Fer-
nendez, who had been chaplain of the presidio of
Loreto. Fr. Palou now placed Fr. Escudero in charge
of San Francisco Javier, his own mission, and sent

(24) Vida, 63-70; Noticias, I, 36-39; 51; 55; Banc., Hist. N. M. States, I.
690-691.

Benito Sierra to Mulegé. Fr. Juan Gaston went to Purisima Concepcion, left vacant by the departure of Fr. Crespi for the north. (1)

ABOUT June, 1769, a deadly epidemic broke out in the southern part of the peninsula, and raged with fury particularly at San José and Santiago. Fr. José Murguía was attacked by the disease while at San José, and had to be removed to Todos Santos. Fr. Juan Moran, then stationed at San José, attended the sick with much zeal. One day while hearing the confession of a sick member of his flock at some distance from the mission, he was himself stricken with the dreaded malady and died on the 18th of July, 1769, before the curate of Santiago could reach him. Fr. Palou was much grieved because the missionary had died without the sacraments, but he was also comforted by the knowledge of Fr. Moran's virtuous life and heroic self denial during the epidemic. San José after that was only a station of Santiago.

No sooner had this pestilence subsided than another broke out, followed by a third more fatal, causing dreadful ravages in all the missions. Over three hundred persons died at Todos Santos, while many perished in the mountains, whither they had fled for safety. Rendered desperate by the mortality, the Guaicuris about Todos Santos rose in rebellion, so that the governor had to go in person to check them. In August a ship brought to Loreto cloth to the value of $8,000, which was sent by Don Galvez as a compensation for goods taken from the missions for the establishments in Upper California. Fr. Palou at once distributed the cloth among the suffering natives. (2)

THE acting governor retired and was suceeded on October 23d, 1769, by Matías de Armona as governor

---

(1) Noticias, I, 60-65.   (2) Ibid, 68-72.

The latter brought instructions intended, so wrote
Don Galvez to Fr. Palou, to remove all difficulties
in the affairs of the peninsula. These instructions
were to the effect that whatever was needed at
Loreto, was to be furnished from the storehouse at
Loreto at Fr. Palou's request; but they required that
the native laborers at the saltworks of Carmen Island
should work for their rations without other pay, and
that the salinas should be regularly settled with
mission Indians. Fr. Palou objected to the clauses
relating to the saltworks, and declined to obey them,
for the reason that there must be some error, as
no provisions had been made for the families of the
laboring Indians. All the missionaries agreed with Fr.
Palou that they must decline to manage the temporal affairs of the missions, if the instructions were to
be carried out. A full report was forwarded to the
Father Guardian of San Fernando through Fr. Dionisio Basterra, who was retiring to Mexico on account
of ill health. He sailed on the 19th of March, 1770,
and on July 10th presented a petition which embodied all ideas of Fr. Palou. It was a sweeping reform
bill. Don Galvez accepted the petition, but it seems
he did nothing in the matter at that time.

THE following requests of Fr. Palou were subsequently granted: that the comisario, a government
official, should settle his mission accounts; that the
prices for mission products should be better regulated; that Loreto should receive the balance due at
the expulsion of the Jesuits, and whatever had been
taken since from the rancho; that the solteros, (single persons), at Santa Ana should return to their
respective missions; that the mission Indians should
not be compelled to work on the San Blas trans-
ports; besides similar demands which Fr. Palou does
not specify. (3)

(3) Noticias, I, 7-8; 8-90

In August, 1770, the news of the success of the Monterey expeditions, of the great number of Indians discovered along their march of 800 leagues, and of the many sites suitable for missions and pueblos, (4) reached the viceroy and Don Galvez at Mexico through Fr. Junípero Serra. The zealous president at the same time took occasion to plead for more missionaries supplied with everything necessary for church and farm. In his letter to the Fr. Guardian he wrote that, though one hundred religious came, there would be work for all.

Fortunately, on May 29th, shortly before these news reached the capital, forty-nine Franciscans had arrived from Spain. The viceroy and Don Galvez at once asked the guardian to sent thirty of these to California. Ten Fathers were to be put in charge of five new missions, which were to be founded in Upper California, and named for San Francisco de Asis, Santa Clara, San Gabriel Arcangel, San Antonio de Padua, and San Luis Obispo de Tolosa, respectively. Ten other religious should be placed in charge of five missions to be established between San Fernando de Velicatá and San Diego, and named respectively San Joaquin, Santa Ana, San Juan Capistrano, San Pasqual Baylon, and San Felix de Cantalicio. The ten remaining Fathers were to be distributed as assistants among the old missions having only one priest. When the Fr. Guardian communicated the viceroy's wishes to the religious at the college of San Fernando, thirty friars at once volunteered for the California missions. (5)

Having been provided with vestments and every kind of church furniture, and 400 pesos each for travelling expenses, the thirty volunteers set out from Mexico in October 1770. After reaching Tepic, they were obliged to wait till January, and some even till

---

(4) Towns or settlements. (5) Vida, 102—115; Noticias, I, 101—102; 107.

February, of the next year for an opportunity to embark for the Californias. Nor could more than ten Fathers sail on the 2d of January, when they left San Blas for Monterey in the packet-boat San Antonio. After a voyage lasting fifty-two days, they reached San Diego on March 12th. (6)

THE twenty remaining religious embarked on the San Carlos for the Lower California missions in the forepart of February, 1771, but contrary winds carried them as far south as Acupulco. Being in need of fresh water, they put into the port of Manzanilla, where they found themselves in imminent danger of shipwreck. The vessel was stranded, but by means of boats the Fathers succeeded in gaining the deserted shores of Colima. The ship was so much damaged that the captain informed the viceroy of the danger they should incur by again venturing out into the sea with her. Upon receiving this information, the viceroy directed the missionaries to reach Sinaloa by land, and thence to cross the gulf in a barge. Obeying these instructions, they made the journey of one hundred miles on foot. The hardships of this trip were so great that one of the Fathers, Leguna probably, died on the road. (7)

THE ship had meanwhile been repaired, and two Fathers, Figuer and Senra, took passage in her for the north, reaching Loreto on the 30th of August.

(6) The Fathers sailing to Monterey in the San Antonio were: Antonio Paterna, Antonio Cruzado, Francisco Dumetz, Angel Somera, Miguel Pieras or Pieroos, Buenaventura Sitjar, Domingo Juncosa, José Caballer, Luis Jaime or Jayme, and Pedro Benito Cambon. (7) The missionaries that set out with the San Carlos were the following Fathers: Juan Prestamero, Ramon Usson, Marcelino Senra, Tomás de la Peña, Vincente Imas, Francisco Echasco, Martin de Palacios, Manuel Lago, Pedro Arriguibar, José Leguna, Gregorio Amurrio, Juan Figuer, Vincente Fuster, Antonio Linares, and Vincente Santa Maria, only fifteen as given in Palou, Noticias I, p. 103—104. Father Juan Antonio coming at another time reached Cerralvo on the 22d of March. Palou Noticias I, 136, says that both, Fr. José Herrera and Fr. Francisco Tejada, remained at Tepic on account of sickness. Herrera, it seems, never reached California. Vida, 101—115; Noticias I, 101—103; 107; Banc. Hist. N. M. St. I, 722.

The others chose to go by land rather than to trust themselves to an unseaworthy vessel. They were, however, picked up by the packet-boat Concepcion, and landed at Loreto on November 24th. Fr. Palou was absent at the time, but, as soon as he heard of the arrival of the religious, he wrote to the new governor, and asked him to send the necessary guards for at least two new missions, which were to be founded as directed by the viceroy. The governor replied that he could not spare any soldiers for the present; new missions, therefore, could not be established.

AFTER reporting the state of affairs to the viceroy and to the Fr. Guardian at Mexico, Fr. Palou distributed the nineteen newcomers among the existing missions as follows:

Mission San Fernando de Velicatá—Fathers Vincente Fuster and Antonio Linares as assistants to Fr. Miguel de Campa.

Mission Santa Gertrudis—Fr. Gregorio Amurrio as companion to Fr. Juan Sancho.

Mission San Ignacio—Fr. José Legomera with Fr. Juan de Medina Veytia.

Mission Santa Rosalía de Mulegé—Fr. Pedro Arreguibar as assistant to Fr. Sierra.

Mission Guadalupe—Fr. Manuel Lago with Fr. Andrés Villaumbrales.

Mission Purisima—Fathers Francisco Echaso and Martin Palacios to assist Fr. Gaston.

Mission San José Comundú—Fathers Juan Prestamero, Tomás de la Peña, and Vincente Imas.

Mission San Javier—Fr. Ramon Usson as companion to Fr. Fernando Parron.

Mission Loreto—Fr. Vincente Santa Maria with Fr. José Murguía.

Mission Todos Santos—Fr. Miguel Sanchez as companion to Fr. Marcelino Senra.

Missions Santiago and San José del Cabo—Fr. Villuendas as companion to Fr. Juan Antonio Riobon.

Fr. Francisco Javier Tejada, who had been left sick
at Tepic, did not arrive until April 1772. Fathers
Juan Figuer and José Leguna are not named in
the distribution of the missionaries. (8)

Fr. Palou now sent to Governor Barri a formal
renunciation of Mission Todos Santos. He recommended that the few and incorrigibly bad Indians be
distributed among other missions, and also suggested a
transfer of Spanish settlers from Santa Ana to Todos
Santos. The governor positively refused to accept the
renunciation until he could consult the viceroy. "This
refusal made it evident", says Bancroft, "that the
captious ruler would oppose the Fathers at every
point. Governor Barri, who had come with his family
to Loreto in April, at first seemed disposed to act in
harmony with Fr Palou, the president, or superi-
or, of the Lower California missions; but this state of
things, unfortunately, did not last long, and Barri
turned out to be the bitterest enemy of the Franciscans in California." (9)

Before this occurrence, Fr. Palou, who was in the
northern part of the peninsula making preparations
for new establishments, had been notified by Governor Barri of a revolt at Todos Santos, and requested
to return. The revolt was not serious in itself, as Fr.
Palou had concluded, but it led to unpleasant conse-
quences. The Indians had complained of the cruelty
of the majordomo. Such complaints from the Guaicuris were frequent, and generally unfounded, hence
the Fr. President refused to act in the matter. Then
the Indians, instigated by some shrewd malcontents,
appealed to the governor, including in their complaint charges against the Father, notably that
he denied the governor's right to interfere in the
mission management. Barri, a hotheaded and stub-

(8) Vid i, 116-117, Noticia, I, 135-133; Bancroft, Hist. N. M. St. I, 732.
(9) Noticias I, 139-141; Banc, Hist. N. M. St, I, 731-732.

born man, was very angry at this; nor could any explanation from Fr. Palou mollify his wrath. Thus began a feud which increased in bitterness until the governor, contrary to all the regulations, openly ordered the missionaries to cofinne themselves to preaching, teaching, and saying Mass, and not to meddle with the temporalities, nor with the punishment of the Indians. It was a great triumph for the unruly among the natives, who flocked to Barri with complaints on all occasions. They became insolent and independent, and wasted the property until it seemed the evil days of the comisionades had returned. Filled with indignation, Fr. Palou wrote a letter to the Fr. Guardian, and entreated him to appeal to the viceroy. The letter was sent through Fr. Juan Escudero, who sailed on the 25th of October, and reached Mexico in December 1771.

Fr. Rafael Verger, was then guardian of the college of San Fernando. On learning the state of affairs, he, together with the discretory, prepared a long memorial for the viceroy in behalf of the California missions. The document, quoted at length by Fr. Palou on pages 127-180 of his Noticias, contained eighteen different requests. Clause sixteen is especially notable. It requested that the Dominican Fathers, or others, take charge of four missions in the southern part of the peninsula, namely: San José del Cabo, Santiago de las Coras, Todos Santos, and San Javier, besides three missions in the north, namely: La Purisima Concepcion, Nuestra Señora de Guadalupe, and Santa Rosalía de Mulegé. By this arrangement the Franciscans retained control of missions Loreto, San José Comundú, San Ignacio, Santa Gertrudis, and San Borja. The memorial, though answered in a favorable tone by Viceroy Bucareli, produced no direct or immediate results. (10)

---

(10) Noticias I, 116-180; Banc, Hist. North Mex. St. I, 721; Vida, 117-119.

In his report of February 12, 1772, Fr. Palou, in answer to an inquiry whether or not "Armona's (11) orders for the good of the Indians were carried out," says: "Armona's name cannot even be mentioned in the presence of Governor Barri, who declares that he came to ruin the peninsula. In the presence of Fr. Escudero he declared that he did not wish to be in harmony with me." Something should be done to prevent his interference with missionary efforts in behalf of the Indians. (12)

THE Indians were not slow to take advantage of this unfortunate state of things: they became more insolent and refractory every day; and more than once open rebellion was barely averted. Having exhausted his ingenuity in seeking a remedy, Fr. Palou, at last, sent Fr. Juan Ramos de Lora to Mexico to lay the whole matter before the viceroy. Fr. Ramos departed in January 1772, and reached the capital in March. At this time the question of ceding a part of the missions in Lower California to the Dominicans, as recommended by the Franciscans, was under discussion, and the arrival of Fr. Ramos with his grievances contributed materially to the final surrender of the entire peninsula to the Dominican Order. Under date of June 1st, 1771, the Fr. Guardian requested Fr. Palou to send a full report regarding the spiritual and the temporal affairs of each mission in Lower California. This order of his superior did not reach Fr. Palou until the 18th of January, 1772, shortly after Fr. Ramos had gone to Mexico. (13)

FR. Palou's report, which was dated February 12th, 1772, and covers 52 pages of the Noticias, contained a sketch of the history, location, and condition of each establishment; also a summary of the past grievances and necessary reforms. The registered popula-

(11) Former governor of California.   (12) Noticias I, 188-189.
(13) Noticias, I, 141-143; Vida, 118

tion, a large part wandering in the mountains, was
5,074 in thirteen missions. San Francisco de Borja
with 1,579 souls was the largest; San José del Cabo
with fifty the smallest. Most of the mission cattle
were running wild. (14)

Long, however, before this document reached its
destination, the missions had been ceded to the Dominicans. The Franciscan guardian of San Fernando,
Fr. Rafael Verger, and the Dominican vicar-general,
Fr. Juan Pedro de Iriarte, signed a concordato, or
agreement, on April 7th, 1772, which was witnessed
by Viceroy Bucareli on the 80th of the same month.
In general terms it gave to the Dominican Order the
entire peninsula, with all its missions, up to San
Juan de Diós, a point just below San Diego; while
the Franciscans were to retain San Diego and the
missions north of that place, with the privilege of
extending their establishments without limit to the
north and northwest. (15)

In a letter of June 10th, in which the Fr. Guardian
announced the result, he directed Fr. Palou, to
surrender the property and to send the Fathers back
to the college, except Fathers Senra, Murguía, Usson,
and Figuer, who were destined for the Monterey missions. Fr. Palou also was permitted to join the Fathers in the north, if he wished to do so. The news
reached California on the 81st of August, and was
welcomed by the ringing of bells and a High Mass of
thanksgiving. Fr. Palou instructed the religious at the
various missions to prepare their accounts, in order to
be ready for the transfer when their "successors and
brothers" should arrive. Meanwhile, one was to remain at each mission, and the rest were to come to
Loreto. On October 14th ten Dominicans, nine priests
and one lay-brother, arrived on the ship Lauretana
and were hospitably received by the Franciscans.

(14) Noticias, I, 141-196.   (15) Noticias, I, 196-215;   Vida, 118.

They, however, declined to accept the surrender of the missions until their superior, Fr. Iriarte, should arrive. Six Franciscans, nevertheless, departed on the 19th of October. These were: Fathers Martínez, Echaso, Somera, Palacios, Imas, and Arreguibar. Two more, Fernando Parron and Manuel Lago, embarked for Mexico on the 2d of December. (16)

MEANWHILE the rest of the Dominicans who had sailed from San Blas were shipwrecked, and suffered terribly both on land and by sea. Four of them died, including Fr. Iriarte; nor did the remainder arrive at Loreto until May 12th, 1773. On the death of Fr. Iriarte, Fr. Vincente Mora had become president of the Dominican missionaries in Lower California, but he declined to accept the missions formally until he should be confirmed in his office. He consented to receive the property, however, and to begin work on the inventories. The Franciscan Fathers insisted on the greatest care in taking the accounts, because the vindictive Barri had accused them of plundering the missions. The result showed that all was in perfect order, and that the mission funds and dues had increased from $8,900 to $10,040 since the expulsion of the Jesuits.

WHEN the ceremonies of thanksgiving and welcome had been concluded, the Dominicans were sent to their respective missions, and it only remained for Fr. Palou to attend to a few matters preparatory to his departure for Alta California, whither he had resolved to go with seven of his brother missionaries; but he met with opposition in completing his arrangements. Barri prevented him from collecting some cattle which by the viceroy's order were to be furnished for the north; and, though Fr. Palou had authority to take twenty-five Indian families for Monterey, he could barely obtain half that number. In

(16) Noticia, 1, 213-30.

May, 1773, Fr. Palou with ten Dominicans left for Mulegé. Later on he visited and delivered to them the missions of Guadalupe, San Ignacio, Santa Gertrudis, Borja, Santa Maria, and San Fernando. Then he started with six companions for San Diego, where he arrived at the end of August. Fr. Cambon was left at San Fernando de Velicatá in charge of certain church property which had been taken from the old missions for the new foundations by order of Don Galvez. Governor Barri saw here a last opportunity to annoy the Franciscans. Insisting that the property had been stolen, he ordered Lieutenant Velasquez in command at Velicatá not to permit its removal. Fr. Cambon could do nothing but report this fresh annoyance. In July 1774, an order finally came from the viceroy which directed that the goods should be forwarded without delay, but it was nearly a year before the last of the articles were delivered. (17)

The Franciscans now had no further interest of importance in the peninsula missions. Six Fathers, therefore, departed for Mexico on the Concepcion May 27th, 177?. These Fathes were: Juan Gaston, Juan Sancho, Vincente Santa Maria, Juan Antonio Rioboo, Antonio Linares, and Francisco Javier Tejada. The Fathers Andrés Villaumbrales and Benito Sierra, together with the Sindico Manuel García Morales, sailed in another vessel on June 15th to touch at Cerralvo for the missionaries in the south of the peninsula. Only Fr. Campa and Fr. Juan Medina Veytia still remained in Lower California for awhile longer to wind up the affairs of their brethren. (18)

---

(17) Noticias, I, 2?1-230.   (18) Ibid. 231-232.

CHAPTER III.

ACCORDING to Fr. Francisco Palou's report, dated Loreto February, 12th, 1772, the Franciscan missions in Lower California, at the time of the transfer, were the following from south to north:

1. *Mission de San Jose del Cabo.* This mission was founded in 1780 by the Jesuit Father Nicolas Tamascal, who with Fr. Santiago later on suffered death at the hands of the Indians. Towards the close of April 1768 the place was given in charge of the Franciscan Fr. Juan Moran, who labored there until his death fourteen months after. Fr. Juan Rioboo succeeded him. There were but fifty Indians left in 1772. (1)

2. *Mission de Santiago de Las Coras.* The Jesuit Fathers founded this mission about 1720, and continued there until their expulsion in 1768. The Franciscan Fr. José Murguía, was appointed missionary in April 1768. In April 1769 a secular priest, Rev Fr. Bæza, began to administer the affairs of the new curacy until November 1770, when the mission was again turned over to the Franciscans, and Fr Francisco Villuendas became the missionary. Bancroft claims that Fr. Juan Rioboo was stationed at Santiago with Fr. Villuendas. Owing to an epidemic which had carried away a great number of Indians, there remained, on the departure of the Franciscans in 1772, only seventy souls,. (2)

3. *Mission de Nuestra Senora del Pilar, or Todos Santos.* This mission was established in 1719 at a

(1) Noti las, I, 144-146. (2) Ibid. 146-147.

place called La Paz. The Jesuits were in charge until their departure in 1768, when the Franciscans appeared. Fr. Juan Ramos de Lora was appointed the first missionary. He labored assiduously until January 1772, when he was sent to Mexico on a mission to the government. Fathers Marcelino Senra and Miguel Sanchez succeeded him. When these Fathers departed there were still 170 Indians at the mission or in the neighborhood. (3)

4. *Mission de San Francisco Javier.* The Jesuit Fathers remained in charge of San Javier from the time of its foundation October 1699, to 1768, when, on April 6th, Fr. Francisco Palou was appointed for the place by Fr. Junípero. From that day until November 24, 1771, eighty-three children were baptized, 115 Indians buried, and 14 couples were married. Three stations were attached to San Javier without either chapels or dwellings for the missionary. Fathers Fernando Parron and Ramon Usson were stationed at this mission when the transfer took place. On their departure 212 Indians resided in the neighborhood. (4)

5. *Mission de Nuestra Senora de Loreto.* Fr. Juan Maria de Salvatierra, of the Society of Jesus, celebrated the first Mass there on October 25th, 1697. Up to the time of their departure in February 1768, the Jesuits had baptized 646 souls; interred 1329 dead; and united 292 couples in marriage. The Franciscans succeeded the Jesuits in April 1768. Fathers Junípero Serra and Fernando Parron were the first missionaries. At the close of 1771 the Fathers had baptized 76 Indian and Spanish children, interred 181 dead, and blessed 20 marriages. Fathers Santa Maria, Palou, and Murguía were also stationed at Loreto for a time. When the Fathers departed in 1772 they left 160 Indians about the mission. (5)

---

(3) Noticias, I, 147-149.   (4) Ibid. 151-156.   (5) Ibid. 156-159.

6. Mission de San Jose de Comondu. Twenty league north was the mission of San José, established in 1708. Its first missionary was the Jesuit Father Julian de Mallorca. On the 8th of April 1708 it passed into the hands of the Franciscans, and Fr. Antonio Martínez was chosen for the place. By the 9th of December, 1771, there had been baptized 94 children, 241 dead interred, and 28 couples united in marriage. Fathers Prestamero, Peña, and Imas were stationed at Comondú, after Fr. Antonio's departure. In 1772 the natives numbered 210 souls. (6)

7. Mission de La Purisima Concepcion de Cadeyomo. La Purisima was founded by the Jesuits in 1718. In April 1768 the Franciscan Fr. Juan Crespi took charge. From that date until December 8th, 1771, thirty-nine children were baptized, 120 interments took place, and fifteen couples were married. Fathers Gaston, Echaso, and Palacios were the other missionaries of La Purisima. 168 Indians remained after the Franciscans left Lower California. (7)

8. Mission de Nuestra Senora de Guadalupe. This mission, established by the Jesuits in April 1720, passed into the hands of Fr. Juan Sancho de la Torre in April 1768. In September 1771 the records showed the names of 53 baptized children, 130 deaths, and 28 couples united in marriage. Fathers Manuel Lago and Andrés Villaumbrales succeeded Fr. Sancho, and on their departure in 1772 they left 140 natives at the mission. (8)

9. Mission de Santa Rosalia de Mulege. The Jesuits continued in charge of this mission from its establishments until January 1768, when the Franciscan Fr. Juan Gaston was appointed to succeed them. He in turn was succeeded by Fathers Sierra and Pedro Arreguibar. They had baptized 48 children by the last of August 1771, buried 118 Indians, and blessed

(6) Noticias, I. 109-101.   (7) Ibid. 102-131.   (8) Ibid. 131-136.

17 marriages. In 1772 there were 180 Indians at the mission and in the vicinity. (9)

10. *Mission de San Ignacio.* Fr. Juan Bautista Luyano of the Society of Jesus founded this mission in January 1728. In April 1768 the Franciscan Fr. Miguel de la Campa y Cos was placed in charge of San Ignacio. Fathers José Legomera and Andrés Vill-aumbrales were also stationed at this mission for a time. Up to August 1771, fifteen(?) children had been baptized, 293 Indians buried, and 68 couples joined in matrimony. At the same time there were found in and about the mission 559 natives. (10)

11. *Mission de Santa Gertrudis.* This mission, founded by the Jesuit Fathers in July 1752, was put in charge of the Franciscan Fr. Dionisio Basterra in April 1768. The other Fathers stationed there were Juan Sancho and Gregorio Amurrio. Until August 1771 they baptized 251 children, and buried 408 Indians, besides blessing 102 marriages. Santa Gertrudis was one of the most populous missions, 1,138 Indians being on the records when the report was made in August 1771. (11)

12. *Mission de San Francisco de Borja.* The Jesuits labored at this mission from its establishment in 1759 until January 1768. In May of that year the Franciscan Fr. Fermin Francisco Lasuen began his work among the Indians of San Francisco. He with Fr. Senra baptized 401 persons, of whom 26 were adults; 499 Indians were interred, and 273 couples united in marriage. Five stations were attended from Borja, namely: San Juan with 160 souls; San Francisco Regis with 92 souls; Longeles with 155 souls; Guadalupe with 256 souls; and San Ignacio with 356 souls. These stations had neither chapels nor dwellings for the priests. At Borja itself there were 184 souls. Thus, when the report was sent to Mexico,

there were 1,470 natives in charge of the Franciscans. (12)

13. Mission de Santa Maria de Los Angeles. This
was the last mission established by the Jesuits in
Lower California. They remained from the time of
its foundation, October 16th, 1766, until their expulsion by the Masonic government of Spain, at the
beginning of 1768. The Franciscan Fr. Juan de
Veytia took charge in May 1768. As there was no
church nor dwelling for the priest, he at once erected both structures of adobe, and roofed them with
tules. From his arrival to September 1771, 190 adults
and 91 childred were baptized, 108 dead buried, and
120 couples united in the bonds of matrimony. The
mission record contained the names of 523 Indians
attached to the mission in September 1771. (13)

14 Mission de San Fernando de Velicata. This
was the only mission established by the Franciscans
in Lower California. It was situated about 100
leagues south of San Diego. The first Mass, as we
have seen, was celebrated on the 15th of May, 1769.
The Fathers stationed there at different times were
Campa, Fuster, Linares, and Cambon. When Fr. Palou prepared his report on the missions in September 1771, the number of Indians baptized had reached
380, of whom 306 were adults. Only twelve Indians
had died, but 86 couples had been joined in Christian
marriage. The number of Indians remaining at the
mission was 296. (14)

THUS it will be seen that, from April 1768 to September 1771, the Franciscans in Lower California, San
José del Cabo, Santiago, and Todos Santos not included, baptized 1781 persons, of whom 581 were adults,
buried 2165 dead, and blessed 787 marriages. As the
Fathers did not leave the peninsula until the following year, the number of baptisms, including those of

(12) Noticias, I, 175-178.   (13) Ibid, 175-183.   (14) Ib'd. 182-:91.

the three missions, whose records are not extant, will easily reach 2000.

LEAVING Fr. Cambon at San Fernando de Velicatá to wind up the affairs of the mission, Fr. Palou with Fathers Pedro Benito, Cambon, Amurrio, Lasuen, Prestamero, Fuster, Murguía, and Campa, journeyed northward to join the Fathers in Upper California. On the 19th of August, 1773, a cross was placed on a high rock, five leagues above the Arroyo San Juan Bautista, and fifteen leagues below San Diego, to mark the boundary between Franciscan and Dominican territory. The cross bore the inscription; *"Division de las misiones de nuestro Padre Santo Domingo y de nuestro Padre San Francisco, ano 1773.* The *Te Deum* was then sung with extraordinary joy: "Cantamos con extraordinaria alegría el Te Deum Laudamus." (15)

---

(15) Noticias 1, 236-239. The following is an alphabetical list of the Franciscans that were at any time in Lower California from April 1768 to August 1773. Herrera, however, died before reaching the missions.

Amurio, Gregorio;
Arroguibar, Pedro;
Basterra, Dionisio;
Cambon, Pedro;
Campa y Cos, Miguel;
Crespi, Juan;
Echaso, Francisco;
Escudero, Juan;
Figuer, Juan;
Fuster, Vincente;
Gaston, Juan Ignacio;
Gomez, Francisco;
Herrera, José;
Imas, Vincente;
Lago, Manuel;
Lasuen, Firmin Francisco;
Logomera, José;
Laguna, José;
Linares, Antonio;
Martinez, Antonio;
Moran, Juan;

Murguia, José;
Palacios, Martin;
Palou, Francisco;
Parron, Fernando;
Peña, Thomas de la;
Prestamero, Juan;
Ramos de Lora, Juan;
Rioboo, Juan Antonio;
Sanchez, Miguel;
Sancho de la Torre, Juan;
Santa Maria, Vincente;
Saura, Marcelino;
Serra, Junipero;
Sierra, Juan Benito;
Somera, Angel;
Tejada, Francisco Javier;
Usson, Ramon;
Veytia, Juan de Medina;
Villaumbrales, Andrés;
Villi ond is,   ?
Vizcaino, Juan.

CHAPTER IV.

As we have seen before, the first land expedition for the establishment of missions in Upper California started out from Velicatá on March 24th, 1769, and reached San Diego on May 14th, after marching 52 days. Having placed Fr. Miguel Campa y Cos in charge of the newly-founded mission of San Fernando, Fr. Junípero Serra accompanied the second land expedition under Governor Portolá which left San Fernando on the evening of May 15th, the day after Pentecost Sunday. (1)

ON travelling three leagues, at a place called San Juan de Diós, Fr. Junípero's leg became so swollen as to indicate mortification; he could not rest a moment, so intense was the pain. The governor sug-

---

(1) Vida, page 71. It may be well to preserve the names applied by those first expeditions between Velicatá and San Diego. They are here given from Fr. Crespi's Primera Expedicion as per Bancroft. The additions in parentheses are those applied by the second or Portolá party: Velicatá to San Juan de Diós aroyo, 4.5 leagues; Santos Martires arroyo, 3 leagues; Las Palmas arroyo, 3 leagues; San Angelo de Fulgino arroyo, or Corpus Christi, 3.5 l.; Alamos arroyo, 3.5 l.; Cienegulilla 4. l.; San Ricardo (Santa Humiliana), 3 l.; San Vincente Ferrer (Sta Petronila), 3 l.; San Dionisio Rio, 3 l.; San Leon arroyo (San Andrés Hispolo), 2 l.; San Angel de Clavacio (S. Pacifico), 6 l.; S. Telmo pozo (Stos Martires), 4 l.; San Rafael (Sta Margarita), 3 l.; S. Bernabé, 5 l.; Sta Isabel (S. Guido), 3 l; Alisos arroyo (S. Nazario), 5 l.; Jacobo Ilirico (S. Antonio), 2 l.; S. Anselmo (S. Basilio), 3 l.; San Francisco Solano (S. Antonio), 1.51.; S. Jorge (S. Atonóreros), 2 l.; Stos Martires (S. Gervasio), 3 l.; S. Pedro Mártyr (Sta. Miguelina), 2 l.; Santos Apóstoles, 3 l.; Sta Cruz (Visitacion), 1 l; Sta Monica (S. Juan), 3.5 l.; S. Estanislao valle (S. Juan Bautista), 4 l.; S. Juan Bautista (San Juan Capistrano); S. Antonio valle (S. Francisco Solano), 4 l.; San Pio (San Bienvenuto), 4. l.; Stos Mártires pocita (Cárcel de S. Pedro), 3 l.; Santi Spiritu on San Diego Bay. Banc. H. N. M. St. I. 490.

gested that he go back; but the Father would not
hear of it, as he hoped to reach San Diego. "If
not", he added, "let God's will be done." The
governor now ordered a litter to be made, but the
humble Serra would not consent to be carried by human beings. In this extremity he prayed to God most
fervently for assistance; then calling a muleteer,
Juan Coronel by name, he said to him, "My son,
can you find some remedy for my sore foot and leg?"
"What remedy can I have?" Coronel replied. "I am
not a surgeon. I am only a mule-driver, and can cure
the wounds of my beasts only." "Well, my son", said
the sufferer, "imagine that I am one of those animals, and that this is one of their wounds, which
pains me so much that I cannot sleep; then apply
the same remedy you would apply to one of the
beasts." "This I will do to please you, Father," said
the man. Taking some tallow he mixed it with herbs
and applied the poultice to the sore leg of Fr. Junípero. God rewarded the humility of His servant. The
patient rested quietly that night, and the next morning, to the surprise of every one, he arose early to
recite matins and lauds, and offer up the Holy Sacrifice. (2)

THE expedition now proceeded and reached San Diego on July 1st, after a march lasting forty-six days.
The ship San Antonio had arrived there with Fathers
Juan Vizcaino and Francisco Gomez as early as April
11th, but the crew did not land, as the San Carlos,
which had sailed some time before, was not found.
The San Antonio's orders were to wait twenty days
for the San Carlos before proceeding to Monterey.
Two days before the twenty days had elapsed, that is
on the 29th of April, the long-looked for San Carlos
came in sight. The reason for its delay was that scurvy had broken out among the men and attacked ev-

(2) Vida, 72—74.

ery one, and that, in add'tion, it had missed the port
and had sailed beyond it before the mistake was discovered. The voyage had lasted 110 days. Fr. Fernando was on board all the while. On arriving at the
port of San Diego, the sick were removed to the shore
by the crew of the San Antonio, where they received
from Dr. Pratt and the three Franciscans all the
care that the circumstances allowed. The crew of the
San Antonio was now attacked by the scourge, so
that for two weeks those that were well had more
than enough to do in caring for the sick and burying
the dead. Of about ninety soldiers, sailors, and mechanics considerably less than one third survived.
Fortunately relief came by the first land expedition
under Rivera on May 14th. Fr. Crespi, who kept a
diary of the march, also arrived with Rivera.

On the arrival of Portolá and Fr. Junípero Serra,
the four expeditions were again united at San Diego.
The next day, July 2d, being the feast of the Visitation, the California pioneers, 126 in number, celebrated their reunion by a solemn Mass of thanksgiving in
honor of St. Joseph, the patron of the enterprise. On
the following day, knowing that the San Antonio
was to return at once to San Blas, Fr. Junípero hastened to write an interesting letter to Fr. Palou,
which in substance is as follows: (3)

"My dear friends,—Thanks be to God! I arrived
the day before yesterday, the first of the month, at
this truly fine and justly famous port of San Diego.
Here I found those that had set out before me, both
by land and by sea, except those that have died. Fathers Crespi, Vizcaino, Parron, and Gomez are with
me and quite well, thanks be to God! Here are also
the two vessels, the San Carlos and the San Antonio;
the former, however, without sailors, all having died
of the scurvy, except one who with the cook sur-

(3) Vida. 76-79. Bancroft Hist. California, Vol. I, 127-136.

vives. Though she sailed a month and a half later, the San Antonio reached here twenty days before the San Carlos, the latter arriving just as the former was preparing to sail for Monterey. While assisting the crew of the San Carlos, her own sailors were attacked by the malady which carried off eight of her men. In consequence of this loss, the San Antonio returns to San Blas to obtain sailors for herself and the San Carlos.

THE causes of the late arrival of San Carlos were two: the first was a lack of fresh water, which forced her men to look for water on the coast. The liquid thus obtained proved unwholesome and caused the sickness among her crew. The second cause of the delay was an error in which all shared regarding the exact location of the port of San Diego. They had supposed it to be situated in the thirty-third or thirty-fourth degree of north latitude. Strict orders had been given to Captain Villa of the San Carlos to keep out in the open sea until they should arrive at the thirty-fourth degree, and then to make for the shore in search of the port. But as the port in reality lies thirty-two degrees and thirty four minutes north latitude, the vessel moved beyond the point of her destination, making the voyage last longer than necessary. The men daily grew worse from the cold and from bad water, and they must all have perished had they not discovered the port about the time they did; for they were quite unable to lower the boat to procure fresh water, or to do anything whatever for their preservation. Fr. Fernando did everything in his power to relieve the sick, and, although he arrived much reduced in flesh, he did not grow sick, but is quite well.

OUR journey to this place was a happy one. Though I started out with a sore leg, it daily grew better, with the help of God, and now it is as sound as the other.

We have not suffered from hunger or other privations, neither have the Indian neophytes that came with us suffered any hardships, but all arrived safely and in good health. I have continued my diary and forward it to you at the first opportunity. The tract through which we passed is generally very good land, with plenty of water.. There, as well as here, the country is neither rocky nor overrun with brushwood. In some places the road was good, but the greater part of the way was bad. About midway the valleys and rivulets began to be delightful. We found vines of a large size, and in some cases quite loaded with grapes. We also found an abundance of roses which appeared to be like those of Castile. In fine, it is a good country, and very different from Old California ...We have seen immense numbers of Indians. All those on the coast contrive to make a living by means of various seeds and by fishing. The latter they carry on by means of rafts made of tules (4) in the shape of canoes, with which they venture a great way out upon the ocean. The Indians are very civil. All the males, old and young, go entirely naked; the women, however, and the female children are decently covered from their breast downward. On our whole journey we found that the Indians treated us with confidence and good will, as though they had known us all their lives; but, when we offered them any of our victuals, they invariably refused to accept them. All that these Indians cared for was clothing, and only for something of this sort would they exchange their fish or whatever else they possessed. During the whole march we found hares, rabbits, and some deer, and also multitudes of wild goats. The mission has not as yet been founded, but it will soon be done. I pray God to preserve your health and life many

---

(4) A kind of bullrushes.

years to come..... Port and intended mission of San Diego in North California, July 8d, 1769.—Fr. Junípero Serra."

On the sixth of July the San Antonio sailed for San Blas. It had already been decided that the land expedition in search of Monteroy should leave on the 14th of July, the feast of the Seraphic Doctor St. Bonaventure. The party was composed of Governor Portolá, Fathers Crespi and Gomez, two Indian neophytes from Old California as attendants, Captain Fernando Rivera y Moncada with a sergeant and twenty-six soldiers, Lieutenant Pedro Fages with seven soldiers, engineer Don Miguel Constanzo, seven muleteers, fifteen Christian Indians of Lower California, and one servant of the Governor. Everything having been arranged, Holy Mass was celebrated by each of the Fathers in honor of St. Joseph, the patron of the expedition, and in honor of St. Bonaventure, whose feast fell on that day. The party, then started northward at four o' clock in the afternoon, and travelled two leagues and a half before camping for the night. Fr. Crespi kept a diary of the march in which he noted all the interesting occurrences along the road.

After their departure there remained at San Diego Captain Villa, Dr. Pratt, the mate Canizares, Fathers Serra, Parron, and Vizcaino, a guard of eight soldiers, five convalescent Catalan volunteers, a few sick sailors, five able-bodied seamen, a carpenter, a blacksmith, three servants, and eight Lower California Indians. (5)

The 16th of July was selected for the day on which the first mission of Upper California should be founded. On that date the Church in Spain commemorates the triumph of the Cross over the Crescent in 1212; besides it was the feast of Our Lady

(5) Vida, 81-82.

of Mount Carmel. Fr. Junípero solemnly blessed the
cross which had been raised on a suitable spot facing
the port. High Mass was then sung by the Fr. Superior, and thus the mission of San Diego de Alcalá
was formally established. The place was called Cosoy
by the natives, now Old Town. (6)

SEVERAL huts were at once erected, one of which
was used as a chapel. The Indians now began to draw
near, but, as no one understood their language, little
progress could be made beyond gaining their good
will by offering them some trinkets and clothes. They
invariably refused anything in the line of food; if a
lump of sugar was put into the mouth of a child, he
would spit it out as though it were poison. Had the
natives been as greedy for food as they were for
some other articles, the Fathers and soldiers would
soon have found themselves at the verge of starva-
tion. The Indians were so eager to obtain articles of
clothing that they stole anything within their reach,
even the sheets from the beds of the sick soldiers.
One night some of the thieves were caught on board
the ship cutting sails and ropes, so that two of
the eight soldiers were obliged to guard the vessel
ever after. Persuasion, threats, and even the noise of
firearms were met with ridicule. Trusting to their
numbers and strength, and not knowing the deadly
effects of the Spanish weapons, the savages resolved
to get possession of everything by killing the Fathers
and their companions. They made the attempt on
August 12th and 13th, but withdrew when they found
resistance. On the 15th of August, the feast of the
Assumption, when Fr. Junípero had just finished cele-
brating Mass, the Indians again attacked the little camp. Fr. Fernando with two soldiers had gone
on board the ship to say Mass for the crew. Only
four soldiers remained in the company of two Fathers.

(6) Viʿla, 82-83); Glooson, II, 21.

A large party of Indians armed with bows and arrows and clubs fell upon the crippled band. The corporal and his few comrades, together with the carpenter and blacksmith, gave the alarm and fired at the enemy, who, seeing the effect of the firearms, fled, taking their dead or wounded along with them. Fr. Vizcaino, at the first alarm, raised the mat of his hut to see if any one had been killed, when his hand was pierced by an arrow. At the same time his servant, José Maria Vegerano, rushed in and fell at his feet exclaiming: "Father, absolve me; I have been mortally wounded." Fr. Vizcaino gave him absolution, and in a few moments the soul of José Maria returned to its Creator. A few days later the Indians appeared with peaceful dispositions, and asked that their wounded be received at the mission for medical treatment. (7)

A stockade was now thrown around the camp, and the natives were no more allowed to bring weapons within the mission enclosure. Safety was thus assured, but no progress made in missionary work. One youth, indeed, about fifteen years of age, daily called on the Fathers, and Fr. Junípero, especially, bestowed many favors upon him. The good Father endeavored to teach the boy a little Spanish, and after a while asked his pupil to move some of the natives to have their children baptized. One day a child was brought, and from signs made the Fathers understood that it should receive baptism. Fr. Junípero full of joy requested the corporal to act as godfather, and then, surrounded by the soldiers and Indians, proceeded with the usual ceremonies. When, however, he raised his hand to pour on the regenerating water, the Indians snatched the child away from the surprised priest, and hurried away. The soldiers wished to pursue the offenders, but Fr. Serra forbade it, and attributed the

(7) Vida, 83-85.

frustration of the baptism to his own sins. Even in subsequent years, when relating the incident, tears would fill his eyes. (8)

MEANWHILE new cases of sickness occured and death carried away eight soldiers, four sailors, one servant, and six Christian Indians, so that, when Gov. Portolá returned, only about twenty persons survived. Little wonder, then, that small progress was made in missionary work. 'Prior to April 1770, a year from the first appearance of the Spaniards, not a single neophyte was enrolled at the mission. In all the missionary annals of the northwest there is no other instant where paganism remained stubborn so long.' (9)

THERE is some explanation in the character of the Indians for this barren result of missionary efforts. "The missionaries found these natives as a nation lazy, cruel, cowardly, and covetous. Their features were thick and heavy, showing no ray of mental or moral elevation. They were contemptible physically as well as intellectually, so that Humboldt classes them as low in the scale of humanity as the inhabitants of Van Dieman's Land, who were the nearest approach in the human fabric to brute creation. Their language was a strange jargon; and here arose the first of the many obstacles that beset the paths of the Fathers. Having tenderly nursed the sick crusaders to health, the indomitable Fr. Serra and his companion set to work to acquire the Indian tongue. Then began the dawning of Christian light." (10)

---

(8) Vida, 86.   (9) Bancroft, Hist. Calif., I, 139.
(10) "Old Missions of California", p. 16.   The "Our Father" in the language of the Dieguefios, according to Mofras, Explor., Tom., II, p. 396, is as follows: "Naguo anall amai tacaguach naguanouuzp mamamulpo cayuca amaibo mamatam meyayam canaao amat amaibo quexulk echaaau naguagul fiafia chonfiaquin fiipll mefieque pachls echeyuchapo fiagua quexuic fiagualch fiacagualhpo fiamechamel anlpuch uch-gualich-culapo. Naculuch-pambo-cuchlich-culatpo-fiamat. Napulja.

CHAPTER V.

WHILE the incidents related in the preceding chapter occurred, Gov. Portolá continued his march in obedience to the instructions of the visitador-general, Don Galvez. The course and the events of the journey are fully described in a diary kept by Fr. Crespi which is still extant. From San Diego to their first halting place, where there were several springs, they encountered great numbers of hares and rabbits. Though the night was well advanced, two Indians appeared, one of whom made a long speech of which the Spaniards understood not a word; but on concluding they presented some sardines to the governor. In return they received some beads and clothes. Four days after setting out from San Diego, July 18th, the explorers reached a pleasant valley in which Mission San Luis Rey was later on built. They named the place San Juan Capistrano. A number of Indians, all naked, except the women who were modestly covered with deer skins, welcomed the strangers, and presented some nets of their own make. On the 22d they arrived at a place which they called "Los Cristianos", or "Cañada del Bautismo", because the natives here permitted two dying children to be baptized. The two happy little ones were named Maria Magdelena and Margarita. This was the first baptism administered by the Franciscans in Alta or Upper California. (1)

(1) Life cf Serra, 35; Bancroft, Hist. Cal., I, 145.

On the 24th they camped in sight of the islands of San Clemente and Santa Catalina, and reported San Pedro Bay as being five leagues distant. The 28th of July found the party encamped near a river, which they called "Temblores", because all that day and night they felt terrific shocks of earthquake. This was the Santa Ana River, or Rio Jesus de los Temblores. Here Mission San Gabriel was afterwards founded. On the second of August the expedition forded the Rio de Porciúncula, now the north branch of the San Gabriel, and stopped where the city of Los Angeles stands. On that day the children of St. Francis celebrate Portiuncula, or Our Lady of the Angels, Nuestra Señora de los Angeles, whence the city derived its name Los Angeles. (2)

On Sunday the 6th, while approaching the head of the Santa Barbara Channel, they were visited by Indians who, by marks on the sand resembling ships, conveyed the news that these vessels had been seen. The men everywhere went naked, but the women were covered with skins of deer or rabbits. Along the coast the Indian tents were larger, and each family occupied a separate hut. These dwellings were of spherical shape, and composed of a few poles stuck in the ground and brought together in a conical form, with bundles of sagebrush thrown over, leaving an opening at the top for the smoke to escape, and the air and light to enter. The Indians made canoes of pine boards, often capable of carrying ten fishermen. To work out the timber they only used tools made of flint, as iron and steel were not known to the natives. Along the channel the Spaniards obtained large quantities of fish, which was one of their chief articles of food during that portion of the journey. The country was settled by Indians who lived in towns, one of which they reached on August 14th and named Asun-

(2) Banc. Hist. Cal. I, 14?-146.

cion. It is identical in site with the modern San Buenaventura. On the 18th the expedition passed a village called Laguna de la Concepcion, in the vicinity of what is now Santa Barbara, perhaps on the exact spot, since the presidio was founded later at a place said to have been named San Joaquin de la Laguna by these first explorers. (8)

On the 27th of the same month they came upon Point Concepcion. The natives were still friendly, but poorer and less numerous north of the Point. On the 30th a large stream was crossed, probably the Rio Santa Inéz, called at its discovery Santa Rosa, and on September 1st the camp was pitched at the Laguna de San Daniel, probably at the mouth of the Rio Santa Maria. Next day Sergeant Ortega was taken ill and ten of the men began to complain of sore feet. Turning inland, not far from what is now Point San Luis, they crossed the hills by a somewhat winding course, and on the 7th encamped in the Cañada de los Osos, in the vicinity of the later San Luis Obispo. The sierra of Santa Lucía then impeded further progress, and on the 16th the travellers turned to the right and began to climb the mountain range, "con el credo en la boca", as Fr. Crespi writes, one league per day being counted good progress by infirm soldiers in such a rough country. From the 17th to the 19th the party was on the Hoya, or ravine, de la Sierra de Santa Lucía, at the headwaters of the Rio San Antonio, near where the mission of the same name was afterwards founded. On the 20th the lofty range northwest was ascended, and from the highest ridge, probably Santa Lucía Peak, the Spaniards gazed upon a boundless sea of mountains, "a sad spectacle for poor travellers worn out by the fatigues of so long a journey," sighed Fr. Crespi. The cold began to grow severe, and some of the men were disabled by

---

(3) Banc. I, 146-148.

scurvy; yet, for the glory of God, and with unfailing confidence in their great patron St. Joseph, they pressed bravely onward, after remaining four days in a little mountain cañon dedicated to the Llagas de San Francisco, or Wounds of St. Francis. Wending their way down the slope, on the 26th they came to a river, which they called San Elzeario, or Santa Delfina, believed by the Spaniards to be the Rio del Carmelo, but which was the Nacimiento. They followed its course for several days until at last they again arrived at the long-sought sea. The stream now bears the name Salinas. (4)

On October 1st the governor, the engineer, and Fr. Crespi with five soldiers climed a hill, from the top of which, Crespi says, "we saw the great entrance, and conjectured that it was the one which Cabrero Bueno puts between Point Año Nuevo and Point Pinos of Monterey." The soldiers explored Point Pinos on both sides, but did not recognize the port of Monterey for which they had come so far. Divine Providence, doubtless, blinded them that they might proceed further north and make a more interesting discovery. On the fourth of October, the feast of St. Francis, after a solemn Mass celebrated in a brushwood tent, at the mouth of the Salinas River, a meeting of all the officers and Fathers was held to deliberate on what should be done. The governor proposed going back, because Monterey had not been found where it was said to be, and provisions were becoming scarce, whilst a large number of the soldiers were disabled; but each person present being asked to express his opinion freely, the unanimous opinion of the two Franciscans and the officers was "that the journey be continued as the only expedient remaining, in the hope of finding by the favor of God the desired port of Monterey, and in it the

(4) Banc. I, 148-151.

San José to supply our needs; and that, if God should permit that in the search for Monterey we all perish, we shall fulfill our duty to God and men by working together until death in the accomplishment of the enterprise on which we have been sent."(5)

"IT is", says Bancreft himself, "and must ever re main more or less inexplicable that the Spaniards should have failed at this time to identify Monterey. The description of landmarks, as given by Vizcaino and Cabrera Bueno, was tolerably clear, and in fact these landmarks had been readily recognized by Portolá's party at their first arrival on the bayshore. Yet with the harbor lying at their feet, and with several landmarks so clearly defined that Vila and Serra recognized them at once from the reports at San Diego, and penetrated the truth of the matter in spite of their companions' mystification, the Spanish officers could find nothing resembling the object of their search." (6)

Fr. Crespi's remarks, in addition to what has been related, are as follows: "In view of what has been said . . . . . . and of our not finding in these regions the port of Monterey, so celebrated and so praised in their time by men of character, skilful, intelligent, and practical navigators, who came expressly to explore these coasts by order of the king . . . we have to say that it is not found after the most careful efforts made at the cost of much sweat and fatigue; or it must be said that it has been filled up and destroyed with time, though we see no indications to support this opinion; and therefore I suspend my judgment on this point; but what I can say with assurance is that with all diligence on the part of the comandante, officers, and soldiers, no such port has been found. . . . .At Point Pinos there is no port, nor have we seen in all our journey a country more des-

(5) Crespi in Bancroft., Hist. Cal. I, 151.   (6) Banc. I, 152.

olate than this, or people more rude, Sebastian Vizcaino to the contrary northwithstanding." (7)

FR. Palou, whom Fr. Gleeson (8) follows, regarded
the concealment of the port as a miraculous interpo-
sition of God at the intercession and in the interest
of St. Francis;(9) for on starting from the peninsula, after completing arrangements for the new
missions of San Diego, San Carlos, and San Buenaventura, Fr. Junípero had asked Don Galvez, when
not finding the name of St. Francis among the proposed missions, "and for our Father St. Francis is
there to be no mission?" The visitador general replied: "If St. Francis wants a mission let him cause
his port to be found, and it shall be established
there." "Si San Francisco quiere mision, que haga
se halle su puerto, y se le pondrá." (10)

IT having been determined to proceed, the expedition crossed the Salinas River, an entered Pájaro
valley. Here they encamped on the bank of a stream
they called Pájaro (Bird), from a stuffed bird found
among the natives. Seeing that there were numerous
herds of deer, elk, and antelopes, the whole party
rested for three days on the banks of a small lake,
probably that near which now stands the Catholic
Boys Orphan Asylum in charge of the Franciscan Fathers. After leaving this place the expedition advanced very slowly, as sixteen men had lost the use
of their lmbs, and had to be rubbed with oil every
evening, fastened to the tijéras, or wooden frame, in
the morning, and raised to the backs of the mules.

ON the 17th the explorers forded a river named by
them San Lorenzo, at the site of the present Santa
Cruz; and on the 23d Año Nuevo was passed. Meat

(7) Banc. I. 152. (8) Hist. Cath. Ch. in Calif. Vol. II. 35-39. (9) Vida, 88.
"Luego que lol esta noticia atribul á disposicion divina el que no hall-
ando la expedicion el puerto de Monterey en el parago que lo señalaba el
antiguo derotero, siguiese hasta llegar el Puerto de N. P. S. Francisco."
(10) Vida, 88.

had long before given out, and now vegetables became scarce; rations were accordingly reduced to five tortillas of bran and flour a day. Portolá and Rivera also were added to the sick list. On the 28th the rains began, and the men were attacked by diarrhoea. On the 30th the party reached a point with detached rocks, or farallones, where the hills barred the passage along the shore. It was called Point Angel Custodio and Point Almejas, now San Pedro. On the last day of October the weary travellers climbed the hill, and were rewarded with the sight of the port of San Francisco. There was no mistaking the landmarks so clearly pointed out by Cabrera Bueno. The sorely tried party recognized them immediately. St. Francis had, indeed, and unexpectedly, brought his two disciples, and the expedition which they had accompanied, to the port that bears his name. Strong in this conviction, the pilgrims descended the hill northward, and encamped near the beach at the southern extremity of the sheet of water known to the Spaniards, from that time, as the Enseñada de los Farallones. (11)

On the second of November some soldiers, who had gone out to hunt, discovered a great inland sea which was named San Francisco Bay. Camp was broken on the 4th and the march resumed. Crossing the San Bruno from a place just above Point San Pedro on the 6th, the wanderers pitched their camp on a stream flowing into the bay, probably San Francisquito Creek near Searsville. Here they remained four days, suffering considerably from hunger. On the 11th of November, after Holy Mass, a council of the officers and the Franciscans Crespi and Gomez was held, when it was decided to return, as further search for Monterey was useless. The same afternoon they set out on their return march, and after twenty-

(11) Bancroft, H. C. I, 155-157.

six days reached Carmelo Bay. Here they remained from November 28th to December 10th, making some additional explorations, but still failing to find the port of Monterey. Before leaving Carmelo Bay a large cross was erected, on a knoll near the beach, bearing the inscription, "Dig at the foot and thou wilt find a writing." The buried document was a brief narrative of the expedition with a request that the commander of any vessel arriving soon should sail down the coast and try to communicate with the land party. The copy of it in Crespi's diary closed in these words: "Glory be to God, the cross was erected on a little hillock close to the beach of the small harbor on the south side of Point Pinos, and at its foot we buried the letter." Recrossing the peninsula the Spaniards set up, on the very shore of the harbor which they could not find, another cross with the inscription: "The overland expedition from San Diego returned from this place on December 9th 1769, starving." Below the San Luis Obispo region the natives began to bring an abundance of fish and other food, so that there was no further suffering. Finally, on January 24, 1770, the weary party approached the enclosure of San Diego, and announced their arrival by a discharge of musketry. (12)

DURING Portolá's absence of six months and eight days no progress had been made in mission work at San Diego, save the addition of a few tule huts. Fathers Serra and Parron were just recovering from the scurvy; and Fr. Vizcaino was still suffering from the arrow wound, while eight of the volunteers had died. Nor did the return of the governor contribute anything towards brightening the aspect of affairs, since he himself was much disheartened, because Monterey had not been found, and because the San Antonio with her supplies had not yet returned, al-

---

(12) Bancroft I, 160-163; "Our Contonial," 11; Vida, 88; Bancroft, I, 164.

though double the time required for the voyage had already elapsed. Portolá's plan, therefore, was to make a careful inventory of the supplies on hand, reserve enough for the march to Velicatá, and abandon San Diego when the remainder should be exhausted, which would be the case about the 20th of March. This day he fixed as the date of departure, unless supplies arrived meantime. (13)

THE Fathers, especially Serra and Crespi, were greatly alarmed at the governor's resolution, particularly when they remembered that already 166 years had elapsed since the Spaniards had visited that harbor, and that, in case it were now abandoned, centuries might pass ere others would return. Hence they strenuously opposed the abandoning of the enterprise. Fr. Junípero Serra formed the heroic resolution to remain alone, even though all others should forsake "my poor mission of San Diego." That it was a poor place indeed we may gather from a letter of Fr Junípero to Fr. Palou. He wrote: "One of our greatest drawbacks is the want of news and a proper intercourse with you, but being blessed with good health, a tortilla with some herbs from the field are sufficient for our daily sustenance. If they send cattle from Velicatá, forward a little incense, an ordo, and the holy oils, in case you have received them from Guadalajara. My diary, and that of Fr. Crespi, will be copied and sent you as soon as possible." On receipt of the letter from his superior, Fr. Palou immediately called on the lieutenant governor, beseeching him to order a captain and nineteen soldiers together with sufficent cattle for San Diego, to prevent the mission from being abandoned. The governor readily acceded to the request (14)

EARLY in March, however, the San Antonio had not yet appeared and the condition of affairs was

(13) Vida, 88-94. (14) Vida, 92-94.

growing desperate. Fr. Junípero went to Captain Vila of the San Carlos, still lying in the port, and requested permission for himself and Fr. Crespi to remain on board the vessel until provisions should arrive, so that they might be afforded an opportunity to reach Monterey by sea, in case the governor and his men abandoned the mission. The captain gladly consented to this arrangement. (15)

MEANWHILE men and officers were waiting, preparations were being made for the departure, the Fathers were praying, and the days were passing one by one, but no vessel came in sight. The sole topic of conversation was the abandoning of the northern country, and every word was an arrow to the soul of Fr. Serra; still he could only pray unceasingly, and trust to the intercession of St Joseph, the patron of the expedition. In his honor a novena was begun which was to close on the saint's feast, March 19th, the day before the one of final abandonment of the mission.

"GENTLY smiled the morning sun on that momentous morrow, as it rose above the hills and warmed to happiness the myriads of creatures beneath its benignant ray. Lovely beyond description was the scene on the beautiful bay in its fresh spring border hiding behind the hills. At an early hour the Fathers were abroad on the heights, for they could neither eat nor rest. The fulfilment or failure of their hopes was now to be decided. Fr. Junípero sang High Mass and preached with unusual fervor. The day then slowly wore away. Noon came, and the hours of the afternoon, and yet no sail appeared. The suspense was painful, for the redemption of this bright, fresh paradise was more than life to these holy men; and so all the day they watched and prayed, watched with strained eyes, and prayed, not with lips only, but

(15) Vida, 95-96.

with all those soul-longings which Omniscience alone can translate. Finally, as the sun dropped below the horizon, and all hope was beginning to vanish, a sail appeared in the distance like a winged messenger from heaven, and before twilight deepened into darkness the long sought vessel was in the offing. California was saved, blessed be God! and they might yet consummate their cherished plans. The ship was soon again lost to view; the momentary sight of the vessel, however, served to fill all with new courage. Four days later the San Antonio entered the harbor bearing joy to every heart. Fr. Junípero attributed the momentary view of the ship on the 19th of March to the powerful intercession of St. Joseph, and he never ceased thanking God for the favor; for a long time thereafter he had a Mass sung in honor of the holy Patriarch on the 19th of each month." (16)

WHEN the viceroy and the visitador general had learned from the captain of the San Antonio that the expedition by land had left San Diego in search of Monterey, and that men and provisions were needed, they resolved to provide the supplies at once. The same vessel was ordered northward in December, after certain vexatious, but unavoidable, delays. Captain Perez had orders to sail for Monterey direct, where it was supposed Portolá would be found; but fortunately he was obliged to enter the Santa Barbara channel for water, and the natives there explained that the land expedition had returned southward. Even then Perez in his perplexity would have gone to Monterey, had not the loss of an anchor forced him to turn about, just in time to prevent the abandonment of San Diego.

BESIDES an abundance of supplies, the San Antonio brought instructions from Don Galvez and the viceroy which drove from Portolá's mind all thought of

(16) Vida. 96; Bancroft. I. 166-167.

abandoning the country. Accordingly two expeditions were organized, one to go by land and the other to proceed by water. About the middle of April both set out. Fr. Junípero accompanied the sea expedition, whilst Fr. Crespi joined the land party under Governor Portolá. Before sailing, Fr. Serra again wrote to his dear Fr. Francisco Palou. Among other things he said: "Quite late last night Captain Juan Perez sent word that we were to embark that same night, a summons which was speedily complied with, as I had previously sent on board everything necessary. At an early hour this morning I said Mass. Fathers Parron and Gomez remain at San Diego; Fr. Juan Crespi and I intend to go north. (17) One of us is destined for Monterey, the other for San Buenaventura, which is distant eighty leagues. Should I have no opportunity to write to the Fr. Guardian, I beg of you to do so in my name and to give the reasons for it. The death of our Holy Father Clement XIII, and the election of Ganganelli, one of our religious, are rumors which have reached us. Dominus conservet eum, etc. This news has gladdened me in my solitude. I have also heard of the death of Fr. Moran. We are saying the Masses for him according to agreement. A year has elapsed since I received a letter from the college, and nearly the same length of time has passed since your last reached me. At the first opportunity send us some wax, which we need for Holy Mass, and some incense. Owing to contrary winds we did not sail yesterday. I conclude this letter on the day after Easter, the anniversary of the profession of our holy Father St. Francis. We are sailing out of the harbor, being towed by a boat from the San Carlos, which on its return will carry this letter ashore to our Fathers, who will transmit

(17) Father Viscaino, on account of his wounded hand, had already left San Diego for San Fernando, Mexico, some time before.

it to you. God preserve you many years in His love and grace.—At sea, before the Port of San Diego, April 16, 1770. Fr. Junípero Serra." (18)

GHAPTER VI.

LAND EXPEDITION TO MONTEREY—THE CROSS—FOUNDING OF SAN CARLOS— FR. JUNIPERO'S ACCOUNT—EXULTATION IN MEXICO—PLANS FOR NEW MISSIONS—NEW MISSIONARIES.

As we have seen, the San Antonio sailed from San Diego April 16th, 1770, in search of Monterey, having on board, besides Fr. Junípero Serra and the crew, a cargo of stones for the new mission. Owing to contrary winds the voyagers were driven as far south as the 30th degree of latitude, and then north to the Ensenada de los Farallones, so that they did not enter Monterey harbor until forty-six days after (1)

THE land expedition set out from San Diego on April 17th. The party consisted of Lieutenant Fagés with nineteen soldiers, Fr. Juan Crespi, two muleteers, and five natives, besides Governor Portolá. They made the journey in thirty-six days, encamped on May 24th near the spot where they had left the second cross on the bayshore the previous winter. They found the cross still standing, but curiously surrounded and adorned with arrows, sticks, feathers, fish, meat, and clams: evidently the work of the natives. Fr. Crespi, in his diary of the second land expedition to Monterey, relates under date of May 2d what follows with regard to this cross. "After a journey of three leagues we arrived at one of the salty

(18) Vida, 96-100.   (1) Vida, 100-106.

lagunas of Punta Pinos, where a cross had been erected. Eefore dismounting, the governor, a soldier, and I approached the cross, intending to discover some signs of the expedition which had set out by water; but we found none. The cross was surrounded by arrows and little rods, tipped with feathers, which had been set into the ground by the Indians. Suspended from a stick, at one side of the cross, was a string of half-spoiled sardines, a number of clam shells, and a piece of meat. This astonished us not a little; but we failed to comprehend the meaning of it all. As soon, however, as the neophytes were capable of expressing themselves in Spanish, they assured us that, the first time they saw the Spaniards, their attention was attracted by a beautiful shining cross which each one wore on his breast; that when they departed they left on the shore this large cross, which seemed at night almost to touch the sky, and was surrounded with rays of heavenly light; but in the day time, seeing it in its usual proportions, to propitiate it they had offered it flesh-meat and fish. Observing that it partook not of their feast, they had presented arrows and feathers, as a token that they wished to be at peace with the holy cross and with those who planted it. This narrative was frequently related by the Indians, and in 1774, when Fr. Junípero returned from Mexico, they repeated it to him without any variation." (8)

As Portolá, Crespi, and Fagés walked along the beach that afternoon, returning from a visit to the cross, they looked out over the placid bay, when the truth suddenly dawned upon their minds, and they in one accord exclaimed: "This is the port of Monterey which we seek; it is just as Vizcaino and Cabrera Bueno describe it;" and so it was. They only wondered that they had not recognized it be-

(2) Vida, 105-106.

fore. Soon for lack of fresh water camp was moved
across to Carmelo Bay. (4)

A week later, on the last day of May, the San
Antonio hove in sight off Point Pinos. On June 1st
the governor, Fr. Crespi, and the lieutenant crossed
over from Carmelo to welcome the new arrival. Orders were at once given to transfer the camp back to
the port of Monterey, about whose identity there was
no longer any doubt. On the third of June, 1770, the
mission of San Cárlos Borromeo was formally established. The account of this happy event is best given
in Fr. Serra's own words.

WRITING to Fr. Palou, then still in Lower California, he says: "My dear friend,—On the 31st of May,
by the favor of God, after a tedious and perilous
voyage lasting a month and a half, the packet-boat
San Antonio, commanded by Captain Don Juan Perez, anchored in this beautiful bay of Monterey, the
same unchanged as it was left by the expedition of
Don Sebastian Vizcaino in the year 1603. It was a
great consolation to me, and the pleasure I felt
increased with the news, received that same night,
that the land expedition had arrived eight days before, and with it Fr. Juan and the others in good
health. Our joy increased still more when, on the
feast of Pentecost, June 3d, close by the same shore
and under the same oak-tree under which the Fathers
of Vizcaino's expedition had celebrated Mass, we
built an altar. After the ringing of the bells, and
the singing of the hymn *Veni Creator*, the water was
blessed, and we erected and blessed a great cross, and
unfurled the royal colors. I then sang the first High
Mass known to have been offered at this place. During Mass I preached, and at its conclusion we chanted the *Salve Regina* before a picture of Our Lady
which occupied a place on the altar. The ceremonies

(3) Bancroft, I, 168-169.

A Typical Spanish Franciscan Mission.

were concluded with the singing of the *Te Deum*, after which the officers performed the act of taking possession of the land in the name of the king, our lord.

THE celebration was accompanied throughout with the firing of canon, both on land and on board the ship. To God alone be honor and glory! It is not for me to judge why this harbor was not found by the first expedition. It is enough that it was at last discovered, and that the desires of the visitador general, though rather late, will be accomplished, especially the spiritual conquest we all desire. As in May last it was a year since I received any letter from a Christian country, your Reverence can imagine that we are hungry for news. However, I only beg that at the next opportunity you let me know the name of the reigning Pope. that I may insert it at the canon of the Mass; also whether the canonization of the Blessed Joseph of Cupertino and Seraphin of Asculi has taken place; and whether there is any other saint or blessed so that we can give them their place in the directory. Let us also know whether it is true that the Indians have killed Fr. Joseph Soler in Sonora or Pimería; whether there is any other departed soul to be recommended to God; and, finally, whatever could be of interest to poor hermits cut off from the society of men.

I earnestly entreat you to send two more missionaries who, with the four here, will enable us to establish the mission of San Buenaventura in the channel of Santa Barbara, the land being much better adapted for the purpose than San Diego, Monterey, or any other yet discovered. I should not wish that for want of missionaries this mission be retarded. In truth, as long as Fr. Juan and I can stand, we will not be separated; it will be the greatest trial for me to remain eighty leagues distant from another priest,

Fr. Lasuen desires very much to come to these missions. Our supply of candles has run out here as well as at San Diego; nevertheless, to-morrow we shall celebrate the feast of Corpus Christi with a procession, in order to chase away as many little devils as there may be found about here. Send also the incense I asked for at another occasion. Do not fail to write to the visitador general concerning the discovery of this harbor, and recommend us to God, Who I pray may preserve your Reverence many years in His love and grace. Mission San Carlos de Monterey, on the feast of St. Anthony, June 18th, 1770. Fr. Junípero Serra." (4)

THIS letter was received by Fr. Palou on the feast of Portiuncula, August 2d, while at Mission Todos Santos, more than five hundred leagues from Monterey. Salutes and thanksgiving Masses celebrated the event at Loreto, Todos Santos, and Santa Ana, and Governor Armona despatched a vessel to carry the news to Mexico. At the capital the announcement of the discovery of Monterey was received with loud acclamations of joy; the cathedral bells rang out their glad peals and those of all the other churches responded. The most prominent persons, both ecclesiastic and secular, repaired to the palace to congratulate Viceroy La Croix and Visitador Don Galvez on the happy issue of the enterprise. A solemn High Mass of thanksgiving was celebrated at the cathedral the next day, and all the government officials and dignitaries of the Church were present. An account of the discovery was printed and circulated among the people, and copies of it were sent to Spain. A just tribute of praise was accorded to the zeal and untiring energy of Fr. Junípero Serra, from whom letters had been received by the viceroy and the Fr. Guardian of the college, asking for more

(4) Vida, 101-103.

missionaries. The latter, he wrote, must be supplied with everything necessary for the proper administration of the sacraments. Agricultural implements were also required that the aborigines might be taught to provide for themselves by cultivating the soil.(5)

As soon as Viceroy de la Croix and Don Galvez had read Fr. Junipero's letter, they requested the Fr. Guardian of San Fernando to send thirty Franciscans to California. The guardian agreed to the viceroy's request, but found it necessary to cede the Sierra Gorda missions in Mexico to the bishop of the diocese, in order to supply the desired number of missionaries for California. The viceroy thereupon issued the most judicious orders to make the missions successful. He procured a plentiful supply of sacred vestments and other articles necessary for the churches and vestries. To defray the expenses of the ten missions about to be established, De la Croix sent ten thousand dollars, besides four hundred dollars for travelling expenses for each missionary. Moreover, each missionary was to receive annually a stipend or salary of $275. The commissary of the marines at San Blas received orders to have the packet-boat San Carlos in readiness to take twenty Fathers to Loreto, whilst the San Antonio was to convey the other ten to Monterey. The Fathers intended for Monterey were: Antonio Paterna, Buenaventura Sitjar, Luis Jayme, Miguel Pieras, Pedro Benito Cambon, Domingo Juncosa, Francisco Dumetz, Jose Cavaller, and Angel Somera. (6)

THE missionaries set out from the college in October 1770, but were obliged to wait at Tepic until January 20th, 1771, before the San Antonio could be made ready for sea with a full cargo of supplies for the missions. After a tedious voyage of sixty-

(5) Vida, 104; 107-112; Noticias, I, 101-102.   (6) Vida, 113-115; Bancroft I, 171-173.

eight days, during which all the Fathers became affected with scurvy, the ship entered the port of San Diego on March 12th. From San Diego the vessel proceeded northward on April 10th, and, finally, anchored at Monterey on May 21st, 1771, when the ten Fathers already named landed in their new field with everything requisite for the establishing of the five new missions. With so many priests around Fr. Junipero resolved to celebrate the feast of Corpus Christi with all the spendor possible. A solemn High Mass, the first at Monterey, was sung, and a sermon preached, after which the Adorable Sacrament, surrounded by twelve Franciscan priests, was borne in procession to the amazement of the natives.

AFTER this celebration Fr. Serra distributed his religious as follows:

Mission San Diego: Fathers Luis Jayme (Jaume) and Francisco Dumetz.

Mission San Buenaventura: Fathers Antonio Paterna and Antonio Cruzado.

Mission San Gabriel: Fathers Angel Somera and Pedro Benito Cambon.

Mission San Antonio: Fathers Miguel Pieras and Buenaventura Sitjar.

Mission San Luis Obispo: Fathers Jose Cavaller and Domingo Juncosa.

Mission San Carlos: Fathers Junípero Serra and Juan Crespi.

THE establishment of the missions of San Francisco and Santa Clara had to be posponed for want of priests and troops. On the 7th of June the six Fathers selected for the southern mission of San Gabriel and San Buenaventura, reembarked on the San Antonio for San Diego, together with Fathers Gomez and Parron; the former retired to Mexico on account of ill health, the latter went to the peninsula. (7)

_____

(7) Vida, 11C-121; 127; Bancroft, I, 171-17S.

In accordance with previous orders from Don Galvez, Partolá now turned the military government of California over to Lieutenant Fagés, and sailed away in the San Antonio on July 9th, 1770, taking with him the engineer Constans . Portolá was the first in the line of governors of California. (8)

CHAPTER VII.

Scarcity of Food—Fr. Serra's Letter—His Journey—Disagreement Between The Fr. President And Governor Fages—Fr. Serra Goes To Mexico—Missionaries For Upper California—Fr. Junipero's Illness And Recovery—His Petition And Success—Report On The State Of The Missions.

Food was scarce in 1772, both at Monterey and San Antonio. For a long time the Fathers and neophytes subsisted on vegetables and milk only. Late in May, when the extremity was reached, Comandante Fagés with thirteen men made a raid into the valley called Cañada de los Osos (Bear Valley), fifty leagues from Monterey, where a large number of these animals were killed, and seed obtained to support the mission until other provisions arrived.

In a letter to Fr. Palou, dated August 18, 1772, Fr. Serra thus describes their critical situation, together with other matters of interest, as follows: My dear friend, — Thanks be to God! The Fathers are in good health, and the famine which tormented so many others did not reach us. While waiting for our ship, we received the news that two other vessels were coming to this port. One approached within two leagues of the bay, but could not enter. There is sufficient food at San Diego, but we have none. A

---

(8) Banc. I, 172.

few half-starved mules bring our provisions overland.
Vegetables and milk have been the chief support of
the people; but even these have grown scarce. Nevertheless I do not regret to have founded the missions.
Through our efforts some souls have gone to heaven
from Monterey, San Antonio, and San Diego. A great
number of Christians now praise God, and His holy
Name is more frequently on the lips of the pagans
here than on those of many Christians elsewhere.

SOME persons fear that from meek lambs they will
turn into lions and tigers. God might permit this;
but those at Monterey give us reason to expect the
contrary; for, after three years of experience, we find
them greatly improved. The same is true of those at
San Antonio. The promise made by God to our holy
Father Francis, mentioned by the Ven. Mother Mary
of Jesus, that the people would be converted to our
holy faith by merely looking at his children, I now
see fully realized. If not all have yet become Christians here, it is because of our ignorance of their
language. I often imagine that my sins make me un-
worthy of the gift to converse with them in their
own language. In a country like this, where there is
neither teacher nor interpreter, it will take some
time before any one will have learned the Spanish
language. At San Diego time has already overcome
the difficulty; adults are being baptized and married.
Here, with the help of God, we shall see like results; for some of the children already begin to
learn Spanish, in which language the catechism is
taught them. For the rest we trust in God who will
set everything aright. I intend to go to San Diego
with Don Fagés about the middle or end of September. If your Reverence could come up about that
time, what a gratification it would be to meet each
other after our long separation, and then what a
world of writing it would save us! Do not come for

my sake. Let us both have in view God's glory and the good of souls. Whether with you or alone, by all means let two religious come up to found the mission of San Buenaventura, or to replace those that are sick at San Gabriel. Those that are to be sent here should come supplied with patience and charity; having these they will obtain a rich and plentiful harvest.

DURING my absence Fr. Pieras, with one of the Fathers from San Luis, will attend this mission. The other will go to San Antonio where Fr. Buenaventura Sitjar is alone. Mission San Antonio has very materially assisted us in our distress by sending us seeds and pine-nuts. I owe good Fr. Pieras for four loads of them. If Fathers Lasuen and Murguía come to this wilderness, let them have patience and courage; no doubt you have need of the same where you are. May God preserve you in His holy love and grace many years. Mission San Carlos de Monterey on the Carmelo, August 12, 1772. Fr. Junípero Serra." (1)

WHEN Comandante Fagés found that the vessels with supplies could not come up to Monterey, and that mules were unable to bring the provisions, he started out for San Diego late in August, accompanied by Fr. Junípero, to make arrangements for the better transportation of much needed supplies. On his way Fr. Serra stopped at San Antonio, and was very much pleased to see the large number of Christian Indians. Taking Fr. Cavaller along, on the first of September he founded the fifth mission in California, in honor of San Luis Bishop of Tolouse, as will be related elsewhere. (2)

CONTINUING their journey, Fr. Serra and Captain Fagés arrived at San Gabriel on September 11th. It was the Fr. Superior's first visit to that mission, and

(1) Vida, 186-189.   (2) Ibid. 190.   Vide Mission San Luis Obispo.

he rejoiced exceedingly when he found so many neophytes. Fr. Paterna accompanied his superior from San Gabriel to San Diego, which place was reached on the 16th of September. Fr. Junípero at once urged the captain of the ship to hurry on northward with the supplies. The officer obeyed reluctantly, because he feared the dangers of the voyage at that season of the year. Meanwhile Fr. Dumetz, accompanied by Fr. Tomás de la Peña, had again been sent up from the peninsula to take Fr. Cambon's place who retired to Mexico on account of ill-health. There were then at San Diego, Fathers Crespi, Somera who was ill, Dumetz, and Peña. Two others were expected from the south at an early date. On December 27th, Fathers Crespi and Dumetz accompanied a supply train overland from San Diego to San Carlos to relieve Fathers Juncosa and Pieras. (3)

Fr. Serra now urged Fagés to proceed with the establishment of Mission San Buenaventura on the Santa Barbara Channel, as originally planned by Don Galvez five years before. He spoke to Comandante Fagés, says Palou, about an escort and other assistance necessary to start the mission, but found the door closed and Fagés giving directions whose execution threatened to bring about the loss of what had cost so much work to accomplish, To prevent such a result, the venerable Father used every means suggested by his purdence and skill; but in no way was he able to accomplish his purpose. (4) "A bitter quarrel ensued," says the Protestant Bancroft, who is ever inclined to take sides against Fr. Junípero, "between the two, in the course of which the hot-headed Fagés, in the right (?) at first, may very likely have exceeded the bounds of moderation and good taste; · while the president (Serra), though manifestly unjust (?) in his prejudice against the commandant,

(3) Vida, 144-145; Banc. I, 189. (4) Vida, 146.

was perhaps more politic and self-contained in his words and acts at the time." (5)

Yet only a few months before, March 18th, 1772, the viceroy had urged Fagés to maintain harmony, to treat converts well, and to promote mission work in every way possible. Now, however, the captain presented so many objections to the founding of San Buenaventura and similar establishments, that Fr. Serra began to suspect that orders must have emanated from higher authority prohibiting these undertakings for the future. He, therefore, consulted with the Fathers about the matter. It was the opinion of the four missionaries Serra, Paterna of San Gabriel, Somera and Peña of San Diego, that Fr. Junípero, or some one selected by him, should proceed to Mexico, and represent to the viceroy the great needs of the mission, and give correct information regarding the state of things in California. To obtain God's assistance for the success of this journey, a solemn High Mass was offered up on the following day, October 18th, after which the three Fathers concluded that the only suitable person to transact a business of such importance was the Fr. Superior himself. Though in his sixtieth year and lame, the zealous Father agreed to make the long journey of 200 leagues by land, besides the voyage by sea, in order to secure the welfare of his Indian neophytes. During his absence Fr. Paterna acted as superior of the missions.

Fr. Junípero embarked on the San Carlos at San Diego on October 20th, and after a prosperous voyage arrived at San Blas November 4th, in company with an Indian Christian from Monterey, who afterwards was confirmed by Archbishop Lorenzana. At San Blas Fr. Serra heard of the transfer of the Lower California missions to the Dominicans. Learning

(5) Banc., I, 190,

that the Fr. Guardian had left Fr. Palou free to retire to Mexico or to go to Upper California, Fr. Junípero at once wrote to him from Tepic on November 10th: "If your Reverence is determined that we
shall live and die in California, it will be to me a
great consolation. I only say, act according to God's
will...... If the Fr. Guardian should order that only
four go there, and that the others should return to
the college, I have nothing to say, but I pray God
may apply a remedy. Meanwhile let us obey." (6)

ALMIGHTY God seems to have anticipated Fr. Junipero's wish; for about that time Fr. Palou received
a letter from the Fr. Guardian permitting him to
send eight religious to Upper California. Fathers Juan
Figuer and Ramon Usson had already arrived at San
Diego in November. The eight Fathers who availed
themselves of the permission to labor in Upper California were: Francisco Palou, Pedro Benito Cambon,
Gregorio Amurrio, Fermin Francisco Lasuen, Juan
Prestamero, Vincente Fuster, José Antonio Murguía,
and Miguel de la Campa y Cos. Leaving one Father
at Velicatá, as was related elsewhere, Fr. Palou with
six Fathers journeyed northward. The new-comers
were welcomed at San Diego with every demonstra-
tion of joy. Fr. Palou then made a temporary distribution of the new missionaries, after which the missionary force in Upper California consisted of eighteen Franciscan priests. (7)

MEANWHILE Fr. Serra had proceeded on his way to
the capital as far as Guadalajara, where both he and
his neophyte companion fell sick with fever. They
were reduced to the last extremity and received the
sacraments of the dying. For himself Fr. Junípero
was resigned, but in regard to the neophyte he
feared lest the death of the Indian youth might

(6) Vida, 147-149; Noticias, I, 225-227.   (7) Noticias, I, 230-381; Banc., I,
104-116.

retard the conversion of the other natives, as they might imagine that the Christians had killed him. Almighty God, however, allowed both to recover and reach Mexico on February 6, 1778. (8)

Fr. Junípero found the new viceroy, Antonio Bucareli, no less favorably disposed toward the missions than his predecessor De la Croix. At the request of the viceroy he prepared a memorial on the state of the missions in California, and presented the document to the government on the 15th of March. "In this statement," said he to the viceroy when presenting the papers, "you will find that I have said nothing but what is true, and what in conscience I was bound to say, and what I consider absolutely necessary to attain that which his royal majesty so much desires, namely, the conversion of souls who, for want of knowledge of our holy faith, remain in the slavery of the devil, but who by these means can easily be redeemed. I trust your excellency will speedily determine what is just and expedient, since I must return as soon as possible, whether or not I obtain what I ask, rejoicing if it be granted, and somewhat grieved, but resigned to the will of God if it be refused." (9)

The statement consisted of thirty-two articles. The first and second point concerned the port of San Blas. Therein he strenuously urged the necessity of keeping that port open to furnish the missions with the necessary supplies. It had been decided to close San Blas, and to send supplies by land. Fr. Serra's arguments proved unanswerable, and his request was granted. The remaining articles were submitted by the viceroy to the 'Junta de guerra y real hacienda,' board of war and royal exchequer, of which Bucareli was a member. This body on May sixth granted eighteen of them and part of another, and denied only a

(8) Vida, 150-154. (9) Vida, 154.

part of article 82, in which Fr. Serra asked to have
the expenses of his journey to Mexico refunded. Thus
twenty of the original points were disposed of entirely in his favor. Four of these bore upon the past
troubles between the Franciscans and the military
authorities, and were intended to curtail the powers
which had been assumed by the latter. Fr. Serra
made special charges against Comandante Fagés,
among which were these: his refusal to transfer soldiers for bad conduct at the request of the missionary; meddling with the management of the missions
and the punishment of neophytes, as he has no right
to do except for grave offences; irregular and delayed
delivery of letters and property directed to the missionaries; insolence and constant efforts to annoy the
Fathers who were at his mercy; opening of letters
addressed to the missionaries, and neglect to inform
them when mails were to start; taking away the
mission mules for the use of the soldiers; and reten-
tion of cattle intended for new missions.

By the decision of the Junta the comandante was
ordered to remove any soldier of irregular conduct
and bad example from the mission guard to the presidio, at the missionary's request; the missionaries
were allowed to manage the mission Indians as a father would his family, and the military commander
was instructed to preserve perfect harmony with the
Fathers; property and letters for them or their missions were to be forwarded in separate packages, and
their correspondence was not to be meddled with,
but to pass free of charge like that of the soldiers;
additional vestments and seven bells were to be furnished; two blacksmiths and two carpenters, with
tools and material, were to be sent from Guadalajara for the exclusive use of the missions, etc. Comandante Fagés was subsequently relieved of his position and replaced by Rivera y Moncada. A set
of new regulations provided for several points in

Fr. Serra's petition pertaining to the military and financial affairs of California. (10)

Having obtained far more than he had expected, Fr. Junípero was anxious to return to his Indians, but before leaving he was requested to make a full report on the state of the missions, and to give the history of each from its foundation down to September 1772. On ceding their missions in Lower California to the Dominicans, the Franciscans had already been required to report on the condition of the new establishments in Upper California. Accordingly, Fr. Palou, the superior in Fr. Serra's absence, had prepared a complete statement for the viceroy and forwarded it to Mexico on December 10th, 177?. On 21st of May Fr. Junípero drew up the report of the actual condition of the California mission at the time of his departure the preceeding September. It covers substantially the same ground as that of Fr. Palou, and the two combined may be regarded as one document. According to these reports there were then in the fifth year of the Spanish occupation the following establishments in Upper California:

San Diego de Alcala, at which mission Fathers Luis Jayme, Vincente Fuster, and Gregorio Amurrio were stationed among the Indians; they also attended the soldiers at the presidio.

San Gabriel Arcangel, where Fathers Antonio Paterna, Antonio Cruzado, Juan Figuer, and Fermin Francisco Lasuen were laboring among the natives.

San Luis Obispo de Tolosa, whose missionaries were Fathers Jose Cavaller, Domingo Juncosa, José Antonio Murguía, Juan Prestamero, and Tomás de la Peña.

San Antonio de Padua in charge of Fathers Miguel Pieras, Buenaventura Sitjar, and Ramon Usson.

San Carlos Borromeo, on the Rio Carmelo. Here Fathers Junípero Serra, then in Mexico, Juan Cres-

(10) Vida, 151-156; Bancroft, I, 207-211.

pi, Francisco Dumetz, and Francisco Palou instructed the natives in the rudiments of Christianity and
civilization. They also administered to the wants of
the soldiers and their families at Monterey. (11)

THERE were, then, in the latter part of 1773,
nineteen Franciscan Fathers engaged in missionary
work among the Indians of California. Four hundred and ninety-one natives had been baptized, of
whom twenty-nine had died, and sixty-two Indian
couples had been united in Christian marriage. It
is to be noted, however, that the missionaries
could have received many more into the Church,
but they preferred to see the candidates well instructed before admitting them to the sacraments.
Others, again, held back on account of the distrust
caused by the outrages of the soldiers. Only at San
Diego had there been unprovoked hostilities. Near
each mission, except San Luis Obispo, was a ranchería of pagans, who lived in rude little huts constructed of boughs, tules, grass, and any other material that was at hand. Many of these Indians
came regularly as catechumens for Christian instruction. Often those of more distant rancherías were
induced to come, listen to the music, and receive
trifling gifts of food or beads. The neophytes were
generally willing to work when the Fathers could
feed them, which was not always the case.

AT San Diego, as stated elsewhere (12), there
were ten or eleven rancherías, whose inhabitants
lived on grass, seeds, fish, and rabbits. At San Gabriel the native population was larger than at any
other place; unfortunately the different rancherías
were at war with one another. At San Luis Obispo
the population was also very large, but the Indians
were friendly to the Spaniards from the first. The In-

---

(11) Vida, 154–155; Noticias I, 260–263; Bancroft, I, 195–196.
(12) See Mission San Diego.

dians of San Antonio were ready to live at the mission as soon as the Fathers could receive them. At San Cárlos de Monterey converts were most numerous, but for want of food they could not be kept at the mission. Here, and also at San Antonio, three soldiers had already married native women.

WITH regard to the mission buildings, Fr. Serra reported that at every mission a line of high strong posts, set into the ground close together, enclosed a rectangular space, which contained simple wooden structures serving as church and dwellings; the walls of these also generally took the stockade form. The square at San Cárlos was seventy yards long and forty-three yards wide, with ravelins at the corners. For want of nails the upright palisades were not secured at the top. Within, the chief building, also of palisade walls plastered inside and outside with mud or clay, measured seven by fifty yards, and was divided into six rooms. One room served for a church, another for the missionaries' dwelling, and a third for a store-house. The best rooms were whitewashed. This building was roofed with timbers which were covered with mud. A slighter structure used as a kitchen was roofed with grass.

The soldiers' quarters were apart from the mission buildings and enclosed by a separate stockade, while outside of both enclosures were the huts of Indians. Adobes were used to some extent in constructing a few buildings at San Diego. At San Antonio church and convent were built of adobes. Some of the buildings at Monterey were also constructed of adobe.

In agriculture, Fr. Serra reported, only slight progress had been made so far, though by repeated failures the missionaries were gaining experience for future success. A small vegetable garden at each mission, carefully tended and irrigated by hand, had been more or less productive. The pasturage was excellent, and the little livestock distributed among the missions had flourished from tho beginning. (18)

CHAPTER VIII.

FR. SERRA RETURNS—EXPLORING EXPEDITIONS BY SEA—THE FATHERS AS CHAPLAINS—NEW MISSIONS PLANNED.

Now that Fr. Junípero had finished his task he asked the blessing of the Fr. Guardian, kissed the feet of all the Fathers at the college, begged pardon for any bad example he might have set them, and then bid farewell forever. He set out for the west in September 1778, accompanied by Fr. Pablo Mugártegui and his own Indian neophyte. After a journey of 200 leagues, he was obliged to wait at Tepic for a ship till January 24th. (1)

FR. Junípero and his two companions arrived at San Diego after a voyage of forty-nine days. From there, on April 6th, he journeyed on foot in order to visit all the existing missions. On his way he met Capt. Anza, who was returning from Monterey to report

(13) Banc., I, 199–206.
(1) Vida, 157–159. In addition to the articles granted by the government, namely: three cases of vestments for San Gabriel, San Antonio, and San Luis Obispo, five sets of measures, six in each set, one forge with appurtenances, five quintals, and three arrobas of iron, Fr. Serra had obtained a liberal donation of goods from the viceroy for the exclusive use of the missions consisting of the following articles: 107 blankets, 29 pieces MANTA POBLANA (blankets), 488 yards of striped sackcloth, 380 yards of blue baize, 10 lbs blue maguey cloth for little girls, 4 reams of fine paper, five bales of red pepper, 2,500 lbs of jerked beef, 16 boxes panocha, 4 boxes of brads, 10 boxes of hams, 6 boxes of chocolate, 3 barrels of lard, 9 sacks of lentils, 9 jugs of olive oil, 4 barrels of Castilian wine, 3 barrels of brandy, 9 sacks of peas, 6 sacks of rice, 100 sacks of flour, 900 fanegas (bushels) of maize, and 250 fanegas of beans. Moreover, the government allowed each misson to have six servants, who were to aid in constructing the buildings and tilling the land. They were to be paid by the government during a term of five years. One hundred mules were also donated. Bancroft, I, 219.

to the viceroy that communication by land was open
between that port and Sonora. From him the Father learned of the want of provisions at San Carlos.
He hastened forward and arrived at Monterey on
on the 19th of May. The vessel with supplies had
reached the port three days before. Fr. Mugártegui
had been forced to remain at San Diego on account
of ill health. Fr. Amurrio in his stead took ship to
Monterey. Fathers Prestamero and Usson fell sick
and retired to Mexico. (2)

SEVERAL exploring expeditions, which set out from
Monterey during this and the next few years, may
be mentioned in this connection, as the Fathers
from San Carlos accompanied them. Besides, Fr. Serra is said to have suggested that the California
transport ship might be advantageously used for
purposes of geographical discoveries, in order to find
new fields for spiritual conquest. He also proposed
Captain Perez as a proper person to take charge of
the enterprise. Juan Perez was accordingly instructed
to explore the northern coast as far as the 60th degree. The expense was borne by the Spanish king. The
viceroy, however, asked that one or two missionaries accompany the expedition, wherefore Fr. Serra appointed Fathers Crespi and Peña to act as chaplains.
On the 10th of June, 1774, solemn High Mass was
offered up for the success of the voyage, and on the
11th the vessel sailed from Monterey. On the 9th
of July they were in latitude 45 degrees beyond the
limits of California. Continuing her course, the ship
reached as far north as the 55th degree, where the
crew found an island which they called Santa Margarita, because it was discovered on the feast of that
saint. The island was inhabited by Indians. Though
contrary winds prevented a landing, the explorers had
some intercourse with the natives who approached in

(2) Vida, 159-160; Bancroft I, 224-227.

canoes. Some of the bolder ones boarded the vessel
and exchanged well polished woods, hair blankets,
and mats, made from the bark of trees, for pieces of
iron or for beads. They were dressed in haircloth and
skins, and were of a gentle disposition. The women
were decently clad, but disfigured by wearing an or-
nament of wood in the lower lip, perforated for
that purpose. The Santiago now returned and reached Monterey on August 27th. Fathers Juan Crespi
and Tomás de la Peña kept diaries of this expedition which are still extant. (3)

WHEN the reports of this first enterprise reached
the viceroy, he ordered another expodition to procced
still farther north, and search for a good harbor
where the cross and the Spanish flag could be raised.
A fleet of four vessels was sent out from San Blas in
the spring of 1775 for California and the nothern waters. The viceroy again called upon the Franciscan
college to supply the chaplains, as no other priests
were available. The Fr. Guardian reluctantly detailed
Fathers Miguel de la Campa, Benito Sierra, Ramon
Usson, and Vincente de Santa Maria for this new
service. This was only a temporary arrangement, as
that kind of work was foreign to the Order. Fr. José
Nocedal was also sent along. (4)

ALL sailed from San Blas about the middle of
March. The San Antonio, whose chaplain was Fr.
Usson, landed her cargo at San Diego and returned
to San Blas. The San Carlos, with supplies for Mon-
terey and the northern missions, set sail with Fr.
Vincente as chaplain. The ship reached Monterey
June 27th. After discharging her cargo she sailed for
San Francisco Bay on July 24th. On setting sail the
crew began a novena in honor of St. Francis, at the
termination of which, on the 1st of August, just at

(3) Vida, 160–162; Banc., Hist. Northw. Coast I, 150–153.
(4) Vida, 162; Noticias, II, 216–217, 257, as per Banc., I, 240.

night fall they found themselves off the entrance of San Francisco Bay. The vessel entered, and anchored in the vicinity of what is now North Beach. Next morning the San Carlos crossed over to the Isla de Nuestra Señora de los Angeles, so named from the feast of the day, August 2d, and still known as Angel Island. Captain Ayala remained at anchor in the bay for forty days, making careful surveys meanwhile. Fr. Santa Maria and the officers landed several times on the northern shore toward point Reyes, and visited a ranchería of hospitable Indians. On the 22d of September the San Carlos reentered the harbor of Monterey.

The other vessels' which sailed from San Blas on March 16, 1775, were the ship Santiago under Captain Bruno Ezeta, with Fathers Campa and Sierra as chaplains, and the schooner Sonora, or Felicidad, under Lieutenant Bodega. The crew consisted of 100 men, and the supply of provisions was deemed sufficient for a year's cruise. After battling a long time with contrary winds, they landed in about 41 degrees 4 minutes latitude on the 11th of June, and took formal possession of the country by unfurling the Spanish flag amid a military salute. The sign of Redemption was raised and High Mass sung by Fr. Campa, after which there was a sermon followed by the Te Deum. On account of the feast of the day, the place was called Trinidád, or Trinity Bay, which name it still retains. The stream, since known as Little River, was named Principio. The natives were numerous but friendly, and by no means timid. More than a week was spent there, during which time explorations were made, and the habits of the Indians studied. Leaving Trinidád on the 19th, both ships continued northward.

On the 13th of July they touched upon a lovely spot in latitude 47 degrees and 23 minutes. Here they

errected a large cross with the usual ceremonies.
On July 30th the schooner was separated from the
frigate by violent storms, nor did the two vessels
meet again until October at the harbor of Monterey.
Captain Ezeta, however, kept on to latitude 49 degrees and a half, where on August 11th he decided
to return, because many of his crew were down with
the scurvy. Fogs prevented him from entering San
Francisco Bay. The ship arrived at Monterey on
August 29th. Don Ezeta now resolved to reach San
Francisco by land. Obtaining nine soldiers, three sailors, and a carpenter, and accompanied by Fathers
Palou and Campa, he set out on the 14th of September. Following Rivera's road of the preceding year,
the party arrived at the seashore on the 22d. On the
hill-top, at the foot of the old cross, were found letters from Fr. Santa Maria directing the land expedition to go about a league inland, and light a fire on
the beach to attract the attention of the San Carlos
anchored at Angel Island. The ship, however, had already departed, as we have seen, wherefore Ezeta
and his party left for Monterey on the 24th, arriving
there on the 1st of October.

THE schooner Sonora after its separation from the
Santiago, continued in its course as far as the 58th
degree, where a good harbor was discovered which the
Spaniards called 'Nuestra Señora de los Remedios.'
They took possession of it and erected a cross. A
heavy storm prevented further progress northward,
wherefore the ship returned to Monterey, which was
reached on October 7th. Nearly all the men were down
with the scurvy, but they rapidly recovered under
the kindly care of the Fathers. A week after their
arrival the crew went to the mission of San Carlos,
where a Mass of thanksgiving was offered in honor
of Our Lady. Every one, from the highest officer to
the humblest sailor, received Holy Communion, in or-

der to comply with a promise they had made on their long and perilous voyage. (5)

WHILE these expeditions were at work discovering new countries for the Spanish crown, Fr. Serra desired tó found some new missions under the regulations of 1773, by diminishing the old guards and taking a few soldiers from the presidio. Captain Rivera, however, declared that no soldiers could be spared at the presidio. Fr. Junípero then asked the Fr. Guardian at the capital to intercede with the viceroy for twenty men. The guardian, unable to obtain the soldiers, asked permission to retire the supernumerary Fathers. This request was granted at first, but immediately countermanded. Nevertheless, Viceroy Bucareli wrote to both Fr. Serra and Captain Rivera, in view of Captain Anza's expected arrival from Sonora by way of the Colorado, to establish two or three new missions on the old plan, and to depend on future arrangements for additional guards. The viceroy's letter reached Monterey on the 10th of August, 1775. At a consultation held two days later, it was resolved to establish the mission of San Juan Capistrano at once, between San Diego and San Gabriel. (6)

FR. Serra, meanwhile, directed all his energies to the instruction of the Indians, in order to prepare them for baptism. He was faithfully assisted in this work by the other Fathers, especially by his regular assistant, Fr. Juan Crespi. Though the revolt of the Indians at San Diego, resulting in the death of Fr. Jayme, had occurred in November 1775, and his presence was needed there, it was not till June 1776 that he could leave for the sorely-tried mission.

---

(5) Vida, 162–163; Bancroft. I, 242–248.
(6) Vida, 174–175; Noticias II, 258–261 as por Banc., I, 213.

CHAPTER IX.

AN event of importance to the missions, and which provoked a vast amount of unnecessary controversy, occured about this time. On taking possession of the missions of Lower California in 1768, Fr. Junípero Serra learned that the Jesuit Fathers had enjoyed the privilege of administering the sacrament of confirmation, because of the difficulty for a bishop to reach those districts. Though included in the diocese of Sonora, Alta or Upper California never was visited by a bishop until it had one of its own in 1841. Anxious that the neophytes be not deprived of the sacrament of strength under Franciscan management, Fr. Serra asked the Fr. Guardian to obtain for him, or some other Father, the authority to administer that sacrament for the benefit of his flock. His Holiness Clement XIV, on July 16th, 1774, granted the petition for a term of ten years.

HOWEVER, as "both Church and crown in Spain were zealous defenders of their respective prerogatives; and as not even a bishop could exercise the functions of his office until his appointment had received the royal approval, this special concession of episcopal powers had to be submitted to the king's royal council of the Indies. It was so submitted, and received the sanction of that body December 2d, 17-74. It was also approved of by the Audiencia of New Spain September 27th, and by Viceroy Bucareli Oc-

— 81 —

tober 8th, 1770. On October 17th, 1777, the commissary and prefect of the American colleges, Fr. Juan Domingo de Arricivita, transmitted to Fr. Junípero Serra the desired "Facultád de Confirmar." The patent with instructions came up on the Santiago, and reached Fr. Serra's hand in the latter part of June 1778." (1)

THE particulars regarding the power to confirm, which was granted to Fr. Serra, are given in Bancroft's own words, in order to show that every formality was observed on the part of Fr. Junípero, and that Bancroft's criticism of Fr. Serra emanates from a most ignorant and prejudiced mind.

FR. Serra carefully perused the instructions of the Sacred Congregation in regard to the exercise of his faculties, and immediately began to use them. The next feast after the reception of his new powers was that of the holy Apostles Peter and Paul. Having sung High Mass and given a suitable instruction, the Fr. President confirmed those children who were sufficiently prepared. He continued to instruct the adults and the children, until the 25th of August, when in spite of his infirmities he sailed for San Diego. In the meantime I e had confirmed 181 persons at San Carlos. At San Diego he confirmed the Christian Indians and the children of the soldiers. Proceeding northward he catechised and confirmed at each of the missions on I is way back to Monterey, where he arrived on January 5th, 1779. Soon After Fr. Junípero resumed his work at the missions north of San Carlos, and extended his tour to Santa Clara and San Francisco. 2,432 persons received the sacrament of the Holy Ghost during this tour, 1778-1779. About 100 of the number were Spaniards. (2)

ABOUT the beginning of November 1779, while at San Francisco, Fr. Serra received notice of the death

(1) Vida, 220-225; Bancroft I, 350-421. (2) Vida, 225-231; Banc., I, 327.

of Viceroy Bucareli. The Fathers keenly felt the
loss of their friend. Nor was it without reason that
they dreaded the change in the government. Bucareli
was succeeded by Don Mayorga. A change in the
general government of the missions, which not a little alarmed the missionaries, had already preceded
the death of the viceroy. As early as June 1779
news had reached them that California had been
taken from the jurisdiction of the viceroy, and had
been placed under a captain general who was to reside in Sonora. The first captain general was Don
Teodoro de la Croix. A letter from him to Fr. Serra
somewhat dispelled the latter's fears, and would
have resulted in much good had its promises been
carried out. The captain general wrote from Querétaro under date of August 15th, 1777, as follows: "The
information I have received from his excellency, and
the contents of your letters to him, have convinced
me of your activity, zeal, and prudence in the government of the missions, of your kindness towards
the Indians, and your solicitude for their real happiness. At this date I have not at my disposal the
help you ask, but I hope I shall be able shortly to
satisfy your zeal, and to labor with you for the welfare of those establishments, for which end I trust
you will enlighten me with your advise and opinion.
Your Reverence will find in me all that you desire
for the propagation of our holy faith, and the glory
of religion. I beg your prayers, and those of your
religious, for the happy issue of the important matters confided to my care." (3)

Fr. Serra, however, soon found that little confidence can be placed in human promises. California
had scarcely passed from under the jurisdiction of
the good viceroy, when Fr. Junípero encountered obstacles and difficulties without number. He observed

(3) Vida, 220-220.

that plans and regulations were made that were injurious to the missions; but protests and explanations were of no avail. The civil authorities were prepared to dictate, not only to the soldiers assigned to protect the missions, but also to the missionaries how religion should be propagated. Many of these difficulties, Fr. Palou says, could be mentioned, but one fact will be sufficient to give the reader a clear idea of the disagreeable circumstances under which the zealous missionaries had to carry on the work of conversion in California. About the middle of 1770 the captain general undertook to question Fr. Junípero's right to administer the sacrament of confirmation. The alleged reason for this assumption of authority in a purely spiritual matter was that the Fr. President (4) of the missions had not received the sanction of the goverment authorities to exercise his faculties.

As we have already seen, the faculty of Fr. Serra to confirm had received the sanction of the royal council of the Indians on December 2d, 1774, and had been approved by the Audiencia of New Spain September 27th, and by Don Bucareli on October 8th, 1776. Fr. Serra in replying to the captain general stated that for a year he had exercised his power to confirm, and that the captain general had not objected, and he now earnestly pleaded that the neophytes be not deprived of the graces of the sacrament, as the privilege was granted for ten years only. In addition, he offered to present his faculties for signature and approval to the captain general. De la Croix declined to agree to this, but demanded that the Papal Bull be shown to him. On April 20th, 1780, he even sent an order to the governor of California directing him to take possession of the original patent and instructions which had been sent

(4) This was the title in Spanish of the head of the California missions.

to Fr. Serra by the Fr. Guardian, and which must still be in the former's hands; and, furthermore, under no pretext whatever to permit the Fr. Superior to go on administering confirmation till new orders should be given. (5)

On receiving this communication through Governor Neve, Fr. Junípero refrained from exercising his faculties, as he feared he might also be forbidden to baptize if he continued to confirm contrary to the order of the governor and the captain general; but he informed the Fr. Guardian in reference to the matter. The guardian, Fr. Verger, on December 17th, 1779, stated the case in writing to the new viceroy, and at the same time applied for copies of all the documents bearing on the subject of confirmation. especially a copy enforcing a Brief of the Pope, and the sanction of the authorities of Mexico for Fr. Junípero. The certificates required were obtained without difficulty on February 16ht, 1780, and by Fr. Rafael Verger transmitted to Fr. Serra. A copy was also forwarded to La Croix. The unwarranted interference of the captain general and of the governor of California, moreover, brought out a letter from the viceroy to Governor Neve ordering him not to interfere with Fr. Junípero Serra, and to supply him with soldiers at any time that the Father wished to make his visits to the missions. This decision of the viceroy reached Fr. Serra in September 1781. (6)

H. H. Bancroft (7) labors hard to make it appear that Governor Neve and Captain General Croix were entirely right, that the Fr. Superior was altogether wrong, and that it was owing to the patriotism and moderation of Neve that a scandal was averted which must have proved unfortunate for the country, and perhaps disastrous to the missions. The unpreju-

---

(5) Vida, 23:-233; B. ne., I, 3C-3:1. (6) Vida, 234-290; Banc., I, 325-326; Gleeson, II, 8:-6. (7) H st. Cal. I, 320-328.

diced reader, on the other hand, will come to the
conclusion that both Croix and Neve arrogated to
themselves an authority which of right they could
not possess: the authority to declare what sacraments
should be administered by the missionaries of California. They might as well have forbidden the administration of the sacraments of baptism and extreme
unction. Bancroft, indeed, endeavors to clear himself of the stigma of prejudice and bigotry by saying: "No ardent churchman entertains a more ex-
alted opinion of the virtues of Junípero Serra, *his
pure-mindedness, His self-sacrificing devotion, his industry, and zeal* than myself. Nor would I willingly
detract from the reputation of a man who has
been justly regarded as an ideal missionary, the father of the Church in California; but I am writing
history, and I must record facts as I find them." Yet
on page 322 he twice accuses Fr. Serra of pride for
not submitting to Neve, at once, in a matter that
did not concern the governor; and on page 324 Bancroft insinuates that it may be possible that Serra
practised deception toward Croix. On Page 325 he
claims Fr. Junípero disregarded both Croix's and the
Fr. Guardian's orders; nor does he place much faith
in the truthfulness of Fr. Serra, though the latter
swears *in verbo sacerdotis* and *tacto pectore sacerdotali*
that he tells the truth. On page 326 Bancroft finds
Fr. Serra "happy in the thought that he had snubbed
his enemy." From all that Bancroft says about
Fr. Junípero, concerning this matter of confirmation,
the reader must get the impression that good Fr.
Serra was a trickster, and that Gov. Neve alone was
moderate and patriotic, for all of which this 'historian' has no other foundation that his surmises, and
the hasty deductions of his intense bigotry. Such
words as "effrontery" and "sharp practices" Bancroft applies to Fr. Serra without a scruple. And

this he calls "writing history as I find it." It is but just to remark that otherwise this writer has deserved well of the Franciscans by collecting a mass of historical material concerning them which it is well-nigh impossible to duplicate. Moreover, when stating simple facts and giving dates he is reliable enough, but Bancroft touching anything Catholic must be looked upon with more than suspicion. What is to be thought of a writer whose ignorance or bigotry makes him translate "*Llagas* de nuestro serafico padre Santo Francisco," by "*Sores* of our seraphic Father St. Francis?" (8) He should have said "Wounds," which is correct, and a term familiar even to Protestants; but that would not have sounded ridiculous, hence he translates "Sores." Dr. Gilmary Shea, the eminent Catholic historian, with much reason declares: "We regret our inability to use Bancroft's California, but it is throughout an attempt to treat Catholic affairs with misrepresention, derision, and insult. Catholic terms known to every child are put in a way to seem ridiculous and disgusting." (9) The same may be said of his other works. Only in connection with reputable authorities is it safe to follow this seemingly fair historian. The "pure-minded, self-sacrificing, industrious, and zealous" Fr. Junípero Serra can only gain for being traduced by such authors as Bancroft, to whom a piece of gossip frequently furnishes the sole foundation for his historical "facts." (10)

In September 1781 Fr. Serra resumed administering confirmation at San Carlos and San Antonio. The license to confirm for ten years expired with the life

---

(8) Bancroft I, 289;   (9) Shea, Hist. Cath. Church, IV, 351. (10) Vide, Bancroft, Hist. Central America, Vol. II, 440, for a shocking piece of bigotry and ignorance concerning the Blessed Sacrament. The following is another sample of Bancroft's ignorance and malice regarding Catholic affairs: "Papal Bulls or indulgences were sent to California every two years, and such as were not sold were burned at the end of a specified time.... So far as can be determined from the records the annual revenue from this source was from fifty to a hundred dollars."Bancroft, I,598-599.

of the venerable priest in 1784, before which date he confirmed 5,800 persons. The privilege was again bestowed upon Fr. Lasuen in 1785, and forwarded by the bishop of Sonora in 1790, but never renewed after Fr. Lasuen's death. (11)

Fr. Junípero and Fr. Crespi, in October 1781, went to San Francisco which the latter had not seen since 1769 when none but reaming Indians were to be found along the shore of the bay. Here they remained till November 9th, when they returned to San Carlos by way of Santa Clara, where they assisted Fathers Murguía and Peña in laying the corner-stone for a new church. (12) On returning to San Carlos Fr. Crespi grew sick, and after a short illness died on the 1st of January, 1782, after receiving the last sacraments at the hands of his superior. (13)

---

(11) Bancroft, I, 224.   (12) Vida, 235-237; Bancroft, I, 351.

(13) Fr. Juan Crespi was born in 1721 on the Island of Mallorca; he was educated together with Fr. Palou. From the first he was distinguished for his humility, piety, and simplicity. His companions often spoke of him as El Beato, or El Místico, because of his deep piety. As his memory was poor, and he could not deliver by heart the sermons on Sundays and holydays, he would in early years read the instruction from a book, thus edifying his hearers by his humility. He came to Mexico in 1749, and was sent two years later to the Pame missions of the Sierra Gorda. He served there as missionary for more than sixteen years, and particularly distinguished himself by the erection of a large stone church in the Valle del Filaco. Fr. Juan was next selected for the California missions by the Fr. Guardian, and, without returning to his college, with four companions he hastened to San Blas to take passage for the north. In April 1768 he arrived in Lower California, and was placed in charge of the mission of La Purísima. Fr. Crespi accompanied the first land expedition which reached San Diego in May 1769, and a little later he was one of a party that searched for Monterey and discovered San Francisco Bay. He kept diaries of both expeditions. Returning from San Diego to Monterey in 1770, he assisted in founding the mission of San Carlos. In March 1772 Fr. Crespi went with Lieut. Fagés to the San Joaquin River, of which exploration his diary is the only record. From June to August 1774 he acted as chaplain on board the Santiago, and also wrote a diary of the voyage. His body was interred in the mission church, within the presbytery, on the Gospel side, by his old friend, companion, and superior, Fr. Junípero, surrounded by the soldiers of the presidio and his flock of weeping neophytes, who lost a true friend in "Padre Juan." In the disputes between the secular and missionary authorities his name never appears. Fr. Serra esteemed him so highly that his own last request was that his body be placed by the side of Fr. Juan Crespi, Vida, 237-239.

CHAPTER X.

In the spring of 1782 Fr. Serra established the mission of San Buenaventura, and returned to San Carlos in June. Here he received the news that Fr. Antonio Reyes of the Franciscan college of the Holy Cross, Querétaro, had been made bishop of Sonora and California, and that the Fathers in Sonora and California were to form two independent custodies. On arriving in Sonora the bishop established the Custody of San Carlos de Sonora, and proposed later to go over and establish that of San Gabriel de California but the latter measure was never carried out. Nor did the custody of San Carlos exist long. The Fathers themselves, who had never favored the plan, requested to be again placed under the obedience of their respective colleges. (1)

On returning to San Carlos, Fr. Junípero had expected to find six more missionaries, and additional supplies for the proposed missions of Santa Barbara and La Purisima. He was sorely disappointed when he found they had not arrived Viceroy Mayorga, at the request of Captain General De la Croix, indeed, had called on the college of San Fernando for six missionary priests, to be chosen from those who

(1) Bancroft. I. 378.

should volunteer. The new guardian, Fr. Francisco Pangua, had selected the missionaries, and asked the viceroy to furnish the same aid for the new missions which was granted to the old establishments, that is to say, a complete outfit of church vestments and utensils for both church and vestry, including bells; a sufficient supply of live-stock and seed grain; an outfit of implements for house, shop, and field; and one thousand dollars to be expended in clothes and various articles, in order to attract the good will of the Indians. A full list of the articles needed was annexed to the petition. As the Fathers could not walk eight hundred leagues, and were not accustomed to ride on horseback, the viceroy was asked to permit them to go by sea. (2)

Viceroy Mayorga declined to furnish either church parapharnalia or implements for house and field as the religious had demanded. He declared that the captain general had already ordered the requisites for church and vestry, and as to the implements, neither the captain general nor the governor, though well acquainted with the country, had indicated that any such utensils or implements were needed. On the other hand, the viceroy consented to an advance of stipends, and moreover authorized the payment of two hundred dollars to each Father for travelling expenses.

The Fr. Guardian and his discretorio now saw clearly, what they had previously suspected, that an attempt was to be made in California to overthrow the old mission system. No implements for shop and field signified no agricultural and mechanical industries, no communities of laboring neophytes, and no temporalities for the Fathers to control. Fr. Pangua

---

(2) Vida, 256-260; Banc., I, 370. The Fathers selected from those who volunteered were Antonio Aznar, Diego Noboa, Juan Riobóo, Manuel Arévalo, Mateo Beavide, and José Esteves. Only Noboa and Rioboo ever came to California.

thereupon notified the viceroy on April 9th that the six missionaries excused themselves from going to found missions on terms which had proved so disastrous on the Colorado, (8) and he also gave it as his opinion that no others could be induced to go in their place, but promised to write more fully after Easter.

THE promised communication was dated the 9th of April. The writer, having consulted his discertorio. or council, after calling attention to the fact that, under the rules, no Father could be compelled to serve as missionary among the heathens, proceeded to justify the unwillingness of the six religious. The argument was that only by gifts could the missionaries gain the good will of the savages, as experience abundantly proved; that the only way to the native heart was through the native stomach and pride of personal adornment; that not only were habits of labor essential to civilization, but such love of labor could be formed only under the influence of the Fathers, based on their having the sole right to distribute the fruit of neophyte labor; and that while, at best, the work of conversion was difficult and discouraging, without the advantages of material rewards to native faithfulness, coming exclusively from the missionaries, permanent progress would be impossible, missionary efforts amount to nothing, and their support a useless expense to Church and crown. Moreover the soldiers were not only fed and clothed, but armed and equipped for their work of conquest and defence, why should the militia of Christ be denied arms and amunition for spiritual warfare?

YET another point of "no minor consideration" was brought forward in this able document which was signed not only by Fr. Pangua, but also by the other five members of the college discretorio. This was

(3) See "Franciscans in Arizona."

the "irregular manner in which missionaries were regarded and treated in those establishments" of California. So pronounced was Governor Neve's aversion to the religious that the soldiers were warned not to become *fraileros* (servants of the friars, or fond of the friars); not to perform any service for the missionaries; and not to aid them in bringing back fugitive neophytes. The natives lost their respect for the priest when they found he was not supported by the civil and military authorities, and the result was of course disastrous in every way. Again, minor officers, and the soldiers under them, by their scandalous connections with native and other women, encouraged the Indians to disregard alike the teachings and reproofs of the missionaries, and thus, with the tacit approval of the governor, they entirely neutralized all missionary efforts, and taught the natives to despise Christianity. (4)

H. H. Bancroft makes a strong effort, and succeeds in finding a lame excuse for his client Governor Neve, by asserting that these charges must be exaggerated or false; that Neve only favored a change in the mission system because he believed the missionaries were inclined to abuse the powers given them under the old regimé, and this to the prejudice of the royal authority which he represented in California. (5) Another Protestant writer, on the other hand, comes nearer the truth regarding Neve's intentions by declaring: "Other reasons less magnanimous, however, lay at the bottom of the decree. *An uncontrollable desire possessed the military authorities to usurp the temporal power of the Franciscans. Jealousy of the cowl had ever been rampant in the military breast. Neve, possessed of more diplomatic power than his predecessors, made the bold innovation be-*

(4) Vida, 236-238; Bancroft, I, 379-382; Gleeson, II, 93-94.
(5) Bancroft I. 382.

neath the guise of humanitarianism." (6) The governor's scheme was put into practise among the Yumas on the Colorado River by order of the captain general, and Bancroft himself says of it : "*The plan was a criminally stupid blunder.*" (7)

AFTER receiving the Fr. Guardian's communication, the viceroy allowed the matter to rest, but reported to the king for instructions. Thus it was that the missionaries, whom Fr. Serra had so anxiously expected, were not sent, and the missions contemplated could not be established. This news, communicated to Fr. Junípero by the Fr. Guardian in May 1782, afflicted the old man so much that it probably accelerated his death. He was resigned to the will of God, but asked that at least two missionaries be sent to take the place of others in case of sickness or death. His petition was granted, and the two religious arrived at San Francisco on June 2d, 1783, whence after a few days of rest they set out for San Carlos. They found the venerable superior suffering from a running tumor in the leg, and from oppression of the breast. Fr. Palou says that Fr. Serra suffered from this trouble in the chest ever since he entered the Order, though he never complained. When some of the religious advised him to apply a remedy, Fr. Serra would reply: "Let us leave it as it is; we might lose all." Without doubt, the malady was aggravated by his severe penance. In imitation of St. Francis Solano, he would scourge himself before the people with an iron chain, and, while reciting aloud the act contrition, he would strike his breast with a stone so forcibly that the spectators feared he would break his bones. Sometimes, when describing the torments of a damned soul, in order to make an impression upon the audience, he would

---

(6) "Old Missions of California " 67.

(7) Vide "Franciscan: in Arizona;" Bancroft I, 358.

take a lighted torch, and, laying bare his breast, would burn the flesh with it. (8)

Though suffering intensely under one of his severest attacks, the sight of the new missionaries revived Fr. Junípero and renewed his courage. Leaving one of them, Fr. Diego Noboa, at San Carlos, he set out with the other, Fr. Juan Rioboo, for San Diego in August. As the faculty to confirm would expire in July of the next year, 1784, Fr. Serra resolved to make a last sacrifice, and to visit all the missions for the last time, in order to administer the sacrament of confirmation to the neophytes

The pain in his chest increased to such a degree that no one expected to see him return either by land or by sea. Nevertheless, his zeal triumphed over his weakness, and he arrived at San Diego in September somewhat improved. After confirming the Indians, Fr. Junípero began the return journey on foot towards San Carlos, a distance of 170 leagues, allowing himself but a few days' rest at each mission. At San Gabriel his malady had grown so serious that all thought his death imminent. The little Indian boy who served the Mass, with tears in his eyes, complained to the missionaries: "The old Father *wants* to die." The hearts of all were saddened to see their superior set out for San Buenaventura, because they feared he would not survive the journey; but he reached the place, and, where a year before he had found only pagans, he confirmed a number of Christian Indians. On traversing the region of Santa Barbara Channel, and seeing such vast multitudes of unchristianized natives, Fr. Serra exclaimed with a heavy heart: "Pray ye, therefore, the Lord of the harvest, that He send laborers into His vineyard."(9) The thought that he could do nothing for them no doubt increased his physical ailments.

---

(8) Vida 250-262.   (9) Matt. IX, 38.

AFTER confirming at San Luis Obispo and San Antonio, Fr. Junípero again arrived at his beloved San Carlos in January 1784, and was received with many demonstrations of joy by his neophytes. Although he had completed his seventieth year, the good Father allowed himself no rest, but at once resumed his catechetical instructions. Besides, his dwelling was a poor one, and his mode of life very severe. A large cross had been erected, and this for years he was accustomed to visit and venerate at an early hour every morning. After the office of prime he would say Mass; then all went to work, Fr. Serra everywhere supervising and directing. Often during the day he would interrupt his work, visit the cross, and recite the rosary. These moments were the only recreation in which he indulged. (10)

Fr. Junípero celebrated the Lenten devotions, Holy Week, and the Easter festivities of 1784 with his usual fervor at San Carlos. When all had complied with their Easter duty, he set out for his last visitation of the northern country. On his way back he felt that his days were numbered, and at Santa Clara requested Fr. Palou, who had accompanied his superior thus far from San Francisco, to postpone the return awhile. Then employing several days in making a spiritual retreat, he made a general confession to Fr. Palou. The few remaining days he employed in baptizing, and in confirming those who had not yet received confirmation, even visiting the sick in their homes for that purpose. Fr. Palou now hastened back to his mission, whilst Fr. Serra set out for San Carlos. On his arrival there, in the forepart of June, he sent his assistant, Fr. Noboa, to Santa Clara to take the place of the deceased Fr. Murguía. He then continued to instruct and confirm the neophytes until the 16th of July, on which day his faculties to con-

(10) Vida. 264.

firm expired. Seeing that there was no one who had
not yet received the sacrament of the Holy Ghost,
and that he could no longer confer that sacrament,
he exclaimed with St. Paul: "Cursum consumavi,
fidem servavi," "I have finished my course, and preserved the faith." (11)

On the same day a government vessel made the
port of San Francisco with provisions, and a letter
from the guardian to Fr. Junípero, but no missionaries for the proposed missions along the Santa Barbara Channel. The Fr. Guardian informed Fr. Serra
that no more religious could be sent to California,
because a number of them had returned to Spain,
after having served their time, and some had died.
This news was a great disappointment to the Fr.
President, because he had hoped to see the channel
missions established before his death. He now wrote
to the more distant missions, and bid the Fathers a
last farewell, but from the missions of San Luis Obispo and San Antonio he requested one Father to
visit him for the last time. To Fr. Palou he also
wrote and begged him to assist his dying friend in
the last moments. Fr. Palou arrived, August 18th,
and found Fr. Serra very weak. Nevertheless, the sick
man did not cease to visit the church in the evening,
in order to recite the catechism and the usual prayers
with his neophytes, concluding the devotions with the
pious hymn composed by the Ven. Fr. Margil, apostle
of Texas, in honor of Our Lady. On August 19th he
asked Fr. Palou to sing High Mass in honor of
St. Joseph, California's great patron, as he himself
had been accustomed to do on the 19th of every
month. Fr. Junípero sang in the choir with the Indians, and with them recited the usual prayers. On the
next day, Friday, he made the Way of the Cross in
the church with all the people as usual.

(11) Vida, 264-268.

broth. Feeling much worse during the following night, he asked for extreme unction which he received while seated in a chair, and then recited with these present the litany of All Saints and the penitential psalms. Part of the night Fr. Serra passed on his knees, and for a while he sat on the floor supported by some of the neophytes with whom the room was continually crowded. Later on he received the plenary indulgence while on his knees. August 28th found him somewhat improved, though he had neither slept nor taken any nourishment during the preceding night. The morning he spent in his chair near the bed, which latter consisted of rough boards covered with a blanket. Even while travelling Fr. Junípero was accustomed to sleep on the bare ground, using the blanket for a pillow and embracing a large cross. Later in the day he said to Fr. Palou: "I desire to be buried in the church close by Fr. Crespi. When the stone church is completed, they may throw me where they like." Shortly after he asked Fr. Palou to sprinkle holy water through the room. Having remained silent for a time he suddenly exclaimed: "A great fear has come upon me; I am in much dread; read the recommendations for the dying aloud, so that I may hear them." During the recital of the prayer he responded as though in perfect health. Fr. Palou had scarcely finished the invocations, when Fr. Serra exclaimed: "Thanks be to God! Thanks be to God! the fear has left me entirely. Thanks be to God! there is nothing more to fear, and therefore let us go out." Much surprised all left the room; then seating himself at the table he took his *diurnale* and began to say his Office. When he had closed the book, Fr. Palou reminded him that it was after one o'clock, and begged him to take a cup of broth which the dying man accepted. After giving thanks he said: "*Vamos ahora a descansar,*"

"*Let us now go to rest.*" These were the holy man's last words. Walking to his bed-room without assistance, he took off his cloak only, then stretched himself upon the boards covered with the blanket, and held the large cross in his arms.

EVERY one thought Fr. Junípero was at last going to sleep, as during the previous night he had not rested at all. The officers went to take dinner, but Fr. Palou remained behind. After a little while, feeling uneasy, he entered the Fr. Superior's room, approached the bed, and found him in the position he had left him, but already asleep in the Lord. Fr. Junípero truly had gone to rest, a little before two o'clock in the afternoon of Saturday August 28th, 1784, at the age of seventy years, nine months, and twenty-one days. He had been a Franciscan religious for fifty-three years, eleven months, and thirteen days, of which thirty-five years, four months, and thirteen days were passed in the missions. The deceased had lived in continued activity, always occupied in furthering the glory of God and the salvation of souls. Fr. Palou justly says: "Because he labored so well for others, we must believe that he did so for his own sanctification also."(12)

<hr />

CHAPTER XI.

DESIRE FOR RELICS—FUNERAL SERVICE—FR. PATERNA'S CURE—RESULT OF FR. JUNÍPERO SERRA'S LABORS—MORE CONVERSIONS—BIOGRAPHY—FR. SERRA'S SUCCESSOR—NEW CUSTODIES—NEVE RETIRED—UNFORTUNATE POSITION OF THE FATHERS IN THE SPANISH MISSIONS.

WHEN the church bells announced the mornful news

(12) Vida, 203-270;   Life of Fr. Serra by Fr. Adam, 129-135;   Glocfron II. 94-96;   Bancroft, I. 400-411; "Old Missions of California," 72-73.

of Fr. Junípero Serra's death, the little convent was immediately crowded with Indians, soldiers, and sailors who all wanted to see their beloved father. The throng was so great that it became necessary to close the doors. The body, clad in the simple Franciscan habit in which the venerable Father had died, and which was the only garment he wore, save when he travelled, was then placed in the coffin which the deceased had ordered only the day before. Six lighted candles stood about the corpse. The doors were now opened, and the weeping neophytes entered to cover the lifeless form of their benefactor with flowers, and to touch it with their medals and rosaries. Every one wished to have some relic of their deceased friend, but there was nothing to be had besides the sandals which Captain Canizares of the packet-boat, and Rev. Diaz, the chaplain, took with them as mementoes. At nightfall the body was taken to the church, and placed on a table around which burned six wax candles. The doors were left open all night, and devout groups took turns in watching and in reciting the rosary for the soul of their father and friend. Two soldiers were put on guard to prevent any pious indiscretion or theft; nevertheless, on the next day, it was found that several pieces of the habit, and some portions of the hair had been removed.

On Sunday August 29th, the office of the dead was chanted by the priests and a solemn Requiem Mass sung, at which all the military and naval officers with their men assisted, together with Chaplain Diaz and a great multitude of Indians. The cannons were fired every half hour, and the bells kept up their mournful tolling. Fr. Buenaventura of San Antonio reached Monterey that same morning, and, after saying Mass at the presidio, hastened to San Carlos together with Don Soler, adjutant inspector of both Californias, representing the governor who was ab-

rent. The burial took place in the afternoon at four
o'clock, when a procession was formed. The body was
borne on the shoulders of some officers who deemed
it an honor to be permitted to carry the remains of
the holy man. The other officers, the soldiers, and
sailors bearing lighted tapers, preceded the coffin;
lastly followed the celebrant with the deacon and
subdeacon. The procession moved slowly and solemnly around the plaza. On arriving at the church, the
body was again placed before the altar, lauds were
sung, and then the mortal remains of Fr. Serra were
laid at rest in the sanctuary on the Gospel side
by Fr. Palou, assisted by Fathers Sitjar and Noriega,
and Chaplain Diaz. The funeral over, every one im-
portuned Fr. Palou for some memento of the deceased. Not having anything wherewith to satisfy
all demands, he had a tunic of Fr. Serra cut up and
made into scapulars. These he blessed on the 5th of
September, the 7th day after the death of the good
Father, and distributed to the multitude. The royal
surgeon obtained a hankerchief used by Fr. Serra
which, according to that pious physician's statement,
cured more people than other medical remedies. (1)

Fr. Paterna of San Luis did not arrive until three
days after the death of his superior. Owing to his
age, and the fifty leagues he had travelled, he fell
dangerously sick at San Carlos. Fr. Palou prepared
him for the reception of the last sacraments, but
suggested that the patient gird himself with a haircloth belonging to Fr. Serra. Fr. Paterna did so, and
after four days he was restored to health. Fr. Palou
is careful to state that he does not intend to declare
this case, and others which he relates, to be miraculous, but merely wished to show in what great es-
teem Fr. Junípero was held. Fr. Palou expressly
warned the soldiers and sailors not to look upon the

(1) Vida, 278-281.

scapulars and medals he distributed as relics, but only as articles blessed by the Church, and as mementoes of the virtues of a holy man who had worn the garment of which the tokens were made. (2)

THE labors of Fr. Junípero Serra made a lasting impression upon the inhabitants of California where he toiled so zealously during sixteen years. Besides six settlements of white settlers, at the time of his death, there were nine missions among the natives whose Christians had all been baptized by himself or his companions. The number of Christians in Upper California, when Fr. Serra closed his earthly career, was five thousand eight hundred of whom he had confirmed 5,307. In his last moments he promised to pray for the conversion of the Indians, and the converts did increase so rapidly after Serra's death that Fr. Mugártegui wrote from San Juan Capistrano: "During these last four months we have baptized more Indians than in the three years previous, and we ascribe this great increase to the intercession of the Ven. Junípero Serra, because they have come unsolicited to ask for baptism. In numerous instances the applicants came from afar, and spoke a language different from that used by the Indians of this mission." Other missionaries reported similar results. In the four months remaining of the year 1784, they baptized 936 Indians, a number never before reached during a like period, so that at the end of the year there were 6,736 Christians in Alta California. Fr. Palou concludes his Life of Fr. Junípero Serra in these words of Holy Scripture: "Non recedet memoria ejus, et nomen ejus requiretur a generatione in generationem," "The memory of him shall not depart, and his name shall be in request from generation to generation." (3)

NOR was the faithful disciple of the great founder

---

(2) Vida, 282.   (3) Ibid. 281-287; Eccli., XXXIX. 13,

of the California missions mistaken; for even now, after more than a century since his death, Fr. Junípero's name is pronounced with love and respect, not only by Catholics, but also by non-Catholics. It was a Protestant lady who at Monterey had a monument erected to the noble-hearted son of St. Francis. (4) Protestant papers with avidity copy sketches of his life, and able pens write in select magazines interesting accounts of his labors and the missions he founded. (5)

(4) The monument erected by Mrs Leland Stanford of California, was unveiled at Monterey on June 3d, 1891. Fr. Clementine Deymann. O.S. F., delivered the address on that occasion. Six other Franciscans were also present.

(5) Miguel José Serra, son of Antonio Serra and Margarita Ferrer, was born at Petra, on the Island of Mallorca, November 24th, 1713. He received the Franciscan habit at Palma on September 14th, 1730, and with it the name Junipero, and made his vows in the year following on September 15th. In early boyhood he served as chorister and acolyte in the parish church greatly to the delight of his parents, a God-fearing couple of lowly station. The lives of the saints was his favorite reading, and his fondest ambition was to devote his life to religious work. During his novitiate he was small and sickly, but he relates: "With the profession I gained health and strength, and grew to medium stature." The young religious was an earnest and wonderfully proficient student, and taught philosophy for a year before his ordination at Palma. He obtained the degree of S.T.D. from the famous Lullian University with an appointment to the Duns Scotus chair of philosophy which he held with great success until he left Spain. His doctrinal learning was excellent, and still more prominent did he become as a preacher. One of his sermons an able critic says: "Is worthy of being printed in letters of gold." He was wont to imitate San Francisco Solano, and often bared his shoulders to scourge himself with an iron chain, burnt his flesh with lighted candles, or pounded his breast with a large stone as he exhorted his hearers to penance. Thus he is represented in the engraving which Fr. Palou prefixed to his "Vida del Padre Fr. Junipero Serra." On March 30th, 1749, after repeated applications, Fr. Junipero obtained permission to join the Apostolic College of the Propagation of Faith, commonly called San Fernando, Mexico, to devote himself to missionary work in America. With Fr. Francisco Palou he left his convent April 13th and sailed to Cadiz where he arrived May 7th. On the way he maintained a continuous disputation on dogmatic theology with the heretical master of the vessel, and would not yield even to the forcible argument of a dagger at his throat, and repeated threats to throw him over board. Sailing from Cadiz August 28th, he touched at Puerto Rico where he spent 15 days in preaching. On December 6th he landed at Vera Cruz, and walked to Mexico which he reached January 1st, 1750. He was assigned to the Sierra Gorda missions of Querétaro and San Luis Potosí, and made the journey to Santiago de Japlan on foot, arriving there June 16th, For nine years he labored among the Indians

AT the death of Fr. Junípero the management of the missions in California fell to Fr. Palou as the senior Father on the coast. He had already held the position of superior before in Fr. Serra's absence. At

of the Sierra Gorda, part of the time as president, or superior, devoting himself most earnestly and successfully to the instruction and conversion of the Pamés. In 1759, or 1760, he was recalled, and appointed to the so-called Apache missions of the Rio San Sabá in Texas; but the plans were changed; he was retired by the college, and for seven years employed in preaching at the capital and in the surrounding diocese, in college work, and in performing the duties of his office of comisario of the Inquisition which he held since 1752.

ON July 14th, 1767, Fr. Junípero was named president, or superior, of the Lower California missions. He started out immediately and arrived at Tepic with a number of his brethren on August 21st, but could not obtain passage at San Blas for the north until March 12th, 1768. Arriving at Loreto on April 1st, he assigned the Fathers to their missions, and endeavored to accommodate himself to the new field of labor. On March 28th 1769, he started out, always on foot, for the north, and founded the mission of San Fernando de Velicatá on May 14th. San Diego was reached on July 1st, and there he founded the first mission in Upper California on July 16th. He remained until April 16th, 1770, then sailing for the north he arrived at Monterey on May 31st, where on June 3d he established the mission of San Carlos. In the following year, July 14th, he founded San Antonio. On August 20th, 1772, he started south by land, founded San Luis Obispo September 1st, and arrived at San Diego September 16th. On October 20th Fr. Serra sailed from San Diego to make his memorable visit to Mexico which he reached February 6th, 1773, and remained at the capital until September. He again arrived at San Diego on March 13th, 1774, and went up to Monterey by water. On November 1st, 1777, he established the mission of San Juan Capistrano. In the following year he received the power to confirm, and from September 13th, 1778, to January 5th, 1779, made a trip south, administering the sacrament of confirmation at all the missions on his way back from San Diego. In October and November he visited Santa Clara and San Francisco for the same purpose. In 1781 and 1782 he made similar journeys. On March 31st, 1782, he founded the mission of San Buenaventura, and was present at the founding of the presidio of Santa Barbara. In August 1783 he sailed for San Diego to confirm there for the last time. Returning by land he visited all the missionary establishments, and again arrived at San Carlos in January 1784. Between the end of April and the early part of June Fr. Junípero for the last time confirmed at Santa Clara and San Francisco.

IN the last chapter of his biography Fr. Palou recapitulates the virtues which were especially brilliant in the servant of God Fr. Junípero. He declares that "his laborious and exemplary life is nothing but a beautiful field decked with every class of flowers of excellent virtues." First in the list was his profound humility. He always deemed himself a useless servant, and rejoiced at the success of other missionaries. He avoided all honors not actually forced upon him; shunned praise and notice; sought the lowest tasks; kissed the feet of all, even the youngest novice, on leaving Spain, and again on leaving San Fernando; ran away from the office of guardian; and was in constant dread of honors

first Fr Palou declined to act as superior, partly from real modesty. He had to yield, however, to the unanimous wish of the other Fathers who claimed that a vacancy would prove injurious to mission interests; he reluctantly assumed the duties until a successor could be appointed by the college. Fr. Palou's wishes were gratified by the appointment of Fr. Fermin Francisco Lasuen of San Diego. The latter took possession of the office probably in September 1785. Fr. Mugártegui was named to succeed Fr. Lasuen in case of accident, and on August 16th, 1786, appointed vice-president of the southern missions. On March 13th, 1787, Fr. Lasuen received the privilege to administer the sacrament of confirmation for a period of ten years; but he did not obtain the document until July 13th, 1790, and consequently had less than five years for the exercise of his powers. During that time he confirmed 10,139 persons. (6)

As we have briefly indicated before, in 1783 an effort was made by the king of Spain and bishop Reyes, who was the Ordinary for California and Sonora, to organize the Sonora and California Franciscans into two independent custodies. Bishop Reyes in 1783 came with full authority from the king and the commissary general of the Franciscans to make the

from his Order, the Church, or the king. Then came the cardinal virtues of prudence, justice, fortitude, and temperance, resting like columns on his humility as a base, and supporting the sumptuous fabric of Christian perfection. His prudence was shown in his management as president of the missions, though he was always modest and ready to consult with the lowest about him. His justice was manifested by his kindness and charity to all, and in his exact obedience to the commands of his superiors. His fortitude appeared in his endurance of physical pain, his patience with his enemies in his great selfrestraint, in his steadfast adherence to his purposes, in his resolution to remain at San Diego alone, if need be, when it was proposed to abandon the mission, in his conflict with the indifference or opposition of the military authorities; and in his courage in the presence of hostile Indians. Finally his temperance was such that he had no other passion than that for the propagation of the faith, and constantly mortified his flesh by fasting, vigils, and scourgings. On these columns rested the superstructure of the theological virtues of faith, hope, and charity. Palou, Vida 287-327.   (6) Banc., I, 417.

change which the Fathers themselves did not desire. The colleges of San Fernando and Querétaro protested against the change, and showed that religious would have to be brought from Spain at great expense, since the old missionaries would not sever their connection with their colleges; that the new system made no provision for new conversions; that in California, particularly, there were none to support the Fathers with alms which the projectors of the scheme expected would largely maintain the missionaries; that there were many of the custody regulations which it would be absolutely impossible to enforce in these provinces; and, finally, that the custody must die out sooner or later for want of recruits, as the country could not furnish any novices. The protests were of no avail so far as Sonora was concerned, where the Custody of San Carlos was formed in October 1783, only to be dissolved again some years later at the request of the Fathers headed by the custos himself. (7)

THE college of San Fernando succeeded in postponing action in the erection of the custody of California till the practical result elsewhere could be known; yet as late as April 12th, 1785, the Fr. Guardian informed Fr. Lasuen that there was nothing left but to be silent and cautious, as, notwithstanding the opposition, it was the king's will that the custodies be organized. From the fact that Governor Neve seemed to have favored the plan for California we may conclude that it was not in the interest of the missionaries nor their missions. Bancroft thinks the plan "was doubtless intended as a step toward secularization." On March 21th, 1787, the king directed that, if not enough religious be secured from San Fernando, others might be taken from the Michoacan prov-

(7) Arricivita, Cronica Ser., 532-575; Banc., I, 129-421; Vide "Franciscans in Arizona."

ince. The scheme failed in Sonora, however, and
nothing more was heard of the plan after 1787. (8)
Not only did the missions escape separation from the
control of San Fernando, but their number was increased by the founding of two new establishments,
Santa Barbara and Purisima Concepcion, the long-
talked of missions on the channel whose history will
be related later on.

Even before the death of Fr. Junípero, Governor
Filipe de Neve, the enemy of the prevailing Franciscan mission system, was appointed inspector general
and retired to Sonora in the fall of 1782. Early in
1783 he succeeded Don Teodoro de la Croix as captain
general of the interior provinces; but his rule was
cut short by death at the end of 1784. His relations
with the missionaries may be summed up in a few
words from Bancroft: "Finding that the friars would
not submit to amicable recognition of secular authorities, he proposed to restrict their control of the mission temporalities and of the natives in the interests
of colonization, of real civilization, and the rights of
man". Yet even Bancroft acknowledges that his client Governor Neve may possibly have erred, for he
adds: "Whether his system, or any possible system,
could have been successful, considering the class of
colonists obtainable, the character of the natives,
etc., *I seriously doubt.*" (9)

Encroachments on the rights of the Indians and
their spiritual guides from the secular authorities
were frequent during these years. It was, indeed,
most unfortunate for the missionaries that they were
so little independent from the civil and military officials who seemed to know better how to do missionary work than the missionaries themselves. Conversions among the natives would have been more numerous had there resided about the missions no other

(8) Fac., I, 421. (9) Ibid. I, 417-418.

Spaniards than the missionaries, and had not the Fathers been compelled to appear to the shrewd eye of the Indians as servants of a foreign secular power. This is the impression one receives from the study of all the Spanish missions from Florida to California. The Fathers were ever hampered by the soldiers at the missions, the commanders at the presidios, and by the higher officials in Mexico. Nearly all, at one time or another, made it a point to diminish the influence of the priests over the natives, and make the missionary a mere State machine. Hence the controversies between the Church and State authorities hardly ever ceased entirely. A characteristic instance of military interference in mission affairs will be related in the next chapter.

CHAPTER XII.

INSPECTOR SOLER—FIRST DIRECT PROPOSITION TO SECULARIZE THE MISSIONS—THE NUMBER OF THE MISSIONARIES TO BE REDUCED—THE FATHERS PROTEST—LETTER POSTAGE—CHARGES OF SEVERITY—OTHER COMPLAINTS—REFUTATION AND COUNTER-CHARGES—STATE OF THE MISSIONS.

IN November 1787 Adjutant Inspector Soler made a long report to the captain general in reply to a request for his views on needed reforms in the administration of California affairs. "The author," says Bancroft, who in such matters is usually on the side opposed to the missionaries, "was not a man overburdened with ideas, and such as he had were pretty effectually suffocated in a mass of unintelligible verbiage." (1)

(1) Banc. I. 394.

Soler himself begins by saying: "I confess, Señor, that I have no head to present any project or circumstantial plan," which statement may be taken as a summary of the whole document with its thirty-five articles. Soler then goes on to prove that he had no head by declaring among other things: "The natives have been neophytes long enough; they are fitted for civilized life, and the government has spent all the money on them that can be afforded; the government can furnish no increase of military force, and it is useless to found new missions which cannot be protected; Spaniards should be granted lands at the missions, and the military escorts should be withdrawn from both missions and pueblos; then the gentiles would be attracted by the good fortune of the old converts to follow their example, the work of the priests being thus simplified and promoted." (2)

"To Soler therefore," says Bancroft, "must be accorded the authorship of the first direct proposition to secularize the California missions, although some of Neve's propositions had tended more or less in the same direction. Soler's plan involved a complete overthrow of the old mission system, putting Spaniards and natives on the same footing as citizens, dependence on persuasion and good example for future conversions, dependence for supplies on home products, and restriction of the soldiers to garrison duty proper, and the keeping in check of such gentiles as might fail to appreciate the advantages of civilized life. Whether under his plan the new converts were to undergo a preliminary training as neophytes under the friars' care, or were to pass directly to the state of citizens and land-owners, does not clearly appear." Governor Fagés opposed the plan of Soler and argued correctly that the natives are kept in order as neophytes only by the unremitting efforts of the friars,

---

(2) Banc. I. 304-305.

and are as yet wholly unfit to become citizens; that
the introduction of Spanish settlers into the missions
would interfere with the laws of the Indies providing
that the mission lands are to belong to the natives
eventually when they will be fitted to profit by their
possessions." (3)

It is needless to say that the missionaries did not
favor the absurd views reported with regard to their
missions; nor were they adopted as the law of the
province. In the year following, the office of inspector adjutant was abolished. Soler was summoned to
Arizpe, made commandant of Tucson, and died about
1790. Strangely enough, after all his fault-finding,
and his constant search for defalcations, he left California with a deficit of about $7,000 in his own ac-
counts. (4)

Troubles for the missionaries did not end here. It
will be remembered that the royal regulations of 1781
provided for the founding of the so-called Channel
Missions on a new basis proposed by Governor Neve,
but very unfavorable to the Fathers. Among other
things the regulations ordered that the number of
priests should be gradually reduced to one for each
mission, with certain exceptions. On January 8, 1783,
therefore, the Fr. Guardian wrote to Fr. Serra and
complained that the government in the new reglamento seemed to aim at the destruction rather than
the support of the missions; and that for this reason
no more missions should be founded till the regulations were modified. It would, indeed, be better, he
thought, to abandon a mission than to leave it in
charge of only one priest, and any priest left alone
might refuse to serve, without fear of the conse-
quences. In a letter to the Fr. Guardian Fr. Lasuen
also protested most earnestly against the reduction,
and, after explaining the difficulties involved, he de-

(3) Panc., I, 395, 397.   (4) Ibid., 396, 397.

clared his intention to resign his position as president of the missions, quit California, and if necssary sever his connection with the college rather than serve alone; for nothing save the commission of sin could be so terrible. In his report ef October 1787 he says: "No one can convince me that I am bound to remain solitary in the ministry." The clause was finally annulled by the kihg's order which provided that each mission should have two priests. (5)

THE most objectionable features were thus eliminated from the law, but there were left some grounds on which to base a quarrel if the governor and other officials were so diposed. One of the privileges obtained by Fr. Junipero, as early as 1773, was that of sending letters to the college at Mexico free of charge, and certain other letters to and from the superior in California were likewise exempt from postage as official communications. Nevertheless, on January 12th, 1783, Governor Fagés notified Comandante Sal that Fr. Junipero's claim for the free mailing of his letters to the college and to the Fathers could not be allowed. Fr. Serra pleaded poverty and told Sal to keep the letters if he could not forward them free. Finally, Fagés consented to let the letters pass, but kept an account of them until further instructions were received. On August 16th, 1786, the guardian wrote that the Junta Real had permitted letters between the Fathers and the college to pass free, only they must be in separate packages. Thus ended the matter in favor of the missionaries; but they were not to be without annoyance of some kind from the governor. (6)

"IN real or affected pity for the natives," says Bancroft, "the governor complained of excessive severity on the part of the missionaries toward their neophytes." The affection of the Indians manifested for

(5) Bancroft I, 378.   (6) Ibid. 380.

the Fathers proves, however, that they were not
cruelly dealt with, and that little confidence can be
placed in the governor's assertions. Very likely there
were Indians at the missions too lazy to work who
invented cruelties, or exaggerated the punishments
received for idleness and other vices, in order to revenge themselves on the Fathers. Whoever has lived
among Indians will understand the situation very
well; nor did the government, it seems, pay much
attention to the charges.

IN his complaint of September 20th, 1785, Fagés e-
numerated five grounds for displeasure. His first charge
was that the presidio of San Francisco had been deprived of Mass for three years. Fr. Palou replied that
the Fathers were required to act as chaplains gratui-
tously, though such service was not obligatory, as the
governor claimed, but voluntary. Fr. Lasuen, moreover,
stated that the lack of service at San Francisco was
due to the fact that until lately there had been no
decent place for religious worship, and besides the
mission was so close by that the soldiers could easily
go to Mass there; that the Fathers had never refused
or hesitated to attend to the spiritual welfare of the
soldiers; that he personally had served the presidio of
San Diego though six miles distant from the mission;
and that at San Barbara the missionaries of San Buenaventura attended to the soldiers though the presidio was eight leagues distant. The Fathers were offended, however, because the soldiers insolently
claimed their service as regular chaplains, when in
reality it was a matter of voluntary charity. The
viceroy's decision was that a proper allowance be
made to the missionaries for their services at the
presidio.

THE governor's second point of complaint was that
the Fathers refused to recognize the government in
matters pertaining to property and the *patronato*. Fr.

Lasuen answered that the Fathers managed the mission temporalities by order of the king, though the management was at first reluctantly assumed; that the viceroyal patronage had little or no application in a country like California, but that they would gladly observe any rules that might be prescribed. Fr. Palou, moreover, charged the governor with a disposition to interfere illegally and despotically in the management of the temporalities, and declared that Fagés had no proper understanding of the *patronato*, as he required the right to permit or demand work on feast days.

THIRDLY the Fathers were accused of refusing to sell mission produce at the prices fixed by the government. Fr. Palou in reply said there was no proof that the tariff rates had ever been approved by the king; that the prices ought to be regulated by scarcity or abundance, and that the superior should have a voice in the matter. Fr. Lasuen added that he knew of no instance where the missionaries had refused to sell at the prices prescribed when they had grain to sell; that the governor himself had increased the price of corn, which was shown to be true by a letter of Fagés in which he ordered Sal to pay two reales extra for maize from San Carlos and San Jose. Fagés also modified the tariff on January 2d, 1787, and on July 20th, 1787, and asked Fr. Lasuen for harvest returns that he might regulate the prices.

THE next cause for complaint was the refusal of the Fathers to furnish inventories of property, yearly increase, and the disposition made of mission products. Fr. Lasuen replied that the reports furnished to the governor were exactly the same as those rendered to the Fr. Superior of the missions, and by the latter to the college; that until then these reports had been satisfactory to all; and, finally, that there were no laws requiring the missionaries, who were not mere treasury officials, to render itemized accounts of what had been done with each bushel of maize.

THE last complaint of Fagés alleged that in defiance of the law the Franciscans insisted on retiring to their college without obtaining permission from the governor. Fr. Palou in reply said that by order of the viceroy dated March 29th, 1780, a Father had only to show the governor a license from his superior. Fr. Lasuen went more fully into the subject. In Neve's time, he stated, a missionary retired with his superior's permission, and the viceroy decided that there was no law to prevent it. Fr. Palou departed in the presence of Governor Fagés, who was responsible for any irregularity in the proceeding. The next year on being consulted Fagés made no objection to the departure of Fr. Rioboo; but, finally, there came a decree from Don Galvez forbidding the entry or departure of any Father without his license. This order was observed in the case of Fr. Noriega, and it would be obeyed; but the Fr. Superior went on to argue earnestly against the justice and policy of such a requirement subjected to which the Fathers would serve only with reluctance.

FAGÉ; also found fault with the missionaries because they allowed the neophytes to ride too much, the policy of the government opposing this for fear the Indians might become skilful warriors like the Apaches in Arizona. The Fathers admitted the charge, but showed that there were none but natives to serve as herders of cattle, and that the work could be done on horseback only. (7)

FATHER Palou, then guardian of San Fernando de Mexico, now made counter-charges in behalf of the missionaries. Fr. Lasuen, the superior of the missions, also proceeded to lay before the government the com-

plaints of the Fathers in California, namely : that the
soldiers, being occupied largely with matters outside
of their proper sphere, neglected their duty of afford-
ing protection to the missionaries in their work of
Christianizing the natives; that an insufficient guard
was given the missions, as the most useless and the
worst equipped soldiers were detailed for that duty;
that only one soldier was permitted to escort the missionaries on long journeys; that the soldiers of the
guards kept much live-stock to the prejudice of mission interests; that to obtain workmen without paying, the Indians were condemned to work as laborers
at the presidios for stealing cattle and for other offences the punishment of which should rest exclusively with the missionaries;(8) that the settlers of
San José employed pagans to do their work, demoralized them by bad example, and even persuaded them
to avoid Christianity and its attendant 'slavery;' that
illegal and unequal measures were used for mission
produce; etc.

Governor Fagés became more friendly after this
towards the missionaries, and he seems to have made
an effort to prevent a reopening of the old controversy. This more friendly demeanor was probably
the result of policy, for on August 16th, 1786, the
Fr. Guardian informed Fr. Lasuen that proposals for
the welfare of California had been presented to the
viceroy, and the opinion of the fiscal and his agent
was that the plans should be carried out, and the
governor restrained. Fagés was warned that on the
least complaint of the missionaries he would lose
his position. In his report, rendered in 1787, Governor Fagés, accordingly, spoke in the highest terms
of the zeal and efficiency of the Fathers, and his
personal relations with them were for the most

(8) Bancroft I, 408, in a footnote says: "There is no doubt the military authorities did abuse their power in this direction with a view to get
workmen free of cost."

part pleasant. However, on May 28th, 1791, Fagés recounted his troubles to his successor, and acknowledged that quarrels with the Fernandinos(9)had been frequent, since they were very much opposed to the maxims of the reglamento and wished to be wholly independent. At San Buenaventura it had even come to blows with Fr. Santa Maria. (10)

At the close of 1790 there were twenty-six Fathers on duty in California. Sixteen of these had arrived since 1785, namely: Fathers Arroita, Arenaza, Calzada, Dantí, García, Giribet, Mariner, Noboa, Orámas, Rioboo, Rubí, Santiago, Señan, Sola, Tapis, and Torrens. Fathers Rioboo, Palou, Sola, Mugártegui, and Noriega, however, left California before 1790, and Fathers Cavaller, Figuer, Murguía, Serra, and Crespi died within the period of 1780-1790. (11)

Down to December 31st, 1790, 12,877 persons had been baptized, 4,780 buried, and 2,662 couples had been married in the California missions. (12)

Governor Fagés resigned in May 1790, and was succeeded by José Antonio Romeu. On the death of Romeu in April 1792, Captain José de Arillaga became acting governor until May 1794, when he was replaced by Don Diego de Borica. In the same year the Conde de Branciforte became viceroy. (13)

CHAPTER XIII.

Search For New Mission Sites—Fr. Lasuen's Report—New Missions—Arrival And Departure Of Missionaries—Fr. Lasuen's Duties— Mission Reports—Secularization—Reduction Of The Stipends—Various Troubles Of The Fathers—Indian Selfgovernment.

It had long been the intention to found a series of

(9) Franciscans attached to the college of San Fernando. (10) Banc., I, 408-408. (11) Ibid. I, 388. (12) ' Informes Gen." (13) Banc. 481-98; 501-531.

new missions, each equidistant from two of the old establishments, or as nearly so as practicable, and all somewhat farther inland than the other. Accordingly in 1795 explorations were made by the missionaries, assisted in every instance by a military officer and a guard of soldiers in order that the choice of sites might be officially confirmed. An expedition set out from Monterey on November 15th, 1795, headed by Fr. Dantí. On the 16th they explored the San Benito region, on the stream of the same name, where they found all that was required for a mission. On the following day they discovered another suitable location on the edge of the San Bernardino Plain near Las Llagas Creek, or what is now the vicinity of Gilroy. They arrived at Santa Clara on the 21st, and started next day to examine the Alameda. The river of the Alameda was also called Rio de San Clemente by Fr. Dantí. The explorers continued their journey up to a point which they stated to have been opposite, or in sight of, San Francisco Mission and Yerba Buena Island, nearly or quite to the site of the modern Oakland. From this place they turned back, and, having discovered some important saltmarshes, they erected a cross at a spot called San Francisco, somewhat south of the Alameda. Solano. They returned to Santa Clara, well soaked with rain, on the 25th of November. Both Fr. Dantí and Comandante Sal kept a journal of this expedition. The document of the missionary is dated San Francisco December 2d, 1795.

In August 1795 Fr. Sitjar of San Antonio made an examination of the country between his mission and San Luis Obispo; but he found no better place for a mission than Las Pozas, where farming land might be irrigated from the arroyos of Santa Isabel and San Marcos. The result was addressed to Fr. Lasuen n a report dated August 27th, 1795.

THE region between San Buenaventura and San Gabriel was explored in August 1795 by Fr. Santa Maria. The Encino Valley seemed best suited for a mission, but the gentiles at the time showed no desire for missionaries. On this tour the Father visited the Cayegues ranchería, Simi Valley, Triunfo, Calabazas, Encino Valley with the rancherías of Quapa, Tacuenga, Tuyunga, Mapipinga, La Zanja, and Mufin.

IN the southern district Fr. Mariner started from San Diego on August 17th, 1795, to search for a mission site between San Diego and San Juan Capistrano. His report was in favor of the valley of San José, called Tacopin by the natives, a league and a half beyond Pamó toward the sierra.

THE result of the various explorations were summed up by Fr. Lasuen in a report, dated January 12th, 1796, which was incorporated by Governor Borica in a communication to the viceroy. The sites approved were San Francisco Solano, seven or eight leagues north of Santa Clara; Las Pozas, equidistant between San Antonio and San Luis Obispo; and Palé fourteen leagues from San Diego and eighteen from San Juan Capistrano. The other two required additional examination, since two sites had been recommended between San Carlos and Santa Clara, and that between San Gabriel and San Buenaventura was not satisfactory.(14)

GOVERNOR Borica hoped that by means of the new missions all the pagans of the coast range might be converted, and that in this way $15,060, the annual expense for guards, might be saved to the royal treasury. He did not deem it safe to expose the missionaries with a small guard of soldiers east of the mountains. If the viceroy consented to the foundations he was to send missionaries, and the $1,000 allowed each establishment, but no increase of military force would be needed, so he claimed.

(14) Bancroft I, 550-554.

THE saving of $15,060 and the unusual circumstance that no additional soldiers would be wanted were strong arguments in Mexico, wherefore on August 19th, 179J, the viceroy authorized Borica to proceed with his plan. Fr. Nogueyra, the guardian of San Fernando, gave his consent on the 29th of September, and announced that the religious required for the five new missions had been selected. He asked for the usual allowance, but protested against the reduction of the guards at the old missions. On May 5th, 1797, Fr. Lasuen informed the governor that all was ready, but remarked that it would be hard for the old missions to contribute for so many new missions at the same time. San Carlos, Santa Clara, and San Francisco were called upon to aid the two northern establishments, and to lend Indians and tools. Livestock was donated. Santa Cruz and Soledad were excused from contributing. (15)

THUS the missions in California had increased to eighteen at the end of the century, (16) and the missionaries numbered forty. Since 1790 thirty-eight Franciscan Fathers had come up from Mexico, whilst twenty-one retired, some on the expiration of their regular term of ten years, and others on account of failing health. Three religious died at their posts. This left forty still in the service, or two for each mission, and four supernumeraries. Four of the old pioneer priests, who had come before 1780, were still among the workers: Lasuen, Sanchez, Santa Maria, and Sitjar (17)

---

(15) Banc., 554. (16) The Seven new missions in the order of their founding were: Santa Cruz, Soledad, San José, San Juan Bautista, San Miguel, San Fernando, and San Luis Rey.

(17) THE arrivals in 1791 were Fathers Gili, Landæta, Baldomero, Lopez, and Salazar; Father Cambon retired. In 1792 Fr. Espi came, and in 1793 Fr. Catalá arrived, the latter as chaplain in a Nootka vessel. This same year Fathers Orámas and Rubi departed, and Fr. Paterna died. In 1794 five new priests were sent to California; these were Fathers Martin, Martiarena, Estévan, Manuel Fernandez, and Gregorio Fernandez. The departures were the Fathers Noboa, Pieras, Peña, and Gili. In 1795 came

FR. Fermin Francisco Lasuen continued at the head of the missions, loved and respected by missionaries, officers, soldiers, settlers, and Indians. Being a supernumerary he received no stipend, as no salary was allowed except to the two regular missionaries at each mission. The duties of the supernumeraries were arduous, and those of the superior more so than those of the missionaries, yet, though petitions were made and the viceroy was disposed to grant them in Fr. Lasuen's favor, the attorney general always interposed objections.

The new bishop of Sonora reappointed Fr. Lasuen *vicario foraneo* for the missions and settlements, and *vicario castrense* for the military on September 20th, 1796; and on March 20th, 1797, the Father took the oath before Fr. Arenaza. He was also commissary of the Holy Inquisition for California after 1795, but, as far as the records show, his only duties in this capacity were to receive an occasional edict. (18)

IN 1793 an effort was made by the Spanish and Mexican authorities to insure greater regularity and

Fathers Jaime, Ciprés, and Pujol, while Fathers Salazar and Señan retired the latter temporarily. Fathers Danti, Lopez, Calzada, and Arroita sailed away in July or August 1796. Other Fathers wished to leave California, but the Fr. Guardian thought that, as they had been eager to go there, it was best not to permit them to depart except for the most urgent reasons. In June 1796 Fathers Payeras, José Maria Fernandez, Peyri, Viader, Cortés, Catalan, and Horra came from Mexico. In April 1797 the ship Concepcion brought Fathers Barconilla, Carnicer, Gonzalez, Martinez, Merino, Uria, and Panella. The same vessel in September carried back Fathers Garcia and Arenaza, who were ill and had served out their term; and also Fathers José Maria Fernandez and Concepcion de Horra, who had become insane. On her return trip in May 1798 the Concepcion brought to Santa Barbara the Fathers Señan and Calzada, returning from a visit to Mexico, besides six new Fathers: Barona, Faura, Carranza, Abella, Martinez, and Viñals. Fathers Manuel Fernandez and Torrens retired to Mexico this year; Fathers Landaeta and Miguel also departed temporarily. In 1799 Fathers Merelo, Jacinto Lopez, and José Uria arrived, while Fathers Espi, Giribet, Merino, and Catalan obtained permission to retire in January 1800. During this last year Fathers Faster and Mariner died, Landaeta and Miguel came back, and Garcia and Iturrate were added to the force of missionary laborers in California. Bancroft, I, 570-577.   (18) Bancroft, I, 578-579.

thoroughness in the reports of missionary progress. As early as March 21st, 1787, a royal order required reports on mission progress every two or three years. On January 2d, 1795, Fr. Lasuen in a circular to his religion says that the Council of the Indies had read the mission reports, and thanked the missionaries in the king's name for the results accomplished, which were encourging compared with other missions that enjoyed better advantages. The Fr. Guardian also sent the thanks of the college. As early as 1793 Viceroy Revilla Gigedo declared that the Fathers in California performed their duties in a most commendable manner. When Fr. Salazar returned to Mexico the viceroy requested him to make a report on the condition of the country. This document, dated May 11th, 1796, contained nothing new, except that the wealth of the missions in buildings and chattels were said to amount to $800,000. Fr. Salazar, moreover, complained that better results were impeded by the excessive labors imposed upon the missionaries, and also by the preference shown to white settlers in the purchase of supplies. (19)

On the subject of secularization, or rather confiscation, which was often mooted since Neve and Soler had started the project, not referring to California in particular, Viceroy Gigedo expressed his dissatisfaction with the condition of those missions at which the experiment had been tried in Mexico. He declared he would take no steps in that direction without a better prospect of success. Curates could do no better in the instruction and improvement of the natives than religious. In a letter of August 3d, 1796, Governor Borica expresses the same opinion, and furthermore says that according to the laws, the natives were to be free from tutelage at the end of ten years, the missions then to become *doctrinas; "but*

those of New California, at the rate they are advanc-
ing, will not reach the goal in ten centuries; the
reason God knows, and men known something about
it." (20)

The regulation of 1781, as will be remembered, provided for the gradual reduction of the missionaries
to one at each mission. Until this was effected, religious dying or retiring were not to be replaced. The
arrangement was disregarded by the Fathers, and the
secular authorities made no attempt to enforce it. In
a letter of 1793 the viceroy himself disapproved of the
measure, because it exposed the missionaries to great
dangers. On November 16th, 1797, Governor Borica in
a letter to Viceroy Gigedo urged that the matter be
settled, as there was a deficit of $52,142 in the mis-
sion fund. He, too, disapproved of the reduction, but
suggested that the two Fathers stationed at each mission be allowed the stipend for only one, $400, since
they did not use more for themselves any way. Fr.
Lull, then guardian of San Fernando, opposed this
scheme of the governor, not only because it was contrary to the wishes of the king, but because the missionaries, though they spent less than $400 on them-
selves, used the remainder for the natives; and this
was practically the only way of obtaining necessary
articles, as there was no market for mission produce.
In 1800, or perhaps latter, Fr. Lasuen argued the
same side of the question most earnestly in a letter
to the Fr. Guardian. He wrote rather bitterly of any
plan to economize at the expense of poor and overworked missionaries, when the king was so liberal in
other expenditures, and repeated his determination of
retiring if the change were insisted upon. It most be
remembered here that Fr. Lasuen was not pleading
for himself, as for the last four years he had been
working without stipend or compensation. (21)

(20) Banc., I, 580.   (21) Bancroft I, 581-582.

FROM 1787 to 1794 missionaries, who came to California or retired to Mexico, were allowed $200 for travelling expenses on land and 95 cents per day while on the water. The Fathers subsequently had much trouble on account of the naval authorities who demanded $2.25 per day instead of 95 cents. In some cases, when the return voyage was very long, through no fault of the travelling missionaries, the government refused to pay the full stipend. After 1794 the authorities declared that the ten years of missionary service were to count from the date of departure from Mexico, and after 1800 no leave to retire was to be given, even on the expiration of the term, until substitutes had arrived. Many of the old matters of dispute still remained open at the beginning of the nineteenth century, but as a rule they gave rise to no bitter controversy.

No regular chaplains for the soldiers had as yet been appointed, though Governor Borica, on September 26th, 1793, and again on April 8d, 1795, had asked the viceroy for a Franciscan Father for each presidio at a salary of $400, as the missionaries had too much to attend to. It does not appear that the Fathers received any compensation for attending to the spiritual wants of the soldiers and settlers. The soldiers, at this period, however, were instructed to treat the missionaries with due respect. These regulations of Borica show an earnest desire to maintain harmonious relations with the religious. Yet even of this period of comparative peace Bancroft says; "Doubtless the patience of the friars was often sorely tried by the indolence and insolence of individual soldiers, but of the government they had no cause to complain." In January 1777, for instance, Corporals Moraga and Vallejo were forced to apologize to Fr. Catalá for their rudeness. On the other hand the Fr. Guardian and the Fr. Superior of the missions sought

to reciprocate this show of friendliness. Thus Fr. Catalá's reported hostility to settlers was rebuked by
his superior, and directions given that in all cases of
innovations the Fathers should be cautious and consult the Fr. Superior. Nevertheless, the guards were
reduced in most of the old missions on the establishments of new ones, and this brought out a protest
from the missionaries which was in some instances
successful. (22)

ONE of the annoyances which the Fathers had to
deal with was the desertions of neophytes from the
missions. The pretended motive of the fugitives were
ill-treatment, overwork, and hunger; but the true
cause of apostasy was a longing for the old freedom,
and a dread of the high death-rate among the mission Indians. Rarely, if ever, the alleged excuse had
any foundation. On May 28th, 1791, for instance, the
governor complained that the Indians were getting
too much meat to eat, were becoming too skillful ri-
ders, and were acquiring the insolence of the Apaches. The soldiers of the guard were not allowed to
pursue runaways, but occasionally an expedition of
presidio soldiers was sent out to make a general raid
for apostates. Thus in 1798 ninety fugitives of Santa
Cruz were recovered by the soldiers.

THE laws required that an alcalde, or magistrate,
and several regidores be elected annually in each
mission, a policy not approved by the Fathers, who
insisted that the natives were by no means fitted
for self-government even to this extent. After 1792
the elections ceased altogether until Borica brought
up the matter in 1796, and insisted on the enforcement of the law. Fr. Lasuen obeyed; the elections
were regularly held and reported to the governor.
These alcaldes and regidores, according to a letter of
Borica to Fr. Lasuen, were to act generally under

the missionary's instructions, but in criminal matters
under the corporal of the guard. (28)

CHAPTER XIV.

FR. HORA'S ACCUSATION—INVESTIGATION—SPANISH LANGUAGE OBLIGATORY—
THE FATHERS' SENSIBLE COURAGE—FR. LASUEN'S ABLE REPLY—THE MIS-
SIONARIES OFFICIALLY EXONERATED—THE BISHOP'S REQUEST—INTEREST-
ING ITEMS—STATISTICS—VARIOUS INDUSTRIES—GOVERNOR BORICA RE-
TIRES ANOTHER ATTEMPT TO CHANGE THE MISSION SYSTEM.

CONSIDERABLE trouble was caused the missionaries
by one of their number towards the close of the century. In 1797 Fr. Antonio de la Concepcion Horra,
who had come to California the same year, was sent
back to Mexico by Fr. Lasuen on a charge of insanity. On July 12th, 1798, Fr. Horra, while at the college, secretly addressed a memorial to the viceroy in
which, besides complaining bitterly of the treatment
to which he had been subjected, he made some
charges of cruelty and mismanagement against the
California missionaries. Fathers Lasuen, Sitjar, and
Miguel were the particular objects of his wrath.

THE viceroy sent the accusations of Fr. Horra to
Governor Borica, and ordered him to investigate the
charges. Borica, accordingly, despatched private instructions to the four commandants, and requested
answers to fifteen questions regarding the manner in
which the missionaries were discharging their duties.
Of the reports made by Arguello, Goycoechea, Sal,
Grajera, and Acting-Commandant Rodriguez, only the
replies of Sal and Goycoechea were unfavorable to
the Franciscans. It was not, apparently, until the
governor's report, including those of the command-

(28) Banc., 581-596.

ants, reached Mexico that anything was known at the
college of Fr. Horra's charges against his brethren.
In February 1790 the Fr. Guardian sent a statement
of the accusations to Fr. Lasuen, and a little later he
forwarded copies of other documents which were lost
in crossing the gulf, so that Fr. Lasuen did not receive the fifteen questions and the commandants' replies until September 1800. In October Fathers Tapis
and Cortés of Santa Barbara sent to the Fr. Superior
a long and complete refutation of Goycoechea, whose
statements had been more full than those of the
others. Other Fathers made similar replies. "Finally
Fr. President Lasuen devoted himself from November 12th, 1800, to June 19th, 1801, to the preparation
of a comprehensive exposition of the whole subject,
which is not not only the leading production of the
venerable author's pen, but the most eloquent and
complete defence and presentation of the mission
system in many of its phases which is extant." (1)

Of all the charges preferred against the Fathers
only one is worth mentioning at any length. *It was
the policy of the government to introduce the Spanish
language in place ot the vernacular.* Fr. Concepcion
accused the Fathers of an almost total neglect of this
duty. According to the commandants, religious services and some teachings of Christian principles in
the north were daily conducted in Spanish; in the
south the natives were taught in their own language,
though the *doctrina* was often repeated to them in
Spanish. *In general intercourse the vernacular was
used wherever the Fathers had learned it, and in
some missions exclusively.* Nowhere were the natives
compelled to learn Spanish, and everywhere the missionaries were more or less indifferent on the subject.
Fathers Tapis and Cortes affirmed that at Santa Barbara the *doctrina* at Mass was taught in Spanish,

(1) Banc., I, 587-589.

and in the afternoon either in one language or another; *but they admitted that the natives were not
required, only persuaded, to use the Spanish.* Finally,
Fr. Lasuen, declared that it was useless to preach to
the natives in a language they did not understand,
but that, nevertheless, an honest effort was made to
teach Spanish; that exercises were conducted in that
language once a day; that the natives were compelled
to use it in their petitions; and that premiums were
offered for acquiring it. (2)

AT the close of the report Fr. Lasuen manifested
some dissatisfaction that the charges of a man, who
left California under such peculiar circumstances,
should have been made the basis of this investigation
without a preliminary taking of testimony as to the
state of his mind. He was indignant at the commandants, not only for misstatements in certain details,
but chiefly for what they failed to say, and for what
their silence implied. They had failed to refute the
statements of ever-complaining Indians, whom their
own observations must have shown to be unreliable
witnesses; and, because of certain petty quarrels
about the services of the natives as peons at the
forts, they had given weight to the charges of a mad-
man, and had done great wrong to the missionary
cause.

FR. Lasuen declared that he and his band of religious were working honestly for the conversion of
the natives, according to the well known rules of
their Order, and the regulations of the Spanish government by which they stood in the position of *parents* towards the aborigines. He admitted that, being
but men, they differed from one another in judgment and patience, and consequently that errors were
committed; but he protested most earnestly that the
natives were shown all kindness that was consistent

(2) Banc. 589-590. The missionaries clearly acted like men of common sense.

with the restraint implied in the missionary and parental relation. "The venerable friar's words and manner," says Bancroft, "impress the reader most forcibly, *and a close study of the subject has convinced me that he was right;* that down to 1800, and considerably later, the natives were, as a rule, most kindly treated.... In the matter of neophyte labor at presidio, pueblo, and rancho the friars, here as elsewhere, *were usually right and the military wrong;* and so far as they touched this point, cruelty to natives, or accumulation of wealth, Horra's charge must be regarded as for the most part unfounded." (3)

At length, April 19th, 1805, in a letter to the governor, the viceroy rendered his decision, completely exonerating the missionaries, and urged the commandants to promote harmony. In a letter to the guardian of the same date the viceroy, moreover, declared that the good name of the Fathers was in no manner tarnished. (4)

On April 30th, 1791, the bishop of Sonora called Fr. Lasuen's attention to the royal order of March 6th, 1790, granting an ecclesiastical tax on all revenues, including those of the missionaries, and asked him to collect six per cent for four years on the stipends of all the Fathers and all other revenues. Fr. Lasuen replied that the California Fathers had no revenues except the stipend of $400 each, given as alms, and even with that they had nothing to do besides naming the articles needed for their churches; a síndico at the college collected the stipends and with them paid the invoices. If the king wanted to reduce the stipend by a tax, the matter must be arranged at the college. Franciscan religious had nothing to do or say about revenue matters. He sent a sworn statement, and regretted that his word did not suffice. Nothing more was heard on the subject. (5)

(8) Bancroft, I, 560-566.   (4) Ibid. 596-597.   (5) Ibid. 587.

THERE were as yet no regularly appointed chaplains, and the Fathers continued to care for the spiritual interests of soldiers and settlers, apparently without any compensation. A small income, however, was derived from alms for the celebration of Holy Masses. Thus Santa Barbara received 757 'Intentions' from 1794-1800. (10)

MOST of the missions at this period had a palisade or adobe enclosure which served as a cemetery. No pueblo or town, and of the presidios only San Diego, possessed a cemetery. It was customary to bury the dead settlers in the churches or chapels, a practice the Fathers endeavored to abolish; thus Fr. Señan in 1790 refused to bury Carmen Alviso in the presidio chapel.

BOTH soldiers and natives often escaped a flogging by taking advantage of their right of church asylum, and occasionally this taking refuge in the sacred edifice led to misunderstandings between the officers and the missionaries. An instance of this kind occurred on July 29th, 1794, when the governor ordered that an Indian culprit be taken out of the church at Santa Clara by force, since his offence was not subject to ecclesiastical immunity. (11)

THE eleven old missions in 1790 had in round numbers 7,500 converts; in 1800 they had 10,700, a gain for the decade of 3,200, about 320 a year on an average, or about 30 a year for each mission. During this period the Fathers had baptized 12,800 natives, and buried 8,300, leaving 800 to be regarded as approximately the number of deserters or apostates. Meanwhile in the seven new establishments baptism had been administered to 3,800 persons of whom 1,000 died, leaving 2,800 converts on the roll. Thus for old and new missions together we have a total population of 13,500 Indian neophytes, a gain of 6,000 in ten

years, during which time baptisms had been 16,100
and deaths 9,800.

THE mission herds and flocks multiplied about three
fold during the decade. Horses, mules, and horned
cattle increased from 22,000 to 67,000; small stock,
almost exclusively sheep, goats having diminished
rapidly and swine being few, from 26,000 to 86,000.

AGRICULTURAL products were 30,000 bushels in 1790.
The smallest subsequent crop was also 30,000 in
1795, and the largest 75,000 in 1800. About three
fifths of the whole crop in 1800 was wheat, which was
less, proportionately, than usual, one fifth corn, one
tenth barley, the remainder beans, peas, and various
grains. Wheat yielded on an average fifteenfold barley eighteenfold, and corn ninety-threefold for the
ten years. (12) "THE missions, as may be seen from
the preceding sketch, if we regard only the primary
object for which they were founded, were successful
and prosperous," says Bancroft.

The united white population of the three California
pueblos or towns, San José, Los Angeles, and Branciforte, (the latter opposite the Santa Cruz Mission), in
1800 was about 550 in something over a hundred families, and about 1,275 in whole California. The only
industries of these settler were agriculture and stock-
raising. They had 16,500 head of cattle and horses,
about 1,000 sheep, and they raised about 9,000 bushels of grain each year. (13)

AT the first occupation of Upper California some
Christian Indians from the peninsula were brought
north as servants of all work in the new missions.
The presidial companies usually had a few smiths, ar-
morers, and carpenters whose services were available
at times, as well for the missionaries as for the soldiers. The soldiers themselves were obliged to render
assistance in building and some other kinds of work.

(12) Bancroft I. 577.   (13) Ibid. 600-601.

Pagan Indians were hired from the first, especially on the channel coast. After 1773 men were enlisted and paid as sailors to serve in California as laborers, and among the settlers at the pueblos were persons of various trades. This was the condition of mechanical industry down to 1790. Besides the repairs executed on arms, implements, and articles of clothing, there were rude attempts at tanning and various other simple and necessary processes suggested by the needs of the soldiers and ingenuity of the Fathers.

A decided effort to promote manufactures was made in the last decade of the century, and with considerable success. The plan adopted was to send skilled artisans from Mexico under government pay to teach their trades to the neophytes and to white apprentices. About 20 of these artisan instructors were sent into California chiefly in 1792 and 1795. At first the mechanics were distributed in the missions and presidios, or in some cases travelled from one place to another giving instruction. Thus in 1793 and 1794 several San Carlos Indians were instructed in stone cutting, bricklaying, etc. After 1795 the Fathers were obliged to pay for the work done, to pay the mechanics' salaries, or to send their neophytes to the presidios to be taught, which latter they considered as scarcely beneficial to the good morals of the Indians. However, before 1800 the neophytes had acquired a stock of knowledge in the various mechanical departments which, it was thought, would suffice for the mission needs. The results of all these efforts were that before 1800 rude looms were set up in many missions, on which by Indian labor the wool of the country was woven into blankets and coarse fabrics with which the neophytes were clothed. In fact no blankets were brought from Mexico after 1797. A little cotton cloth was woven from material brought from San Blas. The Indians also had some natural skill for

dyeing. Hides were tanned and made into shoes;
and some of the coarser parts of saddles and other
leather goods were also manufactured, though not
enough to avoid importation from Mexico. About
2,000 hides were tanned at Santa Clara as early as
1792, but very few of them could be sold as there
was no market. Soap was made of suitable quality
and quantity to supply home needs after 1798; coarse
pottery was produced at San Francisco and several
other · places; and water-power flouring mills were
built at Santa Cruz and San Luis Obispo, possibly
also at San Gabriel and San José, which supplied
the province with flour. (14)

EACH mission had a vegetable garden, a fruit orchard, or a vineyard. There are no dates respecting
the time when grapes, oranges and other fruits were
introduced into California; but many varieties of
fruit, including probably grapes, were brought up
from the peninsula by the earliest expeditions between 1769 and 1773, as nearly all the varieties were
in a flourishing condition before Fr. Junípero Serra's
death in 1784. La Perouse left the first potatoes in
California in 1786. Wine was manufactured in the
southern missions before 1785. (15)

ON the 16th of January 1800 Governor Borica retired, and Arrillaga of Loreto took his place. The
former's relation swith the missionaries were always
friendly. From the first he assured Fr. Lasuen of his
desire to avoid controversy between the secular and
missionary authorities, a desire reciprocated by Fr.
Lasuen. Only Fr. Lasuen often thought Borica too
much inclined to hear and credit the complaints of
lying Indians, but no noticeable coolness ensued. In
this respect Borica was a decided improvement over
his predecessors Neve and Fages. (16)

IN 1802 a renewed effort was made from Mexico to

(14) Banc. I, 613-019. (15) Vida. 1?9; 220; Banc. I, 618-619. (16) Ibid. 727-29.

to change the mission system by adopting the plan formerly favored by Governor Neve for the channel missions. The natives after their conversion were to remain at their rancherías, and occasionally to be visited by the missionaries for the purpose of giving instruction and performing other spiritual duties. The Fr. Guardian opposed the change, but called on Fr. Lasuen for a new statement of the reasons against the scheme. The latter in reply, besides dwelling on the fact that the Indians could not be induced to change their habits except under the constant supervision of the missionaries, recalled the tragic results of a former experiment on the Rio Colorado, and referred to the comparative failure in Lower California and at San Diego, where the sterility of the soil rendered necessary a practice somewhat similar to that proposed. He believed the innovation would be in every respect injurious, and the viceroy thereupon decided that it should not be attempted. Fr. Lasuen's argument was dated June 16th, 1802, and the viceroy's decision bore date of February 2d, 1803. The missionaries, in this year and the next, were also troubled by disputes with the settlers concerning their lands; but the Fathers gained the victory. (1)

CHAPTER XV.

Death Of Fr. Lasuen—Biography—Bancroft On Fr. Lasuen—Fr. Tapis Superior—Governor Arrillaga's Sensible Report—Fr. Garol's Circular—Fathers Diaz, Font, And Garcés Cross California By Land From Sonora—Exploring Expeditions—Mission Santa Inés Founded—Statistics.

In 1803 California was called upon to part with the

---

(1) Banc. Hist. Cal. Vol. II, 6.

venerable Fr. Lasuen, for thirty years a missionary
in the province, and for eighteen years superior of
the missions. He died at San Cárlos on June 26th,
1803, at two o'clock in the afternoon, and was buried
next day in a stone sepulchre at the foot of the altar on the Gospel sideof the mission church by six
of his brother religious. (1)

"Though Lasuen's name stands second and not first
chronologically in the list of Franciscan prelates," says
Bancroft, "though no pen of brother friar or friend
has recorded his life and virtues, I cannot but regard
Lasuen as first thus far in California, both as man
and missionary. In him were united the qualities
that make up the model or ideal padre, without taint
of hypocrisy or cant. In person he was small and
compact, in expression vivacious, in manners always
agreeable, though dignified. He. was a frank, kindhearted old man, who made friends of all he met.
Distinguished visitors of French and English, as well
as of Spanish blood, were impressed in like manner
with his sweetness of disposition and quiet force of

(1) Banc,, II, 8.   (2) Fr. Fermin Francisco de Lasuen was a native of
Vitoria, province of Alava, Spain. Of his early life nothing more is on
record than that he belonged to the Franciscan province of Cantabria.
was incorporated in the apostolic college of San Fernando, Mexico, and
sailed from San Blas on March 14th, 1768, for California. He reached
Loreto on April 1st, and was assigned to the mission of San Francisco
de Borja. In March 1769 he went up to Velicatá to bless Rivera's expedition starting for the north. In May 1771 he left Loreto, was at Velicatá in July, and on August 30th arrived at San Diego. He served at San
Gabriel from December 1773 to September 1775; at San Juan Capistrano
through 1776; and at San Diego until 1785, when he was appointed superior of the California missions. From September of that year his headquarters was at San Carlos, but. in addition to his frequent tours through
the missions, he was at Santa Clara almost continually from 1786-1789, at
San Buenaventura in 1797, and at San Luis Obispo from October 1799 to
August 1800. In May 1795 he received a few votes for the office of guardian of the college, but Fr. Nogaeria was elected. Vancouver in 1792
says of him: "This personage was about 72 years of age, whose gentle
manners, united to a most venerable and placid countenance, indicated
that tranquillized state of mind, that fitted him in an eminent degree for
presiding over so benevolent an institution." Vancouver gave his name to
Pt. Fermin and Pt. Lasuen, still so called on modern maps. Bancroft II.
9-10.

character. His relations with the college, with the government, and with his band of missionary workers were always harmonious, often in somewhat trying circumstances, though no one of the Franciscans had more clearly defined opinions than he. None of them had a firmer will, or were readier on occasion to express their views. His management of the mission interests for eighteen years affords abundant evidence of his untiring zeal and of his ability as a man of business. His writings, of which I have many, both original and copied, prepossess the reader in favor of the author by their comparative conciseness of style. Of his fervent piety there are abundant proofs; and his piety and humility were of an agreeable type, unobtrusive, blended with common sense. He overcame obstacles in the way of duty, but he created no obstacles for the mere sake of surmounting them. Let us remember the good qualities of Junípero Serra and others like him; let us make every allowance for their weaknesses; but first among the California prelates let us ever rank Fermin de Lasuen as a friar who rose above his environment and lived many years in advance of his times." (2)

IMMEDIATELY after the death of Fr. Lasuen, Fr. Estévan Tapis, who since 1798 had been empowered to fill the place in such an emergency, assumed the office of superior of the California missions. In his first general report for 1803-1804 he complained that the missions were exposed to attack on all sides. The guard was usually reduced to two or three men, one of whom was generally sick, one in charge of the horses, and one absent on royal service. Fugitives

(2) Banc. II, 7-10 Many allusion derogatory to Fr. Junípero's character have been omitted in the preceding quotation, but elsewhere this historian's mind, and his impartiality towards Fr. Serra, have been placed before the reader sufficiently clear to make it evident that whatever Bancroft may say against the first superior of the California missions is of no value. Fr. Junípero Serra's character is altogether too lofty for this materialist's comprehension.

were increasing, and the only remedy was an immediate increase of the military force. This subject was
presented to the viceroy in a report of Fr. Guardian
Pangua in September 1804. Governor Arrillaga also
made a full and interesting report on November
10th, 1804, regarding the missions and their management. "The paper," says Bancroft, "is a straightfor-
ward and business-like one, written by a man of
good judgment and long experience. The substance of
it is that the mission system, if not perfect, was a
good one; the missionaries were in the main sensible
and honest men, and the natives were as a rule well
treated. Slight defects and excesses were sufficiently
guarded against by Franciscan and ecclesiastical regulations, while secular interference on account of a
few isolated complaints against individuals was not
advisable." It was in this year Fr. Superior Tapis received the appointment of vicar-general for California from the bishop of Sonora. (4)

On October 1st, 1806, Fr. José Gasol, the guardian, issued an important series of regulations for the
guidance of the California Fathers. Most of the sixteen articles relate to details of ecclesiastical, missionary, and private life of the religious. Among
other things the Fr. Guardian required an annual
meeting of the Fathers of the different districts at
San Francisco, San Carlos, San Luis Obispo, Santa
Barbara, San Gabriel, and San Diego, for the spiritual exercises, for consultation, and mutual consolation

The introduction reads as follows: "Fr. José Gasol,
of the Regular Observance of Our Holy Father Saint
Francis, etc., to the Reverend Father President and
other religious of the said college, serving in the missions of Monterey, San Diego, Santa Barbara, and
others founded, or which may be founded, in New

(4) Banc., II 9; 26-27.

California under charge and direction of the said college. Grace in Our Lord Jesus Christ which is the true grace.

"THE hour has at last come which I so much desired, Reverend Fathers and dearest Brethern in Jesus Christ, to open to Your Reverences my breast and manifest to you the sentiments of zeal and vigilance with which my heart is penetrated not only for those sons of our beloved college who live within its cells, but also for those who outside of it exercise the functions of our apostolic ministry. To both alike should extend my paternal solicitude; and Your Reverences yourselves, if, on account of being so far from your college, deprived of the exhortations, counsels, and corrections conducive to spiritual consolation, might with reason complain of my negligence. In order, then, that you may not have the slightest reason for complaint, nor for accusing me in the presence of the Lord of remissness in speaking, advising, and correcting whatever is worthy of advice or correction, I have resolved, with the consent of the Venerable Discretory, to direct to Your Reverences this circular for the purpose of establishing some points which all must observe in order that, by means of this religious conformity, there may be preserved among you the peace for which so zealously strove the founders of those missions, sons of this apostolic college, and that there may be an end of the clamors which, by reason of some infractions by certain missionaries, have reached not only me and my predecessors, but the viceroyalty of this capital." Then, follow the 10 articles of the instruction proper. (5)

THE Spanish territory in 1800 was limited to a narrow strip along the coast from San Francisco to San Diego. Soledád mission, the most inland establishment, was not over thirty miles from the sea. The

(5) Banc. II, 41-42.

vast interior was a *tierra incognita*. In 1774 Juan
Bautista de Anza, accompanied by Fr. Diaz of the
Querétaro Franciscan college, came from the Colorado River to San Gabriel across the country, from
southeast to northwest, by a route practically the
same as that followed by the Southern Pacific Rail-
road. In 1775 and 1776 Anza brought a colony to California by the same route, accompanied this time by
Fr. Pedro Font of the Querétaro college. In connection with this expedition Fr. Francisco Garcés made
an extensive and important exploration a little further north. He went up the Colorado to the Mojave
region, and crossed westward by the thirty-fifth parallel and Mojave River to San Gabriel; then proceeding northward he traversed the famous mountain
passes into the great Tulare Valley, nearly reaching
the latitude of Tulare Lake; and finally he passed
out of the valley eastward and returned along the
thirty-fifth parallel to the Colorado. Fr. Garcés had
thus explored what is now Kern and San Bernardino
counties, but, though his diary was preserved in Mexico, and the results of his explorations were preserved in Fr. Font's map, these results were soon
completely forgotten. (6)

SEVERAL expeditions were made into the interior
during 1804-1810 with a view to finding new fields
for missionary zeal. Thus Fr. Martin, then it seems
stationed at San José, made a visit to the valley of
the Tulares and reached a rancheria of the Bubal
named La Salv , but accomplished nothing. Another
expedition under Luis Arguello and Fr. Uría was in
preparation at San Francisco, but of this one nothing
further is known. On June 20th, 1806, Fr. Sanchez ac-
compan'ed a party from San Luis Rey towards San
Miguel, and returned on July 14th, after visiting the
rancherias for nearly thirty leagues around.

(6) Bancroft, II, 45-11. Vide "Franciscans in Arizona."

Fr. Zalvidea accompanied another expedition which set out from Santa Barbara on July 10th, 1809. The route first ran north from Santa Inés, and then eastward into the great plain. In what seems to have been the Visalia region, Fr. Zalvidea found an excellent site for a mission, but most of the country passed was arid and unfit for missionary purposes. The northern limit of their march seems to have been the southern boundary of Fresno County. Proceeding southward, they traversed Tejon or Tehachapi Pass, followed the eastern foothills of the San Gabriel Range until they turned west, and crossed the mountains to San Gabriel on the 14th of August. The natives as a rule were friendly and willing to receive missionaries; several also received baptism at the hands of Fr. Zalvidea. The Father kept a diary of this trip which is reproduced in substance by Bancroft.

On September 21st an exploring expedition started out from San Juan Bautista under Ensign Moraga, accompanied by Fr. Pedro Muñoz who kept a diary of this tour which also may be found in Bancroft. The course was somewhat north of east from San Juan, and crossed the San Joaquin near the present boundary between Merced and Fresno where it turned northward. The first large stream crossed, and deemed the best place in all the northern region for a mission, was named Nuestra Señora de la Merced, still called Merced River. A soldier, who claimed to have been with the expedition, declared that they explored the whole country from the head of the San Joaquin up north along the Sacramento and the Sierra Nevada. From their camp many trips were made into the snow mountains. The natives in the north were timid, and only in a few instances friendly intercourse could be established. Some of the Indians professed a willingness to become Christians. Above the Rio de la Pasion, possibly the Calaveras, in the vicinity of Stockton, there was a total change of language which prevented all intercourse. On November 2d the explorers returned and reached San Fernando.

In his missionary report Fr. Tapis stated that four expeditions accompanied by Franciscans had been made within the year 1806. The gentiles had everywhere manifested a desire to have missionaries. Twenty-four rancherías had been discovered with 5, 300 inhabitants, of whom 192 had been baptized by the Fathers. Only four or five good sites for missions had been found, all lying between the parallel of San Miguel and San Francisco. These prospective establishments would require a new presidio for their protection, because of their remoteness and of the numerous gentiles who dwelled beyond the region explored. (7)

In 1810 Ensign Moraga and Fr. Viader made two expeditions toward the San Joaquin, in order to find new mission sites. Fr. Viader kept diaries of both trips. The first was made from San José on the 15th of August and continued to the 27th, when they reached San Juan Bautista. The second tour began from San José on October 19th, and continued to the 27th, when the party returned to Santa Clara. Nothing seems to have resulted from these two expeditions. (8)

Only one mission, Santa Inés, was added during the first decade of the nineteenth century to the eighteen existing in 1800. During the same period twenty religious retired to their college on account of ill health, or on the expiration of their term of service; ten died in California, and twenty-eight new missionaries came from Mexico; so that there were thirty-eight Fathers at work among the Indians in 1810. Of the old pioneers, who came to California

(7) Bancroft, II, 46-55.   (8) Banc., II, 56.

with Fr. Junipero Serra, the venerable Fr. Francisco Dumetz alone was left to see fourteen days of the second decade. (8)

DURING this first decade of the century the missionaries in California baptized 22,000 persons of whom 12,000 were Indian adults. The smallest number baptized in a year at the missions was 808 in 1800, and the largest 4,259 in 1808, not only the largest in this decade, but in the whole course of the mission history during a like period. 16,725 persons died, of whom 6,000 were children under eight years of age. The total gain in neophyte population was from 13,668 in 1800 to 18,770 in 1810, that is to say 5,162. On an average 779 marriages were solemnized each year. (9)

LARGE stock increased to 141,000 head Small. stock, mostly sheep, gained from 86,000 to 157,000 head. Agricultural products amounted to 83,000 bushels per year, most of which was wheat. (10)

---

(8) Banc. II, 137-38. The Fathers who left California did not depart at the same time. Thus Fathers Jacinto Lopez and Lorenzo Marelo sailed on October 9th, 1801. Fathers Ibañoz and Gil came to take their place in August, whilst Fr. Pujol died. Fr. Estevan was the only missionary to retire in 1872. In 1803 Fathers Lasuon and F. M. Sanchez died, and Fr. Panella retired. On November 30th the Fr. Guardian wrote that of the fourteen religious asked for only seven had offered to go. Nevertheless ten new Fathers arrived in the following year; these were Amestoy, Amoros, P. Cabot, Cueva, Dulanto, Gutierrez, Muñoz, J. B. Sanchez, Sancho, and Urresti. Fr. Urresti was the superior of this band of missionaries while on the road. On the other hand Fr. Cruzado died, and Fathers Barcenilla, Martiarena, Martinez, and Viñals sailed away in Nov. or Dec. In 1805 the now-comers were Fathers Juan Cabot, Lásaro, Quintana, Suisar, and Zalvidea. The departures were Fathers Fernandez, Cortéz, Gonzalez, and F. J. All had worked zealously and completed their term. Uria. Fr. Uria returned some time later. The arrivals in 1806 were Fathers Boanena, Duran, Fortuni and Saens. Fathers Cueva and Gutierrez, sailed for Mexico in Nov. In this year, Fr. Santa Maria died. In 1808 Fr. Lázaro died. In 1808 Fathers Arroyo de la Cuesta and Suñer arrived, whilst Fathers Carnicer, José Garcia, and J.A.Uria retired. In Nov. Fathers Sitjar and Dulanto died on the mission. Three Fathers; Sarria, Ulibarri, and Rodriguez came to California in June 1809; and two: Fathers Faura and Iturrate retired in Oct. In 1810 the arrivals were Fathers Marquinez and Panto; the departures Fathers Carranza and Santiago; but Fathers Ciprés and Landaeta died. (9) Banc. II, 138-160. "Informes Generales" 1800-1810. The figures in these official reports of the Fathers do not agree entirely with those furnished by Bancroft. The same is true of the numbers given by him in 1800. (10) Banc., II. 160.

CHAPTER XVI.

THE situation of the missionaries during the revolutionary period of 1810-1820 was a trying one indeed, says Bancroft. Not only were they deprived of their stipends, (1) and their missions of the articles which those stipends had formerly procured, but they were obliged to exchange the mission products, the proceeds of which had also been devoted to the same end, for orders on the royal treasury which they had every reason to fear would never be paid, as indeed they never were. Yet he sneeringly adds: "After all, if they did have to support the whole province, and notwithstanding their troubles, they were much better off than any other class. ... And I have no doubt that several of the friars accumulated by their irregular commercial operations large sums of money during this period and a little latter." For this benevolent fling at the devoted missionaries Bancroft gives no other evidence than his "I have no doubt."(2)

ELSEWHERE (3) he forgets his bigotry and rightly declares: "Upon the Franciscan establishments fell the whole burden of supporting the provincial government and the troops, and their dues for unpaid drafts amounted to nearly half a million dollars in 1820.

---

(1) These annual payments to the Fathers were interrupted from 1811-1834. (2) Bancroft II, 196. (3) Ibid. II, 405-406.

Not a dollar of stipend was received by the friars during the entire decade; and not a single invoice of goods for the missions, goods usually bought with the proceeds of habilitado's drafts and the friars' stipends, could be forwarded, except one or two of very small amount obtained from other sources. The fact that the stipends came from the Pious Fund, to which the treasury had no claim save as a kind of trustee for the missions, and the fact that the other missionaries were not so entirely neglected as those of California, made the situation all the more exasperating; yet the protests and complaints of the friars were neither so frequent nor so bitter as might be expected, considering the legal rights that were being violated."

In September 1811 there came two letters, dated February 20th, and April 18th, from Fr. Guardian Garijo to Fr. Tapis. In these letters the guardian explained the impossibility of sending missionaries or supplies this year, and the uselessness of trying to bring to the viceroy's attention any measure for the good of California, on account of the revolution then raging in Mexico. A company of five Fathers, newly arrived from Spain, succeeded, however, after much trouble from the rebels, in reaching Loreto by water from Acapulco, and thence came overland to San Diego in July 1814. (4)

The greatest trouble of the California missions, or that about which most was written, was that of obtaining new missionaries to take the place of those that had died, of the aged and infirm, and of those that, having served out their term, were anxious for one reason or another to retire. The failure to pay stipends seems to have been the smallest difficulty in the way; the failure of the government to pay traveling expenses was a more formidable obstacle; and

(4) Banc., II, 197; 199.

worse yet, the college had rarely any Fathers to
spare for the northern field. As early, therefore, as
1811 a proposition was made to the Fernandinos to
cede half the California missions to the Franciscan
college of Orizaba, but it was rejected by the discretory. In 1816 Governor Sola wrote to the viceroy on
the great need of Fathers to relieve the old and infirm, attend to chaplain and pueblo duties, and to
found new missions in the east. Twenty was the
number asked for, and he suggested that they might
be obtained from Orizaba, either acting for their own
college, or incorporated with that of San Fernando.

In 1817, however, nine missions from Purisima
south were ceded to the Orizaba college, the reason
being inability to carry on so great a missionary
work for want of missionaries. The cession was accepted July 16th, and approved by the viceroy. It
was announced in California by Fr. Serra in a circular of October 11th; and in a report of November
5th, he expressed his pleasure at the transaction. On
September 12th, 1818, the Fr. Guardian wrote that
arrangements had been made for seven of the Orizaba Fathers to come in that year to take charge of
the missions transferred to them, and that the viceroy had ordered their travelling expenses to be paid.
At the same time he urged the Fathers to receive
the new-comers kindly, and to remember that all
were Franciscans. However, on account of the war
there was a delay of two years in sending the new
missionaries.

MEANWHILE, obstacles arose in California which prevented them from being sent at all. While Father
Prefect Sarría was pleased with the transfer of the
southern missions, the Fathers stationed at those missions were surprised and very much displeased. Fr.
President Payeras shared their feelings, but consoled
the missionaries until in 1819, becoming sole superior

of the missions, he was in a position to express his
views. He then protested to the Fr. Guardian that
the northern missions, which were to be retained,
were but worthless skeletons in comparison with those
in the south, which were to be given up. He insisted
on delay, at least, so that the Fathers in California
could be consulted. Both guardian and viceroy saw
the justice of this request; a stay of proceedings was
ordered until the question could be thoroughly ven-
tilated.

MEANWHILE four Fathers from each college were ordered to California to take the places that might be
assigned them temporarily. The Orizaba religious, however, refused to come to California on the experimental basis proposed, so that the four from San Fernando arrived alone. It is not known how the question
was settled in Mexico; but it could not make itself
heard above the political din of the next few years,
and never reappeared in California. (5)

FR. Estévan Tapis was the president of the mission,
until 1812. On July 13th of that year the college of
San Fernando elected Fr. Jose Señan to succeed Fr.
Tapis. He took charge of his office in December, and
held it until 1815. He was also appointed vicar-general by the bishop of Sonora, and continued to reside
at San Buenaventura; but his powers were abridged
at this time by the creation of a new and higher office. On the same day that Fr. Señan was elected
president of the missions, there was also an election
of a *comisario prefecto* in the person of Fr. Sarría.
It was not until a year later, July 1818, that he announced his assumption of the office. The duties of his
position were not specified in the announc.ment of his
election, but they were made clear, not only by the
prefect's subsequent acts, but through an explanation
of Fr. Sarría given in later years. From this ins ruc-

tion we learn that the Fr. Prefect was the president's superior, and the delegate of the Franciscan commissary general. He was likewise commissary of the Inquisition, and had full control of all matters pertaining to the *temporal* management of the missions. The president, on the other hand, while subject to the prefect in business matters, was responsible only to the Fr. Guardian in spiritual matters, and was also the bishop's vicar general. "There was never any clashing between the two, nor any apparent jealousy," Bancroft informs us. Prefect Sarría's headquarters was at San Carlos, but he travelled from place to place frequently.

In 1815 Fr. Mariano Payeras was chosen president in place of Fr. Señan, whose term had expired. He was reelected in 1818. For a time Fr. Payeras possessed all the old authority of president, as the Fr. Guardian notified him that, in the absence of orders from Spain, no election for perfect had been held, and that the office no longer existed. No official information reached Fr. Sarría; but in a circular he announced that on the expiration of his term of six years he would no longer hold the position. Fr. Payeras issued a circular accepting with sorrow the full responsibilities of the presidency as it existed in former years. In October 1819, however, a new election was held, and Fr. Payeras was raised to the position of prefect, while Fr. Señan was again made president. The two Fathers assumed their respective offices on April 1st, 1820, and on the 4th Fr. Payeras appointed Fr. Señan his vice-prefect. (6)

On assuming the office of prefect Fr. Sarría issued a pastoral letter dated San Carlos July 8th, 1813. It was directed to the missionaries, and divided into 48 articles. Among other things he enjoined a strict compliance with the Rules of St. Francis, warned the

(6) Bancroft, II, 396-398.

religious not to neglect the annual spiritual exercises, and especially urged them to *acquire the Indian language so as to be able to teach religion and the catechism in the native idiom.* Though he favored the teaching of Spanish to the Indians in accordance with the king's wishes, he objected to the parrot-like repetitions by the neophytes of religious truths in a language they did not understand. Accordingly, we find the missionaries, in their reports of 1815, stating that religious instruction was given in Spanish and the vernacular alternately. More than half the articles of Fr. Sarría's circular is devoted to details of the spiritual training of neophytes. He reminded the missionaries that, in the absence of curates, the souls of the Spanish settlers must not be neglected, and alluded to the management of the temporalities as a duty which must not detract attention from more solemn spiritual obligations, and closed as he had begun with an exhortation.

On January 25th, 1817, the Fr. Prefect again addressed the religious in a letter divided into 27 articles. He had just completed a tour of inspection which, he affirmed, had filled him with joy and satisfaction. Yet he had noted that some of the rooms of the Fathers were much too large and sumptuously furnished for the "cells of poor evangelical toilers." He was grieved at this, and at certain comforts in clothing and food more in accord with the "spirit of the world" than with Franciscan Rules. (7) He entreated them to avoid scrupulously every appearance of wordly ease, and not to wear shoes except in case

---

(7) In his instructions of 1806 Fr. Gasol, the guardian in Mexico, insisted that the Fathers part with certain silver watches, which had to be sent to Guadalajara and sold for the benefit of the Indians. It was not permitted to sell them to naval or military officers in California for fear that stories of mission luxury in that province, inconsistent with the vow of proverty, should become current in Mexico and Spain. In the same document the Fathers were also instructed to avoid suspicien by employing none but male servants. Bancroft, II, 163.

of great necessity, and by formal permission from
the superior or confessor. He warned them to avoid
suspicious company and all counsel and association
with women, that no breath of scandal might be
raised. *The matter of neglect to teach in the native
tongue was touched upon more emphatically than before.* (8)

On December 19th, 1817, Fr President Payeras issued a circular to the Fathers on their duties as
priests, confessors, and guardians of public morals,
with particular reference to their obligations toward
the Spanish population.

In 1820 Fr. Lopez, the guardian of San Fernando,
addressed the missionaries in California on their
worldly extravagance, and warned them earnestly a-
gainst even the appearance of evil. It had been reported in Mexico that the Franciscans in California,
forgetting the example of their predecessors, of whom
only the old and infirm had travelled on horseback,
or otherwise than on foot, were using carts with two
wheels, and even wagons with four wheels. This fact
had given rise in Mexico to the scandalous report
that the Fathers in California, far from e idt ring hardships, were living in wealth and ease. Hence the discretory of the college had voted unanimously that every carriage must be burnt at once, if it could not be
converted to some other use than carrying the missionaries. The Fr. Prefect was charged with the immediate execution of this order, which was, however,
accompanied with much praise of those same Fathers
for their faithfulness in other respects. (9)

In May 1816 Fr. Juan Buenaventura Bestard, commissary general of the Indies, called upon the American members of the Franciscan Order for information about themselves, their past lives, and present
positions. The reports were to be rendered to their

---

(8) Banc. II, 400-401.   (9) Ibid, II, 402.

immediate superiors, who were to add notes on the
various topics. In accordance with this request, Fr.
Sarría, on May 28d, 1817, sent out a circular of
eight blank leaves, enclosing a copy of Fr. Bestard's
order, and in a few lines on the first page of his circular he called for the record of their lives and services. Each, on receiving the document, inscribed on
it a brief autobiography of himself, signed his name
and position, and passed the paper to the nearest
companion missionary, until within a month the circular contained the life of each of the thirty-five Fathers then stationed in California. The original statements thus obtained were embodied with additions
in Fr. Sarria's report of November 5th, 1817. (10)

In August 1818 the commissary general instructed
the prefect to release Fr. Señan from other duties in
order that he might be induced to prepare a historical account of the missions, a work which he was exhorted to begin in the Lord's name and with the Fr.
commissary's blessing. In September 1819, Fr. Payeras, having consulted Fr. Señan and obtained his consent to undertake the task, instructed all the Fathers
to render him every possible assistance. Fr. Señan,
however, died in 1823, and there is no evidence that
he left any part of his work completed, though,
doubtless, he collected some material for his missionary chronicle. (11)

On September 17th, 1819, (12) Fr. President Payeras made a report to the governor, which was an eloquent statement of the mission troubles, particularly
in their relations to the pagans and the runaway neophytes. Formerly, says Fr. Payeras, the soldiers protected both Fathers and settlers, kept the Indians
under the sweet yoke of the Gospel, and inspired respect and fear among the gentiles; but now the spirit of insubordination and independence spreading

through the world had reached California and affected both soldiers and Indians. The neophytes were deserting the missions, and the pagans, under the leadership of renegade Christians, were daily becoming more bold and hostile.

THE population of Spanish and mixed blood, known as gente de razon, at the close of 1820 amounted to 3,270 souls. The total neophyte population had increased from 18,770 to 20,478 in the ten years, and there were twenty missions. (13)

OF the thirty-nine Fathers in the province at the end of 1810, four had retired to the college before 1820; seven had died at their posts; and nine new Fathers had entered the field, so that thirty-seven still remained at work among the natives of California. Fr. Señan was the only one left of those who had come before 1790. (14)

THE number of baptisms in all the missions during this period 1810-1820 was 18,718. As many as 16,525 persons died, and 4,695 marriages were blessed. Large stock at the end of 1820 amounted to 149,489 head, a gain of 13,188 over 1810; small stock, or sheep, gained 84,679 head, there being 191,698 in the mission pastures at the end of 1820, while 4,953 horses, a gain of 1257, belonged to the missions. Agricultural products averaged 118-625 bushels a year. (15)

THE raising of cotton was unsuccessfully attempted at San Gabriel as early as 1808. Olives from the mission orchards were utilized in the manufacture of oil

---

(13) "Informes Generales" 1810-1820. (14) Banc. II, 393-397. The thirty-seven on the missions in 1820 were as follows: Abella, Amorós, Arroyo, Barona, Boscana, Cabot, J., Cabot, P., Catalá, Duran, Fortuni, Gil, Jaime, Martin, Martinez, Payeras, Peyri, Rodriguez, Salzar, Sanchez, Sancho, Sarria, Señan, Suñer, Tapis, Ulibarri, Uria, Viador, and Zalvidea, with the new-comers: Altimira, Escudé, Esténega, Martin, Nuez, Olbés, Oliva, Ordaz, and Ripoll. Among the "gente de razon," or Spanish settlers, as registered in the mission books, there were 1,873 baptisms, 585 deaths, and 250 marriages. (15) "Informes Generales" 1810-1820. Bancroft's figures do not agree with the reports of the Fathers.

at San Diego, and at some other places, between 1801 and 1808. Hemp was also cultivated at the missions. In 1810 there were shipped from San Gabriel, 15,582 pounds; from San Fernando, 7,600 ℔s; Santa Inés, 12,508 ℔s. ; San Buenaventura, 9,008 ℔s.; San Luis, 2,044 ℔s.; Santa Barbara, 4,588 ℔s.; San Diego, 44,781 ℔s.; Monterey, 4,537 ℔s.

MANUFACTURING industries were confined to the missions, where the neophytes under missionary superintendence worked the wool, shorn from their large flocks, into blankets and coarse fabrics which sufficed for their clothing. They also made soap, tanned various kinds of skins and hides, made shoes and saddles, and did the rude carpenter's, cabinetmaker's, and blacksmith's work needed at the missions. There are, however, no statistics or details respecting the products of the mission workshops. (16)

CHAPTER XVII.

SECULARIZATION PUBLISHED IN CALIFORNIA—THE FATHERS READY TO LEAVE—INSTRUCTIONS TO THE MISSIONARIES—FR. PAYERAS' PROTEST—EXPEDITION TO THE NORTH—INDEPENDENCE OF MEXICO—DEATH OF FR. PAYERAS—DEATH OF FR. SEÑAN—THE FATHERS REFUSE TO TAKE THE OATH OF ALLEGIANCE—FR. MARTINEZ BANISHED.

As early as 1813 the Spanish Cortes had passed a decree secularizing, or rather confiscating, all the missions in America. After an unexplained delay of seven years, the royal confirmation of the decree was published by Viceroy Venadito on January 20th, 1821. The news was at once forwarded by the Fr. Guardian to Fr. Payeras, with instructions to comply at once with the requirements of the decree

------

(16) Banc., II, 175-180.

by surrendering the administration of the temporalities to the government, but to insist on exact inventories and other requisite formalities. He was also to
notify the bishop that the Fathers were ready to give
up the missions as soon as demanded. Accordingly,
in July he notified Governor Sola that the missionaries rejoiced at the prospect of being free to engage
in new spiritual conquests, or to seek retirement at
their college. A similar notice was sent to the bishop
of Sonora, and a corresponding information was forwarded to all the missionaric.

In the communications of the Fr Guardian and the
Fr. Prefect, says Bancroft, there appears no word of
protest, no complaint, but only joy as at relief from
a burden. Doubtless there was at the college, and in
the minds of the Fr. President and the Fr. Prefect,
a feeling of weariness and disgust arising from the
complications of the temporal management during the
past ten years, and a corresponding sense of relief
from the measure proposed. In his letter to the Fathers Fr. Payeras exhorts them to have all in readi-
ness, both temporal and spiritual, so as "to reply
with sonorous voice to the first lawful call, whether
ecclesiastical or political, *Domine, ecce adsum.*"

Governor Sola in his reply to Fr. Payeras stated
that he had received no official news of the matter
in question, but that on receipt of such news he
"would act with the circumspection and prudence
which so delicate a subject demands." The bishop of
Sonora replied that secularization had not been enforced anywhere in America, and that the California
Fathers might remain in charge of their missions. (1)

On January 28d, 1821, Fr. Payeras issued a circular dated at Soledád, in which he embodied the views
of the Fr. Guardian communicated to all the religious the year previous upon the use of coaches, and

(1) Bancroft. II, 431-433.

warned them against other luxuries and comforts incompatible with a Franciscan's vow. He doubted the propriety of riding on horseback; but surely no Father should ride in any other vehicle than the ordinary cart of the country drawn by oxen or mules, and then only when necessary, as in the case of sickness. During the same year, and also the next, the Fr. Prefect issued two other letters on the same subject, in which, however, he seems to have modified his views somewhat, as he declared that the Fr. President need have no scruples in using a cart, and advised the aged to take care of themselves, since there was no hope of being relieved from duty. (2)

On June 18th, 1821, Fr. Payeras sent a long and earnest protest to the college against Governor Sola's ever-increasing interference in the temporal management of the missions. The immediate occasion of this protest was Sola's demand for the original invoices and accounts of all mission trade, in order, as the Father claimed with reason, to pry into mission affairs, to show his authority, and to learn what the missionaries possessed.

From the first, he urged, Sola had held radical views of missionary subordination to provincial authority, and had regarded the Fathers as mere administrators of estates. Hitherto the governor's inquisitive schemes had been baffled, chiefly through the old time decision that the missionary stood *in loco parentis* to the Indians, and had exclusive control of them and their property; but now, in view of the changes in Spain, Sola proposed to revive his plans, and this demand for papers was doubtles a first step in that direction. He pointed to the progress of the missions from struggling poverty to their present position as proof of the missionaries' successful management, and referred to the fact that the missions had

(2) Bancroft, II. 438.

supported the province for the last ten years, during which the religious had not received their annual allowance. He declared that this year, as in former years, the response to the governor's frequent calls for aid had been liberal and cheerful, and denied the charge that the missions had wealth other than what was visible, the most having from $100 to $1,000 in money, and a few $3,000 or $4,000, which was needed for current expenses. Fr. Payeras, moreover, insisted that the mission property, though large in the aggregate, would afford but little to each of its thousands of owners. (3)

HOWEVER, as destitution continued to press upon the soldiers, and the only source of relief, as in former years, were the missions, from them were obtained food and other articles for actual consumption, contributions of produce for trade with foreign vessels, laborers for presidio work, cattle for the company ranches, and even advances of money. Only in one instance did a Father protest to his superior that the soldiers were not content with the necessaries of life, often coupled their demands with threats, and were always grumbling, no matter how much the missionaries exerted themselves. Governor Sola acknowledged the aid received from the missions, and in one instance the Mexican official journal took notice of it. Thus in January 1821 Fr. Payeras deemed the call upon the missions for $3,000 in coin for an arsenal at Monterey just, and urged each mission to contribute. Each mission gave from $25–$200. In February Sola acknowledged receiving eighty horses, eighty

---

(3) Bancroft, II, 433-435. Bancroft here professes to be astonished that the Franciscans, who without a word of protest cheerfully agreed to give up all the missions, could so earnestly and eloquently resist demands upon the missions, which he thinks were not so much oppressed after all. It is strange he does not comprehend the difference. The Franciscans claimed nothing for themselves, but standing in the position of parents towards the Indians they had to protect the rights of their wards, and they did so fearlessly.

saddles, and fifty blankets through Fr. Martínez as a donation for the troops. San Francisco gave $1,200 worth of soap this year, as the mission had no wheat. In May 800 cattle were furnished by the missions, and $6,000 were advanced in June. The missions also offered to furnish supplies for the troops in Lower California. (4)

LATE in the year of 1821 Governor Sola sent an expedition north of San Rafael. Fr. Blas Orduz accompanied the troops as chaplain and chronicler. Some neophytes were also attached to the force which sailed from San Francisco on October 18th. Starting from the strait on the morning of the 22d, the company for nine days marched northward up the valley of the Sacramento, which they called Jesus Maria. The northern limit reached seems to point to the latitude of Shasta or Weaverville. For nine days the explorers then marched southward over the mountains. It would seem from the diary that the party entered the region of Ukiah from the direction of the Caw Mountains on the east and northeast. (5)

THE party also came to a place thirteen leagues above the mouth of the Russian River in the region of Cloverdale. Returning, probably by way of the modern Healdsburg and Santa Rosa, the party arrived at San Rafael on November 12th. This was the most extensive northern land expedition ever made by the Spaniards in California. Fr. Ordaz's diary of the famous trip is still extant. (6)

MEXICO's independence from Spain and Iturbide's imperial regency, established in September, was not announced in California before the end of 1821. The

(4) Banc. II 436-439.   (5) From 1587-1823 Round Valley, Ukiah, Hopland, and surrounding Indian missions, the district traversed by Fr. Ordaz if Bancroft is correct, were in charge of the Franciscan Fathers, among whom was the writer. Big Valley, east of the Caw Mountains, perhaps also visited by the Franciscan traveller, is still in charge of the Fathers, who at St. Turibius have a residence.   (6) Banc. II, 445-449.

Franciscan Fathers all took the oath of allegiance to
the new government. (7)

ı In 1823 the missions suffered a great loss in the
death of Fr. Prefect Payeras and Fr. President José
Señan. The former died on April 28th at his own
mission of Purisima, and was buried next day under
the pulpit of the mission church. "There was no missionary of better and more even-balanced ability in
the province," says Bancroft. "He was personally a
popular man on account of his affable manners, kindness of heart, and unselfish devotion to the welfare of
all. It was impossible to quarrel with him; and even
Governor Sola's peevish and annoying complaints
never ruffled his temper. Yet he had extraordinary
business ability, was a clear and forcible as well as
a voluminous writer, and withal a man of great
strength of mind and firmness of character."

THE vice-prefect and president of the missions, Fr.
Señan, succeeded Fr. Payeras temporarily. Fr. Señar,
however, also died on August 24th of the same
year. He had named Fr. Sarría as his successor on the
4th, until the college of San Fernando could make
an appointment. Fr. Sarría learned of the death of Fr.
Señan on September 5th, and held the office of prefect *ad intermin* until November 1824, when he was
appointed and continued in office throughout the decade. He was also president of the missions till April
1825, when Fr. Narciso Duran became president. The
latter was succeeded by Fr. José Bernardo Sanchez,
who held the office until 1831, though Fr. Duran was
reelected in May 1830. (8)

EARLY in 1825 Governor Arguello received the fed-
eral constitution of the Mexican republic adopted by
Congress October 4th, 1824. Fr. Prefect Sarría declined to take the oath of allegiance. However, he

(7) Bancroft, II, 451-452. (8) Both, Fr. Duran and Fr. Sanchez, held the title of vicar under the bishop, Fr. Duran having received his appointment
as early as 1824. Bancroft II, 400-401; 656.

left each of the Fathers free to decide for himself, and refused to issue instructions on the subject. He defended his action in letters to the governor, and stated that anterior obligation to the king of Spain was the ground on which he based his refusal. On the 7th of April the *diputacion* (9) took up the matter. Francisco Castro urged immediate steps to learn which of the Fathers would follow the example of their superior. He also proposed that those who took this course should be deprived of all control of the temporalities of their respective missions, which should be intrusted to administrators. Governor Arguello opposed the measure, because it might force the missionaries to abandon the missions altogether, and also because it would be impossible to find competent administrators. The final result was an order to the commandants that each Father should be required to state in writing whether he would take the oath or not. (10)

When Fr. Duran became president of the missions in 1825, he likewise refused to take the oath of allegiance, not, as he said, from "any disaffection to the independence," nor for any "odious passion," for he indeed believed Spain was better off without Mexico; but he was tired of taking so many oaths during the past few years, when oaths seemed to have become mere playthings. "I offer", he wrote, "an oath to do nothing against the established government, and if this be not accepted, I am resigned to the penalty of expatriation which the constitution imposes." Meanwhile the news that Fr. Prefect Sarría had refused to take the oath was sent to Mexico, and in June an order from Victoria, the Mexican president, was despatched to California that the obstinate prefect should be arrested and sent to Mexico by the first vessel. This order was carried into effect in October,

---

(9) Legislative assembly.   (10) Bancroft III, 7; 16-18.

as appears indirectly from Governor Echandia's communication to Fr. Duran, in which the latter was directed to proceed to San Diego and take the oath, in
order that he might assume the duties of Fr. Sarría
during the latter's arrest. That is as far as the matter went; for Fr. Sarría retained the position of comisario prefecto of the missions, and was not dis-
turbed in the performance of his duties, though nominally under arrest as a recalcitrant Spaniard. (11)

As a rule the missionaries refused to take the oath
of allegiance to the constitution of 1824, but it was
not deemed wise to expel any of them for that reason. The great fear was that they might leave the
territory in a body if pressed too hard. As matters
were, the rulers and leading citizens understood that
any radical and sudden change, effected without the
aid of the Fathers, would ruin the territory by cutting off its chief resources, and exposing them to the
raids of hostile Indians. Besides there were none to
take their places. Hence Gov. Echandía excused himself for not enforcing the decree against the Fathers,
on the ground that all the Franciscans except three
were Spaniards, and it would be manifestly absurd to
expel them with nobody to take their place. He
urged the Mexican government to allow them to remain permanently in the territory. Moreover the
ayuntamientos(12)of San José, Monterey, and perhaps
other places, sent petitions on the evils that must
result from expelling the missionaries; they expressed
the deepest love and veneration for the Fathers, and
pleaded eloquently that the people might not be deprived of their spiritual guides. The matter seems to
have rested there. One of the Fathers, however,
passed beyond the reach of political intrigues by
dying before the end of 1820. This was the aged and
infirm Fr. Jaime. Two others, Fathers Ripoll and Al-

---

(11) Banc., III, 18-19; 87.   (12) Town councils.

timira, took passage for Spain on board the American brig Harbinger, at the end of 1827, or perhaps in January 1828. (18)

THOUGH attached to the old system, "the most serious charge that could be brought against the Fathers was an occasional injudicious use of the tongue," says Bancroft. Of all the missionaries Fr. Martínez of San Luis Obispo was the most outspoken and independent in political matters. Governor Echandía from personal motives deemed his absence desirable, and he determined to make an example of this Father The governor charged Fr. Martínez with complicity in the Solis revolt, to give more significance to the arrest. 'The evidence," Bancroft himself says, "was very weak; but there was no risk, since as a Spaniard the accused might be at any time exiled legally." He was arrested in February 1830, and confined in a room of the comandancia at Santa Barbara. In his testimony he denied all the allegations against him, except that of giving food to the soldiers as others had done, and as was customary for the missionaries to do, whoever their guests might be. He claimed to have tried to dissuade Solis from the foolish scheme of raising the Spanish flag. In a long and eloquent communication addressed to Echandía against the manner of his treatment, Fr. Martínez, while not denying his well-known political sentiments claimed that he was not such a fool as to suppose that Spain could be benefited by petty revolts in California, that he desired the welfare of the territory, and that in his opinion it could not be advantageously separated from Mexico. The two Fathers Cabot testified to having seen letters in which Fr. Martínez declined to take part in the political scheme of Solis, and declared that, if the king wished to conquer any part of America, he might do it himself.

(18) Banc. III 90-97.

Fr. Sarría, too, presented an argument to prove Fr. Martínez innocent. On the 9th of March, however, a council of war, composed of six officers, besides the governor, decided by a vote of five to one that the accused should be sent out of Mexican territory by the first vessel available. Many of the items rested on the testimony of a single soldier. An English ship thereupon took the Father to Callao which he reached in June. (14)

CHAPTER XVIII.

SECULARIZATION—DESTITUTION—MISSIONS TAXED—INDIAN REVOLT—STATISTICS—DECREE OF SECULARIZATION PUBLISHED—OPINION OF SOME OF THE FATHERS—FR. DURAN'S COMMENTARIES—THE PIOUS FUND—ITS HISTORY—ECHANDIA'S REGULATIONS—FR. SANCHEZ' CRITICISM—FR. PEYRI.

THE most important problem effecting the missions was that of secularization. The governor recognized the impossibility of immediate action, but he resolved to make a step in that direction. On July 25th he issued a proclamation of partial "emancipation" in favor of the mission Indians. By its terms those desiring to leave the missions might do so, provided they had been Christians from childhood, or for fifteen years, were married, or at least not minors, and had some means of gaining a livelihood. The order, however, applied only to the districts of San Diego, Santa Barbara, and Monterey. In 1828 San Francisco was included, excepting the frontier missions of San Rafael and San Francisco Solano. It does not appear that the missionaries made any special opposition. The experiment was tried with a few neophytes who, as might have been foreseen, fell into excesses, gam-

(13) Banc. III 98-100.

bled away their property, and were compelled to beg
or steal. (1)

NEVERTHELESS, at the session of July 20th, 1830,
Echandía brought his secularization scheme before the
diputacion, and this body, after much discussion and
some slight modifications, approved the plan. It provided for the gradual transformation of the missions
into pueblos or towns. Each neophyte was to have a
share in the mission lands and other property. The
Fathers might remain as curates, or establish a new
line of missions on the gentile frontier. Provisions
were also made for the establishment of two Franciscan convents, at Santa Clara and at San Gabriel, for
which twenty or more religious were to be sent from
Mexico at the expense of the Pious Fund, and to
which the Spanish Fathers allowed to remain might
attach themselves. These convents were intended to
supply the future missionaries, curates, and chaplains.
The measure, with which the Fathers had nothing to
do, was not to be enforced without the approval of
the supreme government. The plan was forwarded to
Mexico in September 1830, but the general government took no action in the matter. (2)

THERE was considerable distress in some seasons of
this period all over California. Fr. Duran on one occasion told Fr. Martínez of San Francisco that no
more supplies could be sent, and that it would be
best to discharge the guards if there was a lack
of rations. Fr. Viader wrote that Santa Clara had to
buy wheat for its neophytes, while the pueblo had
plenty of grain to sell to the presidios. The destitution was very great at San Diego, but the commandant in his letters stated that the Fathers gave all
they could. In Mexico the Fr. Guardian made a detailed representation to Minister Aleman on the critical condition of affairs in California, and showed

---

(1) Banc., III 100-104.   (2) Ibid. III, 105-108.

that the Indians were naturally disgusted, since by
their labor they had to support themselves, the missionaries, the government, and the troops. He declared
the amount of unpaid drafts to be $250,151, whilst
the unpaid stipends amounted to $158,712; and he
begged most earnestly for at least a partial payment
to save the missions from ruin. (3)

BESIDES furnishing supplies for worthless drafts and
paying commercial toll and taxes, the missionaries
had to contribute a tithe of all the mission products
to the government. The method of collection was to
exact from each mission the largest possible amount
of supplies for guards and presidial garrisons, and at
the end of each year to give credit on account for
the excess of amounts thus furnished over the taxes.
"I find no evidence," says Bancroft, "that any part
of the balance was paid in any instance." (4)

THE neophytes of Santa Inés, Santa Barbara, and
Purisima in 1824 revolted against the military authorities, and caused some bloodshed. The Fathers in
Mexico, advised by those in California, declared the
real cause to be the discontent of the Indians at
having to support the troops by their hard labor
without pay, which discontent was fanned into revolution by continued acts of cruelty. At any rate there
was no ill feeling shown by the Indians against the
Fathers.(5)

MEANWHILE the missions received nothing from the
Pious Fund through the Mexican treasury. During
1819-1820, $24,000 of the stipend were paid, but it is
not certain that even this amount ever came to California. (6)

As registered in the mission books, during the decade 1820-1830, there were 1,866 Baptisms, 717 death,
and 357 marriages among the Spanish and mixed

(3) Banc. III. 21.   (4) Ibid. 87-88.   (5) Ibid. II. 527-528.   (6) Ibid.
III. 80.

white population, which in 1880 numbered 4,250 for whole California. The Franciscan Fathers were in charge of the settlers, as there were no resident secular priests in the territory. (7)

THE neophyte population had fallen from 20,473 in 1820 to 18,815 at the close of 1831. (8) There were probably about 2,000 pagan Indians living in the ranchos, pueblos, and presidios, though there are no data on which to base any estimate respecting the number of gentiles. In only a few missions were there any more pagans accessible for conversion, except at very great distances. During this period in all the Indian mission 18,726 persons were baptized, and 16,885 deaths occured, whilst 5,544 couples were joined in matrimony. Mission cattle increased from 149,489 to 152,900 head; horses decreased from 4,953 to 4,905; and sheep likewise decreased from 191,693 to 153,655. The average crop of grain amounted to 86,250 bushels The largest crop during the whole existence of the missions, 180,000 bushels, was in 1821. (9)

OF the thirty-seven Franciscans at work in 1820 ten died before 1831, four left California, and only three came to take their places. Only twenty-six, therefore, were in charge of twenty-one missions. The death of Fr. Señan left none alive of those who had come before 1790; and the pioneers of earlier date than 1800 were reduced to five. (10)

SECULARIZATION of the missions continued to be the talk among politicans, and though Governor Echandía well knew that the territorial government had no power to secularize the missions, a decree of secularization was issued January 6th, 1831. "It was an ille-

(7) Laue. II. 653.   (8) "Informes Generales." The official reports of the Fr. Superior of the California missions close with 1831, at least as far as the writer has been able to obtain them. The report of 1831 is not signed. The one of 1820 is signed by Fr. Sanchez. The dates and other statistical matters after 1831 must be supplied from Bancroft, whose figures we have found to be incorrect so far, though not very materially so.   (9) "Informes Generales." 1820-1831; Bancroft II, 654-659.   (10) Bancroft II, 654-655.

gal and even revolutionary measure," says Bancroft.
With the proper instructions the document was sent
not only to local officials, but to the Fr. Prefect and
to the bishop, who were urged to instruct and prepare the Fathers for the change. The ayuntamiento of
Monterey chose a comisionado for each of the seven
missions of the military district. San Carlos and San
Gabriel were to be organized into towns at once,
and the surplus property, after distributing the lands
to the neophytes, was to pass under the control of
secular administrators. A similar change was to be
effected at most of the other missions as rapidly as
the comisionados could attend to their duties. Castro
and Alvarado were sent to San Miguel and San Luis
Obispo, where they read the decree and made speech-
es to the Indians. At San Luis the comisarios were
elected; but at San Miguel, after listening to the
speakers the neophytes expressed a decided preference
for the missionary and the old system. Alvarado,
from a cart in the mission courtyard, vividly pict-
ured the advantages of freedom to the Indians; he
then requested those who wished to remain under
the missionary to stand on the left, and those pre-
ferring freedom, on the right. Nearly all went to the
left and were soon joined by the small minority. The
Indians at San Luis and San Antonio expressed the
same views. On account of the arrival of Victoria,
the new governor, the matter went no further than
the election of the comisarios; nor is there any record that it went even so far in the districts of San
Francisco and San José. (11)

In August 1831 Fr. President Duran issued a circular, in which he asked the Fathers for their opinions of a scheme for emancipating the neophytes,
and distributing the estates on a basis including the
maintenance of religious service, the support of the

(11) Bancroft, III, 301-308.

missionaries, and the retension of community property to a certain amount with which to found new
missions. There are extant three replies of as many
religious.

Fr. Juan Cabot wrote from San Miguel that, while
he would be glad to be freed from his cares, he
could see no way of distributing the estates without
ruin. The Indians of his mission would have to be
scattered at long distances in order to get a living,
and he could not be responsible for their spiritual
needs. Fr. José Joaquin Jimenez of Santa Cruz wrote
that, in view of the reasons urged by the government, and of the fact that the burden was becoming
insupportable to the religious, it would be wisest to
dismiss the Indians and distribute the property on
the basis proposed, but also that the Indians should
be obliged to keep their share of the land and to
work. Fr. José Sanchez deemed the execution of the
project probably inevitable, but sure to result, as it
was intended to, in total destruction of the missions.
Taking into consideration what had happene din Lower California and Sonora, he could see no possibili-
ty of good results here. "So far as it concerns me
personally," he wrote, "would that it might be to-
morrow, that I might retire between the four walls
of a cell to weep over the time I have wasted in behalf of these miserables." (12)

On December 31st, 1831, Fr. Duran prepared a series of commentaries on the decree of January, for
use probably in Mexico. "It was one of the ablest
documents," says Bancroft, "that was ever written
by a friar in California, but one which cannot be
presented en resumé, and much too long for literal
reproduction. On the decree, article by article, Fr.
Narcisco Duran expends the full force of his talent
and learning, with not infrequent volleys of wit, sar-

casm, ridicule, and bitter denunciation. Not a weak
spot, and there are many, is overlooked, and not a
weapon neglected. The standard position of all the
missionaries, that the Indians were absolute owners
of the soil and all the mission property, but that
they were still children requiring parental control,
and that the missionaries alone were qualified to exercise that control, and Echandías lack of authority
to make the changes was particularly insisted upon."

Fr. Duran concluded his argument in these words:
"It would be better, with less bluster about the
Indians, to begin with the *gente de razon*. (13)

"LET the latter begin to work, to found establishments and schools, and to practice arts and industries;
then it will be time to lead the Indians to follow a
good example. Are they, but yesterday savages to go
ahead and teach the way to civilized men? To form
such projects of giving freedom to Indians, after having taken a million dollars of their hard earnings for
the troops, and to leave in their endemic sloth the
others, who as a rule know nothing but to ride on
horseback? Truly, I know not from what spirit can
proceed such a policy, or rather I know too well.
Why not write what all say? Why say in whispers
what all say openly? What all believe is that, under
the specious pretext of this scheme, there is a se-
cret plan for a general sack of the mission property:
the leaders in the plot intend to convert as much as
possible of the booty into money to be enjoyed in
foreign lands." (14)

MEANWHILE in the Mexican congress Carlos Carrillo
exerted all his influence and eloquence in opposition
to any change in the mission system. He was a
friend of the missionaries, and foresaw nothing but
ruin in secularization. A branch of the same subject,
and one of more urgent importance at the time than

(13) Settlers of Spanish or mixed blood.   (14) Bancroft., III, 309-310.

secularization of the missions, was the disposition to be made of the Pious Fund, a topic under discussion in congress. (5)

THIS Pious Fund consisted of money and property which had been donated by various Catholics for the purpose of establishing and maintaining Catholic missions. Down to the year 1768 it had grown so much that it yielded a revenue of fifty thousand dollars annually. The beginning of the Fund dates from the year 1697. Before the royal warrants had yet been obtained by the Jesuit Fathers for the reduction of California, Fr. Salvatierra, S. J. proceeded to Mexico for the purpose of collecting funds for the establishment of missions. Among those who subscribed liberally were Don Alonso Davolas, Count de Mira Vallez, and Don Mateo Fernandez de la Cruz, who donated two thousand dollars. This, with the other private subscriptions collected by the Father, amounted to fifteen thousand dollars. At the same time the Congregation of Our Lady of Dolors gave eight thousand dollars as a fund for one mission, to which they afterwards added two thousand dollars more, as nothing short of ten thousand dollars sufficed for the establishment and maintenance of a mission. During the same year Don Juan Cavallero y Ozio, a devout priest of the city of Querétaro, subscribed twenty thousand crowns for the establishment of two other missions, which, added to the sums already mentioned, constituted the beginning of what was afterwards known as the Pious Fund of California. (6)

ON the fifth of February 1697 the royal warrants were issued to Father Salvatierra, and two days later he left Mexico to set out for California, which he reached in the same year. For the next few years Fr. Kino, S. J., who was in Sonora, also collected what subscriptions he could obtain, and sent them to his

(5) Bancroft. 311.   (6) Gleeson, Vol. II, 138-139.

brother religious. The next important donation, was
made in 1702 by Don José de la Puente, who subscribed for the establishment of three missions; while
Don Nicolas de Artega and his wife founded another
mission, which made the sum equal to forty thousand
dollars. To these other donations were constantly added, so that in 1768 the aggregate sums collected a-
mounted to one million two hundred and seventy-
three thousand dollars, of which only eighteen thousand dollars had been received from the government.
It must be observed that these donations were given
for the establishment and maintenance of the missions *in perpetuum*. To avoid the loss of any part of
the Fund, the money was invested in land and other
real estate, the annual revenue of which would serve
for the maintenance of the missions. Down to 1768
the Pious Fund remained under the control of the
Jesuit Fathers; but on the expulsion of these religious it was taken charge of by the Spanish authorities, and farmed for the benefit of the missions. The
Fund in 1768, as we have already seen, yielded an
annual revenue of fifty thousand dollars. Twenty-four
thosand of this sum was expended in stipends for the
Franciscan and Dominican missionaries, and twenty-
six thousand dollars for general mission purposes.
This arrangement lasted down to about 1807, from
which date to 1831 the missionaries received only
$24,000, if indeed it ever reached California.

Don Carrillo's efforts in behalf of the missions
proved of no avail. "Under the plea that the missions were no longer in need of external support, the
congress of Mexico by a decree, passed on the 25th
of May, 1832, empowered the executive to rent out
all the mission properties for a period of seven
years, the proceeds to be paid into the national
treasury." (7)

---

(8) Gleason II. 195; Banc., III. 311—313.

On November 18th, 1832, Governor Echandía issued supplementary regulations, to bring about the secularization of the missions, which did not go so far as the decree of January. Moreover, they were intended to apply to the four southernmost missions only. It was first submitted to the missionaries, who were at the same time asked to accept the positions of parish priests. Fr. Sanchez replied in a long series of critical notes on both preface and reglamento. "This criticism," Bancroft says, "is one to which it is impossible to do justice here, and to which may be applied much of what I said about Duran's notes on the original decree. Giving his attention chiefly to the preamble, Fr. Sanchez begins by suggesting that the precepts of obedience to law would come with better grace from one who had given a better example than Echandía. His pretensions to teach the padres their obligations and rights, or to change their status, are met with protest and ridicule. If the laws and his instructions required him to secularize the missions, why had he waited six years, until the arrival of his successor, before acting? If the Indians of the south, as was certainly true, were assuming a threatening attitude, it was due to the license they were enjoying under Echandía, and to his unwise act in having put arms into their hands against Zamorano, which would be a reason for a return to the old restraint rather than for additional license. As to the enthusiasm of the Indians for Echandía, the Father has little to say beyond reminding him that there are several ways of winning popularity among school-boys, one of the most successful being to let them do as they please."

Fr. Sanchez concludes the document as follows: "It seems to me that I have given some convincing proofs, not perhaps of absurdities, I do not venture to say that, but of difficulties as they appear to me at first reading. I do not wish to engage in a prolonged dispute with Echandía; let him do what may seem best. I have expressed my views, not so much for him, as for an instruction to the Fathers that they are by no means to lend themselves to any such cooperation as is demanded by that gentleman, since to do so would be to subscribe to the ruin of their missions, and to the ignominy of all the insults, suspicions, and distrust expressed in his plan, which were by no means necessary if only the welfare of the Indians were sought. Let Señor Echandía, then, do what he pleases about the missions, but let him not count on the cooperation of the Fathers, which he himself must know to be out of the question. The missionaries will serve as such and in no other capacity, until the curia ecclesiastica, in accord with the supreme government, communicating with us through our prelate, may see fit to order a competent change, and so long as they are given the necessary food to support life; and if this be wanting they have the natural and divine right to shake off the dust from their shoes, and go to other work wherever it may be found." (8)

Fr. Duran also issued a series of notes similar to those of Fr. Sanchez. The answers from the Fathers of San Diego, San Luis, San Juan, and San Gabriel were to the effect that they left the matter entirely with their superiors. Fr. Martin added that, since May 20, 1832, the neophytes at San Diego had already managed temporal affairs for themselves, except the wine cellars. Fr. Zalvidea declared that he would gladly be relieved of the burden; that he had toiled over twenty years, but had not saved half a dollar. There is nothing on record to show that Echandía took any further steps before the end of 1832. (9)

Fr. Antonio Peyri left California at the beginning of the year; and Fr. Antonio Menendez, a Domini-

(8) Bancrof:, III. 315-316.   (9) Banc, III. 316-317,

can, who for six years had served as chaplain at different places, died in August. Two priests from the Sandwich Islands remained in the country for five years about this period; they were Jean Alexis Auguste Bachelot, prefect apostolic of the Sandwich Islands, and Patrick Short. They had been driven from their missions through Protestant intrigues. Rev. Bachelot served as assistant priest at San Gabriel, whilst Rev. Short went north and was engaged in some educational enterprise at Monterey in 1834. (10)

CHAPTER XIX.

New Missionaries From Zacatecas—Concordato Funeral—Corporal Punishment—Gov. Figueroa's Report—His Regulations—Fr. Duran's Letter—Indians Unwilling To Be "Emancipated"—Renewed Efforts Fathers Diego And Duran Reply—Six Missions Secularized—Statistics—Missionary Changes—The Rule Of Plunder—The First Bishop Of California.

WITH the new governor, Francisco Figueroa, there came to California a missionary reenforcement of ten Franciscans, all Mexicans by birth. In order to rid the country of the Spanish religious, the government had applied to the College of Our Lady of Guadalupe at Zacatecas for a number of missionaries, and insisted that some Fathers be sent to take the place of the Spaniards. The college reluctantly gave way to the demand, and thus in April 1833 (1) ten Fathers departed for the northern country. The superior of this band of missionaries was Fr. Francisco García Diego with the title of commissary. In California these religious were commonly known as Gaudalupanos or Zacatecanos, as the earlier Fathers had been

---

(10) Banc., III, 317. (1) Sotomayor, Historia del Colegio de Guadalupe page 515; Banc., III, 318, says February.

Missionary College Do Nuestra Senora De Guadalupe,
Zacatecas, Mexico.

called Fernandinos from the name of their college.
Immediately after their arrival the Zacatecanos
were put in charge of the seven missions from San
Carlos northward; their superior, Fr. Diego, went to
reside at Santa Clara. The Fernandinos who had been
at these missions retired to the southern establishments. (2)

CONSIDERING the importance of the subject, there is
a remarkable absence of original records respecting
the coming of the Fathers from Zacatecas and the
division of the missions; though it cannot be doubted
that much which is no longer extant was written at
the time. This is also the case respecting many important topics of mission history during these last
years. It will be remembered that in 1817 the southern missions were ceded by the college of San Fernando to the Franciscans of the college at Orizaba;
but on account of troubles in Mexico and the dissatisfaction of the California Fathers the change was
not consummated. The transfer of the northern missions was evidently agreed upon in Mexico, but, beyond the presence of the ten Zacatecanos in California, there is no account of the journey, and no official record of their arrival extant. Fr. Duran in a
circular to the Fernandinos, January 23d, 1833, alluded to the cession as a matter in which he should lose
no time, as he had already permitted the superior of
the Zacatecans to station his religious so that they

(2) The Fathers from Zacatecas were: Francisco Garcia Diego, the super-
ior, who succeeded Fr. Vlader at Santa Clara. Fr. José Maria de Jesus
Gonzalez Rubio, who took Fr. Duran's place at San José; José Maria de
Jesus Gutierrez, who relieved Fr. Fortuni at San Francisco Solano; Ra-
fael de Jesus Moreno, was the assistant of Fr. Diego at Santa Clara;
Lorenzo de la Concepcion Quijas, followed Fr. Estenega at San Gabriel,
but soon removed to Solano; Antonio Suarez del Real, who succeeded
Fr. Jimeno at Santa Cruz; José Maria del Refugio Sagrado Suarez del
Real, brother of Fr. Antonio, who took the place of Fr. Abella at San
Carlos; Jesus Maria Vasquez del Mercado, who was stationed at San
Rafael in place of Fr. Amorós; José Bernardino Perez, secretary to Fr.
Diego; and Francisco del Jesus Sanchez, of whom nothing is known
for 8 or 9 years. Bancroft, III 318-319.

could learn their respective duties, and prepare to be installed in the missions. He hoped that the change would enable some of his own brethren to go to the relief of the mother college, which had been reduced to only four Fathers. He, moreover, declared that no one might hope for permission to retire to any other destination. (3)

THE best of feeling existed between the two bands of missionaries in California. A *concordato funeral* was soon concluded between them by virtue of which each Father agreed to say twenty Masses for the soul of any member that might die of the other band. (4)

IT did not take the Zacatecanos long to learn that their lots had not fallen in places altogether pleasant; for in September their superior complained "we cannot subsist here longer, because the climate is destroying our health." Their troubles in 1833, to say nothing of the climate, arose especially from the unmanageable character of the Indians, and from the difficulty of furnishing supplies to the presidios. The Indians did not behave in a satisfactory manner so that some of the missionaries found it necessary to use the lash. In his circular of July 4th, 1833, however, Fr. Diego disapproved of this; for he says: "Mi genio, mis ideas, mi sensibilidad todo junto se opone á esta costumbre que jamas aprobaré. "My nature, my ideas, my feelings are altogether opposed to that custom which I shall never approve." (5)

GOVERNOR Figueroa had been instructed to restore the missions to the condition in which they had been before the publication of Governor Echandia's order of secularization; but at the same time to ascertain what missions were in a condition to be secularized, and to report such a plan as he might deem expedient. His views were for the most part identical with

_____

(3) Banc., III, 320. (4) Ibid. (5) Ibid. 322.

those of his arbitrary predecessor; but the result of
his investigations was the conviction that any general measure of secularization would be ruinous, and
that a change of system must be very gradually effected. In his report to the government Figueroa describes the neophytes as children with a natural pre-
dilection for the customs of their ancestors, and for
a savage life without work. During their reduction
they had learned, perforce, only to cultivate the
soil imperfectly, to practice some rude industries,
and to manage horses. If freed at once from their
present state of mild servitude, they would soon from
proprietors become beggars, after having bartered
away their possessions for liquor and gewgaws. They
would then return to the wilderness and join the
wild Indians in stealing cattle and horses, in order
to sell them to the New Mexicans and foreigners.

NEVERTHELESS, he issued a series of regulations on
gradual emancipation which were to go into effect
provisionally until approved by the government.
Shortly before these regulations were published, Fr.
Duran on July 16th, 1833, wrote a strong letter on
the subject to the governor. He based his opposition
to the measure on the state of things which he had
found at Los Angeles. The two or three hundred Indian inhabitants of that town and neighborhood, he
showed, were beyond all comparison more unfortunate and oppressed than any in the missions. Not one
had a garden, a yoke of oxen, a horse, or house fit
for a rational being. Instead of the equality so much
talked about, the Indians swept the streets and did
all the menial work. For offences scarcely noticed in
others, they were bound naked over a cannon to receive one hundred blows. They were in reality slaves,
being bound for a whole year by an advance of some
trifle, since no Indian looked beyond the present.
They had no ambition for liberty except for savage

liberty and vicious license, which they would purchase at the cost of a thousand oppressions. Fr. Duran said he was convinced by experience, and from
conversing with practical men, that emancipation
would result in slavery or savagism to the Indians,
and in destruction to all their property. He begged
the governor to consider well the results before decid-
ing a subject "worthy the wisdom of a whole congress." However, when he saw the regulations published, Fr. Duran offered no further opposition beyond recommending a change in some of the articles.
His closing suggestion was as follows: "If after
three or four years it shall be noted that the "em-
ancipados" depend on wild fruits for subsistence,
that they allow their live-stock to decrease, that
they neglect their planting and other labors in a
spirit of vagabondage, or that they manifest no zeal
or liking for a rational and civilized life, and if, being several times warned, they do not mend, then
they shall be returned to their missions." (6)

THE governor made an earnest effort to give the
Indians the civil liberty so little prized by them, but
so valuable in the eyes of the Mexican theorists. He
visited the southern missions and exhorted the assembled neophytes to accept the proffered freedom;
but of one hundred and sixty families at San Diego
and San Luis Rey, qualified according to the standard established, only ten could be induced to be
emancipated. At San Juan Capistrano the scheme of
forming a pueblo of the emancipated Indians was
tried; but the results were not encouraging. There
were no Indians "emancipated" north of San Juan
Capistrano. (7)

STILL, in August 1832, Governor Figueroa again
called upon the superiors of the two missionary
bands to state what missions were in condition to be

---

(6) Banc. III 327-331. (7) Ibid. 332.

secularized under the law of 1813; what objections
to secularization existed; and what would be the
best means to be employed. Fr. García Diego for the
Zacatecanos replied that all the missions under his
charge, except Solano, which lacked some weeks of
the required ten years of existence, were subject to
secularization according to the law of 1813; but he
believed that the law could not be applied to California without inevitable ruin to the missions and to
the neophytes. The law, he declared, was framed 2,000
leagues away by men who had no knowledge of the
character and needs of the California Indians. Emancipated Indians would return to nakedness and savagism. Good men would not be chosen for alcaldes,
and the Fathers would have to content themselves
with saying Mass and hearing the confession of those
who applied. Only under restraint could the Indians
be made to attend to their religious duties. At all
events, the Fathers would not serve as mere curates,
and as the bishop had no priests to take their places
the missions would perish. (8)

Fr. Duran in behalf of the Fernandinos also opposed a change in the mission system. He pointed
out two great obstacles which must be overcome before secularization could be beneficial to all parties
concerned: first, the natural apathy, indolence, and
incompetency of the Indians; and second, the burden
imposed upon the missions for the support of the
troops which had been borne by these establishments
for more than twenty years. Of course, the natives
would do nothing for the support of the soldiers after
the missions were secularized; and, if any of their
property were taken by force, the Indians would find
means to do away with the rest and escape to the
wilderness and to barbarism. Fr. Duran, disclaimed
any opposition from motives of self-interest, but the

(8) Banc. III, 313.

law of 1818 was altogether inadæquate, as it had
been made by men who knew nothing of the subject
in its Californian phases. The ten year rule should
be set aside and another adopted, if the results of
half a century's work were to be saved. Without
waiting for the report of the governor, however, the
national congress passed a bill for the secularization
of the missions on the 17th of August, 1833. The law
directed that the missions should be converted into
parishes under the management of the ordinary ec-
clesicsti al authorities. (9)

SIX missions were secularized in 1834; these were
San Diego, San Luis Obispo, San Antonio, Soledád,
San Juan Bautista, and San Francisco Solano. No
change took place at San Buenaventura, Santa Inéz,
San Miguel, Santa Clara, and San José. Thus in sixteen missions the missionaries were deprived of the
temporal management. Comisionados at first took
charge; inventories of all mission property we:e
made; a portion of the property distributed to the neophytes; the Fathers became curates temporarily; and
majordomos, often unofficially called administrators,
succeeded the comisionados, or were managing the estates under their super7ision. The Fathers, especially
the Fernandinos, quietly submitted to the new system, and in good faith devoted themselves to the
performance of their new duties, though aware of the
hopelessness of the task in which they were engaged. (10)

REGULAR mission statistics cease almost entirely
with secularization in 1834, even for those establishments which were not secularized until some

(9) Bancroft, III 331-336. The Fr. Guardian of the Zacatecas college, in a
lottor to Fr. Diego, May 1834, congratulated the Fathers on t'ie adoption
of a measure which would enable them to retire to the motherhouse. In
another letter of June 13th, 1833, he declared that the mission must no
be called parishes, nor the missionaries curates. Banc., III, 347; 352.
(10) Banc. III, 353-355.

years later. Nothing but occasional and fragmentary
reports are extant for the period 1835 to 1846. In
1835 there were twenty-six Fathers in charge of
twenty-one missions. The neophyte population in five
years decreased from 18,726 to about 15,000; only
one mission, San Luis Rey, showed a gain. Baptisms
numbered 8,500 for the four years since 1830. During
the same time 4,250 persons died. (11)

THE reader will have noticed throughout this work
that the mortality among the converts was unusually
large. To what this death-rate should be attributed
it will be difficult to say, Gleeson remarks; nor
could the missionaries themselves assign a positive
cause. Syphilis, measles, and smallpox carried off large
numbers. Some of the diseases, in all probability,
were generated by the sudden change in their lives
from a wandering existence to a quiet, domestic
state. The same result had been previously experienced by the Jesuit Fathers in Lower California,
where great numbers of converts died rapidly. (12)

THE author of "Old Missions" gives another explanation of the high death-rate among the mission Indians. "Many historians," she says, "attribute the
decimation of the native race to the new modes of
life forced upon it by the advance of civilization and
Christianity. Be that as it may, the race was fast
becoming incapable of its own reproduction, even before the advent of the white man, and this must
needs result disastrously to any people." (13)

DURING the four years preceding 1835 cattle decreased to 140,000 head; horses likewise showed a
loss of 4,600 head; and sheep decreased from 150,000
to 130,00. The average yield of grain in all the missions decreased from 57,500 fanegas to 32,700 fanegas a year, or more than forty per cent. The
greatest loss was singularly enough at San Juan Cap-

(11) Banc. III, 366.   (12) Gleeson II, 112.   (13) "Old Missions of California," p. 36.

istrano which had practically been turned into a
pueblo. The new system was beginning to show results not flattering to the enemies of the missionaries. The loss at San Juan Capistrano was seventy-
three per cent. (14)

Two of the Fernandinos, Fr. José Bernardo Sanchez, who had been superior of the missions, and
Fr. Luis Gil y Taboada, died during the year 1833;
and one, Fr. José Viader, left the country. Fr. Narciso Duran succeeded Fr. Sanchez as president or superior of the missions in June 1821. He also held
the offices of vicar to the bishop and ecclesiastical
judge. Fr. Duran's authority, after the coming of the
Zacatecanos, was confined to the missions south of
San Antonio. Fr. Sarría, as already noted, had held
the office of comisario prefecto down to 1830, after
which period the office seems to have been abolished,
as far as the Fernandinos were concerned. In the
north Fr. García Diego was comisario prefecto of the
Zacatecanos, and Fr. Rafael Moreno was president
and vice-prefecto. Both were reelected in 1835. Fr.
Diego at the same time was one of the discretos or
councillors of the college at Zacatecas. (15)

THE venerable ex-prefecto of the Fernandinos, Fr.
Francisco Vincente Sarría, died in 1835; his associate,
Fr. Francisco Javier Uría, had died the year before.
These are the only changes to be noticed in mission-
ary circles, except that Fr. Perez, of the Zacatecanos
disappeared from the records in 1835. (16)

FR. Narciso Duran continued to be the president
or superior of the southern missions until 1838, when
he was succeeded by Fr. Joaquin Jimeno; but in
1837 the office of comisario prefecto seems to have
been revived, for Fr. Duran was appointed to that

(14) Banc., III, :56-357.   (15) Bancroft, 337-338; Sotomayor, p. 644.
(16) Banc. III, 370. Sotomayor mentions a Fr. Bernardino Perez as vicario
and discreto of the college of Zacatecas in 1840; as guardian in 1843, and
again as discreto at the chapter of 1857. Historia p. 644; 647.

position and held the office until 1840. He also held the office of vicar under the bishop of Sonora, except for a short period in 1888-89, when it was attached to that of president and occupied by Fr. Jimeno.

Of the Zacatecanos in the north Fr. Rafael Moreno was president and vice-prefecto. The Fr. Prefect, García Diego, was absent in Mexico from early in 1836 until November 1838, when Fr. José Maria Jesus de Gonzalez assumed the office of prefect. He had been elected on June 19th, 1837. On July 22d, 1840, he was reelected. Fathers Victoria, Martin, Fortuni, and Arroyo of the Fernandinos, besides Fr. Moreno of the Zacatecanos, died during 1835-1840, so that the number of Franciscans serving in California was reduced to twenty. (17)

"ALL writers and witnesses, that mention the subject, are unanimous in describing Governor Alvarado's rule from 1836 to 1842, as a period of plunder and ruin in mission history. So uniform is their testimony, that there is no need to cite individual expressions of opinion," says Bancroft.

"THE method of mission spoliation at this time was substantially as follows: The governor, and subordinate officials by his authority, used the cattle and the grain of the missions as freely as they used the revenues from other sources. If the government contracted a debt to a trader, the governor gave in payment an order on any mission for wheat, tallow, or hides, just as he would draw a check on the treasury. The majordomo, being an employé of the government, obeyed the order, as a rule, whenever the articles called for existed at the mission. There were occasional refusals and pleas in behalf of the Indians, but of course these pleas were much less frequent and zealous than those of the religious in earlier times.

(17) Bancroft IV, 63-64.

"As to the comisionados, majordomos, and administrators, who successively "managed" the missions,
many were simply incompetent and stupid, and exhausted their little energy and ability in the task of
collecting their salary, filling the governor's orders
as long as the granaries and herds held out, exercising no restraint or influence on the ex-neophytes, and
allowing the affairs of their respective establishments
to drift, but not, as may be imagined, in the direction of general prosperity. Others were vicious as
well as incompetent, ready to sell any article of
mission property, not only live-stock, but kitchen
utensils, farm implements, tools from the shops, and
tiles from the roofs, for money with which to grati-
fy their propensity for gambling. Still others were
dishonest and able, and devoted their energies to laying the foundations of future wealth for themselves
and friends, oppressing the Indians, quarrelling with
those Fathers, officials, and assistants whom they
could not control or deceive, and disposing of the
mission wealth without scruple for their own interests.

"Of the Fathers, a few accepted the new situation
and made the best of it. They strove to reconcile the
discordant elements, and retained a degree of influence over the Indians for their spiritual and temporal welfare, and were ever ready to aid with their
counsel any person high or low in station who would
listen. Others retired to the habitations assigned
them by law, avoided all controversy and intercourse
with the world, and performed the duties of parish
priests for all who recognized them as such. Others,
again, did not submit so quietly to the robbery and
injustice witnessed on all sides, but protested on every occasion, *too often with ample cause.* As to the
Indians, those to whom property was distributed, as a
rule, made no good use of it. The cattle required

care; the tools implied work; and it was generally deemed best to convert all as rapidly as possible into liquor, steal cattle and various articles as needed, and when all was gone, and the vigilance of local alcaldes interfered with the pleasures of a vagabond life about the towns, to decide between a return to mission labor, or flight to join the gentiles, just as the missionaries had predicted. Pilfering and drunkenness increased rapidly, as did the ravages of syphilitic disease and relapse in to barbarism." (18)

THE neophyte population during this period of misrule decreased in all the missions from about 15,000 in 1834 to 6,000 in 1840 still living at the missions, besides two or three thousand more whose whereabouts as vagrants or servants was somewhat definitely known. In the same years cattle had decreased approximately from 140,000 to 50,000 head; horses from 12,000 to 10,000; and sheep from 180,000 to 50,000. (19)

A great change in the ecclesiastical affairs of the Pacific coast took place at the close of 1840, when a bishop was appointed to govern this part of the Church of God. For several years Fr. Diego had been urging the necessity of such a change with the result that he himself was chosen for the position, as we shall see in the next chapter.

---

(18) Banc. IV, 40-53. (19) Bancroft, 42-43.

CHAPTER XX.

THE province which comprised Upper and Lower California, or, as it was called at the time, "Both Californias," "Ambas Californias," had hitherto been under the jurisdiction of the bishop of Sonia. In 1835 the Mexican Congress resolved that the two Californias should be formed into a separate diocese and have a bishop of its own who would naturally be more interested in the affairs of the country. In accordance with this resolution the government on September 19th, 1836, published a decree, "That one of the three persons named by the metropolitan chapter should be selected and proposed to the Holy See for bishop of both Californias." The bishop was to receive the sum of $6,000 a year from the public treasury until the diocese should have an income sufficient for his support; moreover, he was to receive $3,000 to defray the travelling expenses to his diocese: and finally he was to have the administration of all the property belonging to the Pious Fund.

TROUBLES in Mexico and California prevented further progress in this matter until June 22d, 1839, when the metropolitan chapter chose three candidates, the Franciscan Fr. García Diego heading the list. On April 27th, 1840, the Papal Bull which appointd Fr. Diego y Moreno bishop of the Californias was issued, and in August the news arrived in Mexico. On

September 19th the bishop-elect took the constitutional oath before the President of Mexico, and on October 4th he was consecrated in the church of Our Lady of Guadalupe, Zacatecas. (1)

On October 28th the new bishop published his first pastoral letter to the missionaries and the laity of his diocese in the Spanish language. It was dated at the college of San Fernando, Mexico, and printed during the following month of November. The bishop signs himself simply "Fray Francisco, Obispo de Californias." The pastoral letter is too long to be given here in full; it may be sufficient to say that it dwells especially on the spiritual misfortunes of California in the past. He compares the condition of the people with that of the Israelites in Egypt, describes his efforts with the government since 1836 to have California erected into a diocese, the subsequent delays, and his own final appointment for the position of bishop, much to his confusion and surprise. After quoting the Bull of the Holy Father, the bishop addresses himself to the missionaries in these words: "Permit me now, before we close our letter, to direct our voice to the venerable priests who may be found in our diocese. You have without doubt in the bishop of the Californias a companion in your labors, a brother who loves you, and a missionary like yourselves, who will respect you and will consider it the greatest pleasure to serve you, etc." The bishop then asks them to read the pastoral to the laity from the pulpit, and to explain to the people the sublime dignity of a bishop, his own affection for them, and the great benefits that result from this new favor of God. (2)

The bishop did not reach his diocese until late in 1841, when he landed at San Diego on the 11th of

---

(1) Bauc., IV, 64-65; O'Keefe, 22-28; Carta Pastoral del Fr. Garcia Diego.
(2) Carta Pastoral, 3-12; Bauc. IV, 63.

Presidio and Town of Santa Barbara in 1835;
Mission Santa Barbara in the Distance.

December with a suite of twelve persons. He had intended to establish his permanent residence at San
Diego, but, owing to the abject poverty of the mission at that place, he soon changed his mind. On
January 11th, 1842, he arrived at Santa Barbara. His
reception there was a royal one. Alfred Robinson, an
eyewitness says: "All was bustle; men, women, and
children hastening to the beach, banners flying,
drums beating, and soldiers marching. The whole
population of the place turned out to pay homage to
this first bishop of California. At eleven o'clock the
vessel anchored. He came on shore and was welcomed
by the kneeling multitude. All received his benedic-
tion; all kissed the pontifical ring. The troops and
civic authorities then escorted him to the house of
Don José Antonio, where he dined. A carriage had
been prepared for his excellency, with several others
occupied by the president (3) and his friends. The
females had formed with ornamented canes beautiful
arches, through which the procession moved; and as
it marched along, the heavy artillery of the presidio
continued to thunder forth its noisy welcome. At
four o'clock the bishop was escorted to the mission,
the enthusiastic inhabitants taking the horses from
his carriage and dragging it themselves. Halting at a
small bower on the road, he alighted, went into it,
and put on his pontifical robes; then resuming his
place in the carriage, he continued on, amidst the
sound of music and the firing of guns, till he arrived
at the church, where he addressed the multitude that
followed him." (4)

Bishop Francisco Diego came with the sincere desire to benefit his diocese, and with abundant means,
unfortunately only on paper, for carrying out his
plans. He had from the national treasury a sala-

(3) The Fr. Superior of the California missions.   (4) Banc. IV, 382-383;
Robinson, 'Life in California,' 195.   Gleeson. II, 172.

ry of $6,000; and he had the administration of the
Pious Fund, the large revenues of which he could
use in accordance with the intention of the founders,
to say nothing of the tithes and other contributions
from the faithful; and before leaving Mexico the new
bishop had received other important concessions from
the government, so that he had good reasons to hope
for a successful administration. (5)

A petition signed by 123 residents of the town of
Santa Barbara was soon presented to the bishop, urging him to fix his residence at that place. The petition was granted, and thus Santa Barbara became
the episcopal city of the first bishop of California. A
beginning was made for a cathedral, residence, and
seminary. "Large piles of stones were heaped up in
several places for the laying of the foundations....and
there they will undoubtedly remain for some years,
as monuments of the frailty of human speculations,"
says Robinson, an eyewitness. It is said that Bishop
Francisco carried some of the stones with his own
hands. The funds necessary for the erection of these
buildings the bishop expected to obtain from the
government out of the funded property of the missions; but, as that was confiscated in the same year,
the project fell to the ground; for utter failure was
a foregone conclusion, when the bishop had to depend
upon California resources alone. (6)

When Fr. García Diego had been consecrated, the
Pious Fund was turned over to him, and he appoint-
Pedro Ramirez as his manager; but in February 1842
it was confiscated by President Santa Anna, and incorporated into the national treasury. (7)

On the 29th of March, 1843, the new governor,
Micheltorena, issued a decree restoring the management of the temporalities of twelve missions to the

(5) Banc. IV. 339; 333-334. (6) Gleeson, II. 172; Banc. IV. 333. (7) Banc. IV. 335-337.

Rt. Rev. Garcia Diego y Morono, O. S. F., First Bishop of
California.

Fathers, on condition that one eighth of the total proceeds of every kind be paid into the public treasury. These twelve missions were San Diego, San Luis Rey, San Juan Capistrano, San Gabriel, San Fernando, San Buenaventura, Santa Barbara, La Purisima, Santa Inés, Santa Clara, San Antonio, and San José. Under this regulation the missionaries became independent of the administrators with whom, as a rule, their relations had not been pleasant. Fr. Duran, the prefect of the Fernandinos, instructed the Fathers to receive the property after taking an inventory of everything; to perform with the utmost exactness the duties imposed on their honor and conscience; to invest any surplus of revenue in live-stock, or in means for new conversions, but in no case to sell anything for money; and to make the best use of this opportunity to save the neophytes and their property from utter destruction. (8)

THE only changes to be recorded among the missionaries in 1842-1845 were the arrivals of Fathers Gomez, Muro, and Rosales from Zacatecas; the departure in 1844-1845 of Fathers Mercado, Real, and Quijas to the same college; and the death in 1842 of Fr. Ramon Abella, the senior of the Fernandinos in California, and the sole survivor of those that had come to the territory before 1800. Meanwhile, Fr. Duran continued to hold the office of comisario prefecto, and Fr. Jimeno that of president of the southern missions; while, on the resignation of Fr. Gonzalez, the vice-prefecto and president of the Zacatecanos, Fr. Lorenzo Quijas was appointed to the former office, and Fr. Antonio Anzar to the latter office. (9)

BISHOP García, as we have already seen, was prevented from carrying out this plans from lack of funds. He could obtain from Mexico no part either of his salary or of the Pious Fund revenue which the

---

(8) Banc. IV, 308-371.   (9) Ibid. IV, 371-372

government pledged itself to pay for the propagation
of the Gospel in California. His only resources were
the voluntary contributions of his flock and the collection of the tithes. The revenues of the latter
source, however, did not exceed the cost of collec
tion. The bishop was very much discouraged in consequence of his failure to provide for the pecuniary
necessities of his diocese, and on account of the indifference to church obligations and episcopal authority manifested by many prominent Californians.
Nevertheless, he sought to confer all the benefits he
could upon an undeserving people. On January 4th,
1843, he announced Our Lady of Refuge as the chief
patroness of the diocese, and named St. Francis of
Assisi and St. Francis de Sales as the other two patrons. In the same year he issued a pastoral letter in
which he exhorted the clergy never in public or private to speak a word that might be construed into a
censure of the country's rulers. The bishop delares
they must inculcate a spirit of obedience, but keep
aloof from politics. They were also to avoid speaking
against their brethren, whether Mexican or Californian. The zealous bishop, moreover, succeeded in
removing a public scandal by urging Governor Micheltorena to marry the woman whom that official had
brought from Mexico as his mistress. (10)

A general report on the condition of the southern
missions in charge of the Fathers from the missionary college of San Fernando, Mexico, was drawn up
by Fr. Narciso Duran in February 1844. It is in
marked contrast to similar documents of earlier
times. He says: "San Miguel has neither lands nor
cattle, and its neophytes are demoralized and scattered for want of a missionary. San Luis Obispo is
in the same condition. La Purisima, though without
property or sowing-lands, has yet a vineyard of mod-

(10) Banc IV, 372-374.

erate extent, and retains 200 neophytes. The missionary, Fr. Juan Moreno, is ill, but has an assistant in the person of Rev. Miguel Gomez. Santa Inés, with 264 neophytes, and sufficient resources for their support, is in charge of Fr. José Jimeno. Santa Barbara, attended by Fathers Antonio Jimeno and Duran, has the greatest difficulty to support its 287 souls. San Buenaventura remains in tolerably good condition, and has plenty of resources. Its temporal affairs are managed by Fr. Jimeno from Santa Barbara, whilst spiritually it is in charge of Rev. José Maria Rosales. San Fernando, with few cattle, has two vineyards, and is in charge of Fr. Blas Ordaz. San Gabriel, once the 'queen of all the missions,' has nothing left but its vineyards in a decayed condition. There are still 300 Indians in the care of Fathers Esténega and Antonio M. Jimeno. San Juan Capistrano has no missionary, and its neophytes are scattered. San Luis Rey, with a population of 400, has hardly anything left, and its missionary Fr. Zalvidea, is in a state of dotage. San Diego, always a poor mission, has nothing now. Fr. Vincente Oliva cares for its 100 souls. From all of which it appears that three missions are abandoned for want of priests and means; that there remain only eight religious with three secular priests to attend the missions; that only Santa Inés and San Buenaventura possess the means for moderate subsistence; and that the other nine, ruined by secularization, and their neophytes demoralized, are in a moral impossibility of raising their heads." (11)

As to the success of the Fathers in managing the fragments of mission property restored to them in 1843, it is difficult to form any definite idea from the few local items that constitute the only record

(11) "Informe del actual estado de las misiones de la Alta California al cargo del Colegio de San Fernando de Mexico, Febr., 1844," por el Padre Narciso Duran, in Banc. IV, 421-422.

extant. The reports, and many other valuable documents, sent to the college of San Fernando for safekeeping, were preserved with the utmost care; but in 1860, as soon as the expulsion of the religious Orders from Mexico became general, all these documents relating to California and its missions, together with a vast number of priceless historical manuscripts and other valuable papers, were boxed up and taken to the private dwelling of the syndic of San Fernando. Such, however, was the demoniacal hatred excited against the religious communities that nothing they possessed was safe anywhere. Even these documents and manuscripts, that one should imagine the government would make effort to preserve, when found by the officers of Masonic rule, were taken from the private house of the syndic and publicly burned on the streets of the City of Mexico, as an eyewitness, the Very Rev. Fr. Isidore Camacho, in 1886 guardian of San Fernando, informs us.

Moreover, during the rule of the mission robbers, 1836-1842, when Alvarado was governor of California, and also during the subsequent war between the United States and Mexico, the soldiers did pretty much as they pleased. Many missions were completely gutted, and no regard was paid for books, papers, reports, manuscripts, or documents of any kind. Instances are reported where valuable documents were used for gun wads and cigarette paper. In view of these facts it is surprising that even the few papers we possess at the present day should have been saved from the general ruin. (12)

Bishop García in 1844 resolved to establish an ecclesiastical seminary at Santa Inés. By his authority Fathers Jimeno and Sanchez applied to the government for a grant of land for the support of the institution. Their request was complied with on the

_____

(12) O'Keefe, 26-27,

16th of March 1844, when six leagues of land were turned over to the bishop. Early in May he started northward with his attendants. When the bishop arrived at Santa Inés he found the grant of land, together with a communication from Governor Micheltorena to the effect that he had assigned $500 in money a year for the seminary, on condition that every Californian in search of higher education be admitted into the institution. Finally on May 4th, 1844, the founders assembled in the mission church. After the pontifical Mass in honor of Our Lady of Refuge, and a discourse by the bishop, the constitution which was to govern the seminary was read, and the institution declared open for the reception of students. The bishop, priests, and collegians then signed their names to a record of the proceedings. The names were those of Bishop García Diego; his secretary Fr. José de Gonzalez; Subdeacons Doroteo Ambria and Gervasio Valdés; Fr. José Jimeno, rector; Fr. Francisco de J. Sanchez, vice-rector; Fathers Juan Moreno and Antonio Jimeno; Rev. José M. Gomez; and the collegians, José de los Santos Avila, Alejo Salmon, Agapito Cabrera, Ramon Gonzalez, and Diego Villa.

FROM Santa Inés the bishop journeyed northward. At Monterey his reception was hardly less enthusiastic than at Santa Barbara, and his presence imparted unusual splendor to the procession of Corpus Christi. After visiting Santa Clara and San Francisco he returned to Santa Barbara at the end of July 1844.(13)

Gov. Pico now determined to make the secularization of the missions complete by leasing or selling what remained of the estates. The governor explained his views to the superiors in order to obtain their co-operation. Fr. Duran refused to have any share in 'the tremendous responsibility about to be incurred before God and man.' He expressed surprise that a

(13) Banc. IV, 423-427.

governor *ad interim* should dare to undertake such
innovations, and declared the real motive to be clear,
which was not, as the governor pretended, the liberty
and welfare of the Indians, whose ideas of liberty
were those of schoolboys glad when the master is
sick and school closed, etc. He would never consent
to a sale of the missions, which belong, not to the
nation, but to the Indians. Despite this remonstrance
the governor did not abandon his project, for on May
28th, 1845, the assembly passed the following resolu-
tions which were published as a decree by Gov. Pico
on June 5th. 1. The Indians of San Rafael, Dolores,
Soledad, San Miguel, and Purisima are ordered to
reunite and occupy those missions within a month,
or they will be declared vacant, and disposed of for
the general good of the department. 2. Carmelo, San
Juan Bautista, San Juan Capistrano, and Solano are
to be considered pueblos for the present, and after
reserving a curate's house, church, and courthouse,
the remaining property shall be sold at auction for
the payment of debts, the surplus to be devoted to
the support of divine worship. 3. The rest of the
missions may be rented at the option of the government; and the Indians shall be free to work for the
lessees, on the lands to be assigned them, or for
other persons. 4. The principal building of Santa
Barbara is reserved for the bishop and the missionaries, and the rent of this mission is to be equally
divided between the Church and the Indians. 5. The
proceeds from the rents shall be divided into three
equal parts, one for the support of the missionary
and divine worship, one for the Indians, and one for
the government to be devoted to education and the
public welfare after the debts are paid. 6. The first
part shall be placed at the disposal of the prelates for
equitable distribution. 7-8. Money due the mission is
to be **exacted** and used for the purposes named.

BEFORE the end of 1845 San Juan Capistrano, La Purisima, and San Luis Obispo were sold, and Santa Barbara, San Buenaventura, Santa Inés, and San Fernando leased to private parties. (14)

SIX other missions were to be sold in January, but a purchaser was found for only one, that of Soledád. At different dates between May and July the following missions were sold privately: San Juan Bautista, San José, San Luis Rey, San Rafael, San Buenaventura, San Diego, San Gabriel, Santa Barbara, Santa Inés, San Fernando, orchard of Santa Clara, and San Miguel. (15)

CHAPTER XXI.

CALIFORNIA IN THE UNITED STATES—ORDERS FROM GENERAL KEARNEY AND GOV. MASON—MISSION PROPERTY RESTORED—OTHER ITEMS—MISSIONARIES IN 1846—DEATH OF BISHOP GARCIA—DEATH OF FR. DURAN—A NOVITIATE ESTABLISHED AT SANTA BARBARA—THE NEW BISHOP—FIRST FRANCISCAN PRIESTS ORDAINED IN CALIFORNIA—DEATH OF FR. GONZALEZ. THE COMMUNITY DOOMED TO EXTINCTION—INCORPORATED INTO THE PROVINCE OF THE SACRED HEART—THE FIRST GUARDIAN.

IT soon became evident to the new rulers of California, the United States Authorities, that there was room for much doubt respecting the true ownership of the mission estates, wherefore they adhered to the policy of maintaining the matter in statu quo. On March 22d, 1847, General Kearney gave orders that four missions in the north should remain in charge of the missionaries, without prejudice to the rights of the claimants, until proper judicial tribunals should be established. This caused some trouble at Santa Clara, where American immigrants had taken possession, but Governor Mason announced

---

(14) Banc., IV, 546-553. (15) Banc., V, 558-564.

that "the government fully recognizes and will sustain the rights of the priests at the missions and to all mission property, against all who cannot in due course of law show a just and sound title;" and he once ordered a military force to eject the immigrants; but Fr. Real finally permitted them to remain till after harvest, and longer, by paying a small sum for the support of the church. Finally, the supreme court of the United States decided that Governor Pico had no right to sell the mission property. The property of the Church, including the church buildings, priests' houses, and lands to the extent of six to one hundred and ninety acres at each of the twenty-one missions was given to the archbishop as the representative of the Catholic Church. (1)

Of general mission matters during 1845, outside of those connected with the disposal of estates, there is little on record. Fr. Duran continued to be the superior of the missions in the south, while Fr. Anzar directed the Zacatecan missions in the north. Two Fathers, José M. Gutierrez and Miguel Muro, left the country during the year; and one, Fr. Juan Moreno, died. Bishop García Diego still resided at Santa Barbara, but was unable to accomplish much. On July 4th he wrote to Governor Pico that he had no means to defray the expenses of divine service, and expressed the wish of having a successor. In September he described the lamentable condition of all religious interests in California to President Herrera of Mexico. The only method of relief he could suggest was to bring a new force of priests and missionaries for old and new establishments from Europe, and pay their expenses from the Pious Fund. (2)

At the beginning of 1846 there were thirteen Franciscan Fathers in California, six Fernandinos and seven Zacatecanos; but at the end of 1848 only one of

(1) Banc., V. 563-564.   (2) Banc., IV. 553-554.

the former, Fr. Orduz, was left with six of the latter.
The year of the American conquest, 1846, brought
death to five of the missionaries. Fr. Duran held
the position of comisario prefecto until his death in
June, and Fr. Anzar occupied the same position for
the Zacatecanos until succeeded by Fr. Gonzalez. The
formality of assigning stipends for each of the missions had been kept up in Mexico, though of course
no money was forwarded to the missions.

In April 1846, while seriously ill, the bishop appointed Fathers Duran and Gonzalez his vicars-gene-
ral, and shortly after, April 30th, he died. His remains were buried in the mission church on May 3d,
in a tomb on the epistle side of the main altar. (3)

Fr. Duran, the venerable head of the Fernandinos,
died at his post on June 1st, 1846, and his remains
were interred in the vault of the mission church at
Santa Barbara. (4)

Fr. Gonzalez Rubio now governed the diocese of
California alone until the latter part of 1850, when
he surrendered the administration to the Rt. Rev. J.S.

(3) Banc., V, 565; 632-633; Shea, Vol. IV, 383; O'Keefe 28.
Bishop Francisco Garcia Diego y Moreno was born at Lagos, Mexico, on
September 17th 1785. He made his profession in the Franciscan Order at
Guadalupe on December 21st, 1803, and was ordained priest at Monterey,
Mexico, on November 13, 1808. He had been "lector de artes y de sagrada
teologia" at the college of Guadalupe de Zacatecas, when in 1833 he was
sent to California as comisario prefecto of a band of missionaries from
the same college. Fr. Diego became the missionary of Santa Clara, but in
1835 went to Mexico, and remained there till 1841, when he returned as
the first bishop of the territory. After a second visitation of the diocese
he was completely discouraged, and thereafter labored at Santa Barbara to effect what good was possible until his death, which occured
at midnight, at the age of 60 years, 5 months, and 24 days. A tablet over
his tomb bears the following inscription: "Hic jacet Illmus ac Revmus
P.D. Fr. Fran. Garcia Diego y Moreno, Primus Ejus hujus Diœcesi Cali-
forn. Qui pridie Kalendas Maii, Anni Domini MDCCCXLVI ex hac vita
migravit."
(4) Banc., V, 632-634. Fr. Narciso Duran was born December 16th, 1776,
at Castellon de Ampurias, Catalonia, and became a Franciscan at Gerona
on May 3d, 1792. He came to Mexico in 1803, and to California in 1806. He
was stationed at San José in 1806-1833, and then at Santa Barbara until
the day of his death. Fr. Duran was president of the Fernandinos in
1825-1827; 1831-1838; and 1844-1846. From 1837-1843 he also held the position

Alemany, O. P., who had been consecrated bishop of
Monterey in June of the same year. At the earnest
request of the new bishop Fr. Gonzalez retained the
office of vicar-general, however. During the administration of Fr. Gonzalez the Rev. Fr. Langlois in 1849
received from him the faculties of vicar for the
northern part of the territory with instructions to
purchase some land in San Francisco for ecclesiastical
purposes. This was done, and the first Catholic church
in San Francisco, for the use of immigrants, was e-
rected on the site of the present substantial church
of St. Francis on Vallejo Street. Since then the city
has had two churches dedicated to the Saint of Assisi:
Mission Dolores, whose titular feast is on September
17th, the feast of the wounds of St. Francis, and St.
Francis Assisi church on Vallejo Street. Both parishes are in charge of secular priests. (5)

In February 1852 a petition to establish a Franciscan convent or college, with a novitiate for the education of young men, was sent to Rome and granted
by the authorities. The bishop kindly offered to assign
another place in his diocese for that purpose, in case
the buildings of Santa Barbara should prove unsuit-
able. On January 7th 1853, the Fathers held a meeting at which were present the Rt. Rev. Bishop Alemany, Fr. J. M. Gonzalez Rubio, Fr. J. J. Orruño, then
guardian of the college of San Fernando, Mexico, Fr.
José Jimeno, the comisario prefecto of the California
missions, Fr. Antonio Jimeno, and Fr. Francisco San-

of comisario prefecto. He was a most earnest and successful missionary,
and as superior he was a worthy successor of the Fathers that held the
office before him. Throughout the troublous times of secularization he
managed the mission affairs with marked ability. In 1817 he was present
at the founding of San Rafael. In 1826 he refused to take the oath of
allegiance to the shaky Mexican republic, but likewise refused to aid the
revolutionist Solis in 1829. Governor Figueroa recommended his exile in
1833. In 1845 Fr. Duran ordered the balance due him to be paid to the
Indians. In physique Fr. Duran was of medium stature, somewhat stout,
of fair complexion, with blue eyes. Only two of the Fernandinos, Fathers
Oliva and Ordaz, survived him.   (5) O'Keefe, 29-30; Gleeson II., 201.

chez. On that occasion the monastery of Santa Barbara was declared a hospice prepartory to making it
an apostolic college of the Propagation of the Faith,
and Fr. José Jimeno was appointed its first president. (6)

FR. José Jimeno did not consider the mission buildings suitable for a college, and he therefore selected
a place in the city. The bishop approved of the
choice of location, which was that of the present parish church and residence. The church was immediately commenced; the house prepared for occupation;
and on Sunday July 28, 1854, it was solemnly au-
nouced in the presence of a large multitude, that the
apostolic college was then' and there founded under
the patronage of Our Lady of Seven Dolors. The novitiate was opened at the same time by giving the
habit of St. Francis to five young men. These first
fruits of the Order in California were: José Godyol,
Francisco Codina, José Alcina, Geronimo Lopez, and
José Hermenegildo. The last two were lay brothers,
the first of whom I find a record in California. (7)

AFTER the promotion of Bishop Alemany to the
archdiocese of San Francisco, Rt. Rev. Thaddeus
Amat became bishop of Monterey. The new bishop
preferred to have his residence in the town of Santa
Barbara. He, therefore, removed to the parish church
and in exchange, with the consent of Rome, left the
Fathers in possession of the old mission. By this arrangement they obtained the perpetual use of the
mission buildings, church, two orchards, and a vineyard. Before the transfer had been completed, the
president of the college, Fr. José Jimeno died at the
age of 52 years. His brother, Fr. Antonio succeeded
him, but soon retired to Mexico (8)

---

(6) O'Keefe, 30–31. (7) O'Keefe, 31–32. (8) Banc., IV, 602; O'Keefe, 32.
Fr. José Joaquin Jimeno came from the college of San Fernando to Cali-
fornia in 1827 or 1828. He was stationed at San Luis Rey in 1827-1830; at
Santa Cruz in 1830-1833; at Santa Inés in 1833-1850; at San Gabriel in 1850-

IN 1859 Fr. Gonzalez Rubio was appointed president of the institution, and in consequence resigned the office of vicar-general of the bishop. During his term as president of the college, seven young Franciscans were ordained priests. They were the Fathers

Fr. Gonzalez Rubio and his Community at Santa Barbara.

José Godyol, Francisco Codina, and José Alcina on

1853; and at Sta Barbara in 1851-1856. From 1858 he was president of the Fernandinos, vicar-general in 1859-1860, and comisario prefecto after Fr. Duran's death in 1846. In 1844 he founded the Sta Inés seminary, and was its rector until 1850. In 1854 he founded the college of Our Lady of Sorrows at Santa Barbara, and was its president until he died.

Fr. Antonio Jimeno came to California in 1826 or a little later, and served as missionary at Sta Cruz in 1827-1828; at Sta Barbara in 1829-1840; at San Buenaventura in 1840-1843; and again at Sta Barbara in 1844-1856, when he departed for Mexico. In 1871 he was still living in the City of Mexico.

August 15th, 1860; Fathers Bonaventura Fox and B.
Sheehan on December 21st, 1864; Fathers Joseph J.
O'Keefe and P. Wade on September 19th, 1868. (9)

On account of ill health, Fr. Gonzalez several times
asked the Most Rev. General to relieve him of the
office of president, but his petition was not granted
until 1871, when Fr. J. M. Romo was sent to take
his place. Fr. Romo arrived in California in January
1872, but did not take possession of his office until
June, when the documents arrived appointing him
guardian of the college and monastery of Santa Barbara. Fr. Gonzalez lingered on until the year 1875,
when he died at Santa Barbara, the last survivor of
the California missionaries, "a man respected and beloved by all from the beginning to the end of his
career," says Bancroft. (10)

When Fr. Romo arrived the community at the monastery consisted of the following members: Very
Rev. J. Romo guardian; Very Rev. J. Gonzalez, chro-
nologist; Rev. F. Codina, vicar; Rev. F. Sanchez,
master of novices; Rev. J. Godyol, procurator and
treasurer; Rev. J. O'Keefe, Secretary; Rev. P. P.
Wade, secretary of the council; Rev. F. Alvarez, librarian; Brothers. L. Marron, A Gallagher, J. O'Malley, P. Haberlin, E. Barry, J. Dallinan, J. Kirwan,
Charles Reid. D. Potter. The three last-named were
Franciscan Tertaries, it seems. (11)

It was evident, however, that the only Franciscan
community in California was doomed to extinction,

blind and indigent, probably the last survivor, of the Fathers there that
had labored in California. (9) O'Keefe, 32; Catalogus Prov. SS. Cordis.
(10) O'Keefe, 32-33; Banc. III, 760. Fr. José Maria de Jesus Gonzalez Rubio was born at Guadalajara Mexico, in 1811. He came to California from
the apostolic college of Zacatecas in 1833, and served as missionary at
San José in 1833-1842; at Sta Barbara he resided from 1843 until the day
of his death. He was also president and vice-comisario prefecto of the
northern missions in 1888-1848. From 1846 he was administrator of the diocese of California until the appointment of a new bishop in 1850. Under
Bishop Alemany he was vicar-general until 1852.
(11) Prospectus of the college 1872-1873.

unless some means were found to obtain priests and
novices from other countries. Vocations to the sacred ministry were not sufficiently numerous in California to furnish the requisite novices. For this reason Fr. Romo, the guardian, resolved to visit his
native country, Mexico, with a view to induce some
of the religious to join the community at Santa Barbara. With the Superior General's permission he
started out on his journey in May 1879, and did not
return until three years later, very much discouraged;
for, nothwithstanding his earnest efforts in that direction, he had failed to obtain a single rescruit for
old Santa Barbara monastery.

AFTER some consultations the guardian explained
the difficulties under which the community labored to
the Most Rev. Sup. General, and asked him to annex
the Santa Barbara house to some province in the east,
as progress was impossible in its isolated and independent condition. The Sup. General then appointed a
member of the province of the Sacred Heart to make
a visitation, in order that he might come to a right
decision. The visitation was made in August 1884 by
the Very Rev. Ferdinand Bergmeyer, O. S. F. After
his report had been received at Rome, the Sacred
Congregation of the Propagation of the Faith issued
the following decree: "As the Most Rev. Minister
General of the Regular Observance of the Order of
St. Francis has earnestly requested that the College
of Our Lady of Seven Dolors of Santa Barbara, in
the diocese of Monterey and Los Angeles, both for
the greater increase of the same college and for the
greater extension of the Order of St Francis in California, be changed from its independent state, and
annexed to the Province of the Sacred Heart of Jesus
in the United States of North America, His Holiness
Pope Leo XIII, in an audience on the 19th of April,
1885, having heard the report of Archbishop Jacobini,
secretary of the Propaganda, kindly consented that

the aforesaid college should be incorporated with the
Province of the Most Sacred Heart of Jesus." (12)

THEREUPON at the provincial chapter held at St.
Louis, Mo., on July 15th, 1885, Fr. Ferdinand Bergmeyer was elected guardian of the monastery of Santa Barbara, and placed in charge during the following month of August. Of the religious, who had composed the Franciscan community up to that time,
there remained, and were incorporated into the province of the Sacred Heart, Fathers José Godyol Bonaventure Fox, and Joseph O'Keefe, and the brothers
Anthony Gallagher, Joseph O'Malley, and Peter Haberlin. Fr. Victor Aertker, and Bro. Beatus, also
came to Santa Barbara with Fr. Ferdinand. (13)

CHAPTER XXII.

MISSIONARY CHANGES—FR. FERDINAND ELECTED PROVINCIAL OF THE
PROVINCE OF THE SACRED HEART—FR. FERDINAND AGAIN GUARD-
IAN OF SANTA BARBARA—HIS TRAGIC DEATH—BIOGRAPHY—FR. SERVA-
TIUS ALTMICKS—CHANGES—NEW FOUNDATIONS—SAN LUIS REY REOCCU-
PIED BY FRANCISCANS FROM MEXICO—PROPOSITION TO ORGANIZE A
CUSTODY OF THE IMMACULATE HEART OF MARY IN CALIFORNIA—THE
COMMISSARIAT OF CALIFORNIA.

AT the intermediate chapter, held in St. Louis,
Mo., on January 20th, 1887, Fr. Victor was transferred to the convent of St. Boniface, which was at
the same time accepted upon the urged request of
Archbishop Riordan, and Fr. Cornelius Schœnwælder
of Quincy, Ills., took his place at Santa Barbara. Fr.
José Godyol was changed to the orphan asylum at
Péjaro, near Watsonville, which institution had been
put in charge of the Fathers some time before by

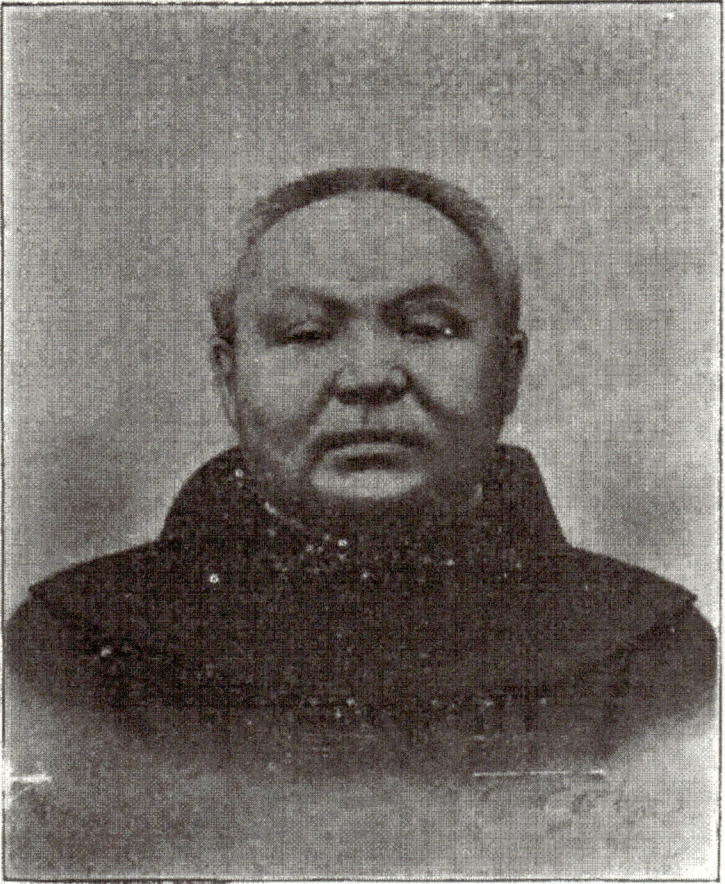

Fr. Ferdinand Bergmeyer.

Rt. Rev. Bishop Móra of Los Angeles. (1)

In the spring of 1888 the Very Rev. Jerome Kilgenstein, then provincial of the Cincinnati province, held the canonical visitation at Santa Barbara. At the subsequent chapter, July 25th, Fr. Ferdinand of Santa Barbara was elected provincial. This made it necessary for him to reside at St. Louis, Mo. Fr. Kilian Schloesser of Chicago, Ill., became guardian in his place. Fr. Cornelius was transferred to San Francisco, and Fr. Raynerius Dickneite took his place at Santa Barbara. (2)

No further changes occured until July 1891, when Fr. Hugo Fessler of Chillicothe, Mo., was elected guardian. Fr. Kilian became vicar, and Fr. Gerard of San Francisco was placed here at the same time. Fr. Vincent Halbfas had held the visitation in California during the spring of 1891. Fr. Ferdinand was succeeded as provincial by Fr. Michael Richardt, till then rector of the college at Teutopolis, Ill. (3)

The provincial chapter of August 22th, 1894, restored Fr. Ferdinand to Santa Barbara as guardian. Fr. Kilian was transferred to the new residence at Fruitvale, Cal., and Fr. Gerard became vicar and librarian. Fr. Hugo was changed to Chicago, and after a few months was appointed superior of St. Mary's, Memphis, Tenn. (4)

A horrible tragedy took place within the peaceful walls of the old monastery of Santa Barbara on the morning of February 27th, 1896. The venerable Fr. Guardian, Fr. Ferdinand, was murdered by one of the domestics, who at times had been afflicted with a fit of insanity. It was owing to the kindness of his victim that the murderer found a temporary home at the monastery. Fr. Ferdinand had just taken break-

---

(1) Tabella capitularis pro anno 1887. Vide the local history of the several now houses in subsequent chapters for further particulars.

(2) Tab. Cap. pro anno 1888. (3) Tab. Cap., 1891. (4) Tab. Cap. 1894.

fast, and was about to retire to his room, when he was fired at by the insane man. Four bullets entered the body of the venerable Father. The community at once hastened to the assistance of their superior, who still conscious asked for the last sacraments. Despite all medical aid Fr. Ferdinand died on the same day about 7 o'clock in the evening. (5)

SHORTLY before the death of Fr. Ferdinand, Fr. Servatius Altmicks of Bayfield, Wisconsin, had been sent to Santa Barbara and appointed vicar of the monastery in place of Fr. Gerard, who had been appointed superior of the residence at Fruitvale. After the death of Fr. Ferdinand, Fr. Servatius held the office of superior ad interium until the next chapter, which was held in August 1896, elected Fr. Bernardin Weis of St. Louis guardian of Santa Barbara. Fr. Servatius was then sent to Memphis, Tenn. While on his way to the latter place he was taken sick at the convent in Los Angeles on August 23d, and died on the same day after receiving the last sacraments. (6)

---

(5) Fr. Ferdinand Bergmeyer was born on October 30th, 1820, at Riesenbeck, Westphalia, Prussia. While pursuing his classical studies he was forced to enter the Prussian army, and served as a soldier for three years, at the end of which he entered the Franciscan Order on June 23th, 1852. On September 4th, 1856, he was elevated to the priesthood, and sent to the United States in November 1859. He was first stationed at Teutopolis, Ills., and then at Quincy, Ills., where he was for a time professor in the college, and later on parish priest and guardian of the monastery until 1871, when he became superior of the convent at St. Louis, Mo. In 1877 Fr. Ferdinand was transferred to the convent at Indianapolis, Ind., where he was parish priest and superior until 1885, when he was made guardian of Santa Barbara. While at Indianapolis he also held the office of custos. In 1891, at the close of his term of office as provincial, he was for more than a year guardian of the monastery at Quincy, after which he was returned to Santa Barbara. In 1889 Fr. Ferdinand went to Rome to take part in the election of a new superior general. He was also theologian to the Rt. Rev. Bishop of Indianapolis at the provincial synod of the bishops of the Cincinnati province in 1882 and again at the Plenary Council of Baltimore in 1884. When informed that there was little hope of recovery he said to the Father at his side: "IT HAS COME TO PASS AS I WISHED: "CURSUM CONSUMMAVI, BONUM CERTAMEN CERTAVI."

(6) Fr. Servatius Altmicks, was born at Warendorf, Westphalia, Prussia, on July 23d, 1829, and entered the Order of St. Francis on October 3d, 1850. On April 5th, 1854, he was elevated to the priesthood, and landed at New York on September 14th, 1858, together with Fathers Capistran

Fr. Raynerius at the same time was transferred to St. Bernard, Nebraska, whilst Fathers Peter Wallischeck of Quincy, Aloysius Wiewer of Teutopolis, Mathias Rechsteiner and Felix Raab of St. Louis, were stationed at Santa Barbara. (7)

Since the Province of the Sacred Heart was extended to the Pacific coast in 1885, a number of residences have been established in different parts of California. As already mentioned, the Boys' Orphanage at Pájaro was put in charge of the Fathers in 1887. In the same year the only German parish in San Francisco, St. Boniface's on Golden Gate Ave., was transferred to the Franciscans by the Archbishop of San Francisco. In the following year St. Turibius Indian mission in Lake County, besides some Indian and white settlements in Mendocino County, were entrusted to the Fathers. In 1891 the Rt. Rev. Bishop of Los Angeles requested the Franciscans to accept the new German parish at Los Angeles. His request was granted. About the same time the Most Rev. Archbishop of San Francisco asked the Fathers to organize a German parish across the bay. Thus

Zwinge and Damian Hennewig. These were the first Fathers to come from Prussia to establish the Franciscan Order in the Western States. At the request of the Bishop of Alton, Ills., they founded a convent at Teutopolis. In the following year Fr. Servatius was sent to Quincy to establish a convent in that city. In 1862 he went to St. Louis and founded St. Anthony's convent. For some years he was in charge of the first parish in Effingham, Ills. In 1872 he became vicar of St Anthony's and lector of moral theology in St. Louis, Mo., which offices he held until 1879, when at his urged request he was sent to the Indian mission at Bayfield, Wisc. In the next year he with the writer established the mission among the Menominee Indians at Keshena, Wisc. In 1882 he was sent to Superior City, Wisconsin, to take charge of the new convent at that place, in the following year he was recalled to St. Louis to again teach moral theology; but after one year his urgent petition to be returned to the Indians was granted. He was now stationed at Bayfield and Ashland until 1885, when he was sent to Harbor Springs, Michigan, where he established a boarding school for Indian children, erected a convent and three churches at that place, in Goodhart, and Burt Lake for the Indians. On account of ill health he was relieved of active work and transferred to Ashland in 1893. Finally, Fr. Servatius was removed to Santa Barbara. At his own request he was recalled to the east in 1896, but died on the way to Memphis. (7) Tab, Capit. 1896.

church and convent of St. Elisabeth arose at Fruitvale.

A second German parish had long been a necessity
in San Francisco. With the consent of the Archbishop St. Anthony's congregation was therefore organized
in 1894. Finally, at the urgent request of the Bishop
of Sacramento, the Fathers established a residence and
formed a mixed congregation at the capital of California in the latter part of 1894. San Luis Rey, too, is
again in charge of the Franciscans. The Franciscans
of Mexico in 1893 took possession of the ancient mission, so long abandoned, and opened a novitiate there
for the purpose of educating young men for the
Order in Mexico, where under the Free Mason government they are prohibited from receiving novices.

Owing to the great distance from the motherhouse,
it appeared advisable to organize the convents west
of the Rocky Mountains into an independent custody.
In 1896, therefore, the Very Rev. Father Provincial
Michael Richardt proposed a plan of forming the custody under the patronage of the Immaculate Heart
of Mary. The conditions proposed by the Fr. Provincial, and approved of by the definitors at a meeting
held in St. Louis, Mo., on February, 20th, 1896, were
extremely favorable to California. They were, however, submitted to a meeting of the local superiors
of the Pacific Coast on April 8th, and unanimously
adopted. All the Fathers and brothers were permitted
to remain or to join the mother province. Likewise
all the members of the province were at liberty,
during a period of three months, to choose to remain
in the east or to join the new custody. (8)

THE whole matter was then submitted to the Most
Rev. Superior General. It seems the proposed plan
was considered premature at Rome; for instead of an
independent custos the intermediate chapter, which

(8) Circular of Fr. Michael Richardt, April 11th, 1896.

Very Rev. Michael Richardt, O. S. F.

convened at St. Louis July 22d, 1896, elected a commissary for the western houses in the person of Fr. Clementin Deyman, at the time superior at Pájaro. The first commissary held the office only three months, for after a long and painful disease Fr. Clementin died at Phœnix, on December 4th, 1896. Fr. Kilian Schlœsser, the senior Father of the province, was chosen to succeed him. A novitiate was likewise granted to the incipient western province, and Fr. Bernardin Weis appointed master of novices. In addition, a classical school was opened at the monastery of Santa Barbara for young men who wished to enter the Seraphic Order. Fr. Peter Wallisheck was made rector of studies. (9)

As we have seen, the twenty-one old missions in their palmiest days numbered forty Franciscan Fathers, but no lay brothers. Though only two of the old establishments, Santa Barbara and San Luis Rey, remain in charge of the Order, among another race of people other missions have been founded which bid fair to outnumber the ancient establishments before the lapse of many years. Thus after three centuries since the Franciscans first entered Lower California, and after one hundred and twenty-eight years of uninterrupted work in Upper California, the prospects are that, ere long, the dream of a century ago, (10) the Custody of California, will be realized. At present the new commissariat, including the residence at Phœnix, Arizona, consists of nine convents, with twenty-seven Fathers and about thirty lay brothers.

(9) Tab. Cap. 1896.   (10) See Chapter X, Part I.

CHAPTER XXIII.

BEFORE proceeding to relate the local history of each mission, it will be necessary to describe briefly the method which the Franciscans followed while in control of the Indians; for, though the missions began about the period of the American Revolution, and attained a wonderful degree of prosperity, they differed essentially from those planted in other sections of our country. Here it was not a single missionary, venturing alone into a distant land facing every danger from the elements, the wild beasts, or the untamed savages of the forest. The missionary went to his station attended by a small guard, (1) with a colony of Indian converts, herds of cattle, and a plentiful supply of agricultural and other implements. Around this nucleus of converted Indians, other natives soon gathered, buildings were erected, the new-comers formed to habits of industry, and instructed in the doctrines of Christianity. As many of the missionaries were ingenious in mechanical arts, the Indians were taught various trades, and each mission yearly sent off its cargoes of surplus products

---

(1) The thoughtful reader ere this will have come to the conclusion that, though this system had its advantages, the missionaries personally would have fared better without this military assistance and supervision, and that often enough, for the sake of their Indian neophytes, they must have sighed for that freedom of action which was sadly wanting under Spanish officials and rulings.

and manufactures to receive in return the necessary goods from Europe. This prosperity constantly attracted new-comers who were in time trained to the life of the mission. (2)

A rectangular building, eighty or ninety yards in front, and about as deep, composed the mission. In one end was the church and dwelling of the missionaries. The interior was a large court, adorned with trees and fountains, in some cases, surrounded by galleries or corridors, on which opened the rooms of the missionaries, stewards, and guests, the shops, schools, store-rooms, granary etc. A part, or another building rather, separated from the main building, constructed so as to leave a square court in the middle, called the *monjerio*, or monastery, was reserved for the Indian girls. This was presided over by a trusted old Indian woman. Here these girls were taught to spin and weave, and to receive such other instruction as was suited to their sex. Most, if not all, the cloth that was used at the mission, and much used at the presidio, besides the blankets, sheets, tablecloths, towels, and napkins, was produced by the deft fingers of the mission maidens at the *monjerio*. Thus they were trained to become thrifty housewives. The boys learned trades.

Each mission was directed by two Fathers, one of whom superintended the mission buildings and religious instruction; the other supervised the field-labors, in which he always took part, teaching by advice and example. How well they succeeded we may judge from the results which they obtained, and from the affection of the Indians. Strangers who visited these missions were amazed to see that with such petty resources, most frequently without the aid of white mechanics, with Indian workmen alone,

---

(2) This description is mainly from Shea's "Catholic Missions" and L. Power's "Old Missions of California."

they accomplished so much, not only in agriculture,
but in architecture and mechanics, in mills, machines,
bridges, roads, and canals for irrigation, and accomplished it only by transforming hostile and indolent
savages into industrious carpenters, masons, coopers,
saddlers, shoemakers, weavers, stone-cutters, brick-
makers, and lime-burners.

THE discipline was severe, and the whole establishment conducted like some large factory. This
has excited a great outcry from superficial travellers
and bigoted writers. Well, the missions have been a-
bolished, and the Indians left to the enlightened men
of our day. Under their care the natives have passed
away like smoke before the wind, and right-minded
men now sigh for the beneficial management of the
missionary Fathers. Dwinelle, in his *Colonial History
of San Francisco* (8) says: "If we ask where are now
the thirty thousand Christianized Indians, who once
enjoyed the beneficence and created the wealth of
the twenty-one Catholic missions of California, and
then contemplate the most wretched want of all system, which has succeeded them under our own government, we shall not withhold our admiration from
those good and devoted men, who, with such wisdom,
sagacity, and selfsacrifice, reared these wonderful in-
stitutions in the wilderness of California. They, at
least, would have preserved these Indian races, if
they had been left to pursue unmolested their work
of pious beneficence."

ALEXANDER Forbes, another unprejudiced writer, in
his *History of Upper California*, says: "Much credit
is unquestionably due to them (the Fathers), and the
result exhibits in a striking point of view the effica-
cy of the system followed by the Fathers, more especially when compared with that adopted by missionaries in other countries . . . . . There are, I fear, few

(3) As quoted by F. Gleeson II, 122.

examples to be found, where men enjoying unlimited confidence and power have not abused them. And yet I have *never heard* that the missionaries of California have not acted with the most perfect fidelity, that they *ever betrayed their trust* or exercised inhumanity; and the testimony of all travellers that have visited this country is uniformly to the same effect. On the contrary, there are recorded instances of the most extraordinary zeal, industry, and philanthropy in the conduct of those men. Since the country has been opened, strangers have found at their missions the most generous and disinterested hospitality, protection, and kindness, and this without one solitary instance to the contrary that I have ever heard of." (4)

AROUND the mission building arose the houses of the Indians, and of a few white setlers. At various distances were rancherias, or Indian hamlets, each with its chapel. In a little building near the mission was a picket of five or six horsemen who acted as soldiers and couriers.

THE regulations were the same for all the missions. At daybreak the Angelus bell summoned the natives to church for prayers and Holy Mass, after which they took their breakfast. This consisted invariably, at San Diego at least, of *atole*, or ground barley. Then all joined their respective bands, and proceeded to the regular task for the day. Between eleven and twelve o'clock the midday meal was taken, consisting of the ever-present *atole* in its different forms, with mutton or beef. Occasionally the Spanish frijoles (beans), were noticed on the table at this meal. To the sick or aged milk was freely given. There was rest until two o'clock when labor recommenced and lasted till five o'clock. During the heated hours of the summer afternoons, a mule laden with buckets would pass around the fields, regaling the toilers with draughts

(4) As quoted by Gleeson II. 129-130.

of vinegar and sweetened water. This was considered a rare luxury. After the work was done the evening meal was served. *Pinole*, a favorite preparation from *atole*, formed the principal dish. To this the neophytes were at liberty to add nuts and wild berries which they gathered in large quantities and stored away. At sundown the "Angelus" called the faithful to prayers; the neophytes, workmen, and missionaries repaired to the chapel or church, where the beads were said, the litany sung, and the evening blessing imparted.

THE commissary department was conducted in the following manner. Every morning at daybreak the mavera, or keeper of the granary, distributed sufficient food for the day to each individual or family. The unmarried men carried their share to the pozolera, where it was prepared and eaten at the community table. The married men carried their rations to their respective rancherías, where they shared them with their families. Here was laid the foundation of California civilization. The family circle had become a fixed institution.

THE dress of the men was a shirt, trowsers, and a blanket, though the alcaldes and chiefs of gangs of workmen frequently wore the complete Spanish costume. The dress of the women was the usual one, with the invariable blanket. When the crops had been harvested each mission sold or shipped its breadstuffs, wine, oil, hemp, hides, and tallow, and from the returns distributed to the Indians clothes, handkerchiefs, tobacco, and other articles. The surplus was spent in the purchase of necessaries for the mission, furniture for the church or the Indians, implements of agriculture, tools, etc. Besides the funds thus resulting from their own labors, the Indians enjoyed, in the early years of the missions, the revenue of a portion of the "Pious Fund" which had been bestowed by charitable persons on the old Jesuit missions; the missionaries who were bound by the vow of poverty received only food and clothing.

THE Indians of a mission were not all of the same tribe, but perfect harmony prevailed; and when the season of work was over, many paid visits to their countrymen, and seldom returned alone. Sometimes a zealous Christian would visit his own tribe as an apostle to announce the happiness enjoyed under the mild rule of the Gospel. In this way the missions constantly received new accessions; for the good Fathers had the art of making labor attractive.

HOWEVER, human nature is the same everywhere. Not all were docile and submissive at all times, and the Fathers, who had studied the character of their wards, chose the only means that will bring refractory spirits to terms, and the only means that Indian nature at least will appreciate, as only those know that have resided among Indians for any length of time. There were various modes of punishments in vogue in the various missions. Imprisonment was one kind. If the crime was a capital one, the culprit was turned over to the military authority at the presidio. Smaller offences were usually settled by the missionaries themselves. Indeed, it is recorded that rebellious young men and boys had been laid over the good old Fathers knee to receive physical emphasis of his admonitions, and with salutary effect.

SUCH was the management of the California missions under the rule of the Franciscans. The stock had increased with wonderful rapidity; the orchards flourished, the fields yielded an abundance of wheat and other grain, and prosperity reigned; but better than all civilization and Christianity had taken root in the new soil and had thriven vigorously, when in 1834, there came a thunderbolt that smote the tried mission system till it shook and fell, a shattered fabric. It came in the form of a decree that the missions were to be snatched from the jurisdiction of the Fathers and transferred, just as they stood, to the government. Comisionados were dispatched to the missions to assume charge. The neophytes, whom the missionaries had cared for and looked upon as their children, were taken from them and turned adrift. The flocks they had tended, the orchards they had reared, and the buildings they had erected, were now no longer theirs. The result was disaster on every side. The Indians of California took to the mountains and returned to their barbarous ways, or became the outcasts of towns that had arisen in the neighborhood. Later on the U. S. government tried the reservation plan, which is the old mission plan revived in some of its features, but with religion left out. The agent takes the place of the missionary, with what results, and with what cost to the United States, is known to all. It is anything but gratifying. The Indian under the rule of the Catholic Religion thrives, as Mexico proves, but the Indian without his priest to control him disappears, or simply follows his animal instincts, as is the case in the United States wherever Catholic missionaries are not in full control.

PART II.

LOCAL HISTORY.

CHAPTER I.

SAN DIEGO.

San Diego Mission Founded—First Missionaries—Other Missionaries—
Fr. Serra Goes To Mexico And Returns—Preparations For A New
Church—Removal Of The Mission—Success Of The Fathers—Indian
Revolt—Attack On The Mission—Death Of Fr. Jayme—Destruction
Of The Buildings—Brave Defense—Fr. Serra Pleads For The Reb-
els—Raid On The Indians—Church Asylum—Rivera Excommunicated.
Rebuilding—Disappointment—The Viceroy's Order.

THE mission of San Diego was formally founded by
Fr. Junípero Serra on July 16th, 1769. The first mis-
sionaries were Fathers Junípero Serra himself and
Fernando Parron. (1)

WHEN Fr. Serra on April 16th, 1771, started out
for Monterey, he left Fr. Francisco Gomez as assistant to Fr. Parron at San Diego; but owing to their
ill-health both obtained permission to retire to a
more congenial climate that they might recuperate.
Fr. Parron went to Lower California, whilst Fr. Gomez chose Mexico. (2)

FATHERS Luis Jayme and Francisco Dumetz, originally from the Mallorca Franciscan province, were
appointed their successors about the middle of July
1771. (3)

---

(1) See Chapter IV. of Part First for particulars.   Vida, 82-104.
(2). Vida, 84; 98; 120. Bancroft, I, 178. Fr. Fernando Parron had originally
been a member of the Estremadura province, Spain, and Fr. Francisco
Gomes had been a son of the province of the Immaculate Conception,
Spain. Palou, Noticias I, 2.   (3) Vida, 120.

Fr. Dumetz, however, also grew sick and departed for the peninsula together with Fr. Cambon, probably in May. It seems Fr. Somera from San Gabriel remained here for a while, though he was in very poor health himself. (4)

Late in August Fr. Junípero with Don Fagés started out from Monterey for San Diego to make arrangements for the transportation of supplies from there to San Carlos and San Antonio. At San Gabriel Fr. Paterna joined his superior and both reached San Diego on September 16th. Fr. Junípero embarked for Mexico on October 20th 1872. (5) Fr. Somera had retired a little while before. Fr. Peña was sent up from the peninsula by Fr. Palou, and labored together with Fr. Jayme until August 30th, 1773, when Fr. Francisco Palou with seven missionaries arrived at San Diego. After that date the missionaries here were Fathers Luis Jayme and Vincente Fuster, together with Fr. Gregorio Amurrio as supernumerary. (6)

After pleading the cause of the California missions successfully in Mexico, Fr. Serra returned to the coast and, having reached San Diego on March 13th, 1774, departed for Monterey on the 6th of April. On account of ill health Fr. Mugártegui remained at San Diego, whilst Fr. Amurrio in his stead took ship for Monterey. About this time there existed around San Diego, within a radius of ten leagues, eleven rancherías, whose inhabitants subsisted on grass, seeds, fish, and rabbits. Nearly all those in the ranchería that had formerly attacked the mission were converted. In a material way some little progress was likewise made. Four thousand adobes had been manufactured, some stones collected, and the foundation for a church ninety feet long was laid when work had to be suspended. (7)

(4) Vida, 131-135; Noticias, III, 28. (5) Noticias, III, 33, has October 19th. (6) Vida, 145-147; Noticias, I, 260-61; III, 31-33. (7) Bancroft, I, 218-224; Noticias, III, 148-149; Vida, 116-160.

In August 1774 the mission of San Diego, with the consent of the viceroy, was removed about two leagues up the valley northeastward of Cosoy, to a place called by the natives "Nipaguay." It was probably identical, or nearly so, with that of the later buildings whose ruins are still visible about six miles from city and port. There are no accounts of the ceremonies with which the transfer was celebrated, nor is the exact date known; but the Fathers and neophytes were pleased with the change and worked with a will, so that, by the end of the year, the mission buildings, consisting of a dwelling, a storehouse, a smithy of adobes, and a wooden church measuring eighteen by fifty-seven feet, and roofed with tiles, were in a better condition than those at Cosoy. At the old site all the buildings were given up to the presidio, except two rooms, one for the visiting priests, and the other for the temporary storage of mission supplies coming by sea. (8)

ACCORDING to Fr. Serra's report of 1775, sterile San Diego showed a total return of only thirty fanegas of wheat. The number of its Christian Indians was only ninety-seven. Prospects, however, were very bright in the fall of 1775. New buildings had been erected, a well dug, and more land made ready for sowing. Fathers Luis Jayme and Vincente Fuster were busily engaged instructing the neophytes. They had been so successful of late that on the 3d of October they were able to baptize sixty Indians. This excited the jealousy of Satan at whose instigation two of the recently baptized natives, under pretense of visiting some relatives, left the mission, and went from rancheria to rancheria telling the Indians that the Fathers were about to baptize them by force. Many disbelieved the story, but the apostates succeeded in moving over one thousand savages to resolve the des-

(8) Serra, "Informe," 1775, in Bancroft, I, 210,

truction of both mission and presidio. The Fathers
had removed the mission to a more fertile spot about
two leagues distant from the harbor and fort, as we
have seen before. This emboldened the savages to
make the attack.

On the night of the 4th of November they arrived
in the valley of the San Diego River. Here they separated, one party proceeding to the presidio below,
which was to be attacked after the mission had been
destroyed, the other falling on the mission. They
then placed sentries before all the cabins of the
Christian Indians, and threatened the inmates with
death if they dared to move or give the alarm. A
large number of assailants rushed to the church and
vestry which they robbed of its sacred vessels and
vestments. They next advanced upon the barracks,
and, finding the guards asleep, snatched firebrands
from the hearth and set fire to the buildings. The
blaze and the horrible yells of the enemy now awoke
both Fathers and soldiers. When the latter at last
were ready, the Indians had begun to discharge their
arrows. Fr. Vincente, seeing the danger, took the son
and nephew of the presidio officer and hastily fled to
the soldiers' quarters. Fr. Jayme, awaking and seeing
the conflagration, thought it accidental. Rushing out
he met a large group of savages whom he greeted
with his usual salutation: "Amad a Diós, hijos,"
"Love God, my children." When the brutes caught
sight of the good missionary, they fell upon him with
fury, and, dragging him to the creek, stripped him
of his habit, beat him, and pierced him with arrows
until he fell dead. When later on they learned that
the missionary whom they had killed was the 'reza-
dor,' the one who always prayed, the pagan Indians
gave vent to their fiendish joy by wild shouts of delight.

In one of the buildings lived the blacksmith and

Death of Fr. Luis Jayme.

the carpenter. With them also resided Ursulino, the
carpenter of the fort. He had become ill and had
been brought to the m's ion to recuperate. José Manuel Arroyo, the blacksmith, was among the first to
hurry out sword in hand, but he fell dead immediately, pierced by two arrows. Felipe Romero, the
mission carpenter, also seized a musket and killed
one of the assailants. Then taking advantage of the
confusion which followed, he escaped and joined the
soldiers. Poor Ursulino received two arrow wounds
which some days later proved fatal. The band which
had gone to attack the presidio, seeing the mission
buildings on fire, and on that account fearing discovery by the presidio guards, returned and joined those
at the mission for a general attack. The mission
guard, at the time consisting of the three soldiers besides the corporal, reinforced by the wounded carpenter and the surviving Father Fuster, defended themselves valiantly. When the savages saw the terrible
effects of the muskets, they set fire to the building
that held the little party who were then forced to
take refuge in a small room of adobe which had
been used as a kitchen. This had but three walls;
the roof of dry branches and the remaining side was
exposed to the enemy. To protect themselves the
soldiers erected a barricade with two bales or boxes
and a copper kettle, brought at great risk from the
burning house; but by the time the opening was
closed two soldiers were wounded and disabled. There
only remained the corporal, one soldier, and the carpenter to defend the little fort which was barely
three feet high. The corporal, who was a sharpshoot-
er, told the others to load the muskets while he did
the shooting. The result was that every Indian who
approached the place open to them was either killed
or wounded. The infuriated savages now determined
to set fire to the branches with which the little

room was roofed. Fortunately the roof was a flimsy
structure, and its fire did not last long; but while it
raged there was great danger that the sack containing fifty pounds of gunpowder might be touched by
the falling firebrands. To prevent such a disaster,
Fr. Fuster courageously sat upon it. Finding that
their stratagem did not force the Spaniards to come
out, the savages next threw burning coals and pieces
of adobe over the walls, and succeeded in wounding
Fr. Fuster, though not seriously. The gallant little
party defended themselves till daybreak, when the
Indians, fearing that help might come from the presidio, fled carrying along their dead and wounded.
The survivors then crawled from behind their adobe
battlements. They were met by the Christian Indians
who with many tears and lamentations related the
story of their confinement, and their inability to render assistance during the night.

SEARCH was at once made for Fr. Jayme. After a
short time, in the dry bed of a creek, they discovered the naked body, bruised from head to foot
with blows from stones and clubs. The face, especially, was disfigured beyond recognition, while the body;
besides bruises, showed eighteen arrow wounds. At
the sight of the mangled remains of his beloved
companion, the good Fr. Vincente almost fainted
away. It was learned later that the martyr had
expired while calling on Jesus to receive his spirit.
On receipt of the news, Corporal Verdugo, with four
men out of the ten he commanded at the presidio,
hastened to the mission. Fr. Fuster had two biers
made on which the bodies of Fr. Jayme and of the
blacksmith were borne to the chapel of the garrison
for burial A few neophytes were left behind to
save something from the wreck, if possible. The
carpenter Ursulino died five days later, having in a
truly Christian spirit willed all the pay due him to

be used for the benefit of his murderers. He was buried by Fr. Fuster. (9)

THE news of the disaster at San Diego reached Montorey on the 13th of December, and, though late in the night, Captain Rivera at once set out for San Carlos to communicate the sad tidings to Fr. Junípero. When the latter heard of the death of Fr. Jayme he exclaimed: "Thanks be to God; that land·is watered; now will follow the conversion of the San Diego Indians." The next day a Requiem Mass was sung, at which six Fathers assisted, among them Fr. Palou. Fr. Palou assures us the zeal and the virtues of the murdered priest was so great, that in the opinion of all his soul needed no supplications, but that it had gone directly to heaven to receive a martyr's crown. However, adoring God's unsearchable judgments, the Fr. Superior ordered each priest to say twenty Masses for the repose of the soul of Fr. Jayme.

FR. Serra immediately wrote to the Fr. Guardian in Mexico, and also to Viceroy Bucareli, deploring the rash act of the poor Indians, because he feared it might retard their conversion. Like a true father ·he pleaded for the misguided natives, and declared that the missionaries were not disheartened, but that the number of soldiers should be increased, in order that the establishment of other missions might proceed. The viceroy received Fr. Junípero's letter in the beginning of April, 1770, and replied as follows: "In view of the prudent and Christian reflections expressed in your letter, inclining to soften the rebels by kindness rather than to subdue them by punishment, I have written Comandante Rivera so to act, thinking it the best method of pacifying and winning them. Such a policy would perhaps also aid us in gaining the neighboring tribes, when they see that they are treated with leniency, whereas on account of

---

(9) Vida, 176-183; Banc., I, 382.

their excesses they deserve punishment. I have ordered my officers to rebuild the mission, and to establish that of San Juan Capistrano." This letter was dated April 3d, 1776. Much anxiety would have been spared Fr. Junípero Serra had he received the letter earlier. (10)

On January 4th, 1776, Captain Anza, with Fr. Pedro Font of the Querétaro Franciscan college, heading a land expedition from Sonora, reached San Gabriel on his way to San Francisco. Captain Rivera had arrived from Monterey the day before with ten or twelve men for the protection of San Diego, and to punish the Indians who had destroyed the mission. The disaster and danger at San Diego caused Anza to suspend his own expedition for a time. At the request of Rivera he set out at noon on the 7th for San Diego to help punish the savages. He was accompanied by Fr. Font and seventeen of his soldiers, and reached the presidio on the 11th. Investigations now followed respecting the late outbreak. Raids were made on the different rancherías; gentile chiefs were brought in, forced to testify, flogged, liberated, or imprisoned. In these proceedings the missionaries took no part, Fr. Junípero having advised an opposite course. (11)

Hearing now that provisions had become scarce at San Gabriel, Captain Anza with Fr. Font hastened to remove the immigrants to Monterey. Only one event occurred at San Diego after Anza's departure which deserves notice in this connection. Carlos, an old Indian and neophyte, but a ring-leader in the late revolt, returned to the mission and professed sorrow for his misdeeds; but as he feared the military he took refuge in the church. Rivera ordered Fr. Fuster to deliver up the culprit on the plea that the right of

(10) Vida, 184-199. (11) Bancroft, I, 205; Vida 180-87; Vide "Franciscans in Arizona."

church asylum did not protect such a criminal, and
that the edifice was not a church any way, but a
warehouse used temporarily for worship. Advised by
his brethren Fr. Fuster refused, and warned the commandant to use no force. Rivera, however, turned
a deaf ear to this warning, entered the church sword
in hand, accompanied by a squad of soldiers, and
without paying any attention to the earnest protest of
Fathers Fuster, Lasuen, and Amurrio, dragged the
Indian out. For this open defiance of the ministers
of the Church, and for violating a sacred place, the
Fathers excommunicated the commander and the soldiers who had assisted him, and on the next day ordered them to leave the church before the beginning
of Mass. They then reported the case to their superior, Fr. Serra, and sent the information through Rivera himself. Arriving there on April 15th, the captain informed the Fr. President of the excommunication pronounced at San Diego, and asked for absolution. After consulting with the Fathers at San Carlos, Fr. Junípero approved of what Fr. Fuster had
done, and at the same time refused to grant the captain's request for absolution until he had given satisfaction to the Church by returning the Indian Carlos
to the sanctuary, when the San Diego missionaries
could raise the excommunication without interference
from their superior.

Fr. Serra informed the Fr. Guardian about the
troubles in California, and, after much difficulty in
obtaining an escort from the comandante, sent Fr.
Cambon with the letter to overtake Capt. Anza. The
next day, April 19th, Rivera started south again, but
on the plea of great haste, refused Fr. Junípero's
request to go with him. (12)

It was not until June 30th that Fr. Serra could
proceed to San Diego for the purpose of rebuilding

(12) Bancroft, I, 209-273;   Vida, 187-191.

the mission. In company with Fr. Santa Maria he
embarked at Monterey in the packet-boat Principe,
and reached San Diego after twelve days. The two
Fathers who had been destined for San Juan Capistrano were still at the presidio with Fr. Fuster.
Anxious to hasten the establishment of the mission,
Fr. Junípero applied to Captain Diego Choquet of
the Principe, and asked him, for the sake of his patron saint, to allow some of his sailors to assist in e-
recting the mission buildings. The noble officer replied : "Not only the sailors shall help, but I will go
myself like a common laborer." With two missionaries, the marine officer and six of his men, besides
twenty soldiers and some laborers, Fr. Junípero then
set out for the place where the old mission had stood.
For two weeks they worked with such enthusiasm
that hopes were entertained of completing the church
and dwelling before the ship would have to sail. The
enemy of mankind, however, could not bear to see
the work proceed so well. He accordingly availed himself of the caprices of the commandant to frustrate
the plans of the missionaries. On the 8th of September Rivera went out to the mission grounds, and notified the principal officer that rumors were current
that the Indians contemplated another attack on the
mission, and that he deemed it necessary to retire on
board the ship with his men. The officer of the ma-
rines, seeing there was no ground to fear an outbreak, entreated Rivera to investigate the rumor;
but the comandante would not listen to reason, and
insisted on carrying out his orders. Don Choquet reluctantly obeyed, but protested that it would be a
shame for the Spanish army to suspend work at the
mere rumor of an outbreak. With much regret he
communicated the gloomy news to the missionaries.
"Let the will of God be done," Fr. Serra exclaimed,
"He alone can remedy this evil."

Having been informed by Don Diego Choquet of

the interruption of the work, the viceroy at once ordered Governor Neve, who resided at Loreto, to take
up his residence at Monterey and assign Rivera to
Loreto. Moreover he communicated this decision to
Fr. Junípero in a long letter, written December 25th,
1776. The following paragraph from the letter shows
that Viceroy Bucareli was animated by a truly Christian spirit. "The suspension of the work on the destroyed mission of San Diego must have caused severe pain to your Reverence. It has greatly displeased
me as well, the more so as I became aware through
Don Diego Choquet of the frivolous motives that
brought it about. I presume that, with the twenty-
five soldiers sent to reinforce the presidio, Don Fernando Rivera will devote himself to the erection of
the mission of San Juan Capistrano; but if he does
not, the governor of the province, who has orders to
reside at Monterey, will do so. I have ordered the
governor to have San Diego reestablished, and not to
punish the ringleaders of the late outbreak, hoping
that they will themselves learn to regret their misdeeds. I likewise ordered him to establish the mission
of Santa Clara in the neighborhood of the San Francisco presidio . . . The governor, Don Felipe Neve, is
directed to have recourse to your counsels, and to
consult me in whatever is necessary to insure the
propagation of the faith, the conversion of souls, and
the extension of the royal dominion. (18)

(18) Vida, 191-196.

----◆----

CHAPTER II.

SAN DIEGO—(CONTINUED).

TWENTY-ONE days after the work of rebuilding San
Diego Mission had been discontinued, twenty-five soldiers arrived from Lower California with two letters
from the viceroy for the Fr. President. These letters
contained the information related at the close of the
preceding chapter. The joy of Fr. Serra now scarcely
knew bounds, and he gave vent to his happiness by
having the bells ring out the news to his flock. A
High Mass was celebrated on the following day,
which happened to be the feast of St. Michael, the
Archangel, patron of the missions. Captain Rivera,
having received orders to that effect, liberated all
the Indians he had imprisoned. One of them, however, had meanwhile hanged himself on the 15th of
August. It was the anniversary of the day on which
six years before the same Indian had attempted to
kill Fr. Junípero in the first general attack on the
mission. (1)

Rivera, moreover, detailed twelve soldiers as a
guard to protect the workmen who were rebuilding
Mission San Diego, and left thirty at the presidio.
With twelve soldiers destined for San Francisco he
then proceeded to Monterey, that he might not have

(1) Vida. 87; 196-197; Banc., I, 302.

to witness the reestablishment of San Diego, and the
foundation of San Capistrano, to which undertakings
Rivera seemed so much opposed. Work was at once
resumed and the buildings were ready for occupation
on the 17th of October. Fathers Fuster, Lasuen, and
probably Santa Maria,. were its first occupants. Fr.
Serra, accompanied by Fathers Pablo Mugártegui and
Gregorio Amurrio, had hastened to San Juan Capistrano to lay the foundation for this new mission. The
lost mission registers of baptisms, marriages, and
deaths at San Diego had already been replaced with
new ones in which the mission entries were restored,
as far as possible, from the memory of priests, neophytes, and soldiers, by Fr. Junípero himself. He,
moreover, added valuable notes on the past history
of the mission at various dates from August 14th
to October 25th. Fr. Fuster also added an interesting
narrative of the tragedy of November 5th, 1775. Fr.
Palou says that progress in the work of conversion
was now very rapid, as whole rancherías came in
from afar to ask for baptism. (2)

ON the 11th of April, 1778, the first public execution in California took place at San Diego. The four
chiefs, Aachil, Aalcuirin, Aaran, and Taguagui, were
tried on April 6th, convicted of having plotted to
kill the Christians, and condemned to death by Ortega, then commanding at San Diego, though that officer had no right to inflict the death penalty without the governor's approval. Fathers Lasuen and Figuer were summoned to prepare the culprits for
their end. "You will cooperate," Ortega wrote to the
missionaries, "for the good of their souls with the
understanding that, if they do not accept the salutary
water of baptism, they die on Saturday morning;
and if they do accept——they will die all the
same." (8)

(2) Vida, 196-197; Bancroft, I, 302-303.   (8) Bancroft, I, 316.

Fr. Junípero Serra, who had obtained faculties to administer the sacrament of confirmation, arrived at San Diego on the 15th of September, 1778. He remained at the mission until October 8th, during which time he confirmed all the neophytes and the children of the soldiers. (4)

A new church of adobe, strengthened and roofed with pine timbers, was completed in 1780. It was ninety feet long, seventeen feet wide, and seventeen feet high. (5)

Fr. Junípero came to San Diego to administer confirmation for the last time in September 1783. Fr. Juan Figuer, after seven years of faithful service at San Diego, went to his everlasting reward on December 18th, 1784. His body was buried in the mission church the next day by Fr Lasuen, who had taken Fr. Jayme's place. (6)

The presidio, six miles below the mission was attended by the Fathers every Sunday and holyday. The priest said Mass, gave instruction, and otherwise cared for the spiritual interests of the soldiers and their families on those days.

For about a year Fr. Lasuen served alone until, in November 1785, the duties of this new position, as

(4) Vida, 228. (5) Bancroft I, 331. (6) Vide, 263.

(7) Fr. Figuer was a native of Anento in Aragon, and became a Franciscan at Zaragoza. It is not known when he came to America, or joined the college of San Fernando. With twenty nine Franciscans he arrived at Tepic from Mexico at the end of 1700, and in February 1771 he sailed with about nineteen companions for Loreto. The vessel was driven to Acapulco, and in returning foundered at Manzanillo. Most of the Fathers returned to Sinaloa by land, but, after the San Carlos had been set a-float, Figuer and Serra again entrusted themselves to the sea, and after a tedious voyage reached Loreto in August 1771. Fr. Figuer was assigned to the Lower California mission of San Francisco de Borja. In November 1772 he was sent up to San Diego by Fr. Palou in company with Fr. Urson, both being intended for the proposed mission of San Buenaventura; but the founding of that mission was postponed, and Fr. Figuer then became missionary of San Gabriel in May 1773. There he served until October 1774, when he was transferred to San Luis Obispo. From here he was called to San Diego in June 1777. At this place he toiled as an earnest missionary up to the time of his death in December 1784. Bancroft, I 451-455.

superior of all the mission, called him to San Carlos.
His place was taken by Fr. Juan Mariner. Fr. Juan
Antonio García Rioboo was associate missionary until
October 1786, when he was succeeded by Fr. Hilario
Torrens. The three last named Fathers were new-
comers, Fr. Rioboo having been sent up by the Fr.
Guardian in 1783, at Fr. Serra's request for assist-
ants, and the other two, having arrived in 1785 and
1786, were now doing their first mission work at San
Diego. (8)

In June 1783 Fr. Lasuen sent to Fr. Junípero a report on the state of the mission of San Diego, which
included an outline of its part history, and a statement regarding the agricultural progress, which
showed that the place was fit for a mission. Nevertheless the spiritual interests of the converts made it
necessary to keep up the establishment, as there was
no better site available. According to the description
accompanying the report the buildings were: a church,
thirty by five and one half varas, or yards; a granary, twenty-five by five and one half varas; a storehouse, eight varas; a house for sick women, six varas; a house for men, six varas; a shed for wood and
oxen; two houses for the Fathers, five and one half
varas; a larder, eight varas; a guest-room; and a
kitchen. These were all of adobe and from three to
five and one half varas high. With the soldiers' barracks these buildings formed three sides of square of

(8) We read no more of Fr. Rioboo after he left the mission. He probably retired to his college in Mexico. Of his early life nothing is known.
He came from San Fernando college to Tepic in the same company with
Fr. Figuer, probably in October 1770. Crossing over to the peninsula with
Governor Barri in January 1771, he was put in charge of the two pueblos near Cape San Lucas. In May 1773 he sailed from Loreto on his way
to Mexico. Nothing more was heard of him until he was assigned to
the Sta Barbara Channel missions; but, disliking the newly inaugurated
system, he refused to serve. Later on he was sent up with Fr. Noboa to
San Francisco, where he arrived June 2d, 1783, and acted as assistant
priest. We find him in the same capacity at San Juan Capistrano and San
Gabriel, until he came to San Diego in 1785, where he remained up to the
time of his departure for Mexico. Bancroft, I, 455-457.

fifty-five varas, while the fourth side consisted of an adobe wall three varas high, with a ravelin a little higher. A fountain for tanning, two adobe corrals for sheep, etc., and one corral for cows, were outside the walls. Most of the stock was kept in San Luis Valley, two leagues away, protected by palisade corrals. There were at this time 740 neophytes under missionary care, and Fr. Lasuen estimated the gentiles within a radius of six or eight leagues at a somewhat higher figure. In 1790 the converts had increased to 856, of which number 486 had been baptized since the last report, and 279 had died, whilst others probably withdrew from the mission.

Large stock had increased from 654 to 1,720 head; small stock from 1,891 to 2,116 head; and the harvest aggregated about 1,500 bushels. In his general report of 1787 on the state of the missions, Governor Fages, repeating in substance Fr. Lasuen's earlier statements respecting the sterility of the soil, affirmed that only about one half of the neophytes lived at the mission, because more could not be fed there; that the gentiles were numerous and dangerous; and that it was only through *the unremitting toil and sacrifice of the Fathers*, aided by the governor and commandant, that this mission had managed to maintain a precarious existence. He added, however, that notwithstanding all difficulties San Diego was the first mission to register a thousand baptisms; and that, owing to the peculiar traits of the San Diego Indians, they were left more completely under missionary control than the Indians at the other missions, there being as yet no alcaldes. (9)

FATHERS Juan Mariner and Hilario Torrens served as missionaries until the last years of the century. The latter left California at the end of 1798, and Fr. Juan Mariner died at San Diego on January 29th,

1800. Their successors were the Fathers José Panella and Joé Barona, both recent arrivals who had already resided at San Diego, the former since June 1797, and the latter since May 1798. Fr. Pedro de San José Estévan, as supernumerary, also lived here from April 1796 to July 1797. The only missionary with whose conduct fault was found was Fr. Panella. He was accused of cruelty to the neophytes, and reprimanded by the superior of the missions, Fr. Lasuen, who declared that he would not permit one of his subordinates to do injustice to the natives.

Durixg the last ten years of the century the neophytes increased from 856 to 1,523. There had been 1,320 baptisms and 628 deaths. San Diego had thus become the most populous of the California missions. There were 554 baptisms in 1797. This was the largest spiritual harvest ever gathered in a single year with one exception, that of the year 1803 at Santa Barbara Mission, when 831 Indians were washed in the waters of salvation. Moreover, the deaths at San Diego were fewer in proportion to baptisms than elsewhere, except at Purisima and Santa Barbara, though the rate was frightfully high, over fifty per cent, even there. The greatest mortality occurred in 1800, when 96 natives died. Fr. Lasuen here confirmed 656 persons between 1790 and 1798. (10)

THE neophyte cabins, as late as 1798, were like those of the pagan Indians of wood and grass, and considered by the comandante sufficient protection a-

---

(10) Banc. I, 654-655. Fr. Hilario Torrens, or Torrente, was a native of Catalonia, where for a long time he held the office of preacher, was guardian for three years, and then vicar of a monastery. He came to California in 1787 with the highest recommendations from his college for talent and experience, and served at San Diego from November 1796 to November 1798; after leaving California on November 8th he died in the following year on May 14th, in a convulsion as the Fr. Guardian wrote.

Fr. Juan Mariner, of whom still less is known, came to California in 1785, and was stationed at San Diego from November of that year until his death. In July 1795 he made a trip with Grijalva to explore a site for the now mission of San Luis Rey. "Inform's." 179.-1:04

gainst the weather. The names of the rancherías belonging to the mission were: Cosoy, San Francisco, Soledád, San Antonio or Las Choyas, Santa Cruz or Coapan in San Luis Valley, Purisima or Apuoquele, San Miguel or Janat, San Jocome de la Marca or Jamocha, San Juan Capistrano or Matamo, and San Jorge or Meti.

THE mission herds multiplied from 1,780 to 6,960 in the year 1800, and its flocks from 2,100 to 6,000. The harvest of agricultural products in the same year amounted to 2,600 bushels. The largest crop, 9,450 bushels, was harvested in 1798 and 1799. In 1795, a year of drought, only 600 bushels were raised. In 1795 a vineyard was surrounded by five hundred yards of adobe wall. A tile-roofed granary, ninety-six by twenty-four feet, was erected of adobe in 1798. (11)

THE first year of the 19th century proved a severe one for the mission from a material point of view. The rains were late, and there was much want during the year, as also in 1808. It may be that these droughts impelled the Fathers to construct an extensive system of irrigating works, and that the works, whose remains are still to be seen, were probably completed during the next few years. About three miles above the mission the river was dammed by a solid stone wall, thirteen feet in thickness, and coated with a cement that became as hard as rock. In the centre was a gate-way twelve feet high and lined with brick. The dam was standing as late as 1874, though the water had washed out a channel at one end, and the sand left but a few feet of the height of the structure visible. From this dam an aqueduct constructed of tiles, resting on cobble-stones in cement, and carrying a stream one foot deep and two feet wide to the mission lands, was built through a precipitous gorge, impassable on horseback. The

(11) Banc., I, 655-657; "Informes." 1790-1800.

aqueduct often crossed gulches from fifteen to twenty feet wide and deep, and was so strong that in places it supported itself after the foundations were removed.

ON May 25th, 1803, an earthquake slightly damaged the church. In a letter to Governor Arrillaga Fr. Sanchez states that work was begun on a new church September 29th, 1808. In 1801 Fr. Payeras and other Fathers, in the presence of Comandante Rodriguez and his troops, transferred the remains of the three Fathers Jayme, Figuer, and Mariner from their old resting places, and deposited them in one grave, but in separate chests, between the altars of the church. The remains of Fr. Jayme were placed in the smallest receptacle nearest the altar of the Blessed Virgin; those of Fr. Mariner in the largest near the statue of St. James; whilst those of Fr. Figuer were buried farthest south. Three stones were erected over the grave. (12)

IN the mission registers on various dates appear the names of Fathers Cayetano Pallas, Mariano Apolinario, José Conanse, and Ramon Lopez, Dominicans from the peninsula, who officiated at different times. The names of the secular priests Loesa and Jimenez, chaplains of San Blas vessels, and those of a dozen Franciscans from different missions, also appear on records. (13)

FROM December 1800 to 1810 the Fathers administered baptism to 1,015 Indians, gave burial to 822, and married 374 couples; while the neophyte population increased to 1,611; San Diego, therefore, was still the largest mission at that period. In other respects, too, it was tolerably prosperous, except that it lost nearly one half of its cattle. Father Barona remained as missionary throughout the decade; but Fr. Panella left the country in 1803, and was succeeded

(12) Banc., II, 104-107; Informes," 1800. (13) Ibid. I, 655.

by Fr. Mariano Payeras for about a year, when Fr.
José Bernardo Sanchez took his place in 1804. Fr.
Pedro de la Cueva from Mission San José was here a
short time in 1806, and Fr. José Pedro Panto came
in September 1810, died in 1812, and was replaced
by Fr. Fernando Martin. Fr. Barona had been transferred to San Juan Capistrano in 1811, and was succeeded by Fr. Sanchez. In the spring of 1820 the
latter's place was taken by Fr. Vincente Pascual
Oliva. (14)

OLIVES of the mission orchards were utilized in the
manufacture of oil at San Diego and at some other
missions between 1801 and 1808. Hemp was likewise
cultivated, and 44,781 ℔s shipped in 1810. (15)

THE new church, vaguely alluded to before, was
completed and dedicated on the day of the titular
saint, November 12th, 1818. The ceremonies were
conducted by Fr. Barona of San Juan. The first sermon was preached by Fr. Boscana of San Luis, and
the second by the Dominican Ahumada, whilst Lieutenant Ruiz acted as sponsor. The erection of a chapel at Santa Isabel, about forty miles from the mission, where two hundred baptized Indians lived,
was urged by the Fathers in 1816 to 1819; but the
governor took no interest in the work, and there is
nothing on record to show that it was carried out
until after 1820.

THERE were 1,334 baptisms administered from 1810
to 1820, whilst 1,089 persons died and 872 couples
were joined in matrimony. The death-rate at San
Diego was exceedingly large for a time. On Decem-

(14) Bancroft II, 341-346. "Informes," 1820. Fr. José Pedro Panto was
a native of Valverde del Fresno, Estremadura, Spain. He received the
habit of St. Francis in the province of San Miguel, and came to California apparently soon after joining the college of San Fernando, arriving at
San Diego July 25th, 1810. From September 1810 until his death on June
30th, 1812, he was stationed at this mission; he was especially known as a
strict disciplinarian. His body was interred in the mission church by Fathers Boscana and Ahumada on July 2d. Of Fr. Panella we know only
that he arrived in 1797.   (15) Bancroft, II, 176-178.

ber 23d, 1814, the Fathers reported that for four yearsdeaths exceeded births and baptisms. The average yield of crops was 7,500 bushels of grain annually; in 1819 the neophytes were reported as dressing in coarse woolen cloths made by themselves. (16)

Fr. Fernando Martin was one of the few missionaries of California who finally took the oath of allegiance to the republic of Mexico, while his companion, Fr. Pascual Oliva, persisted in his refusal. In 1823 the Fathers protested against the granting of the Peñasquitos rancho to Captain Ruiz; and in 1827 they refused to furnish more supplies for the soldiers of the presidio without compensation, which drew out from the governor an order that the provisions should be taken by force. Materially San Diego was one of the most prosperous missions between 1820 and 1830, but it had reached its highest limit of 1,829 souls in 1824. Baptisms still exceeded deaths, 1,832 persons having been baptized from December 31st, 1820 to December 31st, 1831, whilst 1,992 died, and 885 marriages were blessed during that period. The crop of 1821, about 21,000 bushels, was not only the largest ever raised here, but with a single exception the largest ever raised at any mission. The yield consisted of wheat, barley, and corn. In 1830 the mission owned 8,822 head of cattle, 1,192 horses and mules, and 16,661 head of sheep.

By 1822 a chapel had at last been erected a Santa Isabel, and there were also at this branch establishment several houses, a granary, and a graveyard. The number of baptized Indians living there was four hundred and fifty.

The boundaries of the mission lands in 1828 are described with some minuteness on the authority of Fr. Martin as follows: Lands occupied westward, down the valley, 1.5 leagues to the Cañada de 'Osu-

---

na; southward 2.5 l. to the rancheria of San Jorge,
which land is used for sheep in winter; eastward 2 l.
to San Jaime de la Marca and San Juan Capistrano
de Matamo, which is used for pasturage, 5 l. to Sta
Monica, or El Cajon, where grain is raised, and 9 l.
to Santa Isabel; from Sta Isabel northward to the
Valle de San José 1 l., which land is used for cul-
tivation and grazing; to the Laguna de Agua Calien-
te, 2 l. on the boundary of San Luis Rey; thence 7 l.
past Bosque de Pamó to the Rancho de San Bernardo; thence northward 2 l. to San Luis Rey; and by
way of San Dieguito the mission lands extend 3 l.
to La Joya where cattle are kept.

In addition to Fathers Martin and Oliva, the resident missionaries, there may be mentioned Fr. Menendez, who served as chaplain of the troops after
1825, and Fr. Tomás Manilla, who was at San Diego
in 1829-1830. Both were Dominicans from Lower California. (17)

Fr. Martin remained at his post until the day of
his death in 1838, after twenty-six years of uninterrupted service. (18)

Down to 1834, when statistics come to an end here
as elsewhere, the Fathers had baptized 160 Indians
since 1830, buried 312, married 127 couples, and had
on the register 1,882 neophytes. At the close of 1839
there were 800 Indians nominally under the control
of the missionaries, though only about fifty resided at

(17) Banc., II. 551-553; "Informes" for 1831.   (18) Fr. Fernando Martin
was born May 26th, 1770, at Robledillo, Spain. He became a Franciscan
at the convent of Ciudad Rodrigo, where he acted as preacher until 1809,
when he volunteered for the American missionary field. Leaving Cadiz in
March he arrived at the college of San Fernando, Mexico, in June 1810.
The next year he was sent to California, and after vexatious delays at
Acapulco and elsewhere, on account of a pestilence and troubles with
the rebels, he reached Lower California in April 1811, and came to San Diego by land on July 6th. His missionary service began at once, and he
never served at any other mission. Fr. Martin was an exemplary religious
of whom little was heard beyond the limits of his mission. He was one
of the Franciscans who took the oath of allegiance to the Mexican republic, His death occurred on October 19th, 1838. Bancroft, III, 619.

the mission proper. Despite these disheartening circumstances Fr. Vincente Pascual Oliva still held out until 1845. From 1843 he again managed the meagre remnant of temporalities, and boasted that, in spite of all difficulties, he had increased the value of the property. Mofras gives the number of Indians in the community as 560 in 1842, whilst an official report of 1844 claims only 100. The mission retained the ranchos of Santa Isabel and El Cajon until 1844 or 1845, and apparently later. Fr. Oliva left the mission of San Diego in August 1846, and thereafter the place had no resident priest. (19)

THE ruin of the temporalities of the mission from 1834-1846 was very rapid. In 1831 the mission owned 8,822 head of cattle, 1.192 horses and mules, and 16,661 sheep, and there were 1,506 Indians on the roll of the mission. On January 6th, 1846, an inventory was taken of the mission property. There were left of the vast herds 110 cattle, 65 horses, and 4 mules. Only a few Indians were still seen here and there. On June 8th, 1846, the mission lands and other property was sold by the governor to Santiago Arguello for past services to the government. The causes which brought on this change from spiritual and temporal prosperity to utter ruin will be found in preceding pages. (20)

FROM the time of its establishment in 1769 to 1834, 6,638 persons were baptized, of whom 3,351 were Indian adults, 2,685 Indian children, and 602 children de gente de razon, or children of Spanish parents; 1,879 couples were joined in the bonds of Christian marriage, 169 of that number being white; 4,428 persons were buried, 2,573 of whom were adult Indians, 1,575 Indian children, 146 white adults, and 134 children of white or mixed blood. (21)

---

(19) Bancroft, IV, 622; V 619.   (20) Ibid. III, 619; V. 619.   (21) Ibid. III 619-20. According to the last report of the Franciscans, now in the

San Diego Mission At The Present Time.

THE largest number of cattle possessed by the mission at one time was 9,245 head in 1822; horses 1,108 in 1831; mules 830 in 1824; asses 87 in 1801; sheep 19,430 in 1822; goats 805 in 1789; swine 120 in 1815; all kinds of animals 30,325 in 1822. The total product of wheat was 132,077 bushels; corn 24,112 bushels; barley 81,187 bushels; beans 4,299 bushels. (22)

Such is the brief narrative of the first mission in California and the landmark of her history. "Not only had the natives been taught the rudiments of religion," says the author of "Old Missions," "but civilization and even culture, as well. Considering the low mental and moral status of the natives, the result of the mission work was remarkable, as far as it went. Of the once proud church but a few crumbling walls remain, and the day is almost at hand when even these will have passed away. The spot will then be marked only by the gravestones of its founders." (28)

GHAPTER III.

SAN CARLOS.

San Carlos Founded—Conversions—Removal—Carmelo—Fathers Crespi And Serra Die—Other Missionaries—New Church—Fr. Lasuen Dies—Missionaries—Fathers Pujol, Viñals, And Carnicer—Mission Lands—Secularization—Statistics—Graves Of The Missionaries Discovered—Church Restored.

On the very day on which the Spaniards took possession of the country, and began the building of the

archives of the monastery at Santa Barbara, the whole number of baptisms down to December 31st, 1831, was 6,461, deaths 4,210, marriages 1,767, and still living under the jurisdiction of the Fathers, 1,800 Indians. "Informes Generales," 1831. According to the author of "Old Missions in California," page 24, there took place at San Diego Mission from 1769-1846 seven thousand one hundred and twenty-six baptisms, one thousand seven hundred confirmations, and two thousand and fifty-one marriages.

(22) Bancroft, III, 619-620. (23) "Old Missions of California," page 24.

presidio, June 3d, 1770, Mission San Carlos was also founded. Close to the soldiers' quarters a temporary chapel was erected together with a dwelling for the priests, and the whole surrounded with a palisade. For several days the gentiles were not seen, having doubtless been frightened by the noise of the cannon and musketry; but later they appeared one by one to the great joy of Fr. Junípero, who at once began to humor them, and in various ways endeavored to gain their good will.

FATHERS Serra and Crespi then visited the country around, and endeavored to attract the Eslenes Indians by means of gifts and other acts of kindness. A Lower California Indian neophyte, who had learnt the native dialect, rendered great assistance to the Fathers while they instructed the pagans. Finally, on December 26th, 1770, the first baptism was administered to a native. Unfortunately the early records of this mission are lost, and the exact number of converts in the first year is not known; but once a beginning was made, the Christians increased rapidly. Converts were received by tens and twenties, till at the end of the third year from the date of founding of the mission, as many as one hundred and seventy-five of the pagans had been received among the faithful; and when the illustrious founder, Fr. Serra, died, 1,014 Indians had been admitted into the Church of God. The first burial took place on the 3d of June, the day of the establishment of San Carlos, when Alejo Niño, one of the San Antonio's crew, was interred at the foot of the cross. The first marriage occurred on November 16th, 1772. (1)

ON June 8th, 1771, Fr. Serra set to work to find a more suitable site for Mission San Carlos. Proceeding to the plain of Carmelo, he left there, besides forty Indians from Lower California, three sailors and five

(1) Vida, 107-04; 106; Vide Chapter VI, Part I; Banc., I, 175.

soldiers. Having given the necessary directions to get out timber and erect the barracks, he continued on his way to establish the mission of San Antonio.

It was several months before the palisade square enclosing the wooden chapel, dwelling, storehouse, guardhouse, and corrals could be completed. The formal transfer took place at the end of December 1771, but the exact date is unknown.

The establishment thereafter was often spoken of as San Carlos del Carmelo. The full name of the Bay and River Carmelo was Nuestra Señora del Monte Carmelo, or Nuestra Señora del Carmen, so named long before. Nevertheless the mission was always San Carlos, and other words were used solely to indicate the locality. Fr. Junípero's avowed reason for the removal of the mission was lack of water and fertile soil at Monterey; but it is likely that he also desired to remove his little band of neophytes, and the larger flock he hoped to gather, from the immediate contact with presidio soldiers, always regarded by missionaries with more or less dread as necessary evils tending to corrupt native innocence. A sufficient guard of soldiers, however, was to be stationed at the mission. While the garrison remained at Monterey Fr. Serra and Crespi took up their permanent residence in their new home, and labored at this mission for the remainder of their lives. Fathers Juncosa and Cavaller assisted them temporarily, both at the mission and at the presidio. (3)

The Indians now visited the mission daily. Fr. Junípero delighted them by offerings of beads and little trinkets; after a while he made the sign of the cross on their foreheads, and accustomed his hearers to kiss that holy emblem. He also went to work to learn the language, and thus made use of every

(2) Vida. 120-121; 127:   Banc. I. 170-78.

means to attract the natives. The same must be said
cf his companion Fr. Crespi. The latter especially
urged the Indians to salute one another with the
words: "*Amad a Dios*," "Love God." This pious custom became so general that the natives would not
only salute the Fathers in this manner, but every
person they met. The good missionary, who had
toiled at San Carlos together with Fr. Junípero Serra from its foundation, died here on January 1st,
1782. (3)

AFTER his death Fr. Matías de Catarina y Noriega
was the assistant of Fr. Serra. When Fr. Serra, the
founder of the mission, had died in August 1784,
(4) Fr. Noriega, alone it seems, attended to the affairs of San Carlos until October 1787, when he retired to his college in Mexico. Fr. Palou, the temporary successor of Fr. Junípero as president of the
missions, resided here only part of the time. Fr. Noriega'a successor was Fr. José Francisco de Paula
Señan, whose assistant from 1789 was Fr. Pascual
Martínez de Arenaza. Fr. Lasuen, the superior of the
California missions also resided here after 1790. Other Fathers arriving by sea, or coming in from other missions, often spent some time at San Carlos, so
that there were nearly always two and often more.
FR. Arenaza served as missionary until 1797, when
he left the country. Fr. Señan was permitted to retire in 1795, but he subsequently returned. Fr. Arenaza was followed in the ministry by Fr. Francisco
Pujol. and Fr. Señan's place was filled by Fr. Antonio Jaime from 1795 to 1796. Fr. Mariano succeeded him from 1796 to 1798, and Fr. José Viñals from
1798. (5)

(3) See page 87, Part I: Vida, 128-129.   (4) See Chap. X, Part I.
(5) Banc., I, 469; 686. Fr. Matías Antonio de Santa Catarina y Noriega
came up as chaplain on the transport of 1779, and first took Fr. Cambon's place at San Francisco. He remained there until 1781, and then was
stationed at San Carlos.
Fr. Pascual de Arenaza came to Mexico from his native Basque

FROM 1770-1790 there were 1,559 baptisms, 778 deaths, and 408 Marriages. Although the baptisms, 790 in number, exceeded the deaths by 228, the neophyte population suffered a loss of fifteen from 1790-1800, as there were 747 Indians on the roll in the latter year. San Carlos had reached its highest figure, 927, in 1794, since which year its population steadily decreased. Horses and cattle meanwhile increased to 2,180, and smaller stock to 4,160 head. The average crop of grain was 3,700 bushels.

ON July 7th, 1793, the first stone for the new church was laid. The building was of soft straw-colored stone, which was said to harden on exposure to the air. The lime used was made of sea-shells. This church, which is still to be seen on the banks of the Carmelo, was completed and dedicated in 1797. It had a tile roof. (6)

FR. Fermin Francisco de Lasuen, the superior of the California missions, died at San Carlos on June 26th, 1803. Fr. Tapis succeeded him in that office, and lived here most of the time after 1806. Fr. Pujol, who was stationed at San Carlos, died in 1801, while serving temporarily at San Antonio and San Miguel. Fr. José Viñals labored here from August 1798 to August 1804, when he obtained permission to retire to Mexico on account of ill health. Fr. Pujol was succeeded by Fr. Carnicer, who had come to California in 1797. He was stationed here in 1798-1799, and again from 1801 to 1808 when he retired. Fr.

province of Alava in 1785. Having volunteered for the Indian missions he was assigned to California in 1786. After a term as supernumerary he was the regular missionary at San Carlos from 1788-1797. On the expiration of his term he was granted permission to retire on July 8th, 1797. He officiated at Soledad on October 3d. which is the last trace of his presence in California. After his arrival in Mexico he died with consumption before May 14th, 1799. Banc. I, 685-687. "Informes Generales", 1790-1800. According to the mission records of San Carlos, as per the author of PADRE JUNIPERO SERRA, page 22, a Fr. Julian Lopez died at San Carlos on July 15th, 1797, aged 35 years. The name does not appear elsewhere.

(6) Banc., I. 687-688. The church was repaired a few years ago by the Very Rev. A. Cassanova, pastor of Monterey.

Viñals was followed in the ministry at San Carlos by Fr Juan Amorós in 1804, Fr. Carnicer by Fr. Francisco Suñer in 1808, and the latter by Fr. Vincente de Sarría in 1809. (7)

DURING the decade of 1800-1810 the Indian population of San Carlos declined from 747 to 511, the number of deaths exceeding that of the baptism by 145. During the ten years 449 persons were baptized, 594 died, whilst 176 couples were united in matrimony. (8)

THE period of 1810-1820 was a quiet one for San Carlos. Beyond the building and dedication of a new chapel adjoining the church, in honor of the Passion of Our Lord, there is nothing to record except the statistics. Fr. Sarría toiled among the Indians throughout the decade, but Fr. Amorós was succeeded in 1819 by Fr. Ramon Abella. Fr. Estévan Tapis was here as

(7) Banc. II, 146-147; 100 Fr. Francisco Pujol y Pujol, was baptized March 7th, 1762, at Alos, Catalonia, Spain. He received the Franciscan habit on February 13th, 1787, and came to San Fernando college, Mexico, August 19th, 1793, after a terrible imprisonment among the French. In 1795 he arrived in California, and was at San Carlos from 1797-1801. When at the end of 1800 the Fathers at San Antonio and San Miguel were taken suddenly ill, Fr. Pujol volunteered to aid them, though the danger of being himself poisoned was believed to be great. At San Antonio he labored until January 17th, 1801, and then went to San Miguel. There he was attacked with the same malady that had prostrated the other Fathers, and was brought back to San Antonio on February 27th, suffering terribly. He died on Sunday morning March 15th. His death was witnessed by Fathers Cipres, Sitjar, and Merelo. There seems to have been no doubt in the minds of the people that his death was the result of poisoning by the Indians. His body was buried March 16th in the mission church with military honors, rarely accorded in the case of a simple missionary. He was generally regarded as a martyr by the people.—Fr. Jose Viñals came to California early in 1797. He was stationed at San Carlos from August 1798 till 1804, in August of which year he obtained permission to retire to Mexico on the ground of threatened impairment of bodily and mental health. He left the college some time after 1809 to join another. Vide Chapter XV, Part I, for particulars about Fr. Lasuen.

Fr. Baltasar Carnicer arrived in California early in 1797. He served as missionary at Soledad from June of that year to 1795; at San Carlos in 1798-1799; at San Miguel in 1799-1801; and then again at San Carlos until 1808, in August or September of which year he was allowed to retire. He acted as chaplain of the soldiers from 1805 until his departure, coming to the presidio every Friday or Saturday, and remaining until Monday morning. Fr. Carnicer was one of the missionaries supposed to have been poisoned at San Miguel, but he recovered his health. (8) "Informes."

supernumerary in 1812, and Fr. Vincente Pascual Oliva in 1818-1814.

The neophyte population continued to decline from 511 to 881 in 1820. The whole number of baptisms for the ten years was 400; marriages, 109; deaths, 597. Large stock gained from 2,100 to 3,000; small stock or sheep decreased from 6,000 to 4,000; and horses also declined from 150 to 86. The average crop was only 2,550 bushels. In 1820 Commandant Estudillo made a full report, which showed that since 1786 the Fathers had faithfully attended to the spiritual interests of the presidio soldiers at Monterey. (9)

Fr. Ramon Abella served as missionary throughout the third decade also, with the Fr. Prefect as associate until 1829, the latter being under arrest as a recalcitrant Spaniard. The population of the mission decreased from 381 to 209. The number of baptisms for the period was 570; deaths, 566; marriages, 133. Large stock decreased to 2,090; sheep increased to 4,400; and horses also increased to 120. The average crop of grain was 1,905 bushels.

In 1823 the Fathers received from the Santa Barbara presidio $1,802 which had been due since 1804. In 1822 the mission lands were 2¼ leagues wide at the mouth of the Rio Carmelo, gradually narrowing as they extended six leagues up the river. As the only good land was in the valley and in the little tract of Francisquito and Tularcitos, the governor in 1801 had given the mission a cattle rancho two by two and one fourth leagues at San Bernardino, or Sanjones, or Ensen, between the rancho del rey and Soledad. At Salinas, south of the river, a sheep rancho of one and one half by three fourths of a league had been established in 1798. (10)

(9) Banc., II, 383-384, Inform. 1810-1820.   (10) Banc. II. 626-61 ; "Inform. es." 1821-1831.

THERE is no record extant of the local events of
San Carlos after 1831. Fr. Ramon Abella remained in
charge of the mission until 1833, when he was succeeded by the Zacatecan Fr. José Real. But little
mission property was left in 1834, and none at all in
1840, except the ruined buildings.

"Secularization."

SECULARIZATION was effected in 1834. In July 1835
Governor Figueroa planned a mission rancho of 660
cattle, 1,000 sheep, and a few horses for the support
of the Fathers and the church; but the Fr. Superior

declined to permit the religious to take charge of such an establishment. In 1836 a traveller visited San Carlos, and described the mission as in ruins and nearly abandoned, though he found 8 or 10 Indians at work repairing the roof. Another found Fr. Real and two or three families of Indians, who dwelt in the buildings, living on shell-fish and acorns. The neophytes numbered about 150 at the time of secularization; at the close of 1840 there were about eighty left in the mission and neighborhood.

THE statistics of San Carlos for 1831-1834 are entirely lost. The total number of baptisms during the time the mission existed, 1770-1834, the last four years only estimated, was 8,957. Of this number 1,790 were adults, 1,306 Indian children, 17 settlers, and 838 children of settlers. The total number of marriages was 1,065; of these 100 couples were not Indian. During the same period 2,885 persons died, 383 of whom were white settlers. The total production of wheat was 43,120 bushels; barley, 55,300 bushels; corn, 28,700 bushels; and beans, 24,000 bushels. (11)

PERHAPS forty neophytes still lived in the vicinity of San Carlos during 1840-1845, but the mission buildings were abandoned. Fr. José Real was nominally in charge, but he resided at Monterey, possibly holding service in the mission church occasionally until 1845, when his brother Fr. Antonio Real, and for a time Fr. Juan Antonio Anzar, seem to have lived here. In Governor Pico's decree of 1845 San Carlos was regarded as a pueblo, or abandoned mission, and the remaining property was to be sold at auction for the payment of debts and the maintenance of divine service. We have no particulars. The glory of San Car-

(11) Bancroft, III, 678-80. The "Informes Generales," or official reports of the superiors of the California missions, give the following figures down to December 31st, 1831: total number of baptisms, 3,769; deaths, 2,403; marriages, 1,015; still living at the mission in 1831, two hundred and nine.

los Borromeo del Carmelo de Monterey had forever
departed. (13)

The old mission church, which contained the mortal remains of the founder of the California missions, after that was left to the mercy of the relic-
hunter and other vandals. In 1852, the tiled roof of
the building fell in, and the sun and the rains of
many winters brought fou:th a rank growth of grass
and weeds, effectually concealing the resting-place of
Fr. Junípero Serra. When the Rev. Angelo D. Cassanova in 1868 became the pastor of Monterey, he
found at Carmelo, about five miles from the town,
only a heap of ruins.

FROM the first Fr. Cassanova was enthusiastic on the
subject of restoring the mission church, but he met
with very little practical sympathy. However, he continued silently preparing for the work. The first step
he took was to clear away the debris that had accumulated within the building, and then to locate the
graves of Fr. Serra and other missionaries. Finally,
on July 3d, 1882, "after giving notice in the papers
of San Francisco," Fr. Cassanova writes, "over 400
people from the city, and from the Hotel del Monte,
at the hour appointed, went to Carmelo. I, with the
Records Defunctorum, kept in the archives of the
parish, in my hands, read aloud in Spanish and in
English the following four entries:"

"Rev. F. Juan Crespi, born in Spain; died January
1st, A. D. 1782, 61 years old; buried near the main
altar, Gospel side."

"Rev F. Junípero Serra, D. D., President of all
the Missions; born in Mallorca, Spain; died on the
28th of August, A. D. 1784, at the age of 71 years;
buried in the sanctuary, fronting the altar of Our
Lady of Seven Dolors, on the Gospel side."

"Rev F. Julian Lopez, born in Spain; died here,

---

(12) Banc. IV, 657.

on the 15th of July, A. D. 1797, aged 85 years; buried in the sanctuary, on the Gospel side, in the tomb near the wall on the left."

"Rev. F. Francisco Lasuen, vic. for second President of the missions; born in Spain; died here, and is buried in the sanctuary, on the Gospel side, in a stone tomb near the main altar, June 28th, 1803."

The heavy stone slab having been removed before the ceremony, the coffin of each stone tomb or grave was left visible. A man then went down and raised the lid of each coffin. The coffins were simple redwood, unplained, and in a good state of preservation. The people all looked at the remains, first of Father John Crespi, the first that died, then on the remains of Father Junípero Serra. The skeletons were in a good state, the ribs standing out in proper arch, part of the vestment in good order, also the heavy silk stole which is put only on a priest, in good order and in one piece, two yards and a half long, with the silk fringes to it as good as new. We did not raise the coffins, but only viewed them and their contents to the satisfaction of all present. We did the same to the four corpses; anything more would have been improper, especially as the coffin of the last buried, the Rev. Father Lasuen, was going to pieces. Then the tombs were covered as before with stone slabs. The tomb of Father Junípero Serra, for better security, was filled with earth, so as to make it more difficult for any vandal to disturb his restplace and over that was placed the stone slab broken in four pieces."

In 1884 Fr. Cassanova started in on his work of restoration. To his untiring zeal and the sympathy of many benefactors the old mission church of Carmelo owes its present condition.

San Carlos Restored.

CHAPTER IV.

SAN ANTONIO.

Founding Of San Antonio—Buildings Erected—Learning The Language—A Strange Story—Frosts Kill The Crops—Indian Shot—New Church—Fr. Pieras—Other Missionaries—Fr. Sitjar Dies—Interesting Items—Fr. Sancho Dies—Mission Lands—Statistics—Sectularization—Indians Ill Treated—Fr. Doroteo Ambris.

ABOUT a year after Mission San Carlos had been founded, Fr. Junípero Serra proceeded to plant the cross for the establishment of Mission San Antonio de Padua. Taking with him Fathers Miguel Pieras and Buenaventura Sitjar, together with the necessary soldiers and supplies, Fr. Junípero led the way southward along the Salinas River till they reached a beautiful oak-studded glen, which they named Los Robles. Here, about twenty-five leagues from Monterey, in the centre of the Sierra Santa Lucía, he gave orders to unload the mules, and to hang the bells to the branch of a tree. This was no sooner done than the servant of God began to ring, and to shout as though in a rapture of joy: "O gentiles, come, come to the holy Church; come, come to receive the faith of Jesus Christ." Fr. Miguel Pieras, amazed at the action of his superior, exclaimed: "Why do you tire yourself? This is not the place where the church is to be erected, nor are there any Indians here. It is useless to ring the bells." "Let me satisfy the longings of my heart," Fr. Junípero replied, "which desires that this bell might be heard all over the world, as Mother Agreda wished; or that at least the gentiles who dwell about these

mountains may hear it." A large cross was now constructed, blessed, and planted in the soil; then a cab-
in of boughs was erected in which a table was
placed and ornamented to serve as an altar.

On the 14th of July, 1771, the feast of St. Bonaventure, Fr. Serra said the first Mass in honor of San
Antonio de Pádua, ·the patron saint of the new
mission. The unusual sound of the ringing of bells
attracted a native who was straying near by. He
watched the proceedings with much curiosity. When
after the Gospel the celebrant turned about to
preach, he noticed the Indian; this pleased the good
Father so much that at the close of his discourse he
said: "I hope to God, through the intercession of
St. Anthony, that this mission may become a great
settlement of numerous Christians, since we here
see, what was not observed at the other missions
established thus far, that at the first Mass the first
fruit of paganism assisted. He will not fail to communicate to the other gentiles what he has noticed."
No sooner were the ceremonies ended, than Fr. Junípero hastened to the Indian, and by means of presents and signs he gave him to understand that
the Spaniards were friends.

The surprised native soon brought his companions
in large numbers who offered an abundance of seeds,
nuts, etc. to the missionaries. The Fathers in turn
presented strings of colored glass beads to the Indians. Frame huts for the missionaries, soldiers, and
servants were immediately constructed with the help
of the natives; a larger building for the church was
erected, and the whole surrounded by palisades. The
buildings were but temporary structures, as Fr. Serra
thought it wise to proceed as soon as possible to till
the soil; for farm they must, or starve, because supplies were growing very scarce. Stone buildings about
half a league from the first site eventually took the

place of these rude structures. San Antonio was early
noted for one thing—her superb horses, the pride of
the natives. Frequently envy assisted some of the
beautiful horses away from the mission. (1)

A corporal and six soldiers were stationed as
guards at San Antonio. Fr. Junípero remained fifteen days and then returned to Monterey. The natives from the beginning were more tractable than
those at either San Diego or Monterey, and the Fathers had hopes of great spiritual conquest. They at
once began to learn the language of the Indians, and
devoted much time to teaching catechism after they
had made sufficient progress to be understood. The
seed fell upon good soil; for the first baptism took
place on the 14th of August, 1772, just one month
after the opening of the mission. (2)

Fr. Palou here tells the story of an old Indian
woman, Agueda by name, a hundred years old in
appearance, who applied to the Fathers for baptism.
On being asked why she wanted to be baptized, she
replied that when she was a young girl she heard
her father speak of a man dressed like the religious,
who came to their country not on foot, but through
the air, and who preached the same doctrines which
the missionaries taught, and that this had moved
her to become a Christian. The Fathers gave no credit to what the old woman related, but on question-
ing the other Indians they heard the same story
from them. The Indians unanimously declared that
so they had heard from their forefathers, and that it
was a general tradition among their people.

---

(1) Vida, 121-123; Noticias III, 239; Old Missions of California 35-37.
(2) Vida, 124-124; The "Our Father" in the language spoken at San Antonio, according to Fr. Sitjar's "Vocabulario de la Mision de San Antonio,"
is as follows:
"Za tili, mo quixco neapea lima tnil. An zucueteyem na etsmatz antsic-
tsitia na ejtmilica. An citaba nat naloz zai ce quicha neapoa lima. Ma-
tiltac taha z'zalamaget zizucanatel ziczia. Za menimtiltac na zauayl, quicha na kac ap ininitilco na zan naol. Zi quetza commannatzelnoç za ali-
meta zo na ziuxnia, Za no yuissili jom Zumtaylitoc, Amen,"

"WHEN the Fathers of San Antonio," Fr. Palou continues, "related this story to me, I remembered a letter which the Ven. Mother Agreda wrote in 1631 to the missionaries engaged in the missions of New Mexico, in which she says that our holy Father St. Francis brought two religious of his Order, who were not Spaniards, to preach the faith of Christ to these nations of the north, and that, after having made many converts, they suffered martyrdom. Having compared the time, I judged that it might be to one of them the new convert Agueda had reference." (3)

THE climate of San Antonio was very warm in summer and cold in winter; frost was very common. A small creek near the mission was covered with ice every morning until sunrise, says Fr. Palou; thus the crops of corn and wheat were frequently exposed to destruction. The frost on Easter morning 1780 was so severe that the wheat crop, which had commenced to sprout, turned as dry as stubble in August. This misfortune led the Fathers to fear the loss of all their grain. They at once had recourse to the patron of the mission; nor did he fail to assist them. A novena was begun in his honor; the crops which the frost seemed to have killed were irrigated, and after a few days it was noticed that the wheat began to grow again, and at the end of the novena the field was once more green. Irrigation was continued, and after fifty days the new crop was as far advanced as the dead one had been, and a far more abundant harvest was reaped than in the year before. This fact and various others largely contributed to confirm the new Christians in their faith, and attracted the pagans in such numbers that the Christians at San Antonio were more numerous than those of all other missions combined. Even before the death of Fr. Junípero Serra, San Antonio counted one thousand

---

(3) Vida 124-125; Noticias III, 242.

and eighty-four Christians on her registers, though
not all had been baptized there. (4)

Toward the end of 1776, or in the beginning of
1777, Fr. Serra paid a visit to the mission on his way
back from San Juan Capistrano which had just been
established. (5)

After the transfer of the Lower California missions
to the Dominicans in 1773, while Fr. Junipero was
absent in Mexico, Fr. Ramon Usson was placed at
San Antonio as a supernumerary by Fr. Palou. (6)

In August 1775 there was great excitement at the
mission; savages had attacked San Antonio and shot
a catechumen about to be baptized. A squad of soldiers was sent out, captured the culprits, and held
them after giving them a flogging. Later the commandant ordered them flogged again, when after a
few days in the stocks they were released. The in-
jured man however recovered from his wounds. (7)

At the end of 1783, or the beginning of 1781, Fr.
Junípero for the last time administered confirmation
here to a number of neophytes. (8)

In 1793 a block eighty varas or yards long was
built to serve as church, dwelling for the priest, and
storehouse. In 1797 the church is mentioned as of a-
dobes with tile roof. The huts of the neophytes were
of a more substantial character than at San Carlos.
In 1794 an adobe room 14 by 9 varas and a tile-
roofed porridge room were completed.

In August 1795 Fr. Sitjar made an examination of
the country between this mission and San Luis Obispo, for the purpose of finding a suitable location for
a new mission. The result was reported to his superior, Fr. Lasuen, in a document dated August 27th,
and entitled: "Reconocimiento de sitio para la Nueva
Mision de San Miguel, 1795."

---

(4) Vida. 125—126.   (5) Ibid. 200.   (6) Bancroft. I, 196;   Noticias. I, 280.
(7) Banc.. I, 256.   (8) Vida. 264.

San Antonio De Padua.

THE two venerable founders of the mission, Fathers
Pieras and Sitjar, served together until 1794, when
the former, worn out with his long labors, retired to
his college in Mexico. (9)

Fr. José de la Cruz Espí was stationed at San Antonio in 1793 and 1794; he was succeeded by Fr.
José Manuel Martiarena in 1794-1795, and Fr. Marcelino Ciprés from 1795 to 1804. Fr. Sitjar was absent
at San Miguel from July 1797 to August 1798, when
his place was filled by Fr. Benito Catalan. (10)

San Antonio reached its highest limit of neophyte
population with 1.296 souls in 1805. The lands were
reported to be barren, necessitating frequent changes
in stock-ranges and cultivated fields. A new and larger church of adobes was begun in 1809, or the following year.

THE venerable Fr. Buenaventura Sitjar, one of the
earliest Franciscan pioneers, and founder of this mission with Fr. Pieras, died at his post in September
1808. (11)

THE only occurrence to be noted is a quarrel be-

(9) Banc., I. 552; 688-689. Fr. Miguel Pieras was a native of the Island
of Mallorca. He was sent to the California missions in August 1770, and
arrived at Monterey by way of San Diego on May 21st, 1771. His only regular station was San Antonio, where he labored among the Indians from
the day of its foundation to April or May 1794. His last signature in the
mission books is dated April 27th.

(10) Banc., I. 689. Nothing is known of Fr. Benito Catalan beyond the fact
that he was stationed at San Antonio from 1798 to 1799, when he returned
to Mexico on account of ill health.

(11) His name in the world was Antonio. He was born or baptized on
December 5th, 1739, at Porrera, Mallorca Island, and received the habit at
Palma on April 30th, 1758. After receiving Holy Orders he came to Mexico, and was assigned to the California missions in August 1770. He arrived at Monterey by way of San Blas and San Diego on May 21st, 1771.
With Fr. Junipero and Fr. Pieras he founded San Antonio mission, and
labored here almost continuously for thirty-seven years. Fr. Sitjar was
a most faithful and efficient missionary, and perfectly mastered the Indian language, of which he left a manuscript vocabulary, since printed.
He also left a diary of an exploration for mission sites in 1795. On August 20th, 1808, while in the field, he was seized with excruciating pains in
the stomach and bladder. On September first he confessed and received
the last sacraments while suffering terrible agony, and died on the 3d.
Next day the body was buried in the presbytery of the old church by Fr.
Cabot, in the presence of several other Fathers. On June 10, 1813, the re

tween Fr. Ciprés and the corporal of the guard in 1801. The corporal aided by José Castro was very disorderly and violent; both were removed at the missionary's request. They tried to revenge themselves by making charges against Fr. Ciprés, which Alberni decided were unfounded.

In September and October, respectively, of the year 1804, Fathers Pedro Cabot and Juan Bautista Sancho began their labors here as missionaries. Meanwhile Fr. Lorenzo Merelo in 1800-1801, and Fr. Florencio Ibañez in 1801-1803, lived here as supernumeraries. (12)

FATHERs Cabot and Sancho toiled together at San Antonio, as they had done since 1804, until the death of the latter in February 1830. (13)

DURING the years 1810-1820 the Fathers were o-

mained were transferred with those of Fr. Pujol to the new church. A long account of this Father's life, death, and burial, translated from the mission register, appeared in the San Francisco Bulletin of September 10th, 1864. Banc. II, 131-132.,

(12) Banc. II, 152. Fr. Lorenzo Merelo arrived at Monterey July 28, 1799, and served at San Francisco from August of that year until October 1800. The cold winds and fogs of the peninsula, while they could not cool his ardor, soon took away what little strength he had, and he was transferred to San Antonio. As his health did not improve, he was allowed to sail for Mexico in September 1801.

(13) Fr. Juan Bautista Sancho y Lliteras was a native of Artá, Island of Mallorca, where he was born on the first of January, 1773. He received the habit of St. Francis on February 9th 1791, at Palma, and was made master of the choir after receiving Holy Orders. Embarking at Cádiz June 20th, 1803, he reached San Fernando college in September, and then came to Monterey on August 4th, 1804. He was at once appointed to San Antonio, where he labored continuously until his death. The immediate cause of his death was blood poisoning from a tumor.

"Outside his own local field of work Fr. Sancho was not much heard of, though he was a royalist and not backward in expressing his opinion, but for his management of San Antonio he received and deserved much praise. Fr. Cabot his veteran associate, who buried him in the presbytery of the mission church near the remains of Fathers Pujol and Sitjar, pays an eloquent tribute to his memory in the mission register. He says, of him that he had a constitution of iron, and was constantly busy either at work in the field, or in attending to the bodily and spiritual necessities of the sick and dying. In bad weather he prepared books of music and catechisms for the neophytes, with whose language he was perfectly familiar. Engrossed in such occupations he often forgot to eat. His burial occurred on the anniversary of his reception into the Order of St Francis." Banc., II. 621.

bliged to bury many more Indians than they baptized. The native population declined to 878 souls. As there were no more gentiles to be converted within seven ty-five miles, the neophyte population owing to the high death rate continued to decrease. (14)

On November 20, 1826, the neophyte Eugenio Nactré was elected as elector de partido. Fr. Cabot acted as secretary at the election and signed Nactré's credentials. The alcalde and regidores signed with a cross. Thus were the Indians beings trained for the duties of citizenship. In 1822 the mission lands were said to extend thirteen leagues from north to south, and eight or nine leagues from east to west. The soil was rocky, but very good crops were obtained by irrigation. Frosts, squirrels, and insects were very troublesome. In 1827 the missionary reported that it was very difficult to find pasturage for the stock. Alvarado in his history says that the flour from San Antonio was famous throughout California.

Robinson states that this mission in 1830 had an air of thrift not observable at many of the others. Everything was kept in perfect order; the buildings were in good condition; and the Indians were clean and well dressed. (15)

In 1834 Fr. Pedro Cabot retired to San Fernando mission, and Fr. Jesus Maria Vasquez del Mercado, one of the newly arrived Zacatecanos took his place. Fr. Vasquez remained until the arrival of Fr. José de Jesus Maria Gutierrez. (16)

From the time when San Antonio was founded to December 31st, 1831, when the last general report

(14) Banc., II, 385. (15) West three leagues was the rancho of San Miguelito; another at Los Ojitos in the south; another at San Benito, six leagues east on the river; and one for sheep at El Pleito, or San Bartolomé, seven leagues. Northward to the sierra de Sta Lucia, three or four leagues, the horses were pastured; southward the mares, 10½ l; westward, across the river, five leagues, the tamed horses. There were three ditches carrying water from the Arroyo de San Antonio to a distance of two leagues south of the mission; but the water lasted only until June or July. Banc., II, 621-622. (16) Banc., III, 686.

of the mission was made by the Fathers, 4,402 baptisms took place; 3,579 dead were buried; and 1,189 couples united in marriage. 661 Indians were still living at or near the mission. The establishment owned 5,000 cattle, 10,000 sheep, and 360 horses. (17)

MISSION San Antonio was secularized in June 1835. On June 22d Fr. Mercado complained that all his efforts for the good of the Indians were rendered futile by the persons in authority, who committed adultery openly, and were guilty of other excesses. In December Fr. Mercado wrote to the governor about the unjust and even inhuman treatment of the Indians, who were beaten and starved in defiance of the laws under the management of Ramirez. The Father declared that heathenism was gaining on Christianity; that the Indians were naked and starving, and that two thirds of them were absent in quest of food which could not be had at the mission. José Andrade was then appointed in place of Ramirez in 1836. He managed the temporalities of the mission; but in August 1840 Fr. Gutierrez wrote that the mission was daily advancing towards complete destruction. (18)

FR. Gutierrez seems to have remained at San Antonio until 1844, and that in the following year the mission had no resident priest. On May 26th, 1845, however, Fr. Gutierrez certified that in the mission church allegiance was vowed to Nuestra Señora del Refugio, the patroness of the diocese. The inventory of 1845 showed a valuation of $8,000, against $90,000 ten years before, chiefly in buildings and vineyards. Live-stock had disappeared entirely. At this time the

(17) "Informes Generales" for the year 1831. According to Banc., III, 667, the total number of baptisms administered at San Antonio from 1771 to 1834, when all mission reports cease, was 4,456. Of this number of persons baptized 1,761 were Indian adults, 2,537 were Indian children, 107 were children of settlers, and one was a settler. During the same period 3,772 persons died, of whom only nine were white. The total product of wheat for the same time was 79,713 bushels; barley, 12,097 bushels; corn, 19,541 bushels; beans, 2,514 bushels; and other grains 4,500 bushels.
(18) Banc., III, 667-688.

population is given as *ten men and five women*. (19)

Fr. Doroteo Ambris, who volunteered to bury himself among the ruins of San Antonio, for thirty years after 1850 ministered to the remnants of a once populous tribe until his death in 1880. His body was buried in the mission church. Fr. Ambris, apparently a secular priest, came to California with Bishop García Diego while yet a cleric in 1841. There is no record of other events, nor of the mission estate, which apparently was never sold. (20)

CHAPTER V.

SAN GABRIEL.

San Gabriel Established—The Picture Of Our Lady—Scandalous Conduct Of A Soldier—Indian Attack—Missionary Changes—Slow Progress—Fr. Serra Confirms At San Gabriel—Conspiracy—Missionary Changes—Fathers Cruzado And Sanchez Die—Fathers Oramas Estevan, And Barcenilla Retire—New Church—San Bernardino—Fathers Dumetz And Miguel Die.

San Gabriel, once the pride of the missions, was established September 8th, 1771. The missionaries for this mission had already been appointed in May; but local troubles caused by the desertion of some soldiers and muleteers delayed the foundation. On August 6th, however, Fathers Angel Somera and Pedro Benito Cambon, with a guard of ten soldiers, left San Diego to establish the new mission. The party chose a fertile, well-wooded, and well-watered spot near the Rio San Miguel, so named by an expedition the year before, and since known as the San Gabriel River. At first a large force of Indians attempted to

---

(19) Banc., IV, 127; 660.   (20) Ibid. V, 561; 630; II, 606.

prevent the foundation of the mission. One of the Fathers then unfurled a banner showing an oil painting of Our Lady. The Indians had scarcely seen the picture when they at once threw down their arms, and their two chiefs ran up to lay their necklaces at the feet of the beautiful Queen. Soon others, men, women and children, came in crowds, carrying seeds which they left as an offering at the feet of Our Lady. The unveiling of the picture produced such wonderful effects that thereafter the natives approached without fear. (1)

On the feast of Our Lady's Nativity the great cross was erected and blessed, and the first Mass celebrated under a canopy of some green boughs. On the following day the chapel and other necessary buildings were begun. The natives cheerfully assisted in the work of bringing timber and constructing the stockade enclosure. (2)

Though friendly as yet, the Indians crowded into the camp in such numbers that the ten soldiers were not deemed a sufficient guard. Fr. Somera, therefore, went down to San Diego on the first of October, and returned on the ninth with a reenforcement of two men. Next day a crowd of Indians attacked two soldiers, one of whom had insulted the wife of a chief. The enraged husband discharged an arrow at the guilty soldier, who stopped it with his shield and killed the chieftain with a musket ball. Terrified by the destructive effect of the gun, the savages fled, when the soldiers cut off the fallen warrior's head and set it on a pole before the gate. Fearing another assault from the Indians, the commandant sent the guilty

(1) Vida, 130-131; Noticias, III, 28; Banc., I, 179.
(2) The Mission was often called San Gabriel de los Temblores, the latter word like Carmelo with San Carlos, indicating the locality simply. It had been intended to mean San Gabriel on the River Temblores; but when another site was selected the name was retained meaning "San Gabriel in the region of Earthquakes," as San Gabriel de San Miguel would have been awkward. Vida 131; Banc., I, 180.

soldier to Monterey, and for greater security stationed sixteen soldiers at San Gabriel. The kindness
of the missionaries soon made the natives forget
their grievances. Strange to say, one of the first children brought to the mission for baptism was the son
of the murdered chief, and the sacrament was ad
ministered at the request of the widow. (3)

CAPTAIN Fagés meanwhile arrived from San Diego
with Fathers Paterna and Cruzado, sixteen soldiers,
and four muleteers in charge of a mule train, the
force intended for establishing San Buenaventura.
In consequence of the recent hostilities, however,
Fagés decided to add six men to the guard of San
Gabriel, and to postpone the founding of San
Buenaventura for the present. Fathers Paterna and
Cruzado remained at San Gabriel, where in the following year, 1772, on the retirement of Fathers Somera and Cambon, they became the ordinary missionaries of the mission.

MISSION progress was extremely slow at San Gabriel. The first baptism was that of a child. It did not
take place until November 27th, more than two
months after the arrival of the missionaries. Two
years later the whole number of baptisms administered did not exceed seventy-three. Fr. Junípero
Serra attributed this want of prosperity in spiritual
matters largely to the conduct of the soldiers, who
paid no attention to the orders of their worthless
corporal, drove away the natives by their insolence,
and even pursued women to their rancherías, killing
such men as dared to interfere. A change of corpo-
rals brought on the much needed reform. (4)

FR. Junípero paid his first visit to San Gabriel on
September 11th, 1772, while on his way to San Diego
and San Luis Obispo, which latter had just been
founded. Fr. Paterna accompanied his superior from

(3) Vida 132-133; Noticias III, 231. (4) Noticias, III, 231; Dane., I, 181.

here to San Diego on the 18th to return with a supply train. On the arrival of the Fathers from California in 1773, Fathers Juan Figuer and Fermin Francisco Lasuen were assigned to San Gabriel to assist Fathers Paterna and Cruzado. (5)

On January 4th, 1776, Captain Anza's second expedition from Sonora overland reached San Gabriel. Fr. Pedro Font of the Querétaro college of Franciscans accompanied the party as chaplain. (6)

Fr. Junípero came here on March 19th, 1782, and remained until the 26th. During his stay at the mission he administered the sacrament of confirmation to a number of neophytes. In 1784 he visited San Gabriel for the last time and gave confirmation to those who were prepared to receive it. (7)

The neophyte population in 1790 was 1,078. Within the nineteen years of its existence 1,958 persons had been baptized; 869 had died; and 396 couples had been joined in marriage. The governor in his report alluded to this mission as having often relieved the necessities of other mission in both Californias, and as having enabled the government to carry out important undertakings which without such aid would have been impracticable.

In October 1785 the neophytes and gentiles were tempted by a woman, so at least said the men, into a plan to attack the mission and kill the missionaries. Twenty of the conspirators were captured by the corporal. One of the ringleaders was condemned to six years of work in the presidio. Two others were put in prison for two years, whilst the woman was sent into perpetual exile; the rest were released after receiving fifteen lashes by order of Gov. Fages. (8)

Fr. Miguel Sanchez came to San Gabriel in 1775, so that there were three missionaries at work among

(5) Vida, 144; Noticias, I. 223; Banc., I, 139; 190; (6) Vida, 150; 201. (7) Vida, 245; 263. (8) "Informes Generales" 1790; Banc., I. 159-160.

the Indians until 1777, when Fr. Paterna was transferred to San Luis Obispo. In the following year FR. Antonio Calzada arrived and remained as supernumerary until 1792; and Fr. Cristóbal Orámas served here as assistant from 1792 to 1793, when broken down in health he retired to the mother college. (9)

OTHER Fathers besides the regular missionaries stationed at San Gabriel were Fr. Juan Martin in 1794-1796; Fr. Juan Lope Cortés in 1796-1798; and Fr. Pedro de San José Estévan in 1787-1802, when he returned to Mexico; and Fr. Isidoro Barcenilla in 1802-1804, who also retired to Mexico. (10)

FATHERS Cruzado and Sanchez, both missionary pioneers, who for thirty years had served together at San Gabriel, died at their post, the former in 1804, the latter in 1803. (11)

(9) Banc., I, 611. Of Fr. Cristóbal we only know that he had been for five years assistant curate and became a Franciscan a year before coming to California, where he arrived in 1786. He served at Santa Barbara from its foundation in December 1786 to December 1789; at Purisima until November 1792; and at San Gabriel until September 1793.

(10) Banc., II, 113-121; 620. Fr. Pedro de Estévan was a native of Castile. He became a Franciscan at Habana in 1780, joined the college of San Fernando, Mexico, in 1785, and was sent to California in 1794. He was at San Antonio for some months in 1795; served at San Diego from April 1796 to July 1797; at San Gabriel till 1802.

Fr. Isidoro Barcenilla came to California in 1797; was one of the founders of Mission San José, and remained there until April 1802. After leaving San José in 1802, he lived at San Francisco a few months, and then went to San Gabriel where he staid until his departure for Mexico. He was regarded as an intelligent and zealous missionary.

(11) Banc II, 113. Fr. Antonio Cruzado was a native of Alcarazejos, diocese of Córdova, Andalucia, and was born in 1725. Coming to Mexico before 1718, he labored in the Sierra Gorda missions for 22 years; was assigned to California, and arrived at San Diego March 12th, 1771. He was appointed for San Buenaventura, but that foundation being postponed, he remained at San Gabriel until October 12th, 1804, the date of his death. His remains were interred in the mission church.

Fr. Francisco Miguel Sanchez was a native of Aragon, and a member of the Franciscan province of San Miguel. He came to California in 1771, and was first assigned to the mission of Todos Santos in Lower California. He became the regular missionary of San Gabriel in September 1775, though from 1790 to 1800 he spent most of his time at San Diego, Santa Clara, and Soledad. He died at San Gabriel on July 27th, 1803. The remains were buried in the mission church under the steps of the main altar on the epistle side.

· Fr. Dumetz lived here most of the time from 1808 to 1811, and Fr. José Antonio Urresti was stationed at San Gabriel from 1804-1806; but Fr. José de Miguel, who came in 1803, and Fr. José Maria Zalvidea, who arrived in November 1806, may be regarded as the regular successors of Fathers Cruzado and Sanchez. (12)

A stone church was begun early in the last decade of the eighteenth century, but it was not completed until after the year 1800. The church had an arched roof, but an earthquake damaged the building to such an extent that in 1804 the arches had to be torn down and a new roof of timbers and tiles substituted. Fr. Tapis in 1808 attempted to raise cotton at San Gabriel, but without success on account of the cold climate. (13)

In 1820 San Gabriel stood at the head of the list in the number of cattle, and in agricultural products was surpassed by San Luis Rey only, though in 1816 Fr. Zalvidea had reported the land so exhausted that the neophytes had to go to La Puente to plant their grain. This was nine or ten miles away. Six hunderd Indians were at work there, and a chapel, the Father thought, was a necessity at that place. A chapel was built in connection with the mission hospital, as at other southern establishments, before 1818. In 1819 the gentiles of the Guachama ranchería, called San Bernardino, about fifteen leagues from San Gabriel, asked for the introduction of agriculture and of stock-raising in their fertile lands, and a beginning was made. The Fathers regarded this as an important step toward the conversion of the tribes in the direction of the Colorado; but it is not certain that any mission station was established at the ranchería at the time. An article in the San Bernardino Times, July 8th, 1876, claims a branch of San Gabriel with

(12) Banc. II, 114.   (13) Ibid, II, 114-115.

buildings was established at San Bernardino about the year 1820, but that the buildings were destroyed by the Indians about twelve years later. (14)

On January 14th, 1811, Fr. Dumetz died at San Gabriel where he had lived as a supernumerary part of the time since 1803. He was the oldest missionary in California, having served for forty years. He was the only surviving companion of Fr. Junípero Serra. (15)

Fr. Miguel, the associate of Fr. Zalvidea at San Gabriel died in 1818. Fr. Miguel was replaced by Fr. Luis Gil y Taboada, who in 1811 was followed by Fr. Joaquin Pascual Nuez. Fr. Urresti also lived here in 1804-1806. (16)

CHAPTER VI.

SAN GABRIEL (CONTINUED).

Earthquake—Death Of Fr. Nuez—Missionaries—Fathers Boscana And Sanchez Die—Mission Lands—Secularization—Poverty Of The Mission—Statistics—Death Of Fathers Estenega And Ordaz—John Russel Bartlett—Los Angeles Star—Mission San Gabriel Sold—"Our Father" In Indian.

There was constant alarm at San Gabriel on ac-

(14) Banc., II, 355-356.   (15) Ibid. II, 355. Fr. Francisco Dumetz was a native of Mallorca. He was appointed to the California missions in August 1770; sailed with ten companions from San San Blas and reached San Diego March 12th, 1771. He labored among the Indians at San Diego until May 1772; at San Carlos until May 1782; at San Buenaventura until August 1797; at San Fernando until 1802, and again in 1901-5; and at San Gabriel in 1803-4, and from 1806 to 1811. He was buried by Fr. Zalvidea on January 15th, 1811, the day after his death.

(16) Banc., II, 356-357. Fr. José de Miguel came to California in 1790. He served at Santa Barbara from June of that year until October 1798, when he was allowed to retire to Mexico on account of ill health. He returned in 1810 and was stationed at San Luis Obispo until September 1803, and at San Gabriel from 1803-1813. He died on June 2d, 1813, at San Fernando, and was buried by Fr. Oltes.

count of the Indians in 1811, and for some years
thereafter; but the savages attempted nothing against
the mission. It suffered some damage from another
cause, however. An earthquake occurred on December
8th, 1812, at sunrise, and overthrew the main altar,
breaking the statues of Our Lord, St. Joseph, St.
Dominic, and St. Francis. Moreover the top of the
steeple was brought down, and the sacristy, the convent of the missionaries, and other buildings were
damaged. In 1819 the mission was credited with 175
inhabitants *de razon*, or white and mixed settlers, of
whom probably fifty-one were soldiers temporarily
stationed there. A private school existed in 1818. (1)

Fr. Zalvidea was transferred to San Juan Capistrano in March 1826, and succeeded by Fr. Geronimo
Boscana. Fr. Joaquin Pascual Nuez, who had come to
San Gabriel in March 1814, died on December 30th,
1821. Fr. José Sanchez took his place and continued
to reside here, though he became superior of the
California missions in 1827. (2)

THE names of Fathers Jesus Martínez, Francisco
Gonzalez de Ibarra, and Vincente Pascual Oliva, and
the Dominscans Francisco Cuculla and Mariano Sosa,
appear occasionally on the mission registers in 1831
and 1832; but the regular missionaries were Fathers
Boscana and Sanchez until their deaths, which occurred in 1831 and 1833 respectively. (21)

(1) Banc. II, 356-357. (2) Ibid. II, 567. Fr. Nuez was born February 20th,
1785, at Luco, Valle of Daroca, Spain. He received the habit on September 24th, 1800; sailed from Cádiz March 20th, 1810; and was ordered to
California in July 1811. He arrived in California, after being detained by
a pestilence, in July 1812. He was stationed at San Fernando until March
1814, and at San Gabriel during the rest of his life. In his last years his
acts of mortification were extreme. After suffering a severe illness for 24
days, he expired on December 30th, 1821, and was buried in the mission
church on the next day. Fr. Señan in one record gives the date of his
death as December 28th.

(3) Banc. III, 641-643. Fr. Geronimo Boscana, the first to die, was
born on May 23d, 1776, at Llumayor, Island of Mallorca, and took
the habit at Palma on August 4th, 1792. After acting as professor for
nearly four years, he started for America on June 5th, 1803, and arrived at

Father Boscana.

Fr. Sanchez was succeeded by Fr. Tomás Eleuterio
Esténega, who came down from the north on the arrival of the Zacatecan Franciscans, and remained at
San Gabriel many years. The Rev. Alexis Bachelot
from the Sandwich Islands also lived here most of
the time in 1832-1836. The neophyte population decreased only about thirty down to 1834, when the
missions were about to be secularized; but by the
end of 1840 nearly 1,000 had left the community, and
only about 400 remained. San Gabriel reached the
highest number in its population with 1,701 souls in
1817. The largest crop ever raised by any mission was
at San Gabriel in 1821, when 29,400 bushels of grain
were harvested. In 1834 there were 163,579 vines in
four vineyards, and 2,333 fruit trees on land belonging to the mission. (4)

In 1834 San Gabriel was secularized, though the
Indians would not hear of the change. The result was

San Fernando college in October. He reached Monterey on June 6th,
1806, and was assigned to Soledad. In the same year he was transferred
to Purisima where he staid until 1811. At San Luis Rey Fr. Boscana was
in 1812-1813; at San Juan Capistrano in 1814-1826; and at San Gabriel in
1826-1831. At San Juan he devoted much study to the manners and customs of the natives, especially their religious traditions. His writings on
this subject were published by Robinson in 1846 under the title of CHINIG-
CHINICH. His death occured on July 5th, 1831; and his body was buried
next day in the sanctuary of the mission church.

Fr. José Berna do Sanchez, who died on July 15th, 1833, was born at Robledillo, Spain, on September 7th, 1778, and became a Franciscan on October 5th, 1794. Leaving Spain in February 1803, he came to California by
way of Mexico in 1804. He was stationed at San Diego in 1804-1820; at
Purisima in 1820-1821; and at San Gabriel thereafter until his death. In
1806 Fr. Sanchez accompanied an expedition against the Indians; in 1821
he went with Fr. Payeras on an exploring tour among the gentile rancherias. From 1827-1831 he held the office of president of the California missions. Mofras says that Fr. Sanchez died of grief at the ruin of the missions through secularization. His remains were interred at the foot of the
altar in the mission church.

(4) Banc. III, 612-613; II, 567-568. The mission lands in 1822 extended
south 3 leagues to Santa Gertrudis; southwest, 6 leagues to San Pedro;
west 1½ leagues; north, 2 leagues; eastward, 7-9 leagues into the mountains and toward the Colorado, including the pagan settlement of San Bernardino; and 15 leagues northeast. In a report of 1828 there are named as
mission ranchos, La Puente, Santa Ana, Jurupa, San Bernardino, Santo
Timotheo, San Gorgonio, four sites on the San Gabriel, and also lands
between the pueblo and San Rafael.

the same as at other missions. In 1830 the mission
owned 25,725 cattle, 2,225 horses and mules, and
14,650 sheep. In 1840, when the management of the
temporalities was again turned over to Fr. Esténega,
livestock included seventy-two cattle and 700 sheep.
In a letter of February 1840 Fr. Duran quotes Fr.
Esténega to the effect that the mission has to support thirty-eight white people; that there is not a
candle, no tallow to make a candle, and no cattle fat
enough to supply the tallow. "What a scandal! and
what a comment on secularization!" Fr. Duran justly
exclaims. (5)

FROM the time that the mission was founded in
1771 down to December 31st, 1831, when the last report of the Fr. Superior of the missions was made,
there were baptized at San Gabriel 7,709 persons, 5,
494 were buried, and 1,877 couples were married.
The mission owned 20,500 cattle, 13,554 sheep, and
485 horses and mules at the close of 1831.(6)

IN 1843 the real estate and other property of the
mission was restored to the Fathers; but in 1845 the
government resolved to rent the estates. The property
was then turned over to the comisionados on July
7th. There was no semblance of prosperity after that,
but a constant decrease of mission property. At the
end of 1845 there were but 250 Indians remaining at
the mission, and probably even fewer. Finally, in
June 1846 the mission estate was sold by the govern-

---

(5) Banc. III, 643–645. As early as 1841 the cook and cowherd were
discharged on account of the poverty of the mission. Ibid. IV. 6ff.
(6) "Informes Generales," 1831. Bancroft gives the following figures:
General statistics for the whole period of the mission's existence, 1771-
1834; Total number of baptisms, 7,854, of which 4 853 Indian adults 2,459
Indian children; one adult and 1,039 children of gente de razon; average
per year, 123. Total of marriages, 1,935, of which 241 do razon. Deaths, 5,
656, of which 2,916 Indian adults; 2,363 Indian children; 211 adults and 186
children de razon. Largest number of cattle, 26,300, in 1828; horses, 2,400,
in 1827; mules, 205, in 1814; sheep, 15,000, in in 1829; goats, 1,380, in 1785;
swine, 300, in 1832; all kinds of animals, 40,360, in 1830. Total product of
wheat, 225,942 bushels; barley, during eleven years only, 1,250 bushels;
corn, 154,820 bushels; and beans, 14,467 bushels. Banc., III, 643.

ment to Reid and Workman in payment for past aid
to the government; the title was later on declared
invalid by the United States on the ground that the
governor had no right to sell the property.

Fr. Esténega died early in 1847, and Fr. Ordaz a
few months later took charge of San Gabriel. (7) Fr.
Ordaz after 1848 was the only survivor of the Fernandinos in California, and the last missionary for
the Indians of San Gabriel. He too passed away in
1850. (8)

John Russel Bartlett, who visited San Gabriel in
1852, only two years after the last Franciscan had
died at his post, writes of the Indians he observed in
this once prosperous district as follows: "I saw more
Indians about this place (Los Angeles) than in any
part of California I had yet visited. They were chiefly "Mission Indians," i. e. those who had been connected with the mission, and derived their support
from them until the suppression of those establishments. They are a miserable, squalid-looking set,
squatting or lying about the corners of the streets,
with no occupation. They have no means of obtaining
a living, as their lands are taken from them; and the
mission, for which they labored, and which provided
after a sort for many thousands of them, are abolished. No care seems to be taken of them by the A-

(7) Banc., V, 629. Fr. Tomás Eleuterio Esténega was born in the province
of Vizcaya about 1790; he became a Franciscan at Cantabria; came to
the college in 1880, and and arrived California in 1820. Fr. Tomás served at
San Miguel in 1820-1842 at San Francisco in 1832-1833; and at San Gabriel,
from 1833 to 1847. Bancroft says "I find no trace of him in the mission
register after 1845, and, rather strangely, no record of his death; but it
appears that he died at San Gabriel early in 1847, since the juez on May
8th writes of what the "late" Padre Esténega did "over two months ago."

(8) Banc., V, 629; IV, 759. Fr. Blas Ordaz was born in Castilla la Nueva,
Spain, about 1792, and came to California in 1820. He was stationed at
San Francisco in 1820-1823; From there he accompanied Arguello on his
famous expedition to the north, of which trip he wrote a diary. In 1820-
1822 Fr. Ordaz was at San Miguel; 1823-1833 at Santa Inés and Purisima;
in 1833-1838 at San Buenaventura; at San Fernando in 1838-1847; and at
San Gabriel in 1847-1850.

Mission San Gabriel.

mericans; on the contrary, the effort seems to be to exterminate them as soon as possible." (9)

THE "Los Angeles Star" in 1852 had this to say on the same subject: "Situated in the midst of a fertile valley, surrounded with abundant timber, and supplied by a thousand springs with an inexhaustible flow of water, the Mission of San Gabriel flourished and became exceedingly rich. Authentic (?) records are said to exist which show that at one time the mission branded fifty thousand calves, manufactured three thousand barrels of wine, and harvested one hundred thousand fanegas of grain a year. (10) The timber for a brigantine was cut, sawed, and fitted at the mission, and then transported to and launched at San Pedro. Five thousand (?) Indians were at one time collected and attached to the mission. They are represented to have been sober and industrious, well clothed and fed; and they seem to have experienced as high a state of happiness as they are adapted by nature to receive. These five thousand Indians constituted a large family, of which the Padres were the social, religious, and we might almost say political heads."

"LIVING thus this vile and degraded race began to learn some of the fundamental principles of civilized life. The institution of marriage began to be respected, and, blessed by religion, grew to be so much considered that deviation from its duties were somewhat unfrequent occurrences. The girls, on their arrival at the stage of puberty, were separated from the rest of the population, and taught the useful arts of sewing, weaving, cording, etc., and were only permitted

(9) "Personal Narrative," Vol II, 82. (10) These figures are very much exaggerated, but they are in keeping with the notions of many scribblers and so-called historians. "Bandini Hist." Cal., for instance, "talks of 80,000 cattle; Robinson even finds 120,000 cattle. It has been the custom in current newspaper articles to grossly exaggerate the wealth of this mission, though doubtless under the care of Zalvidea it was most prosperous and most systematically managed," says Banc., II, 388. We have given the official numbers in the preceding pages.

to mingle with the population when they had assumed the character of wives.

"When at present we look around and behold the
state of the Indians of this country, when we see
their women degraded into a scale of life too menial
to be domestics, when we behold their men brutalized
by drink, incapable of work, and following a system
of petty thievery for a living, humanity cannot refrain from wishing that the dilapidated Mission of
San Gabriel should be renovated, and its broken walls
be rebuilt, its roofless houses be covered, and its deserted halls be again filled with its ancient industrious, happy, and contented original population."

"SEVERAL industries had been developed in the mission workshops; a soap factory was established, besides a shoe-shop and a carpenter-shop. These were
operated by converted Indians, many of whom attained considerable skill in their respective branches.
Manufacturies, too, had progressed satisfactorily, including large quantities of cloth, blankets, saddles,
etc. Among the Padres were some of artistic tastes,
whose leisure moments were devoted to carving in
wood, horn, or leather, some specimens of which were
very beautiful. Eventually, the more delicate and
sensitive of the natives were instructed in the art,
and some marvelous tracings were done by their
hands." (11)

"SAN Gabriel," says the author of 'The Old Missions of California,' p. 14-15, "suffered sadly from
the cruel blow of secularization, administered, as it
was, at a time wholly premature and ill-advised.
Secularization was but a synonym for destruction......

(11; "Personal Narrative" Vol. II 83-84. The Lord's Prayer in the
language of the San Gabriel Mission Indians, the Kizh idiom, is as
follows: "Yyonak y yogin tucupugunisa sujucoy motuanian masarmi magin
tucupra maimano muisme milleoar y ya tucupar jiman bxi y yoni
masaxmi mit_na coy aboxmi y yo onamaiuatar moojaich milli y yaqma
abonac y yo no y yo ocaihuc coy jaxmen maln itan monosaich coy jama
juexme huememesaich."—Banc., Hist. Native Races III, 675.

Such was the fate of San Gabriel Arcangel, the fairest of all the Franciscan possessions; the generous monastery whose portals were open wide to all the wanderers of its time."

CHAPTER VII.

SAN LUIS OBISPO.

FOUNDING OF SAN LUIS OBISPO—MISSIONARIES—CAPTAIN ANZA'S EXPEDITION—FIRE AT THE MISSION—FR. SERRA CONFIRMS—DEATH OF FR. CAVALLER—DEPARTURE OF FR. GIRIBET—REVOLT—OTHER ITEMS—DEATH OF FR. CIPRES—FR. MARTINEZ BANISHED—MISSION LANDS—STATISTICS—FR. GILI DIES—SALE OF THE MISSION.

As early as June 1771 Fathers Cavaller and Juncosa had been appointed as missionaries for the new mission of San Luis Obispo. (1) The foundations, however, could not be laid until the following year. Fr. Serra, then on his way south, took with him Fr. Cavaller, five soldiers, and a few San Carlos Indians. When within half a league of the Cañada de los Osos, 25 leagues from San Antonio, he halted upon a site known among the natives as 'Tixlini.' Here on the first of September 1772 Fr. Junípero founded the fifth mission in California, San Luis Obispo, in honor of St. Louis, Bishop of Tolouse. A cross was erected, as usual on such occasions, and Holy Mass offered up. On the next day Fr. Serra departed for San Diego. He expressed great hopes for the success of the mission, for in his 'Representacion' he wrote: "Let us leave time to tell the story of the progress which I hope Christianity will make among them in

(1) Vida, 119-120.

spite of the Enemy, who has already began to lash
his tail by means of a bad soldiers, whom soon after
arrival they caught in actual sin with an Indian woman, a thing which greatly grieved the poor padre."
Fr. Cavaller with two Indians from Lower California
and five soldiers remained at the new mission. The
only provisions on hand were fifty pounds of flour
and about three pecks of wheat, besides a barrel of
brown sugar. With the sugar they expected to procure seeds from the pagans. These were scanty means,
but the Father was contented and for the rest trusted in God.

Fr. Cavaller at once had a little chapel and a
dwelling erected. In a few days the natives began to
come down from the mountains, and were soon on
friendly terms with the missionary. They frequently
brought seeds and venison, and in this way helped
the Father along until provisions arrived from San
Diego. The first few months were more fruitful of
baptisms at San Luis than was the first year at the
earlier missions. Fr. Palou in the following year
found twelve Christians. He left four families of
Lower California Christians at the new mission, besides a few unmarried Christians. At the time of Fr.
Serra's death the number had increased to 616 neophytes. In other respects San Luis Obispo also fared
well after the first year; but those twelve months
were trying times for the struggling, lonely Fr. Cavaller. Then the clouds lifted as Fr. Juncosa joined
him. Later, in 1773, Fathers José Murguía, Juan
Prestamero, and Tomás de la Peña were added to
the missionary force as supernumeraries. The mission
was distant from the ocean about three leagues, near
the little Bay of Buchon, fifty leagues from Monterey. (2)

On March 2d, 1776, Captain Anza's immigrants,

(2) Vida, 140-143: Bancroft, I, 188-189, 196,

accompanied by Fr. Pedro Font of the Querétaró Franciscans, were welcomed at San Luis. The mission records show that the next day Anza stood godfather for several native children whom Fr. Font baptized. From this place the travellers continued onward to Monterey. (8)

On November 29th. fire destroyed the buildings, except the church and granary, together with the implements and some other property. The fire was the work of gentiles who discharged burning arrows at the tule roofs, not so much to injure the Spaniards as to revenge themselves on a hostile tribe who were friendly to the Spaniards. Rivera hastened to the mission, captured two of the ringleaders, and sent them to the presidio. On this occasion the marriage register was destroyed.

Twice again the mission was on fire within ten years, and this caused the use of tiles for roofing to be generally adopted at all the missions. Fr. Figuer was made assistant of Fr. Cavaller in 1774, and remained here until 1777. Fr. Murguía, 1773–1777, and Fr. Mugártegui, 1775–1776, were also engaged in missionary work among the Indians. (4)

In 1778 Fr. Junípero Serra administered confirmation here for the first time. His second and last visit to San Luis Obispo for the same purpose was at the close of 1783, or the beginning of 1784. (5)

Fr. Cavaller, who had been stationed here since the foundation of the mission died on December 9th, 1789. (6) His associate from 1777 to 1786 was the aged Fr. Paterna. Fr. Miguel Giribet arrived in December 1787. Between the two Fr. Faustino Sola had

(3) Banc., I, 208. See also "Franciscans in Arizona" for particulars about this expedition. (4) Vid'n, 142-143; Bancroft I, 298-299; 455; 459; 476. (5) Vida. 228; 266. (6) Banc., I, 469. Fr José Cavaller was a native of the town of Fulcet in Catalonia. He left the college, Mexico in, October 1770, and reached Monterey in May 1771. He remained there as supernumerary until he went to found San Luis Obispo. His remains were buried in the mission church. He left the reputation of a zealous and successful missionary.

charge of the mission for a few months. What other
Father was at San Luis during the interval it is impossible to say. Fr. Miguel Giribet continued as sen-

San Luis Obispo.

ior missionary at San Luis Obispo until 1799, when
he left California for his college in Mexico. (7)

---

(7) Banc., I, 469; 472; 689. Fr. Giribet came to California in 1785, where he
served two years at San Francisco and twelve at San Luis Obispo. He
was zealous and successful, but, as was so frequently the case with missionaries, his health was unequal to the task. His last signature on the
mission books was ou October 2d, 1799, but he did not sail from San Diego until January 16th, 1800. He died at the college in 1804.

Fr. Lasuen, superior of the missions, seems to have acted as senior missionary after Fr. Giribet's departure until August 1800, when Fr. José Miguel arrived. The position of associate was held successively by Fr. Estévan Tapis in 1790–1793; Fr. Gregorio Fernandez in 1794–1796; Fr. Antonio Peyri in 1796–1798; and Fr. Luis Antonio Martínez, who began his long service at this mission in 1798. (8)

In September 1794 fifteen or twenty neophytes of San Luis Obispo and La Purisima were arrested, with some gentiles, for making threats and inciting revolt at San Luis. Five of the culprits were condemned to presidio work. In the same year this mission reached the highest figure of population with 946 souls. The church, of adobes with tile roof, was built before 1793, in which year a portico was added to the front. In 1794 the missionary's house, the work-room, barracks, and guard-house were completed. The native huts were well built, and afforded sufficient protection against everything but fire. In 1794 a miller, a smith, and a carpenter were sent here to instruct the Indians; in 1798 a water-power mill was finished.

In 1805 the Fathers were commended for their cool reception of a foreign vessel, which came in pretended need of fresh provisions, but really in quest of opportunities for illicit trade. In 1809 the governor approved of the building of a chapel at San Miguelito, one of the rancherías of this mission.

Fr. José de Miguel left San Luis in 1803. Fr. M. Ciprés replaced him in the following year, but died in 1810, and was succeeded by Fr. Marquinez. (9)

---

(8) Banc., I, 689. Fr. Bartolomé Gili spent some time here before his departure in 1794. He had come to California in 1791, and served irregularly, as supernumerary for the most part, at San Antonio, Soledád, and at San Luis Obispo until 1794. "He was one of the few black sheep in the missionary fold," says Bancroft.

(9) Banc. I, 547; 689 II, 148. Fr. Marcelino Ciprés was a native of Huesca, Spain. He received the habit at Saragossa, and came to Mexico in 1793. In 1795 he was assigned to the California mission. He was stationed at San Antonio from October 1795 until the end of 1804; and at San Luis Obispo

FR. JOSÉ Marquínez in 1811 was replaced by Fr. Antonio Rodriguez, who remained here until 1821. From 1798-1830 Fr. Luis Martínez labored at San Luis, generally alone, till he was banished by the government. His place was filled by Fr. Luis Gil y Taboada. (10)

EVENTS at San Luis Obispo were neither numerous nor exciting. In 1821 eighty horses, eighty saddles, and fifty blankets were sent to the troops as a gift from Father Martínez; but in 1830 Fr. Gil said the mission had become very poor. (11)

IN 1822 the mission lands were described as lying in a cañada one league wide and 14 leagues long, bounded by ranges of mountains on the east and the west. Locusts and squirrels were very troublesome at the mission, and in 1826 the crop was destroyed by mice.

FROM the time that this mission was founded until December 31st, 1831, as many as 2,640 persons were baptized, 2,230 died, and 758 marriages took place. 265 Indians still lived at the mission in 1831. The

until his death in 1810. Fr. Ciprés was a very zealous missionary, who learned the native language at San Antonio, and devoted himself assiduously to the work of caring for the sick and attending to the spiritual welfare of his neophytes. In 1801 he had some trouble with the mission guard, and was in consequence the subject of certain charges which proved to be unfounded. With his companion in 1800 he suffered from an illness which was attributed to poison, but he recovered. At the beginning of 1810 he made a visit to Monterey, and returning arrived at San Miguel on January 26th. There he was attacked with an acute inflammatory disease and died. His body was buried on February 1st in the mission church of San Miguel. Banc, II 148—149.

(10) Banc. II 384; 618. Fr. Luis Antonio Martínez was born on January 17th, 1771, at Briebes in Asturias, Spain, and became a Franciscan at Madrid. in 1785. He left Cádiz in 1795, and joined the college of San Fernando. On May 9th, 1798, he arrived at Santa Barbara, and was stationed at San Luis Obispo from June of that year until his arrest in February 1830. For the causes that led to his banishment see Part I, Chapter XVII. In July 1830 he was at Lima; and in October he arrived at Madrid. where he still lived in 1851. Fr. Martínez was highly spoken of by his superiors. He was familiar with the language of the Indians at San Luis Obispo. "He never scandalized his Order by irregular or immoral conduct," Bancroft declares. (11) Banc., II. 618—620.

The mission buildings were finally sold in 1845. The number of cattle was 2,000, sheep, 1,200, and horses, and mules, 400. (12)

Fr. Gil continued as missionary at San Luis until his death towards the close of 1833, in which year also Fr. Ramon Abella came down from the north to take his place. Fr. Felipe Arroyo de la Cuesta was Fr. Abella's companion in 1833-1835.

The mission was secularized in 1835, and after that the number of the neophytes decreased rapidly, so that at the end of 1839 there were only 170 Indians in the neighborhood. Stock decreased fifty per cent in the five last years. The inventory taken in 1836 showed a valuation of $13,458 on buildings, goods, produce, implements, etc.; on live-stock, $19,109; fábrica, $5,000; garden, $6,858; Santa Margarita rancho, $4,039; nine sites of land, $9,000; church and ornaments, $7,257; library and musical instruments, $510; credits, $5,257; due from one Sanchez, $9,300; total valuation $70,770. On September 10th, 1842, Gov. Alvarado issued an order to distribute the lands and other property among the neophytes; and in 1844 the ex-mission was formed into a pueblo. (13)

(12) Informes Generales 1831; Banc., III. 681, has the following figures for the years 1772-1834: Total number of baptisms, 2,067; deaths, 2,318; marriages, 775. Largest number of cattle in any one year, 8,900 in 1818; sheep, 11,000 in 1813; horses, 1,394 in 1799; mules, 340 in 1810; goats, 513 in 1786; swine, 210 in 1788; all kinds of animals, 20,820 in 1813. Total product of wheat 116,161 bushels; barley, 1,385 bushels; corn, 26,923 bushels; beans, 3,596 bushels; and other grains, 3,156 bushels.

(13) Banc. III, 680—681. IV, 424. Fr. Luis Gil y Taboada was born in Mexico at the town of Guanajuato, May 1, 1773, but became a Franciscan at Pueblito de Querétaro in 1792. He joined the college San Fernando in 1810, and was sent to California in 1801. He served as missionary at San Francisco in1801-1802, 1804-1805, 1819-1820; at José in 1802-1804; at Santa Inés in 1910-1910; at Santa Barbara in 1810-1812; at San Gabriel in 1813-1814; at Purisima in 1815 1817; at San Rafael in 1817-1819; at Santa Cruz in 1820-1830; and at San Luis Obispo in 1829 and 1830-1833. Fr. Gil was a zealous missionary, but he was often in bad health. He spoke several Indian dialects. In December 1833, while at the rancho of Santa Margarita, whither he had gone to say Mass for the Indians occupied in planting, he was attacked with dysentry and vomiting of blood. He died on the 15th, and was buried the next day in the mission church on the Gospel side near the sanctuary by Fr. Juan Cabot.

Scott, Wilson, and Mc Kierey for $510; but on August 24th, 1847, after the United States had taken possession of the territory, Governor Mason ordered that all property held by the Fathers at the raising of the United States flag be turned over to the Catholic Church.

Fr. Ramon Abella was the missionary of San Luis until the end of 1841, or the beginning of 1842. Rev. Miguel Gomez, a secular priest, took charge apparently late in 1848. He attended to the spiritual welfare of the ex-mission till 1856. There are no statistics of this period, but Mofras gives the population as eighty in 1841-1842. Such was the end of San Luis Obispo as an Indian missionary establishment. (14)

CHAPTER VIII.

SAN FRANCISCO.

DON GALVEZ AND ST. FRANCIS—DISCOVERY OF SAN FRANCISCO BAY—EXPEDITION TO THE BAY BY SEA—ANZA's LAND EXPEDITION—THE PRESIDIO ESTABLISHED—EXPEDITION NORTH OF THE BAY—FOUNDING OF THE MISSION—DOLORES—THE INDIANS—INDIAN ATTACK.

When consulting with the visitador general, Don Galvez, about the establishment of the three first missions in Upper California, whose names were assigned by the government, Fr. Junípero Serra was disappointed in not finding the name of his beloved Father St. Francis among the patrons selected. He therefore asked Don Galvez—"and for our Father St. Francis, is there to be no mission?" "y para N. P. S. Francisco no hay una mission?" To this the visitador

---

(14) Banc. III, 682; IV, 423; 583; 539; 657-659; V, 638,639,

replied: "If St. Francis wants a mission, let him cause his port to be found and it will be put there." "Si San Francisco quiere mision que haga se halle su puerto, y se le pondrá." St. Francis did show the port that bears his name, and let St. Charles do as much for Monterey. (1)

THE expedition in search of Monterey started out from San Diego on July 14th, 1769; but instead of finding Monterey, or rather recognizing it when they found it, the explorers discovered San Francisco Bay, and readily recognized the port. The party sighted Point Reyes and the Farallones on October 30th, 1769. Fr. Juan Crespi, who fully described the expedition in his diary, and Fr. Francisco Gomez accompanied the party which was under the command of Gov. Portolá. These Fathers, then, were the first priests that appeared at what is now San Francisco. Want of food compelled the expedition to return to San Diego. Bancroft himself declares: "It must ever remain more or less inexplicable that the Spaniards should have failed at this time to identify Monterey harbor. With the harbor lying at their feet, and with several landmarks so clearly defined that Vila and Fr. Serra at San Diego recognized them at once from the reports, and penetrated the truth of the matter in spite of their companions' mystification, the Spanish officers could find nothing resembling the object of their search! Fr. Palou, and with him Gleeson, attributes the failure of recognizing the port of Monterey to a miracle." (2)

AT the end of 1774 the viceroy notified both Rivera and Fr. Serra that he intended to establish a new presidio at San Francisco. This establishment would serve as a base of operations for a future extension of Spanish and Christian power, and under its pro-

---

(1) Vida. 88; Banc., I, 154-55; Gleeson II, 34-35; see also Chapter. V, Part I. (2) Banc., I, 132; "Our Centennial," 7-11.

tection two new missions, San Francisco and Santa
Clara, were to be founded at once. Fr. Serra was
requested to name the missionaries, and he appointed Fathers Cambon and Palou for the proposed
mission of San Francisco. Lieutenant Ayala at the
same time received orders to explore the San Francisco region by water, and Fr. Santa Maria accompanied the expedition as chaplain on board the San
Carlos. The expedition sailed from Monterey, probably on July 24th, and at the same time the crew began a novena in honor of St. Francis, at the termination of which, just at night, the ship was off the
entrance to San Francisco Bay. She entered the bay
and anchored in the vicinity of what is now North
Beach. Next morning the San Carlos crossed over to
the Isla de Nuestra Señora de los Angeles, so named
from the feast of the day, August 2d, and still
known as Angel Island. Fr. Santa Maria and the officers landed several times on the northern shore toward Point Reyes to visit the Indian rancherías.
After waiting more than forty days for the land expedition, the San Carlos returned to Monterey. On
the 14th of September Fathers Palou and Campa set
out from Monterey with the land expedition. Follow
ing Rivera's route of the preceding year, the party
arrived at the seashore on the 22d. On the hill-top,
at the foot of the old cross, were found letters from
Fr. Santa Maria. After looking in vain for the San
Carlos the expedition returned. (8)

On March 10th, 1776, Captain Anza with Fr. Pedro
Font of Querétaro, heading an expedition for San
Francisco, reached Monterey. Anza made every possible effort to forward the establishment of the mission and presidio of San Francisco by repeatedly urging its importance upon the dilatory and obstinate
Commandant Rivera. It was not his fault that he

(8) Vida, 201-203; Banc., I, 244-248.

had to leave the country before his colonists had
been properly settled in their new home. From Monterey the expedition followed the route of Rivera in
his journey of December 1774 to the Arroyo de San
Francisco, now known as San Francisquito Creek, at
a spot where the Spaniards had first encamped in
December 1769, and which Fr. Palou had selected
two years previously as a desirable site for the mission. The cross set up in token of this selection was
still standing. On March 27th the party encamped on
a lake near the 'mouth of the port,' now known as
Lobos Creek. Next morning Anza went with Fr.
Font to what is now Fort Point, "where nobody had
been," and there erected a cross, at the foot of
wl.ich he buried an account of his explorations.
Here upon the table land Anza resolved to establish
the presidio. About half a league east of the camp
they found a large lagoon from which was flowing
considerable water; this was the present Washer-
woman's Bay, corner of Greenwich and Ontario
streets. Next morning, the 29th, they broke camp,
half the men returning by the way they had come
to San Mateo Creek, and the commander with Fr.
Font and five men taking the route by the bayshore.
Arriving at the spring discovered the day before,
they named it from the day, the last Friday in Lent,
Arroyo de los Dolores. On the 8th of April the party
again reached Monterey. (4)

On the departure of Anza, Rivera at once changed
his policy of delay, and on the 8th of May despatched an order to Commandant Moraga to proceed,
and to establish the fort on the site chosen by
Anza. However, he could not refrain from annoying
the Fathers by saying that the founding of the mission was for the present to be suspended. Nevertheless, Fr. Serra had Fathers Palou and Cambon, who

(4) Vida, 204-205; Banc., I, 268-269; 280-287.

were destined for San Francisco, accompany the soldiers to attend to their spiritual interests, and be
ready on the spot for further orders, On June 27th,
1776, soldiers, settlers, and two Fathers encamped on
the Laguna de los Dolores. Here Moraga awaited the
coming of the ship San Carlos which was to bring
supplies from Monterey. A month passed in explorations, in cutting timber, and in other preparations,
and still no vessel came. Moraga then resolved to go
over to the site selected by Anza, and to make a beginning by erecting barracks of tules and other light
material. The camp was transferred on the 26th of
July. The first building completed was intended for a
temporary chapel, and in it the first Mass was celebrated by Fr. Palou on July 28th. The first Mass
after their arrival, however, had been said on the
feast of Saints Peter and Paul by Fr. Palou in a
little hut constructed of branches. Thereafter the
two missionaries had said Mass every day at the
camp. Meanwhile they had also visited the pagan
rancherías, the inhabitants of which expressed their
satisfaction at seeing the religious among them.

When the camp was transferred to the presidio,
the Fathers did not change their quarters. They
thought the first camp better fitted for a mission
than any other locality on the peninsula: and,
though by Rivera's orders the mission was not yet
to be founded, it was deemed safe and best for the
two missionaries to make preparations for their future dwellings. This was the situation at San Francisco for nearly two months.

To the relief of all, the San Carlos arrived on the
18th of August. Work was immediately begun on
permanent buildings for the presidio, and they were
completed, the chapel included, by the middle of
September. The 17th was chosen for the day of religious dedication, it being the feast of Stigmata of

St. Francis, the patron of the port and mission. More
than 150 persons witnessed the ceremonies. Fr. Palou
sang High Mass. He was assisted by Fathers Cambon
Peña, who had come up from Monterey, and Nocedal, the chaplain of the ship. Fr. Palou also blessed
the great cross. The "Te Deum" concluded the religious ceremonies. The officers then took possession
of the fort in the name of the king, amid the firing
of cannon and musketry and the ringing of bells. (5)

WHILE the supplies were transferred to the warehouse, a new exploration of the head of the bay and
of the great rivers was made by Captain Quiros, Ca-
ñizares, and Fr. Cambon in the ship's boat, and by
Lieutenant Moraga on land. The boat went up as
far as Petaluma Creek and some distance into it, being probably the first European vessel to pass along
the windings of that stream; at any rate, Fr. Cambon was the first priest that came to this region. (6)

IN the camp at the Laguna de los Dolores, where
since July Fathers Palou and Cambon, reenforced
after a time by Fr. Peña, had been making preparations for a mission, six soldiers and a settler had e-
rected houses for their families. Two children of presidio soldiers, the first on the peninsula, were baptized in August.

As soon as Quiros arrived he immediately put six
sailors to work to aid the missionaries in erecting a
church and dwelling. No orders came from Rivera
authorizing the establishment of a mission, but Moraga saw no reason for delay, and took the responsibility upon himself. A church fifty-four feet long, and
a house thirty by fifteen feet, all of wood, plastered
with clay, and roofed with tules, were constructed,
and the feast of St. Francis, October 4th, was the
day set apart for the ceremony of dedication. On the

third the church, decorated with bunting from the vessel, was blessed; but the next day Low Mass only was said, for the solemn ceremonies were postponed on account of Moraga's absence. He arrived on the seventh, and on October 9th the mission site was blessed, and the great cross erected, after which the image of St. Francis was carried about in procession and then placed upon an altar. On this occasion Fr. Palou again sang High Mass, assisted by Fathers Cambon, Nocedal, and Peña. The sermon was preached by Fr. Palou. All the Spaniards on the peninsula, except the few soldiers left in charge of the presidio, assisted at the solemn ceremonies. Volleys of musketry rent the air, aided by swivel-guns and rockets brought from the San Carlos, and finally two beeves were killed to feast the guests before they departed. Thus was San Francisco de Asis on the Laguna de los Dolores, the sixth of the California missions, formally established.

RESPECTING the name of this mission, it should be clearly understood that it was simply San Francisco de Asis, and never properly anything else, Assisi was dropped in common usage, as was Borromeo at San Carlos, and Alcalá at San Diego. Then Dolores was added, not as a part of the name but simply to designate the locality, like Carmelo at San Carlos. Gradually, as San Francisco was also the name of the presidio, and as there was another mission called San Francisco Solano, it became customary to speak of the mission as Mission de los Dolores, meaning simply 'the mission at Dolores.' No other name than San Francisco was employed in official reports. Dolores was in full: "Nuestra Señora de los Dolores," the name given to a stream or spring by Anza on Good Friday. (7)

NONE of the Indians witnessed the festivities at

(7) Vida. 214; Banc., I, 291-295. The parish church, however even in our time celebrates the 17th, of September as its titular feast.

San Francisco, as in the previous month of August they had fled to the deserted islands in the bay, or had crossed over to the other side. Their departure was owing to a sudden attack from their mortal enemies, the Salsona Indians, who lived about six leagues to the southeast. The soldiers had been unable to arrive in time to prevent the outrages on their neighbors. In December the natives began to come back to the peninsula; but they came in hostile attitude, and began to steal all that came within reach. One party discharged arrows at the corporal of the guard; another insulted a soldier's wife; and there was an attempt made to shoot a Christian from San Carlos. Then one of the guilty Indians was shut up and flogged by the soldiers, whereupon the savages rushed up and discharged a volley of arrows at the mission buildings, and attempted to rescue the prisoner. They were frightened away, however, by a discharge of musketry. On the next day the sergeant went out to make arrests, when a new fight occurred in which a settler and a horse were wounded, while of the natives one was killed and another wounded. The Indians now begged for peace; it was granted after sundry floggings had been administered. About three months elapsed before the savages again showed themselves at the mission. Gradually, however, the natives lost their fear of the Spaniards, and on June 24th, 1777, three adults. the first converts, were baptized. At the close of the same year the number of neophytes had increased to thirty-one. Before the death of Fr. Junípero the whole number of converts was 394. The first burial of a neophyte took place on October 20th, 1777. The first marriage was between two Spaniards on November 28th, 1776.

In October 1777 Fr. Junípero Serra, the superior of the missions, arrived at San Francisco. Passing over to the presidio on the 10th, he gazed for the first

time on the blue waters of the bay and exclaimed:
"Thanks be to God that now our Father St. Francis, with the holy cross of the procession of missions, has reached the farthest boundary of the California continent. To go farther he must have boats."
At the end of 1777 the missionary force here consisted of Fathers Francisco Palou, Pedro Benito Cambon,
José Antonio Murguía, and Tomás de la Peña. (8)

CHAPTER IX.

SAN FRANCISCO—(CONTINUED).

THE INDIANS AND THEIR CUSTOMS—FR. SERRA CONFIRMS—SERVICE AT THE
PRESIDIO—STATISTICAL—FR. FRANCISCO PALOU—HIS WRITINGS—FR. CAM-
BON—LIEUTENANT MORAGA—TROUBLES WITH THE NATIVES—COMPLAINTS.

THE natives around Mission San Francisco were of
a darker color than those of the other side of the
bay. Their religion was a kind of negative infidelity.
From San Diego to San Francisco, a distance of more
than 200 leagues, Fr. Palou did not discover a single trace of idolatry. He found a few superstitious
practices, especially among the old people, some of
whom pretended to have the power to bring on rain,
or to produce good crops of corn, but he saw no
signs of idol worship. When any of the Indians of
the northern district fell sick, they imagined it was
owing to the evil influence of an enemy. The bodies
of those that died were cremated, a custom still
practiced among the Yumas on the Colorado. The
Indians subsisted on seeds and herbs gathered by the

---

(8) Vida, 214-215; 224; Banc., I, 291-297.

women, who ground them into powder and prepared the dish from them called 'atole.' Of a certain kind of black seed they made a food similar in appearance to "tamales," (1) which tasted like roasted almonds. They also caught fish in abundance along the bay, gathered muscles, hunted deer, rabbits, ducks, quails, and other game.

OCCASIONALLY a whale would appear on the shore, which was always a period of rejoicing, as was also the capture of a sea-lion. The Indians would slice these, roast them, and hang them to a tree. Whenever the natives felt hungry they would go to the tree and help themselves until nothing of the meat was left. Along the cañons they gathered hazel nuts, and on the sandhills they picked the wild strawberries. On the plains and hills a kind of wild onion abounded, which was roasted, and this dish was called 'amole.' Fr. Palou pronounced it sweet, and of as good a flavor as that of the ordinary preserves.

THERE was another kind of "amole," of a saponaceous nature, similar to our castile soap. The poor Indians, however, had very little use for it, as the men wore no other garments than those of Adam before the fall. To protect themselves against the cold, they would cover their bodies with mud. As the day advanced and the atmosphere grew warmer, this coating was washed off. The women wore a sort of apron, made of skins, which reached down to the knees; another skin was thrown over the shoulders to protect them against the cold.

THE marriage ceremonies of these Indians was very simple; it consisted in the mutual consent to live together till some disagreement occurred, when the couple would separate to choose other companions. The children belonged to the mother. The only for-

---

(1) 'Tamales;" minced meat rolled up in corn shocks and baked on coals.

mula of divorce was the word of the husband: "I
put her out." Many, however, never separated, and
these loved their children tenderly. Some Indians had
several wives, because he who obtained a wife considered himself entitled to all her sisters, and even
her mother. Such were the low ideas of the natives
regarding matrimony. The influence of Christianity
soon made a change in this matter. A short time
after the establishment of the mission a man presented himself for instruction who had four wives: three
sisters and their mother. At the request of Fr. Palou
he dismissed all except his first wife, and his example was followed by so many that in a short while
no Indian had more than one wife. (2)

THE sacrament of confirmation was administered at
San Francisco for the first time by Fr. Junípero
Serra on October 21st, 1779. He had arrived on the
15th and remained until the 6th of November, meanwhile instructing and confirming these who were
ready for the sacrament. (3)

ON October 26th, 1781, Fr. Serra again came to San
Francisco for the purpose of administering confirmation. He was accompanied by Fr. Juan Crespi, who
had not been at this mission since 1769, when none
but roving Indians were to be seen along the shores
of the bay. The two Fathers remained until November 9th. (4)

A new chapel was in course of erection at the presidio in the beginning of 1780. Fr. Junípero once
more visited San Francisco to give confirmation on
the fourth of May, 1784, and remained with Fr. Palou two days. (6)

THERE was some trouble about the performance of
chaplain's duties at the presidio. For two years the
soldiers had to attend Mass at the mission, which
was not a great distance away; but about the year

---

(2) Vida, 215-218.   (3) Vida, 232-233.   (4) Vida, 237.

1788 a chapel was completed, and the Fathers thereafter occasionally held service at the presidio. The
natives gave no trouble save by the rare theft of a
horse or cow, for which offence they were chastised
once or twice at the presidio in 1788; and in 1786
some neophytes were arrested and flogged for ravages
among the cattle of the soldiers. These cattle, however, became so numerous as to be annoying, wherefore a slaughter was begun as early as 1784 to reduce
the number to eight or nine hundred

NOTWITHSTANDING the small area and barren nature
of the soil, the yield of grain at the mission in 1790
amounted to 8,700 bushels. It appears that the sowing
was done mostly at a place ten or twelve miles down
the peninsula. By December 81st, 1790, the Fathers
at San Francisco had baptized 904 persons, and buried 888. There were then residing around the mission 525 Indians. The herds consisted of 1800 cattle,
1,700 sheep, 42 horses, and 159 other animals. (7)

Fr. Palou, who with Fr. Cambon founded the mission of San Francisco, remained here until 1785,
when he retired to his college at a ripe old age. (8)

It is chiefly through his historical writings on California that the name of Fr. Palou will be remem-

---

(7) Banc., Vol. I, 472-473, "Informes Generales" for 1790. (8) Banc., 472-
476. Fr. Francisco Palou was born at Palma in the Island of Mallorca,
probably in 1722. He received the holy habit in the same city, and in 1740
became a disciple of Fr. Junipero Serra, with whom and with Fr. Juan
Crespi he formed a life-long friendship. With his venerable friend he volunteered for the American missions in 1749, left Palma in April, Cádiz in
August, and landed at Vera Cruz in December. After joining the college
of San Fernando, he was assigned to the Sierra Gorda missions, where he
served from 1750 to 1759, subsequently living at the college for eight years,
Appointed to Baja California he arrived at Loreto in April 1768, took
charge of San Francisco Javier, and in 1769, after Fr. Serra's departure
for the north, became acting superior or president of the missions in Lower California. At the end of August 1773 he arrived at San Diego, and in
1774, while Fr. Serra was absent in Mexico, he again acted as president
of the missions. For two years and a half he was stationed at San Carlos, and in June 1776 went to found the San Francisco establishment, having previously visited the peninsula twice. His first entry in the mission
registers bears date of August 10th, 1776, and his last was on July 25th,
1785. On the death of Fr. Junipero Fr. Palou as senior missionary was

bered. There was no man so well qualified by opportunities and ability to write the early history of
California as Fr. Palou, and he made excellent use
of his advantages. As early as 1778 he began the accumulation of material by copying original documents and recording events, without any definite idea
of publication. He continued his labor of preparing
careful historical notes down to 1783, devoting to it
such time as could be spared from his missionary duties at San Francisco. During the years 1784-1785,
having apparently suspended work on his notes, he
gave his attention to the preparation of a life of Fr.
Serra, his superior, former instructor, and life-long
friend. This work he completed in February 1785,
and carried it to Mexico later in the same year,
where it was published in 1787. It was extensively
circulated for a book of that epoch, though since considered rare, and it has been practically the source
of all that has ever been written on California mission history down to 1784. Very few of the modern
writers have consulted the original, however.

THE manuscript of the *Noticias*, after lying for
some years in the college vaults, was copied into
the Mexican archives, and finally printed in 1857,
though it was utterly unknown to writers on California until 1874, since which date it has been as care-
lessly and superficially used as was the Life of Fr.
Junípero before. Fr. Palou must be regarded as the
best original authority for the earliest period of mission history. (9)

After the departure of Fr. Palou. Fr. Miguel Giribet was stationed at San Francisco with Fr. Benito

---

obliged against his own wishes to serve as president of the missions until Fr. Lasuen received the appointment in September 1785. He was now
free to leave California, as he had long desired to do, and departed for
Mexico in October or November. He reached his college on February 21st,
1786, and on July 1st was elected guardian. He died about the year 1790.
(9) Bancroft, Hist. Cal. Vol. I, 417-420. The entire title of the first work is:
"Relacion Historica de la Vida y Apostólicas Tareas del Venerable Padre

Cambon. Except during a short time when he was chaplain of the San Carlos for the sake of his health, Fr. Cambon attended the mission of San Francisco from the beginning in 1776 until 1791. Fr. Giribet remained only two years, 1785-1787. Fr. Santiago was at San Francisco in 1786 to 1787, Fathers Sola and García in 1787 to 1790; and Fr. Dantí from 1790–1796. (11)

Fray Junípero Serra y de las Misiones que fundó en la California Septentrional, y nuevos establecimientos de Monterey. Escrita por el R. P. L. Fr. Francisco Palou, Guardian actual del Colegio Apostoliśo de S. Fernando de Mexico, y Discipulo del Venerable Fundador, a exponsas de varios Bienhechores. Impresa en Mexico año de 1787." In his prologue the author says: "I well know that some who read new things expect a historian to indulge in theories and to clear up all difficulties. This method although tolerated and even applauded in profane histories, in those of saints and servants of God, written for edification and to excite imitation is deemed by the best historians a fault, which I have to avoid. As the soul of history is simple truh, thou canst have the assurance that almost all I relate I have witnessed, and the rest has been told me by other missionary Fathers and companions who are worthy of belief. Finally, I do not forget that neither Homer among the poets, nor Demosthenes among the orators, neither Aristotle nor Solon among the philosophers ceased to be capable of error; for although they were eminent as philosophers, orators, and poets, they were men. Great is the frailty of our nature; and while those who write do not cease to be men, there will always be men to notice it. Kind reader, remember your own frailty, and you will have compassion with mine."

The other work of Fr. Palou "Noticias de la Antigua y Nueva California, Mexico, 1857, is by far the more extensive work of the two, though both cover substantially the same ground. The latest date mentioned is in July 1783, about which time it was probably concluded. The work is divided into four parts. Part I includes the annals of Lower California under the Franciscans from 1768-1773, and extends over 245 pages of the first volume in 40 chapters. Part II describes the expeditions to Monterey and the foundation of the first five missions, and extends from page 247 to 688 in 50 chapters, covering the period from 1769 to 1773. Part III is a collection of original documents on events of 1773-1774, not arranged into chapters, and fill 211 pages of the second volume. Part IV continues the narrative in 41 chapters on pages 213-796, from 1775 to 1783. The author was able; to obtain only the two volumes I and III.

(11) Banc. Vol. I, 473-474; 712. Fr. Pedro Benito Cambon, who in 1791 retired to his college entirely broken down in health, was born at Santiago in Galicia, Spain. He was ordered to California from the college in August 1770, and arrived at Monterey on May 21st, 1771. Fr. Cambon was one of the founders of San Gabriel and was stationed there until April 1772. He then spent several years at Velicatá in Lower California for the benefit of his health, and to look after the property of the missionaries. In October 1776 he went to San Francisco, but was absent from October 1779 until May 1782, during which time he was chaplain of the San Carlos. In 1782 he founded San Buenaventura. Fr. Cambon was a zealous and able

Lieutenant José Moraga was commandant of the military from the first founding of San Francisco as a presidio in 1776 until his death, which occurred on July 13th, 1785. He was buried in the mission church at whose cornerstone laying he had been present. The presidial force consisted of thirty-four men besides the officers. From 15 to 20 men were on duty in the garrison, while the rest did guard duty at the mission, at Santa Clara, and at San José. (12)

THE natives caused more trouble in the region of San Francisco during the last decade of the century than in any other part of California. In March 1795 Fr. Dantí sent a party of fourteen neophytes to the rancherías of the Chaclanes or Sacalanes to bring back some fugitives, but these were attacked by gentiles and renegade Christians, and at least seven of the number were killed. In September over two hundred natives deserted from San Francisco. It seems Fr. Dantí was less lenient than his brother missionaries, and kept up a strict discipline to the disgust of the Indians. The governor complained to Fr. Lasuen about the missionary. Fr. Lasuen promised to investigate the matter. Unwillingness to work on the part of the neophytes seems to have been the principal cause of the dissatisfaction at the mission.

In June a new difficulty arose. A large part of the fugitive natives belonged to the Cuchillones across the bay. The missionaries sent about thirty mission Indians to bring back the runaways. They crossed the bay on balsas and soon had a quarrel with the Cuchillones. No lives were lost, but no fugitives could be recovered. This affair gave rise to new correspondence with the governor. The gentiles now threatened to

---

man, says Bancroft, but his health repeatedly broke down. His last signature on the mission books is dated September 10th, 1791.
Of Fr. Antonio Dantí we only know that he was stationed at San Francisco, that he was a strict disciplinarian disliked by the Indians for that reason, and that he was allowed to retire on account of ill health.
(12) Bancroft Vol. I, 470-472.

kill the Christians if they continued to work, and the soldiers if they dared to interfere. By order of the governor Sergeant Amador with 22 men then attacked the Indians in their ranchería. In the fight two soldiers were wounded and seven natives killed. Amador then returned to San José with 83 Christians and nine pagans. In the examination held with a view to learn why the neophytes had run away, the shrewd Indians gave as their reasons excessive flogging, hunger, and the death of relatives. Those acquainted with the Indian character will smile at the first two reasons. Any punishment in any shape is excessive with Indians. Probably the good Father applied St. Paul's command, "that if any one would not work, neither should he eat." (13) Fr. Lasuen, who also investigated the complaints of the Indians, declared that the charges of cruelty were unfounded, as was also proved by the large number of conversions. The neophytes fled, not because they were flogged or overworked, but because of the ravages of an epidemic. No further troubles occurred at San Francisco, but the Sacalanes and other pagan Indians continued their hostile influence at Mission San José. (14)

---

(13) II, Thess., III, 10. (14) Banc., I, 708-712.

CHAPTER X.

SAN FRANCISCO—(CONTINUED).

A CARMELITE MONASTERY PLANNED—RANCHO DEL REY—MISSIONARY CHANGES—FATHERS ESPI, GARCIA, AND FERNANDEZ RETIRE—THE MISSION BUILDINGS—VANCOUVER'S VISIT—FR. SAENZ RETIRES—THE CHURCH. GREAT MORTALITY—OTHER ITEMS—BRANCH MISSION ACROSS THE BAY—STATISTICAL—MISSIONARY CHANGES—THE INVENTORY—STATISTICS.

A singular plan was formed in Mexico at this time. A monastery of Carmelites was to be established at San Francisco. The buildings were to cost from $25,000 to $30,000, and the community was to be composed of twelve religious. It was to be supported by an agricultural establishment, become the nucleus of a settlement, and thus promote both the civilization of the natives and the colonization of the country, to say nothing of the usefulness of the monastery towers to navigation as landmarks. This doubtful scheme was referred to two religious, Fathers Mugártegui and Peña, who had been in California. The Fathers reported adversely, but declared that, instead, any aid from the Carmelites in founding new missions would be acceptable. There the matter rested. Governor Borica himself disapproved of the proposed establishment, because there would be no market for the produce. (1)

In 1796, at the suggestion of Comandante Sal, Governor Borica determined to reestablish a branch of the rancho del rey, which had been abandoned in 1701 at the petition of the Fathers, who claimed that

(1) Banc., I, 580-581.

injury was done to the mission interest. The plan
was carried out in 1707. Two hundred and sixty-five
cattle were purchased from the missions and placed
at Buriburi, between San Bruno and San Mateo.
When the news reached Mexico it brought out a protest from the Fr. Guardian to the viceroy on February 6th, 1708. In this document the past history of
the rancho was related, and the charge made that
Borica had acted in opposition to the king's wishes.
The guardian then demanded the removal of the
rancho as well as of the cattle owned by the soldiers. The pasturage, he showed, was all needed for
the mission herds, which now must be driven far
down the peninsula; and the natives were suffering
great injury in their natural and legal rights. As instances the Fr. Guardian stated that the horses were
kept ten leagues distant; sheep under a salaried man
six leagues away; and the oxen not actually at work
were also pastured at a long distance. Notwithstanding the objections of the missionaries the viceroy ordered the rancho to be maintained. (2)

SEVERAL changes took place among the missionaries
of San Francisco about the close of the century. Fr.
Martin Landaeta, a new-comer, succeeded Fr. Cambon
and remained until October 1798, when sickness
compelled him to return to Mexico for awhile. Fr.
Espi resided here in 1797-1790, and then retired to
his college. (3) For awhile, 1790-1800, Fr. Merelo succeeded him. Fr. Diego Garcia returned to San Francisco in 1797, and remained until the following year

---

(2) Banc. I, 706-708.   (3) Fr. José de la Cruz Espi, a native of Valencia,
came to Mexico in 1786, and two years later went to Nootka as chaplain
with the expedition of Martinez, which touched on the California coast.
He came to California as a missionary in 1793, and served at San Antonio
from September of that year until September 1794; at Soledad until December 1795; at Santa Cruz until 1797; and at San Francisco from June
1797; until August 1799, when he obtained leave to retire, but did not sail
away from San Diego until January 16th, 1800.

Fr. Diego Garcia came to California in 1757. He was stationed at
San Francisco from September of that year until October 1701; at Solo-

when he departed for Mexico. Fr. Fernandez served at the mission in 1796-1797, and Fr. Ramon Abella arrived in July 1798. (4) Fr. Martiarena was also a supernumerary from August 1800, and the names of several others appear on the mission books as having officiated here at different dates. Down to December 31st, 1800, the Fathers had baptized 2,117 persons at the mission of San Francisco; 1,800 burials had taken place, and 648 couples had been joined in holy matrimony. 635 Indians were on the mission rolls on the same date. (5)

THE mission buildings were described by Vancouver in 1792 as forming two sides of a square, without any apparent intention of completing the quadrangle, the architecture and the material being the same as at the presidio, but the apartments were larger, better constructed, and cleaner. At this period all the roofs were of thatch, and the dwellings of the Indians were huts of willow poles, basket-work of twigs, and thatch of grass and tules. These huts were about twelve feet high and six or seven feet in diameter. In 1793 nineteen adobe houses were built, which number was subsequently increased until in 1798 there were enough for most of the married neophytes. In 1794 a new storehouse, 150 feet long, was erected and roofed with tiles, and half a league of ditch was dug around the *potrero* (6) and fields. In 1795 an adobe building 180 feet long was built, and tile roofs were completed for all the structures, including the church, whose cornerstone had been laid in 1782.

---

dad till February 1792; at San Antonio until November 1792; again at Soledad till March 1796; and again at San Francisco until May 1797, when he was allowed to depart. He was generally a supernumerar.

(4) Fr. José Maria Fernandez left his college in February, and arrived at San Francisco in September 1796. He served as missionary until 1797. He was a very kindhearted man; but a blow on the head accidentally received affected his health, and especially his mind, to such an extent that he was incapacitated for missionary labor. He left California probably in August 1797. (5) Banc., I, 712; "Informes Generales," año 1800. (6) Cattle farm.

Mission Dolores, Or San Francisco De Asis.

WHERE the cultivated fields were situated at this time does not appear. In 1795 supplies furnished to the presidio amounted to $2,881. In January 1795 cold weather prevented the Fathers from saying Mass. From 1797 to 1800 regular weather reports were rendered at the end of each year. At the time of Vancouver's visit one large room at the mission was occupied by manufacturers of a coarse sort of blanketing, made from wool produced in the neighborhood. "The looms," he says, "though rudely constructed, were tolerably well contrived, and had been made by the Indians. The produce is wholly applied to the clothing of the converted Indians. I saw some of the cloth, which was by no means despicable; and, had it received the advantage of fulling, would have been a very decent sort of clothing." In 1797 Governor Borica directed that mission blankets should be used at the presidio, and no more procured from Mexico; but in 1799 he disapproved of the missionaries' plan of building a fulling-mill. In 1796 the manufacture of coarse pottery was begun. Some cotton from San Blas was woven before 1797. In 1798 the mission contracted to furnish tiles to the presidio at $20 per thousand. (7)

THE missionaries now had less trouble with their neophytes than in former years, though 236 of them were carried away by an epidemic of measles from April to June 1806. Twelve or fifteen of the San Francisco Indians were also killed in February 1807 by the gentiles in a fight that seems to have occurred in the region of Carquines Strait.

A traveller visiting the mission about this time describes the dwelling of the missionaries as consisting of spacious apartments. Behind the dwelling was a large court surrounded by buildings in which the neophytes were employed, chiefly in the preparation of

(7) Banc., L. 711-715.

wool and the weaving of coarse fabrics. About a
hundred yards from the mission was the rancheria
composed of eight long rows of dwellings for the Indian families. There were buildings for melting tallow and for making soap, smithshops, shops for carpenters and cabinet-makers, magazines for storing tallow, soap, butter, salt, wool, and hides, and storehouses filled with grain. The wine served was of a
very ordinary quality, being a production of the
country. The kitchen garden was in a poor condition,
the high winds and drifting sands of the peninsula
not being favorable to horticulture. The visitors were
as a rule very favorably impressed by what they saw
at the mission, and had nothing but good to say of
the Fathers.

Fr. Landaeta, who had returned in 1800, left San
Francisco for the south in 1807, and was succeeded
by Fr. Juan Saenz de Lucio, who had come here the
year before. Fr. Martiarena in 1801, Fr. Taboada
in 1801-1802 and in 1804-1805, and Fr. Barcenilla
in 1802, for a few months, are the other names of
missionaries that appear on the mission registers together with Fr. Abella. He with Fr. Saenz labored together for the benefit of the Indians until 1816, when
Fr. Saenz left the province. Fr. Abella remained at
San Francisco until 1819, when he was transferred to
San Carlos. Fr. Oliva served here in 1815-1819, and
Fr. Juan Cabot in 1818-1820; while Fathers Ordaz
and Altimira came in 1820. (8)

San Francisco reached its highest figure as regards
the Indian population in 1820 with 1,252 neophytes
on the registers. In 1818 a school was in operation.
At this period the Indians had their own gardens,

(8) Banc., II, 131-132; 373. Fr. Juan Saenz de Lucio was a native of Cantabria. He left his college for California in February 1800. His last signature on the San Francisco books is on August 7th, 1813, but he seems
to have passed some months at San Juan Bautista before leaving the
province in November 1816.

and all the buildings, including the houses of the In
dians, were of stone or adobe, and covered with tiles.
The habitations of the Indians consisting of long, low
houses, formed several streets. The church was "spacious, built of stone, and handsomely decorated. It
had room for 500 or 600 persons; but there were no
seats." Twenty looms were in constant operation, and
two mills moved by mule-power. The terrible mortality among the neophytes was the great trouble of
the Fathers. To prevent a panic among the Indians
the branch at San Rafael across the bay was established in order to transfer a part of the natives to
this more salubrious climate. A beginning of agricultural and stock-raising operations seems to have been
made across the bay where Oakland or Alameda now
stand, but no particulars are on record. (9)

THE registered population fell from 1,252 to 219,
during the third decade of the century, but, after
making deductions for San Rafael and Solano, the real
decline was from 340 to 210; 590 were at San Rafael
and 822 went to Solano in 1828. The tax on products
paid by the missions was about $800 a year. In 1821
the mission furnished the presidio $1,200 in soap. The
supplies furnished the garrison in 1821-1830, except
1827, amounted to over $8,000 according to some ac-
counts; others say $6,288.

OF the buildings at this period nothing new is
learned. The houses were regularly arranged in
streets, and a fine stream of water flowed through the
plaza. The most important event was the proposed
transfer to Sonoma, which was begun in 1828, so

(9) Banc., II, 574-575. In 1814 limits were assigned to the mission lands
by Governor Sola according to Fr. Esténega's statement in 1828; but
"East to Laurel Creek, and south across the sierra, so as to include San
Pedro rancho on the coast," is the substance of the information given.
On July 22d, 1814, Fr. Abella buried an old woman said to have been
250 (?) years old, and the last living native within six leagues who
could remember the founders of the mission. The mission supplied the
presidio in 1818-1820 with $3,290.

that Solano became a separate mission; but it took
only half instead of all the neophytes from the old
establishment.

FR. Blas Ordaz was succeeded in October 1821 by
Fr. Tomás Esténega, who served alone after Fr. Altimira went to San Francisco Solano in 1829. When '
the Zacatecan Fathers arrived to take charge of the
northern missions in 1833, Fr. Esténega went to San
Gabriel. Fr. Lorenzo Quijas was appointed to succeed him at San Francisco. In the next year Fr. José
Gutierrez took Fr Quijas's place, and remained in
charge until the end of 1839. The neophytes numbered 210 on December 31st, 1831, probably fewer
than 150 in 1834, and at the end of 1839 there were
left only 90, who lived at San Mateo, with possibly
50 more scattered around the country.

WITH secularization began a rapid decline in every
branch. The inventory of July 28th, 1835, described
the buildings minutely. It included 27 structures besides the principal one, and valued them at $22,482;
utensils and furniture were estimated at $819; man-
ufacturing apparatus, $288; goods and produce in
the storehouse $2,414; garden with fences and fruit-
trees, $884; corral, $885; farming tools, $84: launch
and boat, $880; live-stock: 4,445 cattle, 691 horses,
2,125 sheep, 5 mules, 0 asses, 122 swine, $17,172;
church property: buildings, $9,057; ornaments, etc.,
$8,770; etc. If any property was ever divided among
the Indians, there are no records to show it. (10)

THERE is no trace of a resident missionary after
1840, though the Fathers Real occasionally came to
the mission, and Fr. Muro seems to have spent several months there in 1845. (11) The church erected

(10) Banc., II, 596-596, III, 712-718; In 1822 the mission lands are described
as extending six leagues north to south, and three leagues east to west,
hilly, but sufficient with hard work to maintain half the neophytes.
There was no irrigation. The mission also owned a piece of land three
leagues north to south, and a half a league east to west on the other
side of the bay. (11) Banc., IV, 675.

Mission Dolores At The Present Time.

by the Fathers, however, is still used for weekday service by the parish of "Dolores" in that part of San Francisco called "The Mission".

Tʜᴇ Rev. Prudencio Santillan was curate of San Francisco from 1846 to 1850. When the Americans took possession of the territory Santillan retired to Mexico, and did not return to reside permanently until after 1848. (12)

During the whole period of its existence as an Indian mission down to December 81st, 1831, when the "Informes Generales" cease, the Fathers baptized 6,888 persons, buried 2,089 dead, and blessed 2,040 marriages.

According to Bancroft during the same period the whole number of baptisms was 6,998, of which number of persons 8,715 were Indian adults, 2,829 were Indian children, and 454 children of settlers or soldiers. The marriages numbered 2,121, of which 85 were between settlers. The number of burials was 5, 558, of which 3,404 were of Indian adults, 1,900 Indian children, 111 white children, and 58 white adults.

The largest number of cattle owned by the mission was 11,240 in 1808; the largest number of horses, 1, 239 in 1831; mules 42, in 1818; sheep, 11,824 in 1818; all kinds of animals, 22,668 in 1805. The total product of wheat amounted to 114,480 bushels; barley 59, 500 bushels; corn 16,900 bushels; beans 19,880 bushels; and miscellaneous grains 19,058 bushels. (13)

---

(12) Bancroft, V, 712, says Santillan was a novice, who had come to California with Bishop Diego in 1841. He was of Indian parentage, and was ordained priest soon after his arrival. 'Novice' may mean seminarian, which is more probable. Later he became assistant curate at Mazatlan, Mexico, before 1850. (13) "Informes Generales," 1831; Banc., III, 714.

CHAPTER XI.

SAN JUAN CAPISTRANO.

First Attempt To Found The Mission—The Founding—Fr. Serra's Danger—First Converts—The Missionaries—Fathers Amurrio And Mugartegui Retire—Death Of Fr. Fuster—Confirmation At San Juan—Statistical—New Church Begun—Weaving—A Fire—Dedication Of The New Church—Fathers Santiago And Faura Retire—The Missionaries—An Earthquake Destroys the Buildings And Kills A Number Of Indians—Decline Of The Mission—Fr. Boscana Insulted—Emancipation—Inventory—Fathers Oliva And Ordaz Die—Last Missionaries—Sale Of The Mission—Statistics—The "Our Father."

At a conference of the Fathers, held at Monterey on the 12th of August, 1775, it was resolved to establish the mission of San Juan Capistrano under Fathers Lasuen and Amurrio. Fr. Lasuen, thereupon, said the first Mass in a hut constructed of branches, on a spot 26 leagues from San Diego and 18 leagues from San Gabriel. He likewise erected and blessed the great cross, and thus formally began the mission on the 30th of October, the octave of San Juan Capistrano, according to Palou, but on the 19th according to Sergeant Ortega. The natives who appeared in large numbers were well disposed, and assisted in the work on the chapel and other buildings. Fr. Amurrio arrived eight days later with provisions, and the prospects were deemed favorable, when on November 7th Lieutenant Ortega was suddenly called away by the news of an Indian revolt at San Diego. He advised the missionaries to abandon the place for the present. The bells were therefore buried, and the whole party returned to the presidio.

In the latter part of October 1776 Fr. Serra left San Diego with Fathers Mugártegui and Amurrio, under an escort of eleven soldiers to establish a new Mission San Juan. When they arrived at the spot abandoned a year before, they found the cross still standing. They also found the bells, placed them in position, and rang them, thereby causing a number of gentiles to assemble, who expressed their satisfaction at the return of the missionaries. A hut was quickly constructed of branches, and an altar erected at which Fr. Serra said the first Mass. Thus the seventh mission in California was firmly estab, lished on November 1st, 1776, on or near the ruins of a later structure.

In order to speed the work, Fr. Serra went to San Gabriel for more laborers and for some cattle. On his return he took with him only one soldier and a Christian Indian. After having proceeded about ten leagues from the mission, some distance ahead of the pack-train and a drove of cattle, they were surrounded by a crowd of savages, who shouted wildly, and threatened to kill them. Fr. Serra actually thought his last hour had come. The Christian Indian however bade the savages beware, as many soldiers were approaching. This caused them to desist. Fr. Junípero now kindly invited the pagans to draw near. He then made the sign of the Cross on their foreheads, and by means of beads gained their good will.

Fr. Lasuen, who had been assigned to San Juan, was changed to San Diego to take the place of the lamented Fr. Jayme. The first baptism at San Juan took place on December 15th. Fr. Amurrio officiated. On Christmas-Day Fr. Mugártegui, who had succeeded Fr. Lasuen, again administered the sacrament of baptism. The whole number of those baptized before the close of the year was four; but during the next year forty Indians received the grace of regeneration. The

native name of the mission site was Sajirit. The land
was fertile, and the natives were well disposed. Fagés in his report of 1787 alludes briefly to the mission as in a thoroughly prosperous condition. The
number of converts in 1790 was nearly double what
it had been in 1783. In the latter year San Juan
had 389 neophytes, whereas at the close of 1790 there
were 765. Since 1783 there had been 509 baptisms
and only 249 deaths. Agricultural products in 1790
amounted to over 8,000 bushels. An occasional scarcity of water was the only drawback to farming operations.

Of the original missionaries, who were stationed at
San Juan from the time of the founding in 1776, Fr.
Gregorio Amurrio had left the mission, and probably
the country, in the autumn of 1779. (1)

Fr. Vincente Fuster was the successor of Fr.
Amurrio until the end of 1787, when he was transferred to Purisima. Fr. Fuster's place was filled by
Fr. Santiago. Fr. Mugártegui, the other founder of
San Juan Capistrano, left California at the end of
1789, Fr. Fuster having returned in September. Fathers Fuster and Santiago then continued at San Juan
together until 1800, when the former died. (3)

(1) Vida, 174-176; 197 200; Banc., I, 303-304; 458; Informes Generales. Fr. Gregorio Amurrio was one of the party that was wrecked at Manzanillo in at-
tempting to cross from San Blas to Loreto in 1771. He came back to Sinaloa
by land, reached Loreto in November, and served at Santa Gertrudis during the occupation of the peninsula by the Franciscans. At the cession he
came with Fr. Palou to San Diego in August 1773. Here he remained until April 1774, when he sailed for Monterey, subsequently serving most of
the time as supernumerary at San Luis Obispo, until the attempted foundation of San Juan on October 30th, 1775. His last entry in the books of
that mission was in September of 1779.

(2) Fr. Pablo de Mugártegui came to California with Fr. Serra on the
latter's return from Mexico, and arrived at San Diego on March 18th,
1774. Being in poor health he remained for some time unattached to any
mission, first serving as supernumerary at San Antonio from January to
July 1773. He was the regular missionary of San Luis Obispo from August 1773 until November 1776, and of San Juan Capistrano until November 1789. From August 16th, 1786, he held the office of vice-president of
the California missions. Banc., I, 433; 637.

Fr. Vincente Fuster was a native of Aragon who had originally

ACCORDING to Fr. Palou, Fr. Junípero Serra administered the sacrament of confirmation probably in October 1778, and again apparently in October, 1783. (8)

THE missionaries by December 31st, 1800, had baptized 900 persons, blessed 447 marriages, and buried 917 dead. 1,046 Indians were on the mission roll. Horses and cattle increased to 8,500, while in sheep San Juan with 17,000 was far ahead of any other mission. The average crop amounted to 5,700 bushels. In 1797 there was due San Juan for supplies furnished to the presidios of San Diego and Santa Barbara over $6,000.

IN 1794 there were built two large adobe granaries roofed with tiles, and forty houses for neophytes, some with grass roofs and others with tile roofs. In February 1797 work was begun on a new stone church which was to be the finest edifice in California. A master mason was obtained from Culiacan, and the structure rose slowly, but steadily for nine years under the hands of the Indians. The building measured 58X10 varas or yards. On November 22d, 1800, the walls were slightly cracked by an earthquake.

MARIANO Mendoza, a weaver, was sent from Monter-

---

left Mexico in October 1770, arrived at Loreto in November 1771, served at Velicatá, and came up from the peninsula with Fr. Palou. He arrived at San Diego August 30th 1773, and was stationed there until 1776. He was with Fr. Jayme on the terrible night of November 5th, 1775, when Mission San Diego was destroyed and his companion murdered. His pen has graphically described the horrors of that night. After living at San Gabriel and other missions as supernumerary, he was missionary of San Juan Capistrano from November 1779 until December 1787, when he founded Purisima and remained there till August 1789. He then returned to San Juan and resided there until his death on October 21st, 1800. He was buried in the mission church. On September 9th, 1806, his remains were transferred with all due solemnity to their final resting-place in the presbytery of the new church on the epistle side.

(3) Vida, 224; 263: Among the visiting Fathers who officiated here were Fr. Figuer, June 1780; Fr. Miguel Sanchez, May 1782; Fr. Lasuen, October 1783; Fr. Riobóo, February 1784; Fr. Mariner, October 1785; Fr. José Arroita, December 1786; Fr. José Calzada, April 1788; Fr. Torrens, October 1788; and Fr. Cristóbal Oramas, December 1788 to January 1780.

ey in the summer of 1776 to teach his trade to the
Indians. He was under contract with the government
at thirty dollars a month. A loom was set up with
other necessary apparatus of a rude nature. Coarse
fabrics and blankets were thereafter manufactured by
the Indians at this mission. Early in 1797 the Fathers
were notified that if they wished the services of
Mendoza for a longer time they must pay his wages;
but they thought his instructions not worth the money, especially now that the natives had learned all he
knew, and the weaving industry had been successfully established.

BESIDES home manufactures, Capistrano supplied
large quantities of wool for experiments at other establishments. On April 16th, 1797, Pedro Polorena reported that blankets, wide woolen cloths, *mangas*
for vaqueros, 80 yards of *manta*, 80 yards of baize
had been successfully woven. The goods were not so
perfect as the Mexican article, but good enough for
this country. The native women could also spin, pick
wool and cotton, and dye tolerably well. (4)

IN March 1801 the store-room was set on fire by a
sergeant's carelessness. The mission lost 2,400 bushels
of grain, besides more than six tons of tallow; some
damage was also done to church property.

A most important event in the mission annals of
San Juan Capistrano was the completion of the new
church. It was the finest church in California, built
of stone and mortar, and surmounted by a lofty tower. It was regarded with equal pride by missionaries
and neophytes, who had accomplished the work with
the aid of a master-mason. The dedication took place
on September 7th, 1806. Fr. Superior Tapis was assisted by the Fathers of the mission, and Fathers Urresti,
Victoria, Zalvidea, Peyri, and Cueva. Governor Arrillaga was present with Captain Rodriguez, Lieutenant

(4) "Informes Generales" del año 1800; Banc., I. 657-659.

Diego and Santa Barbara. Crowds of neophytes from all the country round witnessed the solemn ceremonies. Next day Fr. Victoria celebrated Mass and Fr. Urresti preached the sermon. On the 9th the remains of Fr. Fuster were transferred to the new church. On this occasion Fr. Cueva sang the Requiem Mass. Fr. Faura preached the sermon. Meanwhile Fr. Sanchez from San Diego had come to join in the festivities. The three days formed an epoch long remembered in southern California. The first baptism in the new church took place on October 18th, 1806.

Fr. Santiago remained in charge of Mission San Juan until 1810, when he retired to Mexico. Fr. Faura likewise retired in 1800. Fr. Francisco Suñer came to the mission in 1800, and Fr. José Barona began his long ministry in 1810. (5)

A series of earthquake shocks, the most disastrous if not the most severe that ever occurred in California, caused the wildest terror throughout the southern part of the province in 1812. The year was ever after known as 'el año de los temblores,' and was for San Juan Capistrano particularly unfortunate. It occurred during early Mass on Sunday December 8th, when about fifty persons were in the church. The edifice was of the usual cruciform shape, with very thick walls and arched dome-like roof, all constructed of stone imbedded in mortar or cement. The stones were not hewn, but of irregular size and shape. The lofty tower at the church front fell with a crash on the vaulted roof at the second shock, and in a moment the immense mass of stone and mortar

(5) Banc., II, 100-111. Fr. Juan Noberto de Santiago came to Mexico from Spain in 1785, and was sent to California the next year. His signature appears in the books of San Francisco often in 1790-7; but his only regular ministry was at San Juan from 1780-1810.

Fr. José Faura was a native of Barcelona; he arrived at Santa Barbara May 7th, 1796; served at San Luis Rey from July of that year till 1800; and at San Juan Capistrano till October 1800, when he was allowed to retire, his term of service having expired.

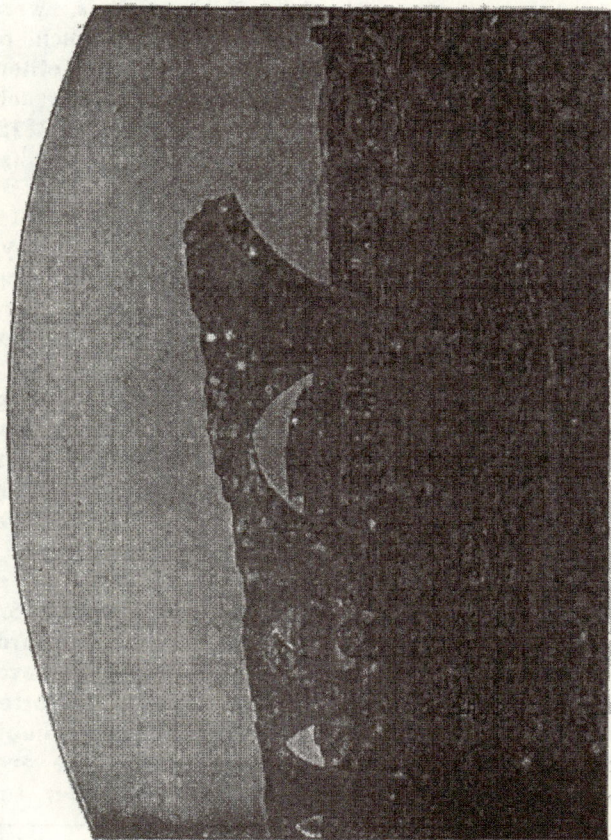

San Juan Capistrano After The Earthquake.

c:me down upon the little congregation. The celebrant, just then at the offertory of the Mass, escaped
by the door of the sacristy, and six neophytes besides were saved as by a miracle; but the rest, forty
in number according to the official reports, were
crushed to death. In the search for bodies much of
the debris was removed from the interior; but otherwise the ruins of the most beautiful mission structure in California still stands as it was left in 1812.
An apartment in an adjoining adobe building has
been used ever since for religious service.

Fr. Suñer, at the end of 1813, or early in 1814,
changed places with Fr. Boscana of San Luis Rey;
and in 1826 Fr. Zalvidea took the place of Fr. Boscana. After 1827 the venerable Fr. Barona spent
much of his time as an invalid at San Luis Rey, but
he finally died at Capistrano in 1831. (6)

Unlike the other missions, Capistrano was no longer prosperous in the third decade of the century. The
population decreased, and so did livestock. The average crop was less than half that of the preceding
decade. The neophytes, while not engaged in open revolt, were disposed to be insolent and unmanageable;
and there was also at times a spirit of hostility a-
gainst the Fathers among the guards. In January 1823
the soldiers went so far as to use violence towards
the venerable Fr. Barona, something that had never
before occurred in California. Fr. Boscana reported
the affair as "el caso mas escandaloso que se habia
visto en California;" "the most scandalous case ever
seen in California." José Cañedo and two other sol-

<hr>

(6) Banc., II, 210; 347-349; 555; III, 625. Fr. José Barona was born at Villa
Nueva, Spain, March 22d, 1764; he became a Franciscan at Velorado July
18th, 1783; he left Spain in 1794, and arrived at the college of San Fernando August 24th, 1795; to California he came in January or May 1798. He
was stationed at San Diego in 1798-1811, and at San Juan Capistrano in
in 1811-1831. As early as 1817 he was in broken health, and desirous of
retirement. In 1823 he was rudely treated by the soldiers at San Juan.
He died on August 4th, and was buried on the 6th by Fr. Zalvidea.

diers were implicated; they were excommunicated by
the Fathers, and a military trial was held. Finally, in
December 1824, the supreme tribunal in Mexico decided that Cañedo had merely carried out the orders of
his chief, and in view of his two years imprisonment
in shackles he was to be set free and made corporal. (7)

THE neophytes were all "emancipated" under Governor Figueroa's experimental system in 1833, the
lands apportioned to the natives, and a regular Indian pueblo was organized in November. In 1840 the
Indians were again put in charge of Fr. Zalvidea, and
he also again managed what was left of the mission
property. The Indian population had decreased to 861
in 1833, and in 1840 was probably less than 500, with
less than 100 at the pueblo. The inventory of mission
property made in 1835 by the missionary and four
comisionados shows a total valuation of $54,450; this
includes the buildings, also the library, which was
valued at $400. The debts amounted to $1,410. (8)

FR. Zalvidea remained at San Juan Capistrano until the latter part of 1842, when he went to San Luis
Rey. Thereafter the mission was without a missionary
until 1846, except that Fr. Esténega officiated there
occasionally in 1843-1846, and Fr. Ignacio Ramirez de
Arrellano in 1844. Fr. Oliva came to San Juan in the
autumn of 1846, and died there in January 1848. He
was apparently the last Franciscan that resided at
Capistrano, Fr. Blas Ordaz, however, occasionally
visited San Juan in 1847-1848. (9)

---

(7) Banc., II, 488; 535-536. In 1822 the lands were described as extending 12-
13 leagues north and south; 3-4 leagues east and west. Some of the fields
were irrigated, and they furnished grain enough to feed the Indians with
the aid of fish and meat. In 1825-1830 the mission ranchos are named as
Santa Ana, San Joaquin, Trabuco and San Mateo.

(8) Banc., III, 625-627. As a specimen of Bancroft's knowledge of Catholic affairs the reader will appreciate this 'historical fact:' "September 12th,
1832, P. Zalvidea sends a keg to San Luis to be filled with CONSECRATED
wine, that at S. Juan having soured." Banc. III, 626, footnote.

(9) Banc. IV, 624; V, 623; Fr. Vincente Pascual Oliva was born July 3d

In December 1845 the mission buildings and gardens were sold to McKinley and Forster by order of the government for $710. The last named of the purchasers remained in possession for twenty years. The Catholic Church authorities then claimed the chapel and its belongings. After much litigation the bishop won the suit. (10)

DURING the whole period of the mission's existence, November 1st, 1776 to 1884, there were baptized at San Juan Capistrano 4,404 persons, of whom 1,689 were Indian adults, 2,628 Indian children, four white adults, and 83 children of settlers. The total number of marriages was 1,108, of which 24 were not Indian. 3,227 persons died, i. e. 1,255 Indian adults, 1,898 Indian children, 24 white adults, and 80 children.

THE "Informes Generales," or official reports of the Fathers, state that from November 1st, 1776 to December 31st, 1831, there were 4,303 baptisms, 1,149 marriages, and 3,064 deaths recorded.

The largest number of cattle owned by the mission in one year was 14,000 in 1819; largest number of horses, 1,355 in 1806; mules, 183 in 1813; asses, 4 in 1813; sheep, 17,030 in 1800; goats, 1,358 in 1784; swine, 206 in 1818; and all kinds of animals, 31,270 in 1819. The total production of wheat was 140,700 bushels; barley, 7,760 bushels; corn, 89,975 bushels; and beans, 6,375 bushels (11)

1780, at Martin del Rio, Aragon, and became a Franciscan at Zaragosa, February 1st, 1790. He came to Mexico in 1810 and started for California in 1811, but did not arrive until August 1813. He served as a supernumerary at San Carlos in 1813-1814, at San Fernando in 1814-1815, at San Francisco in 1815-1819, at San Miguel in 1819-20, at San Diego in 1820-46, and at San Juan in 1846-1848. He died without receiving the sacraments on January 2d, 1848, as the rains prevented Fr. Ordaz from arriving in time; but Fr. Ordaz buried him in the presbytery of the mission church.

(10) Banc., IV, 624-625; V, 628, 'Old Missions of California' p. 60. The "Our Father" in the language of the Netela Indians at San Juan Capistrano is as follows: "Chana ech tupana avo onench, otune a cuechin cal-, me om reino, libi yb chosonee esna tupana cham nechetepe, micate tom cha chaom, pepsum yg cai caychame, y l julugcalme cai och. Depupunopco chame chum oyoto. Amen." Banc., "Native Races," III, 674.

(11) Banc., III, 628.

GHAPTER XII.

SANTA CLARA.

FATHERS Tomás de la Peña and José Murguía had long been appointed for the new mission which was to be named for St. Clare of Assisi, but the establishment was delayed through the animosity of Com. Rivera. Nor did he make any arrangements to found the mission, as ordered by the viceroy, until he received a communication from Bucareli in September 1776. The viceroy wrote as though the mission were already established. Rivera now realized that something must be done. Preparations were therefore made at once. On the 6th of January, 1777, Lieutenant Moraga and Fr. Peña, with a company of soldiers, started southward from San Francisco, and on arriving at the spot chosen, the great cross was erected and blessed, and Holy Mass said on January 12th by Fr. Peña in a hut constructed of boughs. The new mission ever after was known as Santa Clara. It was situated on a spot called Thamien by the natives, fifteen leagues from San Francisco, among the tribe of Indians who went by the name of Tares. Fr. Murguía with cattle and other property joined his companion on the 21st.

San Juan Capistrano in 1865.

THE Indians soon approached, and in May the first baptism could be administered. Some time after an epidemic broke out among the children. The Fathers went from ranchería to ranchería and baptized a large number of little ones who were at the point of death. Some of the parents were likewise baptized after having been properly instructed, so that before the close of the year the registers contained the names of sixty-seven Indians, of whom eight were adults. Thirteen Christians and ten catechumens were living at the mission, whilst the others still remained in their rancherías. The new church was six varas wide and twenty varas long. The dwellings were constructed of timber and plastered with clay. The mission had many advantages not possessed by the others. Its soil was very productive, and the crops of beans, corn, and other grain were abundant. By means of irrigation soon all kinds of fruit were raised. Until the Fathers arrived the Indians had largely subsisted on acorns. The language of the natives was similar to that spoken among the tribes near San Francisco. Sodomy was practised here and among the Indians of other missions to some extent, especially along the Santa Barbara Channel, but the perpetrators of the crime concealed themselves. In a short time every vestige of the vice disappeared before the influence of Catholic doctrines. (1)

FR. Junípero Serra arrived at Santa Clara on September 28th, 1777, on his way to San Francisco. The next day being the feast of St Michael the good Father sang High Mass and preached. Fr. Serra again passed through Santa Clara in October 1779 to give confirmation at the northern missions. He returned on November 6th or 7th, and remained for some days to prepare the Indians for the reception of the sacrament of confirmation.

ON November 9th or 10th, 1781, Fr. Junípero came

---

(1) Vida. 218-222: Banc. I. 304 306.

to Santa Clara from the north with Fr. Juan Crespi. He confirmed the neophytes, and on the 10th, with the assistance of Fathers Crespi, and the two resident missionaries Peña and Murguía, the cornerstone for a new church, was laid. Fr. Junípero again passed through Santa Clara in the latter part of April 1784, but he did not allow himself to be detained, as he expected to be back for the dedication of the new church, which was fixed for the 10th of May. He returned to Santa Clara on the morning of May 15th, and was greeted by a mourning congregation; for one of the founders of the mission, the architect and builder of the new church, had died only four days before. On the evening of the 15th the new a-dobe structure was blessed by Fr. Serra with the assistance of Fathers Palou and Peña, in the presence of Governor Fages, Comandante Moraga, and a great multitude of neophytes, pagans, and settlers. On the following day, which was the fifth Sunday after Easter, and the feast of the Dedication of the Basilica of St. Francis of Assisi, Fr. Junípero sang High Mass, during which he preached to the multitude with his accustomed fervor. At the conclusion of the Mass he confirmed those who were prepared. He also made the spiritual exercises here for the last time as a preparation for his death, which he saw was near at hand. During his stay he at different times gave confirmation to all who could be made ready, even going to the rancherías for the sake of those that on account of sickness could not come to the church. On his arrival at Monterey Fr. Serra appointed Fr. Noboa to take the place of the late Fr. Murguía at Santa Clara. The new church was the finest yet erected in California. The builder, Fr. Murguía, however, did not live to see its dedication. (2)

(2) Vida, 223-224; 221-223; 287; 205-208; Banc. I, 51. Fr. José Antonio de Jesus Maria de Murguía was born December 10th, 1715, at Domayguia,

Fr. Lasuen, the superior of the California missions, seems to have resided at Santa Clara much of the time from 1786–1789. There were no serious troubles with the natives, though the neophytes were sometimes inclined to take part in the petty wars of the gentiles. Two or three neophytes were chastised by the Fathers in 1786 for being present at a gentile fight, and Sergeant Amador was sent to warn the pagans not to tempt the converts.

In agricultural advantages Santa Clara was deemed superior to any other mission except San Gabriel, and the crops of grain and fruit usually were large. In 1790 the mission owned 2,477 cattle, 800 sheep, 36 horses. Down to December 31st of that year the Fathers had baptized 1,836 persons, blessed 228 marriages, and buried 870 dead. At the same time there were 960 Indians on the mission roll. (3)

Fathers Peña and Noboa labored together for the welfare of the Indians at Santa Clara until August 1795, when both retired, the former on account of ill-health and the latter at the expiration of his ten years of service. (4) Their successors were the saint-

Alava, Spain. He came to America as a layman, but entered the Franciscan Order at San Fernando college, Mexico, June 24th, 1738; was ordained priest in 1744, and assigned to the Sierra Gorda missions in 1748. There he toiled for 19 years and built the first masonry church in the district, that of San Miguel. Chosen for California in 1767, he reached Loreto April 1st, 1768, and was assigned to Mission Santiago, where he remained until March 1769. In June he was at San José del Cabo waiting to embark for California; but sickness saved his life by preventing him from sailing in the ill-fated San José. He subsequently served at San Javier, but in July 1773 joined Fr. Palou and accompanied him to San Diego. He resided for a while at San Antonio as supernumerary, and in October 1773 became the pastor of San Luis Obispo. In January 1777 with Fr. Peña he founded Santa Clara, and died there May 12th, 1789, while preparing for the dedication of the church on which he had worked so hard as architect, director, and even laborer. His remains were buried on May 12th in the presbytery of the new edifice by Fr. Palou, who had also administered the last sacraments. (3) Bancroft, I, 476-477: "Informes Generales" for 1790.

(4) Banc. I, 722. Fr. Tomás de la Peña y Saravia, a native of Spain, left Mexico in October 1770, sailed from San Blas in February 1771, was driven on to Manzanillo, came back to Sinaloa by land, and finally reaching Lo-

ly Fr. Magin Catalá and Fr. Manuel Fernandez, but the latter served only one year, when Fr. José Viader took his place. It seems the soldiers insulted Fr. Catalá on some occasion; for on January 7th, 1797, Governor Borica ordered officers Moraga and Vallejo to give satisfaction to the Father for their conduct towards him. (5)

IN 1800 Santa Clara had a larger Indian population than any other mission in California. The average crop of grain amounted to 4,200 bushels per year. Wheat was the leading product. In the garden were peaches, apricots, apples, pears, figs, and grapes. Twenty four oxen were killed every Saturday for food at the time of Vancouver's visit in 1792. Vancouver describes the mission buildings as erected on the same general plan as at San Francisco. They

reto November 24th, 1771, was assigned to Comondú Miss'on. He came up to San Diego on September 1772, serving there for a year, and subsequently as a supernumerary for short periods at San Luis Obispo and at San Carlos. From June to August 1774 he made a voyage with Perez to the northwest coast, and kept a diary of the expedition. After his return he remained as supernumerary at San Carlos and neighboring missions until January 1777, when he became one of the founders of Santa Clara. He served there until August 11th, 1794, when he sailed for Mexico. In 1795 he received some votes for office of guardian of the college, and was subsequently elected, since he held the position in 1798. He was also sindic of the college from 1800 to February 6th, 1806, the date of his death. Fr. Peña was an able and successful missionary, but a strict disciplinarian. He was accused. before 1780, of having caused the death of two boys by blows; but after a full investigation the charge was proven false, the Indian witnesses confessing that they had testified falsely; some evidence was adduced to show that Comandante Gonzalez, whom the Father had reproved for immorality, had used his influence in favor of the accusation. The formal decision was not reached until 1795, after the poor missionary had retired to Mexico; but he interceded with the authorities in behalf of the Indian accusers, who were then released after publicly apologizing to the missionaries for the attempt to bring dishonor on the religious. The affair had weighed on the Father so much, however, that Fr. Lasuen in May 1794 spoke of his condition as very pitiable, for he had become emaciated, talked to himself, appeared constantly afraid, and showed other symtoms, which caused fears that he might lose his reason. Fr. Peña had been appointed by the college to take Fr. Lasuen's place as superior of the missions in case of latter's death. Of Fr. Diego de Noboa nothing is known save that he arrived at San Francisco on June 2d, 1783, remained at that place and Santa Clara until June 1784, when he became the successor of Fr. Murguia, and served till he sailed away with his associate, August 11th, 1794.   (5) Banc., I, 721.

formed an incomplete square of about 100 by 170 feet. The structures were somewhat superior to those of San Francisco, the church especially being long, lofty, and as well built as the rude materials would permit. The upper stories of the other buildings and some of the lower rooms were used as granaries, but there were also two detached storehouses recently erected. Close to the dwelling of the missionaries ran a fine stream of water, but in order to be near this stream the site had been selected in a low marshy spot only a few hundred yards from dry and comfortable eminences. In fact this very year of 1792 the Fathers had been confined for a long time to their house by a flood, and it had already been resolved to move the mission buildings about five hundred yards to higher ground. There is no further direct record of the removal, nor is it likely that the church was ever removed, but a report of 1797 that the houses of the Fathers, the guard-room, storehouse and soldiers' dwellings had been completed indicates a transfer of those buildings which were on low ground. The convent had eight rooms. The church had a roof of tiles, and had been lengthened twenty-four feet in 1795.

At the time of Vancouver's visit some of the natives were at work on adobe houses for themselves. Fourteen of these dwellings, thatched, were completed in 1793, nine more in 1794, and before 1798 nearly all the married neophytes were thus accommodated. There was also a corral 80 yards square, with walls six feet high, built of stout timbers and adobes, A trench was dug in 1795 half a league long, nine feet wide, and five feet deep. The cloth woven at Santa Clara seemed to Vancouver of a better quality than that manufactured at San Francisco. 2,000 hides were tanned in 1792, but very few of them could be sold for want of a market. There was a master tanner and shoemaker, and a carpenter and millwright at the mission. (6)

On August 12th, 1802, a new main altar was consecrated. It had been purchased in Mexico. There were some troubles with the Indians at the beginning of 1801. In a fight which ensued five gentiles were killed. In April 1804 the Fathers sent twenty neophytes out to bring back some fugitives; but the party was attacked, one Christian was killed, and the rest came running to the mission without a captive. In May 1805 a neophyte and a pagan of the Sennenes were caught on the roof of the convent. It was rumored about that the Indians had planned to burn the mission and kill the Fathers. Five or six accomplices were arrested. The excitement was great, and all the available forces of San Francisco with reenforcement from Monterey were sent in haste to the rescue. The rumors of impending hostilities were found to be without foundation, however; some discontented neophytes had simply uttered threats with a view to frighten the missionaries and avoid certain imminent floggings.

Though the number of baptisms was larger at Santa Clara than at any other establishment at this period, except Santa Barbara and San Francisco, the number of deaths was nowhere exceeded. According to the biennial mission report for 1817–1818, a fine new church of adobes with tile roof had been completed during that time. (7)

During all these years, from 1795–1830, Fathers Catalá and Viader labored together at Santa Clara for the benefit of the natives. In November 1830, however, Father Catalá, one of the oldest missionaries in California died after a ministry of thirty-seven years at this very mission. (8)

(6) Banc., I. 722-725.   (7) Banc., II. 180-187; 377.   (8) Ibid. II. 600-602.
Fr. Magin Catalá was born about 1761 at Montblanch, Catalonia,

In population the maximum of 1,464 souls was reached at Santa Clara in 1827. After this date the decline began. The average crop was 4,888 bushels of grain; yet the taxes on mission products in 18-24 amounted to $721, and in 1828 the taxes were $1, 561! The monthly supplies to the guards in 1820-1830 were $40 to $125 per month, generally about $70. The supplies to the presidio in 1821-1830 amounted to $14,068. (9)

Fn. José Viader concluded his missionary service of nearly forty years in 1833, when he left the coun-

Spain, and became a Franciscan at Barcelona in 1777. He sailed from Cádiz for San Fernaudo college in October 1785, and went to Nootka in one of the king's ships serving as chaplain for more than a year, and subsequently returned to the college. He arrived at Monterey in July 1794, and declined to go to Nootka again as chaplain of a ship. He was then sent to Santa Clara, where he was stationed continuously as long as he lived, and during the same time he also attended to the spiritual wants of the pueblo of San José. In 1800 and 1804 Fr. Catalá asked and obtained permission to retire on account of ill-health, but remained at his post. At different times his zeal, gentleness, experience, and all the desirable qualities of a missionary save that of robust health, were attested by his superiors. He suffered much from inflammatory rheumatism, so that for years before his death he could not mount his horse. Among the people Padre Magin was believed to be gifted with prophetic powers; and there are current traditions that he foretold the discovery of gold in immense quantities in California. On one occasion he paused in his sermon, and called on the congregation to pray for the soul of a man who had died; ere the prayer was ended news arrived that a soldier had been thrown from his horse and killed. Fr. Catalá died on November 22d, 1830, and was buried in the mission church by Fathers Viader and Duran, the former of whom testifies to the exemplary, laborious, and edifying life which had made his associate beloved of all, and his loss deeply deplored by the community. He was regarded as a saint by all who knew him. Of late years steps have been taken by the ecclesiastical authorities to procure the beatification of Fr. Magin Catalá. In 1884 an ecclesiastical commission was appointed to receive the testimony of as many as sixty witnesses. Forty of these were eye-witnesses to the remarkable facts they related under oath. The twenty others under oath declared their information was from reliable sources. The Most Rev. T. S. Alemany, O. P., Archbishop of San Francisco, who presided at the hearing of the case, had the evidence transcribed and sent to Rome. From this report the late Rev. Clementin Deyman, O. S. F., compiled a sketch of the life of Fr. Magin Catalá, which is now in possession of the writer, and may eventually be published.

(9) Banc., II, 60!. The lands in 1822 and 1828 extended north to south 6 leagues; and east to west three leagues in the widest part. The limits were the Rio Guadalupe, the sierra, San Francisquito Creek in the northwest.

try on the arrival of the Zacatecan Fathers. (10)

Fr. Francisco García Diego, prefect of the Zacatecan Franciscans in California, succeeded Fr. Viader, and remained at Santa Clara until the end of 1835. From 1834 until his death in 1839 Fr. Rafae! Moreno was also stationed here. (11)

Fr. Mercado took charge of the mission on the death of Fr. Moreno, and remained there until 1844, when he retired to Mexico. (12)

Fr. J. Real succeeded Fr. Mercado in August 1844 as missionary of Santa Clara, from which place he also attended San José and San Carlos. Fr. Real resided here until 1852, when he left the country. (13)

(10)   Banc., III, 726. Fr. José Viader was born at Gallines, Catalonia, on the 27th of August, 1765, and became a Franciscan at Barcelona in May 1788. He sailed for Mexico in 1795 and started for California in February 1796. His only mission service was at Santa Clara from 1796-1833. Fr. Viader was a large man of fine physique; somewhat reserved and stern in manner with strangers, but well liked by all acquaintances, with whom his manner was always frank and courteous: very strict in all matters pertaining to the faith and religious observances: a diligent and effective man of business. It is related that one night about 1814, while going to attend a dying neophyte, he was attacked by three Indians, who tried to kill him,: but they were instead overcome by his great physical strength, and became the Father's faithful friends. In 1818 he made a tour to San Francisco and San Rafael as secretary to the Fr. Prefect. In 1826 he declined to take the oath of allegiance to the republic of Mexico. In early years he had often desired to leave the country, but had consented to remain at the request of superiors and neophytes. In 1833 Fr. Viader arrived at Habana whence he probably went to Spain.

(11)   Banc., III, 727. Fr. Rafael de Jesus Moreno was a Mexican Franciscan of the Guadalupe college, Zacatecas, who came with the others in 1833, and served at Santa Clara until 1839. He was also president and vice-prefect of the Zacatecans in 1836-1839. "The fact that he was chosen for so responsible a position,' says Bancroft, 'indicates that he was a man of some ability, but otherwise no information direct or indirect about him appears in any records that I have seen.' He died on June 8th, 1839, at Mission San José where he had gone for his health some time before. He was buried in the San José mission church on the 9th by Fr. Gonzalez.

(12)   Fr. Jesus Maria Vasquez del Mercado was one of the Fathers who came from Zacatecas in 1833. He was doubtless a Mexican, but of his early life nothing is on record. His missionary service was at San Rafael in 1833-1834, at San Antonio and Soledad in 1834-1839, and at Santa Clara in 1839-1844. Bancroft accuses him of almost all kinds of crimes, but adds "much of the testimony, though not all, comes from men who were not friendly to the padre," and therefore of little value. We have already remarked elsewhere that a piece of gossip is often deemed of sufficient value to find a place in Bancroft's Histories. Banc., IV 682.

(13)   Fr. José Maria del Refugio Sagrado Suarez del Real came to Cali-

SANTA Clara was secularized in December 1886. On May 15th, 1840, the inventory of the property showed 8,717 cattle, 218 horses, 4,807 sheep, 510 fanegas of grain, some tallow and wool, whereas under the management of the Fathers as late as December 31st, 1831, there had been 9,000 cattle, 7,000 sheep, and 230 horses. (14)

IN 1843 the mission was restored to the Fathers, and in 1845 the mission property was valued at $16, 173. On June 30th, 1846, the orchard of Santa Clara was sold by the governor to Castañeda, Arenas, and Diaz for $1,200. The title was subsequently declared invalid. Santa Clara had been one of the wealthiest missions, but its downfall after it was taken out the hands of the missionaries was remarkably rapid. (15)

DURING the whole time of its existence as a mission, 1777-1882, the Fathers of Santa Clara baptized 8,475 persons, joined 2,472 couples in Christian marriage, and buried 6,724 dead.

EVERY vestige of the red man about Santa Clara has disappeared, everything save the mission church. That alone survives, a monument to a departed race. (16)

fornia in 1883, and was stationed at San Carlos until 1848. He succeeded Fr. Mercado at Santa Clara and remained there probably until 1852, when he left the country under threat of suspension if he did not go. In 1855 he had severed his connection with the college, and probably with the Order, and was serving as parish priest at Mazatlan. 'It was most unfortunate for the general reputation of the California Fathers, a most excellent body of men', says Bancroft, 'that the Real brothers, Quijas, Mercado, and a few other black sheep were the friars whose conduct was best known to the foreign immigrants, and on whom many pioneers have founded their estimate of the missionaries." Banc., IV, 682-683; V, 605-607; 600.

(14) Banc., III, 720; 727; 'Informes Generales del año 1831.' (15) Banc., IV, 47; 209; 682-683. On December 31st, 1831, there were 1,184 Indians at the mission. 'Informes Generales.' In 1839 there were left only 291. (Banc., III, 727); and in 1845 there were no more than 130 still in the neighborhood. (Banc., IV, 683). (16) 'Old Missions.' p. 64. According to Bancroft, III, 727, from 1777 to 1834 the whole number of baptisms was 8,640, of which 4,584 were Indian adults, 3,177 Indian children; six white a. dults, and 923 white children. Marriages, 2,548, of which 182 de razon. Deaths, 6,950, of which 4,152 Indian adults, 2,529 Indian children, 137 adults, and 82 children de razon. Largest number of cattle 14,500 in 1828; horses 2,800 in 1811; mules 45 in 1827; sheep 15,800 in 1829; goats 500 in

1741; swine 60 in 1830; all kinds of animals, 10,825 in 1824. Total product of wheat 175,300 bushels; barley 21,270 bushels; maize 60,450 bushels; beans 3,500 bushels; miscellaneous grain 11,600 bushels. These figures are about the same as those given above from the Informe General. The 'Our Father' in the language of the Indians at Santa Clara is as follows: 'Appa macreno mo raura sa-

Santa Clara in 1849.

ruatchia ekepuhmen imragat, sacan macreno meusaraherelig nouman ouran macari phuca numa ban sariachizga poluma macreno sumhali saltis sat macreno neena, la annanit macreno pleona, la annanit macreno macrec equetr macciari nourraban m aro as-sau, nou marote, jaesemper macreno in eckoné tamouniri innam tattahne icatraca onlet macreno erquetx macoritkoun oun ech a-'(sus.' Banc., III. "Native Races."

CHAPTER XIII.

SAN BUENAVENTURA.

FOUNDING OF THE MISSION REPEATEDLY DELAYED—A BEGINNING MADE AT LAST—THE INDIANS—GOVERNOR NEVE'S PLAN—REPORT OF 1790—VANCOUVER'S VISIT AND REPORT—INDIAN FIGHT—MISSIONARY CHANGES—DEATH OF FR. SANTA MARIA—EARTHQUAKE—INDIAN FIGHT AND OTHER ITEMS—DEATH OF FR SENAN—BIOGRAPHY—FR. ALTIMIRA RETIRES—INTERESTING ITEMS—DEATHS OF FATHERS SUNER, URIA, AND FORTUNI—SECULARIZATION—LAST MISSIONARIES—SALE OF THE MISSION—STATISTICS.

San Buenaventura was among the first three missions which it had been the intention of Don Galvez and Fr. Junípero Serra to found as early as 1768. As has been related elsewhere, Don Galvez himself had assisted in packing what was necessary for *his* mission, as he called San Buenaventura. (1)

In May 1771, in the beginning of June, Fathers Antonio Paterna and Antonio Cruzado had already been appointed as missionaries for San Buenaventura, yet, instead of being one of the first, San Buenaventura was the last mission founded by Fr. Serra, through no fault of the good Father, however. Fr. Junípero, who had set his heart on founding this mission, used to say of it: "Tamen quo tardius, eo solemnius," 'the more slowly the more solemnly." (2)

At last, in the spring of 1783, it seemed agreeable to Governor Neve to allow the mission to be established. He accordingly asked Fr. Serra for two missionaries, one for the long contemplated mission and the other for Santa Barbara. Though he had no missionaries to spare at the time, Fr. Junípero wanted

(1) Vida. 50–63.   (2) Vida. 121; 182–183.

to avoid further delay; he therefore went south himself, and reached San Gabriel on March 19th. Here he
met Fr. Cambon who had come up from San Diego
at his request. Both Fathers visited the governor then
staying at San Gabriel. It was resolved to proceed at
once to the foundation of the mission at the head of
the Santa Barbara Channel, and to place it in charge
of Fr. Cambon. By order of the governor the expedition set out from San Gabriel after Holy Mass on
Tuesday in Holy Week, which was the 26th of
March. The whole party consisted of seventy soldiers
with their officers, besides ten soldiers from Monterey
with their families, servants, and some neophytes.
The governor also joined the expedition in company
with the two Fathers. At the first encampment he
was obliged to leave the party with his ten soldiers
on account of news received from Col. Fagés. The
commanding officer was ordered to proceed, however,
to establish the mission.

On the 29th the company reached the first ranchería of the channel, named Asuncion de Nuestra Señora by Portola's party in 1769. This place had long
been selected as a suitable locality for the mission
of San Buenaventura. A large tribe of Indians was
discovered there who dwelt in houses built in conical shape of tules and straw. On the following day
a large cross was erected and a hut constructed of
boughs. In this little structure Fr. Serra on March
31st, which was Easter Sunday, sang the first Mass
and preached after having blessed the cross and the
place that was to be known thereafter as Mission San
Buenaventura. The Indians manifested a very friendly disposition, and even assisted the soldiers in building a chapel and house for the missionaries, besides
the barracks for the guards. The whole group of
buildings was surrounded by a palisade for the sake
of greater security. By opening a ditch, water was

brought to the mission for daily use, and afterwards
for the purpose of irrigating the land. Through some
Christian Indians from San Gabriel Fr Serra now
made known to the natives the object of the missionaries, and remained at the new mission for fifteen
days, during which time he sought to dispose the Indians to listen attentively to the truths of religion.
He had not the happiness of baptizing any of them,
but on his visit in the following year he had the satisfaction of seeing that some of the natives had pro-
fited by the presence of the missionaries and had become Christians. (8)

It had first been the determination of Governor
Neve and General La Croix to found Mission Buenaventura on a radically different plan. The mission
was to have only a few guards, and the temporalities
were to be entirely under the management of the soldiers. This system had been tried on the Colorado
River against the advice of the missionaries. The result had been the waste of four missionary lives and
of a number of soldiers and their families. This disaster directly traceable to the stupid scheme of Neve
and La Croix, for a time at least effectually put a
stop to further plans of a similar nature. When,
therefore, Gov. Neve in April visited the newly established mission, and noticed that the Fathers were
following the same old method which had made other missions prosperous, he wisely held his peace, and
even expressed his satisfaction at the progress made.

Fr. Cambon remained in charge until the coming
of Fathers Dumetz and Santa Maria in May. Only
two adults received the sacrament of baptism during
1782; but through the zeal of the two missionaries
the number of baptisms administered by the 31st of
December, 1790, had reached 534. During the same
period 69 marriages were blessed, and 115 dead bur-

(8) Vida. 2:0-264; Banc., I, 173-376.

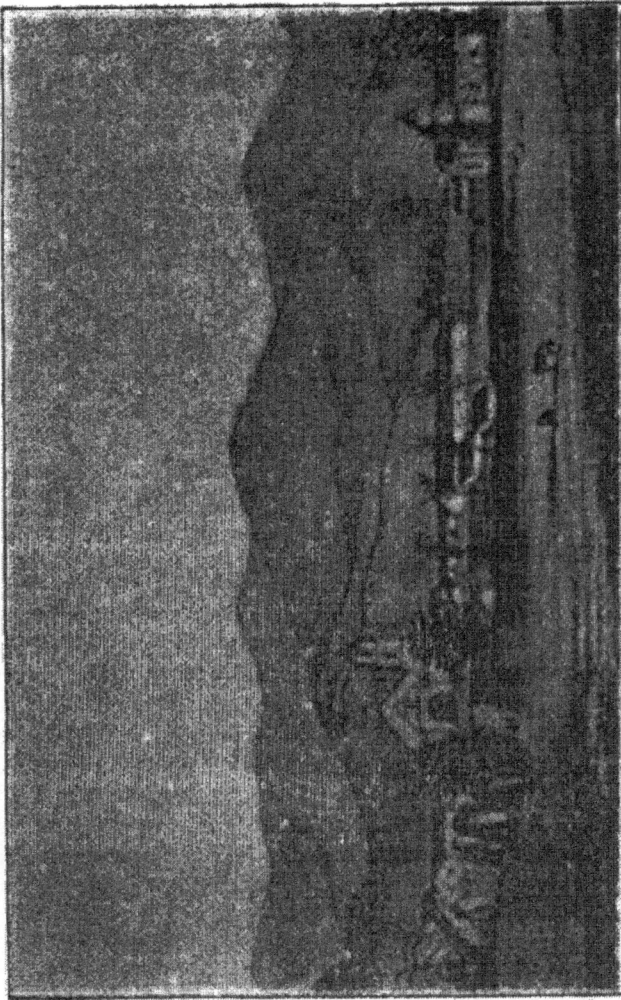

Mission San Buenaventura.

led. The number of Indians living at the mission was 419. The mission owned 771 cattle, 905 sheep, and 56 horses. (4)

VANCOUVER landed here on November 20th, 1793, bringing with him Fr. Santa Maria from Santa Barbara. He was deeply impressed with the missionary's piety and earnest devotion to the neophytes. He also noticed that the natives were always addressed in their own tongue. Vancouver spent a few hours at the mission, which he found to be "in a style very superior to any of the new establishments yet seen." "The garden of Buenaventura far exceeded anything I had before met with in these regions," he writes, "both in respect of the quantity, quality, and variety of its excellent productions, not only indigenous to the country, but appertaining to the temperate as well as torrid zone; not one species having yet been sown or planted that had not flourished. These have principally consisted of apples, pears, plums, figs, oranges, grapes, peaches, and pomegranates, together with the plantain, banana, cocoa nut, sugar cane, indigo, and a great variety of the necessary and useful kitchen herbs, plants, and roots. All these were flourishing in the greatest health and perfection, though separated from the sea-side only by two or three fields of corn, that were cultivated within a few yards of the surf.

THE buildings were also of a superior class, a previous destruction by fire having caused them to be rebuilt. A fight between the neophytes and pagans in 1795 seems to have been the only excitement of the period. The Christians were victorious. They killed two chiefs and made six or seven pagans captive, while only a few of their own number were wounded. The leaders on both sides were reproved or punished, and one neophyte was put in chains.

(4) Banc., I, 406; "Informes Generales," 1790.

FATHERS Dumetz and Santa Maria continued their
work together until 1797, when the former was succeeded by Fr. Señan. Fr. Señan served as missionary
at San Buenaventura for many years, but his companion, the venerable Fr. Santa Maria, its first resident missionary, died in 1806. (5)

FR. Victoria was his successor. Fr. Romuald Antonio Gutierrez came here from Santa Inéz in 1806 in
search of health which he failed to find. The construction of the new church proceeded slowly. In 1807
it is still described as nearly finished, very capacious,
of stone and brick, a part of the roof only covered
with tiles. Finally it was completed on September
9th, 1809, and dedicated by Fr. Señan with the assistance of five other Fathers and a secular priest, the
Rev. José Ignacio Arguello, born at San Gabriel in
1782, and then on a visit from Mexico. The next day,
which was Sunday, the first Mass was sung by the
Rev. visitor, and the sermon deliverd by Fr. Urresti.

IN December 1812 three heavy shocks of earthquake
occurred at San Buenaventura, which damaged the
church to such an extent that the tower and much
of the facade had to be rebuilt. The whole mission
site appeared to settle, and the fear of being engulfed
by the sea drove all away to San Joaquin y Santa
Ana, where they remained until April 1818. A temporary chapel was constructed and several baptisms
took place there. In 1814 all damages save those of

(5) Banc. I, 674–675. II, 121–122. Fr. Vincente de Santa Maria was a
member of the province of Burgos, Spain. He left San Fernando collego
for California in October 1770. He was stationed of Loreto, became the
missionary of San Javier in December 1772, and sailed for Mexico on May
27th, 1773. In the summer of 1776 he came to Alta California as chaplain
of the San Carlos. Fr. Vincente lived as supernumerary at San Francisco,
San Antonio, and Santa Clara until 1782, in May of which year he was
transferred to San Buenaventura, and remained there till his death on
July 15th, 1806. His remains were interred in the mission church, and on
September 11th, 1809 they were transferred with all possible solemnity to
the newly dedicated church and deposited in a recess in the wall on the
Gospel side. Fr. Santa Maria spoke the native language fluently.

the church had been repaired; and in 1818 not only was all restored to a condition better than the original, but a chapel in honor of San Miguel had been added. The work of rebuilding had been done by the neophytes under direction of the Fathers.

THE most exciting local event at this time was the fight with the Amajaves of the Colorado River in May 1819, when two soldiers and ten of the enemy were killed inside the mission enclosure. San Buenaventura reached its highest figure of population in 1816 with 1,828 neophytes. In June 1820 the government owed San Buenaventura $27,685 for supplies, besides $6,200 in stipends, and $1,585 for a cargo of hemp, or a total of $35,170, which there was not the slightest chance of ever receiving. Fr. Señan was superior of the California missions in 1812-1815, but he continued to reside at San .Buenaventura with Fr. Victoria. The latter was absent in 1818-1819. On August 24th, 1823, Fr. Señan died at this mission, and was succeeded by Fr. Suñer. (6)

(6) Banc., II, 355-360. II. 400. Fr. Francisco de Paul Señan was born March 3d, 1760, at Barcelona, and entered the convent of that city at the early age of 14. He was noted for his extraordinary memory and inclination to study. He arrived at the Mexican college of San Fernando in September 1787, and in October was sent to California. He was stationed at San Carlos until 1796, when he retired. While in Mexico he made a full report to the viceroy on the condition of the California missions. He returned to the west and arrived at Santa Barbara May 7th, 1798, and was thereafter stationed at San Buenaventura until his death on August 24th, 1823. Fr. Señan was elected superior or president of the California missions in July 1812, and held the office from the end of that year until the end of 1815. Again he was elected in October 1819; and occupied the office from April 1820 till his death. He was also vicario foraneo for the bishop of Sonora, and vice prefect of the missions during the same time. From April 28th, 1823, he was the prefect of the missions. Bancroft says of him: "Father Señan was older in the service than any other in California, being the only survivor of those who had come before 1790. He also was a model missionary, resembling Payeras in many of his excellencies, but unlike the latter shrinking from the cares and responsibilities of official life. He was the superior of Payeras in scholarship, his equal in the qualities that make a successful missionary, but inferior as a politician and leader. He was particularly averse to all controversy, except on theological points. He disliked to issue orders, but was always ready to respond to the frequent calls of his confrères for advice. Sometimes he was nicknamed Padre Calma. He was familiar with the

Fr. Victoria left the mission in 1824, and Fr. Altimira came in 1826. The latter retired in 1828, but
Fr. Francisco Uría had already arrived in 1827. (7)

THE decline of San Buenaventura was very marked
and rapid in the third decade of the century. In the
number of its cattle it dropped from the head of the
mission list to the fifteenth place. As early as 1822
the Fathers presented a discouraging report respecting the mission lands and the agricultural and stock-
raising projects. The Indians, however, had a number of gardens along the banks of the river, where
they sucessfully raised vegetables for sale. The gardens of the mission, too, were much more thriving
than the grain fields. There was a severe shock of
earthquake on January 1st, 1821, and extreme cold,
snow, and frost in February. On May 16th, 1822, the
Fathers and neophytes took the oath of allegiance to
the emperor of Mexico. On March 16th, 1822, Fabian
an Indian neophyte, was honored by being buried in
the Franciscan habit, says Bancroft. Probably Fabian
had been a Tertiary of St. Francis and his body
shrouded in the habit of the Third Order. In 1827–
1828 the measles carried off many Indians. Forty
head of cattle were killed every week for food at San
Buenaventura. Robinson mentions a small chapel as
standing near the beach, and a fine fountain in the
garden in 1829. From 1822–1827 the mission supplied
the presidio with $26,155. (8)

language of the Indians about San Buenaventura. Comparatively few
of his writings are extant. During his first term as president he managed
the interests of the missions with much skill, but during his second
term he was released as far as possible from such duties by orders from
Spain, in order that he might write a history to California. In 1819 he
promised to undertake the task, but what progress he made, if any, before his death is not known." Banc., II, 490-491.

(7) Fr. José Altimira was a native of Barcelona, where he also entered
the Franciscan Order. He was 32 years of age when in 1819 he came to the
Mexican college. He arrived at Monterey August 18th, 1820. He served at
San Francisco in 1820-1824; at San Franciso Solano, which he founded, in
1824-1826; and at San Buenaventura in 1826-1827. As late as 1860 he was said
to have been living at Teneriffe. Banc. II, 578-579, III, 94. (8) III 579-580.

Fr. Suñer died at his post in 1881, as did also his companion Fr. Uria in 1884. Fr. Blas Ordaz came to San Buenaventura in May 1883 and remained until 1883. Fr. Fortuni was sent here in the middle of 1887, and attended the mission until his death in 1840. (9)

THE records of secularization, the blight of the missions here as well as elsewhere, are very meagre, but it was not effected until 1837. For lack of a missionary in December 1840 the sacristan said the prayers at several burials. Fr. Antonio Jimeno was stationed at San Buenaventura temporarily during the illness

---

(9) Banc., III, 658. Fr. Francisco Suñer was born in January 1738 at Olot, Cataluña. He received the habit at Barcelona on April 14th, 1779. Leaving Cádiz in April 1804, he reched the Mexican college in July, and in 1808 he came to California. His missionary service was at San Carlos in 1808-1809; at San Juan Capistrano in 1809-1813; at San Luis Rey in 1814-1816; at Santa Barbara in 1816-1823; and at San Buenaventura in 1823-1831. Fr. Suñer was a preacher of more than ordinary eloquence, but his usefulness as a missionary was seriously impaired by his broken health. From 1824 he was blind. He took the oath of allegiance to the Mexican republic in 1826. His death occurred on January 17th, 1831, and he was buried next day in the mission church.

Fr. Francisco Javier de la Concepcion Uria was born May 10th, 1770, at Aizarna, province of Guipúzcoa, Spain. He became a Franciscan on January 13th, 1789, at San Sebastian; leaving Cádiz on May 8th, 1795, he came to California in 1797. After laboring at San Fernando in 1797-1815, he retired to his college, but came back at the end of 1807. He then was stationed at Santa Cruz in 1808; Santa Ines in 1808-1824, Soledad in 1824-1826, and at San Buenaventura in 1826-1834. Fr. Uria was an excellent manager of temporal affairs, and noted for his generosity, especially to the Indians. He refused to take the oath of allegiance to the unstable republic of Mexico. In his last illness he went to Santa Barbara, where he died at the house of Captain Guerra in November or December 1834, and his remains were interred in the vault of the mission church by Fr. Jimeno.

Fr. Buenaventura Fortuni, or Fortuny, was born at Mostor, Cataluña, in February 1774, and received the habit of St. Francis at Reus on October 30th, 1792. He left Cádiz in May 1803, and came to California in 1806. His ministry was at San José in 1806-1825; at San Antonio in 1825-1826; at San Francisco Solano in 1826-1833; at San Luis Rey in 1833-1836; and at San Buenaventura in 1837-1840. His superiors pronounced him an able, zealous, and faithful missionary. He was a quiet unobtrusive man, careful in temporal management, moderate in his views and expressions, strict in religious duties, but indulgent to the Indians, and noted for his charitable disposition. In 1836 he refused to take the oath, but was respectful and obedient to the government, says Bancroft. Like Uria he went to Santa Barbara in his last days, and died at the residence of José Ant. Aguirre on December 16th, 1840. He was buried in the mission vault on the 18 h.

of Fr. Fortuni, and seems to have become the regular missionary at the end of 1840. He remained until late in 1843. During 1842 and 1843 he had an assistant in the person of Fr. Francisco Sanchez. In November 1843 the bishop appointed the Rev. José Maria Rosales curate of San Buenaventura, when the church property was turned over to him. Rosales had already lived there for nearly two years. He remained until after 1845, but he had nothing to do with the temporal management of the mission. Which it seems was left in the hands of Fr. Jimeno even after he was transferred to Santa Barbara. Rosales was to receive $50 a month from the mission fund, and to have a garden and servants. (10)

In 1845 the mission estate was leased or rented to José Arnaz and Narciso Botello for $1,630, and finally sold to José Arnaz for $12,000 in June 1846. His title was not recognized by the United States Government in 1846-1848, and Arnaz was even ousted as lessee in 1848. (11)

The statistics of San Buenaventura from March 1782 to December 31st, 1831, are as follows: baptisms, 8,857; deaths, 3008; marriages, 1086. There were still 708 Indians at the mission in 1831. The number of cattle was 4,000; sheep 3,100; and horses 140. (12)

According to Bancroft, III, 660, the whole number of baptisms from 1782-1834 was 8,876, of which 1,896 were those of Indian adults, 1,009 Indian children, 4 adults and 67 children de razon; marriages 1,107, of which 11 de razon; deaths 3,216, of which 2,015 and. adults, 1,158 Indian children, 22 adults and 21 children de razon. The largest population, 1,330, was in 1816; largest number of cattle, 23,400 in 1816; horses, 4,652 in 1814; mules, 342 in 1813; sheep, 13, 144 in 1816; goats, 488 in 1790; swine, 200 in 1803;

(10) Banc., III, 658-661; IV, 644-645.   (11) Banc., IV, 646; V, 558; 561; 634.
(12) "Informes Generales." for 1831.

all kinds of animals, 41,890 in 1816. The total product of wheat amounted to 148,855 bushels; barley,

San Buenaventura At The Present Time.

54,004 bushels; maize, 51,214 bushels; beans, 9,061 bushels. The mission lands in 1822 extended five leagues north, and nine to ten leagues east. (18)

(18) Banc., III, 378-380.

CHAPTER XIV.

SANTA BARBARA.

The Presidio Of Santa Barbara Founded—Fr. Junipero Serra Disappointed—Santa Barbara Mission Founded On The Old Plan—The First Missionaries—The Buildings—Conversions—Tiles Manufactured—More Buildings—Missionary Changes—Death Of Fr. Paterna. The Third Church—Wall Around The Property—Industries—Report Of 1802—A Missionary Station At Saqshpilekl—Mission Santa Inez— Other Items—The Reservoir—Fr. Cortes Retires—Missionary Changes—Earthquake—New Church.

After San Buenaventura had been founded, Governor Neve came up from San Gabriel to establish the presidio in the channel district for the protection of the missions in that region. Accordingly the party consisting of the governor, Fr. Junipero Serra, and sixty or more soldiers, marched along the shore to a spot about nine leagues from San Buenaventura, and near a large settlement of Indians, which like its chief was called Yanonalit. Here an elevation of land was found suitable for a fort. A large cross was erected, a hut constructed to serve as a chapel, and a table therein prepared for an altar. On the next day which was April 21st, (1) 1782, Fr. Serra blessed the site and the cross, after which he celebrated Mass and preached a touching sermon. This was the beginning of the presidio of Santa Barbara.

The natives were more friendly than had been anticipated, and Chief Yanonalit was willing to exchange presents. Work was at once begun and oak timber felled for the chapel, priest's house, store-

---

(1) O'Keefe, 'Mission Santa Barbara' p. 6, says it was the 29th.

house, barracks, and palisade enclosure. The Indians
were hired to do the work and paid in articles of
food and clothing. Yanonalit had authority over a-
hout thirteen rancherias, and his friendship proved of
great advantage. (2)

As Fr. Junípero naturally supposed the mission
would be founded along with the presidio, he remained for some time with the soldiers and their families. Noticing, however, that the governor made no
preparations to that end, Fr. Serra questioned him
regarding the matter. The governor replied that he
did not intend to begin that work until the presidio
was completed. "Then, Sir," said the disappointed
missionary, "as there is nothing for me to do here
at present, I shall return to Monterey and meet the
vessels that are expected; but in order that so many
people may not be without Mass and priest, I shall
call a Father from San Juan Capistrano." This he
did, and then started for San Carlos, after he had
administered confirmation to those of the troops who
had not yet been confirmed. Nor was Santa Barbara
established during the life-time of the venerable Fr.
Junípero.

THE ships which Fr. Serra hastened to meet at
Monterey did not bring the six religious he had expected from Mexico. The fault lay not with the missionaries nor their superiors, but with the government authorities who desired to overthrow the old
mission system, and to introduce the plan which had
proved so disastrous among the Yumas on the Colorado River only a short time before. The foundation
of Mission Santa Barbara was thus delayed indefi-
nitely. (3)

When Fr. Serra died in 1784, Fr. Palou became
superior of the missions temporarily. Fr. Lasuen was

(2) Vida. 255; O'Keefe, 5-6; Banc.. I, 877.
(3) Banc.. I, 877; Vida 255-256.

appointed president of the missions in 1785. The Fr. Guardian instructed him not to allow any new mission to be founded except on the old basis; at the same time he informed Fr. Lasuen that more Fathers would come to California, and that then Santa Barbara might be established if the old system were continued, but not otherwise. Nor did the Fathers pay any attention to the repeated request of the governor to go on with the founding of Santa Barbara until they were permitted to have their own way.

Fr. Lasuen then went down to the presidio, at the end of October 1786, with two of the newly arrived religious, and superintended active preparations for the new mission which was to be dedicated on December 4th, the feast of Santa Barbara, Virgin and Martyr. On that day the cross was raised and blessed at a place called in Spanish 'El Pedragoso,' in the native tongue, Taynayam, about one mile from the presidio. Thus the 4th of December was ever since regarded as the day of the mission's regular foundation, though the ceremonies were interrupted on account of the governor's absence and his order to suspend operations until his arrival. "Possibly," says Bancroft, "Governor Fagés had some thought of insisting on the innovations which had caused so much controversy, but if so he changed his mind; for after his arrival on December 14th, the Fathers were allowed to go on in their own way." On the 15th of the same month Fr. Lasuen celebrated the first Mass and preached in a temporary chapel constructed of boughs. The governor and a few soldiers were present. (4)

FATHERS Antonio Paterna from San Luis Obispo and Cristobal Orámus, one of the new-comers, were appointed the first missionaries of Santa Barbara. The rainy season did not permit the erection of

(4) O'Keefe 9; Banc., I, 422–423; Bancroft claims Fr. Paterna said the the first Mass.

buildings during the remainder of the year, wherefore the first baptism was administered at the presidio on December 81st. The work of building commenced in 1787. First in order was a house for the missionaries which was 5x18 varas; a kitchen 5x6 varas was added; then the first church or chapel 5x 14 varas arose, followed by a servants' room 5x6 varas, a granary 5x21 varas, and a house for girls or unmarried women 5x12 varas. A carpenter shop which for a time served as a home for unmarried men was also erected. (5)

ALL the buildings were built of adobe, and the walls were one vara thick. The roofing consisted of heavy rafters, across which long poles or canes were tied; a layer of soft clay or mud was spread over these, then finished or thatched with straw. By the end of the year 1787 as many as 188 persons had been baptized; and at the end of 1790 the mission registers showed 593 baptisms, 148 marriages, 124 deaths, and 407 Indians living about the mission. The number of cattle was 208, sheep 286, and horses 80. (6)

In 1788 tiles were manufactured and the buildings covered with them. A new house for the unmarried men was built, and the church enlarged. A second church building, 5x80 varas, arose in 1789. The first, considered much to small, was taken down. A larger granary, apartments for unmarried women, and two rooms for the muleteers were next constructed of adobe, well plastered, and roofed with tiles. In 1790 two houses for the Fathers were built, besides a house containing dining room, kitchen, hall, storeroom fuel room, lockup, flour and meal room, a room for the women, and a structure to be used as a granary. (7)

(5) The vara has 34 inches.   (6) "Informes," 1790.
(7) O'Keefe 10-12; Banc., I. 424.

Fr. José de Miguel took the place of Fr. Orámas in 1790, and Fr. Paterna died at Santa Barbara in 1793. He was succeeded by Fr. Tapis. Fr. Miguel remained here until 1798, when he was relieved by Fr. Juan Lope Cortés. (8)

Much progress was made in mission buildings during the last decade of the century. A third church of adobe was commenced in 1793, and finished in 1794. The building measured 9 and one fourth by 45 varas, with a sacristy 9 and one fourth by 5 varas. A portico of brick was added to the front in 1805, and the walls were plastered. The principal industry at this period was the cording and weaving of wool into blankets and cloth for the Indians.

As the Indians were rapidly increasing, it became necessary to form a village, and give a separate house to each family. Land was set aside for that purpose near the mission, and in 1798 nineteen houses were built of adobe for as many families. These cottages measured 12x19 feet, and were plastered, whitewashed, and roofed with tiles. Moreover, a piece of land was inclosed by an adobe wall nine feet high and 1200 yards long, to be used as a garden, vineyard, and orchard. The wall was capped with tiles to throw off the rain. In the same year, 1798, the six chapels of the church were each adorned with an oil painting. In 1800 thirty-two cottages were erected for as many families. These houses were built so as to form streets crossing at right angles. In the same year sixty neophytes were engaged in weaving. The carpenter of the presidio was hired at one dollar a

(8) Banc., I, 672–673. Fr. Antonio Paterna was a native of Seville, and served twenty years in the Sierra Gorda missions before coming to California. He arrived a San Diego on March 12th, 1771. He was supernumerary at San Gabriel until May 1772, and the regular missionary until September 1777. He was acting president in 1772–1773. From 1777 to 1786 he was stationed at San Luis Obispo, and at Santa Barbara thereafter until he died on February 13th, 1793. His body was buried in the mission church on the next day.

day to teach his trade to the Indians; and a corporal
taught tanning at $150 a year. Before October, 165
naguas or petticoats of home manufacture had been
distributed, 800 yards of cotton and 700 yards of
blanketing woven. $1,020 worth of soap was furnished
to Monterey in 1798. The mission supplies, consisting
of implements, groceries, church vestments and sacred
vessels, clothing, etc., for 1790–1800, amounted to
$10,500. These articles were purchased by the Fathers
in Mexico with their salaries and with the proceeds
from the sales of produce. (9)

In 1801 thirty–one houses to accommodate that
many Indian families, and thirty–one in 1802 were
built, making a total of 113 Indian dwellings, enclosed on three sides by an adobe wall nine feet high.
Many other improvements were made which it would
be to tedious to enumerate. According to a statement drawn up by Fr. Lasuen in 1802, there had
been baptized at Santa Barbara from 1786 to December 31st, 1802, as many as 2,251 persons. During the
same period 989 dead were buried, and 404 marriages
were contracted before the Fathers. 1,093 Indians
lived at the mission, which owned 2,100 head of cattle, 9,082 sheep, 215 horses, 427 mares and foals, and
58 mules. (10)

In 1803-1807 there were 189 additional dwellings
erected for as many Indian families. In order that
the missionaries could attend to the distant Indians
more effectively, a mission station was established a-
bout two leagues west of the mission at 'Sagshpileel,'
or 'Mescaltitlan,' a large ranchería near a laguna. An
adobe church 27x66 feet was built there and dedicated to San Miguel. The ruins of this chapel were yet
to be seen near the old houses of Daniel Hill, at the
"Patera," as late as 1886. On September 17th, 1808,
Mission Santa Inés, or Ynéz, was founded. It was

---

(9) O'Keefe 12–16;   Banc., I, 672–673.   (10) "Informes," 1802.

situated nearer to the rancherías of several Indian families baptized at Santa Barbara, but enrolled at Santa Inés after that date. The number thus withdrawn from Santa Barbara was 112, which accounts for the decrease of the population at this time. All the ranchos east of the Santa Inés River, including San Marcos, belonged to the mission of Santa Barbara, and the property extended to the "Rincon." The principal ranchos for wheat and corn were: San Pedro y San Pablo, or Dos Pueblos, called by the Indians 'Mekeguwe;' San Estévan, in the native tongue called 'Tokeene'; and San Miguel, or 'Sagshpileel.' Corn and beans were raised at San José or Abajo, and at San Juan Bautista, or the Sauzal, at present a part of the Hope ranch bordering on the eastern bank of the arroyo del Burro. Tokeene or San Estévan is all that land north of the present stage road, beginning west of the Arroyo Pedragoso at the new bridge, and continuing to the Arroyo del Burro. (11)

A great many improvements were made by the Fathers in the beginning of the present century for which we refer the reader to Fr. O'Keefe's pamphlet. Among the most notable works are a reservoir 40 varas square, still in perfect condition, and a very solid dam across the Pedragoso Creek, about a mile and half from the mission.

FATHERS Tapis and Cortés continued as missionaries of Santa Barbara till 1805, when the latter retired to Mexico. Fr. Tapis, who in 1803 had succeeded Fr. Lasuen as president of the missions in California, removed to San Carlos in 1806. Fr. Marcos Amestoy began his labors here in November 1804. Fr. Marcos Victoria was at Santa Barbara in 1804-1805, and Fr. José Urresti from 1806 to 1809, when Fr. Luis Gil y Taboada arrived. Santa Barbara reached its highest figure in Indian population with 1,792 souls in 1803.

(11) O'Keefe, 16-20; Banc., II, 119-120.

That ground squirrels had already proved a pest at
this early day is shown by the fact that about a
thousand of these animals were killed in nine days
of May 1808. (12)

Durixg the month of December 1812 several eartl-
quake shocks were felt. These shocks were so seveie
that all the mission buildings were badly damaged:
the church in particular had suffered so much that it
was thought more expedient to take it down and
erect a new one than to make repairs. A new stone
church was accordingly commenced in 1815, but not
completed until September 1820. On the 10th of that
month the edifice was dedicated. Three Fathers from
other missions joined the two resident missionaries in
the ceremonies. The church, still used by the Fathers,
is 60 varas, or nearly 180 feet, long, 14 varas wide,
and 10 varas high. The walls are of hewn stone, and
nearly six feet thick. They are further strengthened
by solid stone buttresses. The building is without
doubt the strongest mission church in California. (13)

(12) Banc., II, 121. Fr. Juan Lopo Cortés was assigned to duty in California on February 24th. 1796. He was stationed at San Gabriel from August of that year until June 1798, ai d at Santa Barbara till September
1805; in November he sailed for Mexico. From September 1815 he seems to
have been the procurador of San Fernando college; and in June 1827 he
was síndico of the same monastery.   (13) O'Keefe, 19; Banc., II, 855.

Mission Santa Barbara in 1865 with Autograph of
Fr. Gonzales Rubio.

CHAPTER XV.

SANTA BARBARA—(CONTINUED).

INDIAN REVOLT—OPINION OF THE FATHERS—FR. AMESTOY RETIRES—DEATH OF FR. ANTONIO JAIME—FR. RIPOLL RETIRES—INTERESTING ITEMS—SECULARIZATION—STATISTICS—MISSION REPORTS—FR. ANTON. JIMENO'S DEATH. FR. JOSE JIMENO RETIRES—THE MISSION RENTED AND SOLD—THE INVENTORY—THE COMMUNITY OF SANTA BARBARA—FATHERS ROMO AND CODINA. DEATH OF FR. SANCHEZ—HIS BIOGRAPHY.

THE neophytes of the three missions Santa Barbara, Santa Inés, and La Purisima in 1824 revolted against the military authority, and caused considerable trouble and some bloodshed before peace was restored. The Fathers in Mexico took the ground that the real cause of the rebellion was the ever growing discontent of the Indians at having to support the troops by their hard labor without pay. Some of the missionaries claimed that the first outbreak was due to a petty act of injustice on the part of the soldiers, and that it was fanned into a revolution by continued acts of cruel severity. This is what Fr. Ripoll of Santa Barbara reported to Fr. Sarría on May 5th. Fr. Sarría also seems to have taken this view of the matter. At any rate there was no ill feeling shown by the Indians against the missionaries. (1)

FR. Gil y Taboada was transferred to San Gabriel in 1813, and Fr. Olbés succeeded him until 1816; Fr. Francisco Suñer then arrived and remained at Santa Barbara until 1823. Fr. Amestoy retired to Mexico in 1814. Only one Father seems to have been at this

1) Banc., II, 527-530.

mission after Fr. Amestoy's departure until July 1815, when Fr. Ripoll was placed here. (2)

Fr. Antonio Jaime came to Santa Barbara in 1821 and remained until 1820, when he died. Fr. Suñer left the mission in 1823, but Fr. Ripoll remained until 1828, when he retired to Mexico. Fr. Juan Moreno was stationed here in 1827-1829, and was succeeded by Fr. Antonio Jimeno. (8)

In 1827 Fr. Ripoll had 200 Indians at work in his woolen factory, and about the same time he was giving his attention to the construction of a fountain and a water-mill. About 1824 the Fathers laid the cornerstone and prepared adobes for a church at San Emilio, but the work was abandoned on account of the revolt. In 1822 the mission lands were described

(2) Banc., II, 364. Fr. Marcos Amestoy left Guadalajara for California April 23d, 1804, and arrived at San Francisco August 14th. His only station was Santa Barbara from November 1801 to September 22d, 1814, when he sailed for Mexico, disabled by a paralysed arm.

(3) Fr. Jaime, or Anton o Mariano Francisco Miguel Gaspar Jayme de Seguras, was born at Palma on the island of Mallorca in 1757. He received the habit of S'. Francis in 1774 at Palma. He volunteered for Mexico and arrived at the college of San Fernando in August 1793. He came to California in August 1795, and served at San Carlos till February 179 . He was then stationed at Soledád for 23 years until October 1823, when he was transferred as invalid to Santa Barbara. His name is inseparately connected with the mission of Soledád. In later years he was confined to his room by the torments of rheumati m. He died on December 2d, 1829, and his remains were deposited in the vault of the Santa Barbara church.

Fr. Antonio Ripoll was, like Jaymo, a native of Palma in Mallorca, where he was born in 1785. He became a Franciscan in 1799, and arrived in Mexico in June 1810. A year later he was assigned to the California missions, and came to San Diego by way of Lower California in July 1812. He was stationed at Purisima until May 1815, and at Santa Barbara till January 1828. In 1832 he was residing at his native town. Fr. Ripoll was noted for his enthusiasm in any cause to which he gave his attention, particularly in the improvement of manufacturing industries and of mission buildings. At the time of the Bouchard attack he organized a neophyte force of 180 men. In the Indian revolt of 1824 Fr. Ripoll saw nothing but an act of Iudians who were protecting church property and the missionaries. Hence the subsequent killing of natives was, in his eyes, murder. From that time he was discouraged and unwilling to endure the later troubles to which the Fathers were subjected as Spaniards and royalists. He determined to leave the country secretly that he might avoid detention and annoyance by the military, and made good his escape in company of Fr. A'timira. Banc., II, 576-.74.

as extending seven to eight leagues east to west, and three to four leagues north to south. (4)

THE Indian population decreased to 679 in 1831. In 1836 it was 480, and in 1840 not more than 250. In 1881 the mission still owned 2,600 cattle, 8,800 sheep, 150 mules, and 210 horses. (5)

AFTER the mission was secularized in 1834 the decline was rapid, yet the buildings were kept in better condition than at most of the other establishments. Anastasio Carrillo was the comisionado to secularize Santa Barbara. In 1838–1839 Manuel Cota was administrator. In 1839 his accounts were found in a bad condition, and the Fathers as well as the natives were dissastisfied with Cota's management. Finally he was suspended for cruelty to the Indians and insolence to Fr. Duran. In 1839 Fr. Duran was authorized to expend $500 for clothing for the Indians who under Fr. Duran's supervision again became more contented and industrious. In 1840, however, Fr. Duran urged the appointment of an administrator, as he did not want to have anything to do with the temporalities. (6)

DURING the whole period of the mission's existence before secularization was ordered, 1786–1834, the total number of baptisms was 5,679, of which 2,490 were Indian adults, 2,168 Indian children, and 1,021 children of other than Indian parents. There were 1,524 marriages contracted before the Fathers, of which 200 were not Indian. The deaths amounted to 4,046, of which number 2,446 were Indian adults, 1,288 Indian children, 160 adults and 152 children of other than Indian blood. The largest number of cattle owned by the mission at one time was 5,200 in 1809; sheep, 11,066 in 1804; horses, 1,837 in 1816; mules. 340 in 1823; goats, 200 in 1792; swine, 200 in 1823;

(4) Banc., II, 576-579. (5) "Informes Generales" del año 1831.
(6) Banc., III, 656-658.

and all kinds of animals, 16,090 in 1809. The total
product of wheat amounted to 152,797 bushels; barley,
24,733 bushels; corn, 10,084 bushels; and beans, 2,458
bushels. (7)

THE last report rendered to the government of
Mexico concerning the missions was signed by Fr. Antonio Jimeno in 1836. The missionaries, however, continued to report the state of the mission to their
respective prefects down to the arrival of the first
bishop. The prefects sent these reports to the colleges
of San Fernando, or Guadalupe. Thus Fr. Gonzales Rubio made a report of Mission San José as late
as 1841. (8)

SANTA Barbara remained in charge of Fr. Antonio
Jimeno until late in 1840, when he went to San Buenaventura. Fr. Duran, though president or superior
of the Fernandinos in California, was the associate
missionary. He became the principal missionary on
the departure of Fr. Antonio, and remained at his
post until his death in 1846. Fr. Antonio Menendez,
the Dominican chaplain of the presidio, was buried
at the mission in April 1832. Fr Antonio Jimeno returned in 1844 and remained at Santa Barbara until
1856, or a little later, when he retired to Mexico
Fr. José Gonzalez, of the Zacatecan Fathers came to
Santa Barbara in 1848, and resided there many
years. Fr. José Jimeno came to Santa Barbara from
San Gabriel in 1858 and remained until his death in
1856. (9)

THE temporal management of the mission was restored to the missionaries in 1843, but in 1845 Fr.
Duran asked the governor to relief him of the care
of the temporalities. The good Father in his old age

(7) Banc., III, 657. According to the Informes Generales, from 17**-1831.
December 31st, there had been baptized 5,483 persons, 1,467 couples joined
in marriage, and 3,674 dead buried.   (8) O'Keefe, 26.   (9) Banc., III,
650-658; IV, 643. For the biographies of Fathers Duran and Jimeno see
Part I.

had become discouraged, as the Indians, though respectful to him, were careless and wasteful. The property was accordingly appraised in July 1845, Fr. Duran being one of the committee.

FINALLY in December 1845 the mission estate was rented by the governor to Nicholas A. Den and Daniel Hill for $1,200 a year. The principal buildings, however, were reserved to the bishop and his clergy. The Indians were to retain a part of the buildings, to have lands assigned them, to be at liberty to work for the lessees or for themselves, and to have a third of the rental; but there is no evidence that they received anything beyond the privilege of remaining. (10) In June 1846 the mission was sold to Richard S. Den for $7,500, but the title was subsequently annulled, it seems. (11)

THIS practically put an end to Santa Barbara as an Indian mission, but not to the monastery which continued as the only Franciscan community in California for many years. For the subsequent events at Santa Barbara the reader is referred to Chapter 21 and 22, Part I, and to Part III.

ON an accompanying cut the reader will find the whole community of Santa Barbara as it existed about the year 1880. The following are the names of the religious:

1. Fr. José Maria Romo, guardian; 2. F. Joseph J. O'Keefe, vicar; 3. Fr. Francisco Sanchez, definit.; 4. Fr. Bonaventure Fox; 5. Fr. Francisco Arbondin;

---

(10) Banc., IV, 642-344. O'Keefe 29. The inventory of July 25th, 1845 gives the following valuations: Buildings reserved for the bishop and missionaries, 34 rooms, $1,500; storehouse and goods $1,552; cellar and contents, $768; soap factory and outfit, $898; tannery etc., $250; smithshop etc., $100; weaving rooms, loom, etc., $120; carpentershop, $84; majordomo's house, $185; vaquero's outfit, $24; orchard with 512 fruit trees, $1,500; vineyards with 3,995 vines 1,720; 816 cattle, 306 horses, and 9 mules, $3,545; carrals, $265; San José vineyard with 2,232 vines and 100 trees, $1,835; cieneguita with crops, $100; San Antonio, a corral, $25; rancho of San Marcos with buildings, vineyards, grain, 140 cattle, 90 horses, and 1,730 sheep, $6,050; a total valuation of $25,845. (11) Banc., V, 634.

6. Bro. Anthony Gallagher; 7. Bro. Joseph O'Malley; 8. Bro. Dominic C. Reid. Fathers Romo and Codina died at Alexandria, Egypt, but the date is not known. Fr. Francisco de Jesu Sanchez after a saintly life died at Santa Barbara, on April 17th, 1884. (12)

* * *

CHAPTER XVI.

LA PURISIMA CONCEPCION.

FOUNDING OF THE MISSION—SUCCESS OF THE FATHERS—FATHERS ARROITA AND FERNANDEZ RETIRE—NEW CHURCH—REPORT OF FR. PAYERAS—MISSIONARY CHANGES—EARTHQUAKE IN 1812—DESTRUCTION OF THE BUILDINGS—MISSION REMOVED—NEW CHURCH—FIRE—DEATHS OF FATHERS RODRIGUEZ AND PAYERAS—INDIAN REVOLT—LAST MISSIONARY—STATISTICS.

As early as 1779-1780 it had been determined to found a mission at the western extremity of the Santa Barbara Channel, and to name it La Purisima Concepcion in honor of the Immaculate Conception of the Blessed Virgin. (1) The establishment was delayed, however, until certain government restrictions obnoxious to the missionaries had been removed. In June 1785 Governor Fagés recommended a site on the Santa Rosa River, now the Santa Inés River; and in March 1786 General Rengel instructed the governor to proceed with the foundation of La Puri-

---

(12) He was born at Leon, Mexico in 1813. He came to California with the other Zacatecanos in 1833, but nothing is heard of him there until 1842, when he became the missionary of San Buenaventura. Bancroft thinks Fr. Sanchez remained behind in Lower California while the other Fathers proceeded to Upper California. Fr. Francisco was stationed at San Buenaventura in 1842-1843 and again in 1852-1853; at Santa Inés in 1844-1850 where he was vice-rector of the seminary. In 1874 Fr. Sanchez with Fr. Codina and Brother Joseph O'Malley took charge of the diocesan orphan asylum for boys at Pájaro. He remained there until 1879, when he returned to Santa Barbara. The body of Fr. Sanchez was interred in the mission vaults.   (1) Vida, 240,

sima. This was done after the government had acceded to the conditions the Fathers laid down. Fr.
Lasuen went up from the presidio of Santa Barbara
to the site selected, called by the natives Algsr-
cupi, where on December 8th, 1787, he blessed the
place, raised the cross, celebrated Mass, and preached
a sermon. Thus the mission of La Purisima was nominally founded, though on account of the rains actual work was not begun until several months later.

At length about the middle of March 1788, the
mission escort with a band of laborers and servants
went up to erect the necessary buildings. Early in
April Fr. President Lasuen arrived with Fathers
Vincente Fuster, of San Juan Capistrano, and José
Arroita, a new-comer. After four months the two
missionaries had already enrolled seventy-nine neophytes. By the end of 1790 the records showed 801
baptisms, 62 marriages, and 23 deaths. At the same
time the mission possessed 169 cattle, 464 sheep, 26
horses, and 334 other animals. Only 278 Indians lived
at the mission, though there were over fifty rancherias in the Purisima district. (2)

Fr. Fuster did not remain long at the mission, as
Fr. Cristóbal Orámas of Santa Barbara replaced him
in 1780. Fr. Orámas was succeeded in 1792 by Fr.
Antonio Calzada, who labored here until August 1796,
when Fr. Gregorio Fernandez arrived. Fr. Arroita,
one of the founders of Purisima Concepcion, remained at the mission until June 1796, when he retired to Mexico. In 1798 Fr. Calzada returned and
served as missionary until 1804, when Fr. Mariano
Payeras took his place. Fr. Juan Martin was also stationed here in 1796-1797. In 1805 Fr. Fernandez left
California for Mexico. He was succeeded by Fr. Juan Cabot, who departed in the next year to give
way to Fr. Geronimo Boscana.

(2) Banc., I, 424-425; Informes Generales, 1790.

In 1795 the Fathers began to collect material for a new church, as the old building was in a bad condition. The new edifice was completed before the end of 1802. It was built of adobes and roofed with tiles. (3)

In 1810 Fr. Payeras made a full report to the Fr. Superior of the state of his mission. From this report we learn that, with the help of interpreters, he had made a complete catechism and manual of confession in the Indian language by means of which the neophytes were becoming more or less perfect in the knowledge of religion. He had found many errors in matters of faith, and even idolatry at first, but he had made progress in uprooting the worship of Achup, or Chupu. Nearly all mothers had given birth to dead infants; preaching, teaching, and even chastisement had for a while been powerless to arrest the evil, or to make known its direct cause. There remained no more gentiles to be baptized except at a distance of twenty-five or thirty leagues. The natives were docile, industrious, and not inclined to run away. It was a joy to see them at work, sing, and pray, and especially to see them bear their sufferings, beg for confession, and die like good Catholics. For five years not a kernel of grain could be raised without irrigation; but certain springs had been found which promised well for the future. A great deal of live-stock had been purchased, and the

---

(3) Banc., I, 675; II, 123. Fr. Francisco José de Arroita came from Spain to Mexico in 1784. He was sent to California in April 1786, and stationed at San Luis Obispo until December 1787; and at Purisima he was till June 1790, about which time he sailed for San Blas.

Fr. Gregorio Fernandez was born at Burgos, Spain, in 1751; became a Franciscan in 1772; came to America in 1785, and to California in 1794. He served at San Luis Obispo from November 1794-1796; and at Purisima from May 1796 to September 1815. He also officiated at San Franci co in June 1794. Fr. Fernandez was styled 'un angel' when he came to California: "and there is nothing to show that his angelic qualities deteriorated in California," says Bancroft. He sailed for Mexico on November 6th 1815.

prospects for meat, tallow, and wool were excellent. The report is dated January 18th, 1810. (4)

In 1815 Fr. Payeras himself became president of the California missions, yet he continued to reside at Purisima; but Fr. Boscana left the mission at the end of 1811. Fr. Estévan Tapis, president of the missions, also served here in 1811-1813. Fr. Antonio Ripoll arrived in 1812 and remained till 1815; Fr. Luis Gil from 1815 to 1817; Fr. Ullibarri in 1818-1819; and Fr. José Sanchez in 1820-1821. The population began to decrease in the second decade of the century, but in livestock Purisima was in a most flourishing condition until December 1816 and January 1817, when there was no rain, and sheep died by the hundreds. (5)

On December 21st, 1812, there was an earthquake while the Fathers were making their examination of conscience. The earth shook so violently that it was difficult to stand. A brief examination showed that the church walls had been thrown out of plumb. Just before 11 o'clock there came another more violent shock which brought down the church and nearly all the mission buildings, besides about 100 neophyte houses of adobe. The earth opened in several places and emitted water and black sand. Several persons were wounded, but none were killed. Subsequent floods completed the devastation, so that very few buildings were worth repairing. Huts of wood and grass were hastily erected for shelter and religious service; but in March 1818 the Fathers petitioned their superior for a permit to rebuild the mission on another site across the river at Los Berros, or Amun. The request

---

(4) Banc., II, 123. (5) Banc., II, 386-387. In January and February 1816 some measurements were made by the Fathers, which showed the distance from Purisima to Santa Inés to be 6 and ½ leagues and 619 varas; to San Luis Obispo by way of La Graciosa 15 leagues less 280 varas; and to San Antonio rancho by way of the garden of Mateo three leagues and 3,400 varas.

was granted, and the transfer effected with the consent of the governor; but of the progress in erecting
the new buildings little or nothing is known, though
the church, houses, and irrigating canal are said to
have beeh completed in two years. The church was
only a temporary structure, but a new one of adobes
and tiles was finished in November 1818. In the same
year, September 20th, nearly all the houses of the
neophytes were destroyed by fire, and it required a
year to repair the damages. (6)

Fa. Sanchez was succeeded by Fr. Rodriguez in
1821, but the latter died in 1824, and his place was
taken by Fr. Victoria. Fr. Victoria seems to have
been alone at Purisima until 1834, when Fr. Moreno
came to the mission. Fr. Payeras also died at Purisima in 1823. (7)

THE great event of 1824 was the Indian revolt, during which the place was retaken after having been
for some time in possession of the rebels. In the revolt the mission buildings were much damaged, and
it seems that the church, though a new structure,
had to be rebuilt; at all events a new church was

(6) Banc., II, 201: 367-363.   (7) Banc., II, 429; 530. Fr. Antonio Catarino Rodriguez was one of the few native Mexican Franciscans in California before 1810. He was born at San Luis Potosi on January 1st, 1777, and
received the habit in his native city, where he also filled the offices of
vicar, master of novices, and lector of moral philosophy. He joined the
missionary college of San Fernando in August 1808, and arrived at Monterey on June 2d. 1809. His missionary service was at Santa Cruz till
1811, at San Luis Obispo until 1821, and at Purisima till his death in
1824. He died at San Luis Obispo, however, on November 24th, and was
buried in the church of that mission. Early in the year of his death, already ill and infirm, Fr. Rodriguez was taken by the rebel Indians and
kept as a prisoner for several weeks, but he was treated with great respect, and worked earnestly for the interests of his flock at the time of
their surrender.
    Fr. Mariano Payeras was born on October 10th, 1769, at Inca, Island of
Mallorca, and entered the Order of St. Francis on September 5th, 1784 at
Palma. He left Spain in January 1793, and in February 1796 he was sent
to California. Fr. Payeras was stationed at San Carlos from 1796-1798; at
Soledad from November 1798 to 1803; at San Diego from September 1803
to 1804; and at Purisima from 1804 to the day of his death April 28th,
1823, though after 1815, when he became president of the California missions, a large part of his time was spent in travelling from mission to

dedicated on October 4th, 1823. The mission lands in 1822 extended 14 leagues from north to south, and four and. 6.1 leagues from east to west. The soil was good, but irrigation was necessary. Frosts, grasshoppers, and squirrels were very troublesome at Purisima. The mission furnished $12,921 worth of supplies to the presidio in 1822-1827. (8)

For years the Indian population of Purisima had been decreasing until at the close of 1831 there were only 404 natives at the mission; and about the year 1840 only 120 were left, with perhaps as many more scattered in the region belonging to Purisima. According to the report of the Fathers on December 31st, 1831, the mission possessed 10,500 cattle, 7,000 sheep, and 100 horses. (9)

In 1834 Domingo Carrillo was appointed comisionado to secularize the mission of Purisima Concepcion; this he effected in the next year. An inventory was taken in 1888 and the mission estate valued as follows: Chief building with twenty-one rooms, $4,800; twelve smaller buildings, $1,205; furniture and implements, $2,001; contents of the storehouse, $6,255; grain and produce, $4,821; church ornaments, etc., $4,044; church, $400; library, $655; five bells, $1,000; three gardens, $728; live-stock, $201. The following named ranchos were valued at the price annexed: Sitio de Mision Vieja, $375; Sitio de Jalama, $784; Los Alamos, $1,185; San Antonio, $1,418; Santa Lucía, $1,080; San Pablo, $1,060; Todos Santos, $7,176; Guadalupe, $4,065; live-stock, $17,821.

In February 1839 more than 600 sheep were drowned in the floods. In 1843 the mission estate and other property, or what was left of it, was restored to

mission. He was president till April 1st 1820, and vicario prefecto from May 1816. From April 1st, 1820, till his death Fr. Payeras was comisario prefecto, and also comisario del santo oficio. In October 1819 he was thanked in the king's name for his services against the Bouchard rebel-. (8) Banc., II, 581. (9) Informes Generales año 1831; Banc., III, 665-66.

the management of the Fathers, but in 1845 it was
sold by the governor to John Temple for $1,110. In
1844 Fr. Duran reported 200 Indians for Purisima and
neighborhood, no live-stock or cultivated lands, but
a small vineyard. Towards the close of the same
year small-pox carried away most of the Indians and
broke up the community. (10)

Fr. Victoria remained at his post until August
1835, when Fr. Arroyo de la Cuesta succeeded him.
Fr. Arroyo was transferred to Santa Inés in 1836,
after which date it seems there was no regular missionary at La Purisima. Fr. Juan Moreno was here
in 1834, and possibly he was in charge part of the
time in 1836-1840. For a few months the venerable
Fr. Abella, the last survivor of the Fernandinos who
came to California before 1800, served as missionary
at Purisima, and then died. (11) After Fr. Ramon's
death the mission was in charge of Fr. Juan Moreno
and a secular priest, the Rev. Miguel Gomez, though
both resided at Santa Inés most of the time. After
the sale of the estate in 1845, when the Indians had
scattered, Mission La Purisima Concepcion was abandoned. (12)

---

(10) Banc., III, 661-663; IV, 647-319. (11) Fr. Ramon Abella was born
May 26th, 1764, at Montforte, Aragon, Spain, and became a Franciscan at
Zaragosa March 6th, 1784. He joined the college of San Fernando in 1795,
and arrived in California in 1798. His missionary service of 44 years was
passed in succession at San Francisco in 1798-1819; San Carlos 1819-1833;
San Luis Obispo 1833-1842; and Purisima in February-May 1842. In 1817 and
1811 Fr. Antonio accompanied expeditions to the pagans. His narratives of
the tours are still extant. He was present at the founding of San Rafael, and there is hardly a mission register in California that does not
show his name. He was considered by his superiors to be one of the
most zealous and able Fathers in the country for missionary work. In 1826
Fr. Abella professed obedience to the new Mexican republic, but refused
to take the oath. Before leaving San Carlos he became sick and infirm;
and his term of service at San Luis Obispo was one of illness. Fr. Jimeno in 1842 charged administrator Guerra and others with having robbed
Fr. Abella, and with having treated the old Father "with the greatest in-
gratitude, inhumanity, and vileness " Fr. Ramon's last days were passed
at Santa Inés, where he was buried, on May 24th, 1842, in the presbytery
on the epistle side, about two varas from the church wall.
(12) Banc., IV, 647; V, 635.

Mission La Purisima Concepcion.

FROM the time that Purisima was founded· in 1787 down to December 81st, 1831, when the general mission reports cease, the number of baptisms was 8, 245; marriages, 1,011; and deaths, 2,588. (13)

CHAPTER XVII.

SANTA CRUZ.

PREPARATIONS—FOUNDING OF THE MISSION—FR. LASUEN'S REPORT—INSTRUCTIONS TO THE GUARDS—ERECTION OF BUILDINGS—DEDICATION OF THE CHURCH—GLOOMY PROSPECTS—MISSIONARIES—FATHERS SALAZAR, LOPEZ, AND FERNANDEZ RETIRE—MURDER OF FR. QUINTANA—PUNISHMENT OF THE CRIMINALS—MISSIONARY CHANGES—FATHERS MARQUINEZ AND OLBES RETIRE—DISEASE AMONG THE INDIANS—OTHER ITEMS—SECULARIZATION—INVENTORY—THE LAST MISSIONARY—STATISTICS.

IN 1789 it was determined to found two new missions, one in honor of Our Lady of Solitude, and the other in honor of the Holy Cross. The necessary preliminaries were· arranged between the viceroy and the Fathers, and four missionaries were selected to take charge of the new establishments. Two thousand and eight hundred dollars were to be paid to the síndico at México, $1,000 for each mission, and $200 for travelling expenses for each missionary; and in April

(13) Informes Generales del año de 1831. According to Bancroft the statistics down to 1834 are as follows: Total number of baptisms, 3,314, of which number 1,740 were those of Indian adults, 1,492 Indian children, four adults and 78 children de gente de razon. Deaths, 2,711, of which 1,790 were Indian adults, 902 Indian children, one adult and 18 children of settlers or soldiers. Marriages 1,031, of which only five couples were de gente de razon. The largest population ever reached at Purisima was 1,520 in 1804. The largest number of cattle owned by the mission in any one year was 13,000 in 1820; horses, 1,451 in 1821; mules, 300 in 1821; sheep, 12,000 in 1820; goats, 292 in 1791; all kinds of animals, 23,862 in 1821. The total product of wheat was 0,522 bushels; corn, 23,235 bushels; barley, 9,306 bushels; and beans, 4,818 bushels. Banc., III, 681-600.

1790 the síndico Fr. Gerónimo, sent provisions and tools for Santa Cruz to the value of $1,021. This information reached California at the end of July 1790, together with Fathers Dantí, Miguel, Rubí, and Tapis, and everything necessary except the vestments and sacred vessels. This omission caused delay, and it was not until July 1791 that a positive assurance came from the viceroy that these articles would be sent. He then ordered the Fathers to proceed at once with the founding, and meanwhile to borrow the needed articles from the other missions. What further happened may be seen from a letter of Fr. President Lasuen to Governor Romeu, written on September 29th, 1791. It is as follows:

"In view of the superior order of his excellency I at once named the missionaries. I asked and obtained from the commandant of this presidio the necessary aid for exploring anew the region of Soledád, and there was chosen a site having some advantages over the two previously considered. I applied to the missions for vestments and sacred vessels; and as soon as the commander of the Aranzazu furnished the help allowed for the new establishments, I proceeded to Santa Clara in order to examine anew in person the site of Santa Cruz. I crossed the sierra by a long and rough road, and I found in the site the same excellent fitness that had been reported to me. I found besides a stream of water very near, copious, and important. On the day of San Augustin, August 28th, I said Mass, and a cross was raised on the spot where the establishment is to be. Many gentiles came, old and young, of both sexes, and showed that they would gladly enlist under that sacred standard, thanks be to God! I returned to Santa Clara by another way, rougher but shorter and more direct. I had the Indians improve the road and was perfectly successful, because for this as for

everything else the the comandante of San Francisco,
Don Hermenegildo Sal, has furnished with the greatest activity and promptness all the aid I had asked
for. I ordered some little huts made, and I suppose
that by this time the missionaries are there. I found
in Monterey the two corvettes of the Spanish expedition, and the commander's power to please obliged
me to await their departure. I endeavored to induce
them to transport the Santa Cruz supplies by water,
but it could not be accomplished. The day before
yesterday, however, some were sent there by land,
and with them a man from the schooner which came
from Nootka under Don Juan Carrasco. The plan is
to see if there is any shelter for a vessel on the
coast near Santa Cruz, and to transport thither what
is left. To-morrow a report is expected. This measure
is taken because we lack animals. To-day eleven Indians have departed from here with tools to construct a shelter at Soledád for the Fathers and the
supplies. I and the other Fathers are making preparations, and my departure thither will be, by the favor of God, the day after St. Francis, October 8th at
the latest." (1)

COMANDANTE Sal now started out from San Francisco for Santa Cruz with a corporal and two privates.
The corporal of the mission guard was fully instructed respecting his duties. He was admonished to constant precautions, kindness to the gentiles, harmony
with the Fathers, strict performance of religious duties, etc. The instructions were about the same as
those given to the soldiers at the other missions. It
is to be noticed, however, that when escorting the
missionaries the soldiers were not allowed to pass
the night away from the mission. If a missionary
desired to go to a distant mission, word had to
be sent to San Francisco, and a guard obtained

(1) Banc., I, 491-493.

from the presidio. From Santa Clara Sal proceeded
to Santa Cruz in company with Fathers Salazar and
Baldomero Lopez. On the 24th of September some
Christian Indians of Santa Clara were set to work
cutting timber and building a hut for the missionaries, while these were looking for a suitable piece
of land to sow twenty-five fanegas of wheat. A fine
plain was found near a stream called by the explorers of 1769 Arroyo de Pedro Regalado. The mission site was about five hundred yards from the Rio
San Lorenzo, also named in 1769. The chief, Sugert,
came with a few of his followers, and promised to
become the first Christian of his tribe, and Sal a-
greed to be godfather.

On Sunday, September 25th, Don Hermenegildo Sal
took formal possession of the place, Holy Mass was
celebrated, the Te Deum chanted, and thus Mission
Santa Cruz formally established. Santa Clara sent a
contribution to the new mission consisting of 64
cattle, 22 horses, 77 fanegas of grain, and 26 loaves
of bread. San Francisco gave five yoke of oxen, 70
sheep, and two bushels of barley; and San Carlos
furnished seven mules and eight horses. Church
vestments, etc., were also provided by the older missions.

At the end of 1791 the neophytes numbered eighty-
four, but after another year they had increased to
224. In 1796 the number was 523, the highest ever
reached. (2)

The church, whose cornerstone had been laid with
due solemnity on February 27th, 1793, was formally
dedicated to its holy use on the 10th of May, or possibly March, 1794, by Fr. Peña of Santa Clara, with
the assistance of Fathers Gil and Sanchez, and the
resident missionaries. The next day Holy Mass was
celebrated in the new edifice. The building measured

about thirty by one hundred and twelve feet, and was twenty-five feet high. The foundation walls to the height of three feet were of stone, the front was of masonry, and the rest of adobes. About the other mission buildings but little is recorded, except that the last two sides of the square were completed in 1795. A flouring mill was built and began to run in the autumn of 1796, but it was badly damaged by the rains in December. In 1798 a granary of two stories and a house for the looms were finished.

Towards the close of the century the mission prospects were far from encouraging. At the beginning of 1798 Fr. Fernandez wrote that everything was in a bad shape. A hundred and thirty-eight neophytes had deserted and left only thirty or forty to work, while the land was overflowed and the planting not half done. The church had been damaged by the flood; the live-stock was dying; and a dead whale on the beach had attracted an unusual multitude of wolves and bears.

The missionary founders of Santa Cruz, Fathers Salazar and Lopez, served here till July 1795 and August 1796 respectively, at or about which dates they departed for Mexico to seek the retirement of their college. They were succeeded by Fathers Manuel Fernandez and José de la Cruz Espí. The latter was replaced in May 1797 by Fr. Francisco Gonzalez, while the former had as successor, after his departure from the country in October 1798, Fr. Carranza. (8)

---

(8) Banc., I, 483-408. Of Fr. Alonso Isidor Salazar we know nothing till he became missionary at Santa Cruz; he probably arrived from Mexico a little earlier in the same year 1791. On May 11th, 1796, while at the college of San Fernando he wrote a long report on California.

Fr. Baldomero Lopez came to California in 1791, and was stationed at Santa Cruz until he retired in August 1796. He was most of the time in ill health; in Mexico it seems he regained his health, for on August 8th, 1818, he was elected guardian of San Fernando.

Fr. Manuel Fernandez was born in 1767 at Tuy in Galicia, Spain. He entered the Franciscan Order at Compostela in 1781 joined the college of

NOTHING of importance occurred at Santa Cruz in
the early part of the present century, except that in
1805 Captain Goycocchea recommended that the neophytes of the mission be divided between Santa Clara and San Juan Bautista, and that the Fathers be
employed in new fields, since all the Indians in the
district had been converted. The year 1812, however,
saw an awful crime committed at Santa Cruz: Fr.
Andrés Quintana was brutally murdered, though it
was first supposed he had died a natural death. (4)

HE was found dead in his bed on the morning of
of October 12th, 1812, and his remains were interred
by Fathers Viader and Duran. The suddenness of the
death caused an investigation, which was conducted
by Lieutenant Estudillo during the following week;
but the conclusion was that, as there were no signs
of violence, the missionary had died a natural death.
About two years later suspicions were again aroused.
A new investigation was made, and it was ascer-
tained that Fr. Quintana, though sick himself, had
been called from his room at night to visit a man
said to be dying, and that on the way he had been
murdered in a most diabolical manner. The body had
then been taken back to the room of the missionary,
put to bed, and the door afterwards carefully locked.
Nine or ten Indians were tried for the crime, and
the case was sent to Mexico for final sentence. In
the spring of 1816 the sentence came by which five
of the criminals were condemned to receive two
hundred lashes each, and to work in chains from two

San Fernando in 1788, and came to California in 1794. He was one of five
Fathers who arrived recommended by Fr. Mugártegui as of a different kind from several who had exhausted Fr. Lasuen's patience. Fr.
Fernandez was stationed at Santa Clara in 1794, but was much at San
Francisco in 1795. He was sent to Santa Cruz in 1795 and remained there
till October 170*, when he obtained permission to retire on account of
sickness.

(4) Banc., II, 154; 888-889. Fr. Andrés Quintana was a native of Antoña-
na, Alava, Spain. He landed at Monterey August 31st, 1805, and was stationed at Santa Cruz from November of that year until his death.

to ten years. Two others of the accused had meanwhile died in prison, and one of the five, Lino, supposed to have been the leader, died in 1817 at Santa Barbara presidio, where the convicts had been sent to serve out their time. Only one is said to have survived the punishment.

On November 21st, 1820, another Indian, Alberto, imprisoned at San Francisco, was examined on the subject, and confessed that he had been urged to join the conspiracy, but that he had refused. In the sentence it appears that the defence of the murderers had been excessive cruelty on the part of the murdered missionary. The officials in Mexico seem to have attached some importance to this absurd plea, so that Governor Sola felt himself called upon to reply. He denied the charges of the Indians, and eulogized Fr. Quintana as a model of kindness, who had sacrificed his life in the cause of duty: first in leaving San Carlos to assist sick a missionary, and then in rising from a sick-bed to visit that of an Indian supposed to be dying. And still further the governor declared that after a close investigation he could find no evidence of cruelty on the part of the Fathers, and that their errors were for the most part on the side of mercy. (5)

Fr. Gonzalez labored at Santa Cruz until June 1805, when he retired to Mexico. Fr. Quintana had succeeded him until 1812. Fr. Carranza left the mission in August 1808. The two Fathers, José Antonio and Francisco Javier, Uría served here as supernumeraries in 1806-1808, and Fr. Antonio Rodriguez arrived in June 1809, but remained only till 1811. Fr. Tapis was at Santa Cruz for a time in 1812; but Fathers Marquinez and Escudé held out longer, the former from 1811 to 1817, and the latter from 1812 to 1818, when Fr. Olbés arrived. Fr. Gil was transferred

(5) Banc., II. 385-389.

to Santa Cruz in 1820. Of this number of missionaries Fr. Marquinez departed for Mexico from Santa
Cruz. Fr. Olbés also returned to his college in 1821,
so that Fr. Gil y Taboada toiled alone here after
that date, except for the period 1827-1830, when Fathers Antonio Jimeno, José Joaquin Jimeno, and
Juan Moreno were at Santa Cruz much of that time.
In 1830 Fr. Gil left the mission in charge of Fr. José
Jimeno, who remained at his post until the arrival
of the Zacatecan Fathers in 1833. (6)

THE mortality at San Cruz was very great at this
period. Fr. Gil writing on the subject says that the
Indians were all impregnated with venereal disease,
so that the slightest change in the temperature prostrated them, and from sixty to eighty were sick at
the same time. The mission lands extended three
miles from north to south, and seven to nine leagues
from east to west, though only three miles were of
use. Grasshoppers and other insects did much damage
to the cultivated fields, yet the taxes on mission produce amounted to about $380 a year. Supplies to the
guards averaged about $35 a month, and the supplies
furnished to the presidio during 1821-1830, except
1817, amounted to $5,600. On December 81st, 1831,
the mission possessed 3,500 cattle, 5,403 sheep, and
140 horses; at the same time 298 Indians were still
living at the mission. (7)

THE mission was secularized in 1834–1835 by Ignacio

---

(6) Banc., II, 151-155; 387; 625. Fr. Marcelino Marquinez was a native of
Treviño, Vizcaya, Spain, where he was born in May 1779. He took the
habit in November 1796, and joined the college of San Fernando in 1804.
After his arrival in California in July 1810, he served as missionary at
San Luis Obispo from September of that year to November 1811, and then
at Santa Cruz until May 1817. As late as 1811 he was still living at the
college. Ill-health had been the reason for his retirement.

Fr. Ramon Olbés was born at Ateca in Aragon, Spain, February 8th,
1787; he took the the habit at Zaragoza January 1st, 1802; joined the
college of San Fernando June 10th, 1810, and reached California in 1812.
He was stationed at Santa Inés in 1812-1813; at Santa Barbara in 1813-
1816; at San Luis Rey in 1816-1818; and at Santa Cruz from June 1818 to
November 1821, when he went to Mexico on account of ill-health.

(7) Banc., II, 625-626; Informes Generales del año 1831.

Mission Santa Cruz.

del Valle, the comisionado. The value of the property when turned over to the secular authorities at the end of 1835 was $47,000, exclusive of land and the church property, besides $10,000, which had been distributed to the Indians. There is no record of subsequent distributions, or how the estate disappeared; but in 1839 Hartnell found only 70 Indians, with perhaps as many more scattered in the district, and about one sixth of the liv.-:tock mentioned in a former inventory.

THE church property in 1835 was estimated to be worth $32,142 as follows: Buildings, $8,050; ornaments, bells, etc., $23,505; library of 152 volumes, $386. The live-stock consisted of 3,700 cattle, 500 horses, 2,900 sheep, 18 mules, 10 asses, and 28 swine. In 1839 there were left 36 cattle, 127 horses, and 1,026 sheep. Lands, buildings, and fruit trees were valued at less than $1,000 in 1845. In the same year only about 40 Indians lived in the neighborhood of the old mission.

IN 1833 Fr. Antonio Suarez del Real of the Zacatecans succeeded Fr. Jimeno, and remained at Santa Cruz until about 1844. Fr. Anzar of San Juan Bautista seems also to have officiated here in 1844-1845. Thereafter there is no definite record of any resident Father at Santa Cruz. .(8)

FROM the time of the opening of Mission Santa Cruz in 1791 down to December 31st, 1831, the Fathers baptized 2,424 persons, blessed 820 marriages, and buried 1,946 dead. (9)

(8) Banc. III, 692-695; IV, 662; V, 642.
(9) Informes Generales del año 1831. Bancroft, III, 694 gives the following statistics for the same period down to 1834: Total number of baptisms 2,466, of which 1,277 Indian adults, 830 Indian Children, six adults and 244 children de gente de razon. Marriages, 847, of which 63 de razon. Deaths, 2,035, of which 1,359 Indian adults, 574 Indian children, 45 adults and 47 children de razon. Largest population ever reached at Santa Cruz, 644 in 1798. Largest number of cattle 3,700 in 1825; horses 900 in 1828; mules 92 in 1805; sheep 8,300 in 1826; swine 150 in 1819; all kinds of animals 12,502 in 1827. Total product of wheat 9,900 bushels; barley 13,180 bushels; maize 30-500 bushels; beans 9,250 bushels; miscellaneous grains 7,000 bushels.

CHAPTER XVIII.

LA SOLEDAD.

Fr. President Lasuen selected the site for Mission
Soledad early in 1791, but not till September 29th
did a party of natives depart from San Cárlos to e-
rect the necessary buildings. On October ninth, with
the assistance of Fathers Sitjar and García, and in
the presence of Lieutenant Arguello, the guards, and
a number of Indians, Fr. Lasuen blessed the place,
erected and blessed the mission cross, and thus
ushered into existence the mission of Our Lady of
Solitude. The spot was called Chuttusgelis by the natives, but to the Spaniards the region had been
known as Soledad since the first occupation of the
country.

The first baptism of an Indian took place on November 23d, 1791. One other entry in the mission records deserves special mention. From them it appears
that on May 19th, 1793, there was baptized a Neotka
Indian, twenty years of age, "Iquina, son of a gentile father, named Taguasmiki, who in the year 1789
was killed by the American Gret (Gray), captain of
the vessel called *Washington* belonging to the Congress of Boston." (1)

---

(1) See beginning of preceding chapter. Banc., I, Hist. Cal. I, 408-300.

AT the end of the first year Soledad counted eleven converts, but on December 31st, 1800, the books showed 704 baptisms, 164 marriages, and 221 deaths. 512 Indians lived at the mission which, at the same time, possessed 1,000 cattle, 3,000 sheep, and 64 horses. (2)

FATHERS Diego García and Mariano Rubí were the first missionaries of Soledad. The former was present at the founding of the mission, and the latter arrived soon after, but on account of ill-health he left the mission in January, and the country in February or March 1793. Fr. García also left La Soledad in February 1792, but returned in December and remained until March 1796, when he was transferred to San Francisco. Fr. Gili succeeded Fr. Rubí and staid at Soledad until the arrival of Fr. Espí in the following year. In 1795 Fr. Espí gave way to Fr. Martiareno, who labored at the mission for two years, when Fr. Carnicer took his place until 1798. At the end of the century the missionaries were Fathers Antonio Jaime and Mariano Payeras, since March 1796 and November first, 1798, respectively. In 1803 Fr. Ibañez relieved Fr. Payeras. (3)

THE epidemic in the spring of 1802 was particularly severe at Soledad. On February 5th the Fathers reported that the Indians through fear were abandoning the mission; that each day five or six deaths occurred; and that the missionaries were overworked. Yet three years later the same mission reached its largest population with 727 neophytes. After that date the Indian population slowly decreased until 1810, when it was the smallest mission in the province, except San Carlos. (4)

(2) Informes Generales, año 1800.   (3) Fr. Mariano Rubí was one of the four Fathers who arrived in California in July 1790 sent expressly for the new establishments. He was stationed at San Antonio from 1790 to September 1791, and at Soledad from October 1791 to January 1793, when he retired to Mexico on account of ill health.   Banc., I, 499-500: II, 152.
(4) Bancroft, II, 152-153; 386.

A new church was begun in the autumn of 1808 to take the place of the old straw-covered adobe building, till then used for a place of worship. Governor Don José Joaquin de Arrillaga died at Soledad on July 24th, 1814, at the age of sixty-four. While on a tour of inspection he was attacked by a serious illness, and hastened to Soledad in order to put himself under the care of his old friend Fr. Ibañez. His remains were interred in the mission church by Fr. Ibañez on Tuesday July 26th. His will directed that his body be shrouded in the Franciscan habit and buried at the mission where he might chance to die. One hunlred Masses were to be said for his soul at San Miguel and also at San Antonio. (5)

Fr. Ybañez died at Soledad in 1818, (6) and left Fr. Antonio Jaime to toil alone until Fr. Juan Cabot came in 1820. In the following year Fr. Jaime was transferred to Santa Barbara. Fr. Cabot in turn was

---

(5) Bancroft, II, 152-153; 204-2 5.

(6) Ibid. 285-286. Fr. Ibañez, or as h.) and others wrote it, Ybañez, was a n an of large and varied experience. and quite famous among his brother missionaries. He was born at Tarragona in Catalonia, Spain, on October 26th, 1740, and became a Francican at the convent of Zaragoza on February 8th, 1757. Her he received the several sacred Orders. serving also as master of the choir. He arrived at the college of San Fernando de Mexico in May 1770, and was attached to the choir there until 1774, when failing health induced him to obtain a transfor to a convent in Michocan, whence in 1781 he was transferred to the college of Santa Cruz de Querétaro, as a member of which community he served seventeen years in Sonora, chiefly at Dolores del Suric. He made his journeys usually on foot. In 1800 he again joined the college of San Fernando, and was sent in 1801 to California. Until 1803 he was stationed at San Antonio, and from that time until his death on November 26th, 1818. he labored at Soledad, where he was buried next day by Fathers Jaime and Sarria in the mission church. In person he was tall, broad shouldered, and of great strength. In character he was noted for his kindness to all of low estate, or whom he deemed in any way oppressed. He was fond of teaching the soldiers of the guard to read and write, and never tired of instructing the neophytes in work and music. Governor Arrillaga and Fr. Ibañez were always firm friends. On Arrillaga's second coming to California he was welcomed by the Father at Soledad with vocal and instrumental music, and with verses composed by Fr. Ibañez himself. In his last illness the Father refused to excuse himself from any of the duties imposed by the Church or the Order. Fr. Sarria, who was serving as chaplain at the camp on the Salinas, hastened to Soledad to perform the last offices for the old missiona-

alone at the mission until 1824, when Fr. Francisco
Javier de Uría succeeded him.

THERE were several changes among the missionaries
of Soledad in the third decade of the century. Fr.
Jaime left the mission in 1821, and Fr. Juan Cabot
in 1824; Fr. Francisco Javier de Uría served in 1824-
28; Fr. Pedro Cabot in 1828-29; and Fr. Prefect Sarría came here to live in the middle of 1829. On May
5th, 1822, the Fathers and neophytes met to take the
oath of independence from Spain, and on November
19th, 1826, the Indians formally elected one of their
number to go to Monterey to represent them in an
elecion de partido. (7)

THE mission furnished $1,150 to Monterey presidio
in 1829. Mission lands in 1822 extended 9 to 20
leagues east to west, and 8 leagues north to south.
The soil was poor and yielded tolerable crops only in
the wet seasons. There was some irrigation; but
frosts and locusts did much damage. On April 22d,
1829, Fr. Cabot informed governor Echeandía that he
could not establish a school for want of a teacher, of
funds, and of scholars. The record of an election in
1826 is as follows: "At the mission of Nuestra Señora de la Soledad, this day Sunday November 19th,
1826, I the Chief Alcalde Gerónimo, last night summoned the people all to come to the church; and all
being assembled, we attended our Mass and commended ourselves to the Virgin to give us a good
heart that we might do what the comandante of the
presidio had directed us to do. After hearing the
Mass we went out of the church, and being together
with all the people I named Señor Simon Cota, who
can write, as my secretary, and chose two scrutators

ry, and to leave in the mission record a narrative of his life and virtues.
In fragments of the old mission books of Pimeria, Sonora, are the signa-
tures of Ibañez as COMMISSARIO of Caborca in April 1796; and as missionary of Saric in 1783 and besides he often officiated at San Francisco del
Ati down to 1799. (7) Banc., II, 385-426; 622.

Odilon Quepness and Felipe de Jesus; and out of all the people eleven were set aside as the comandanto prescribes, and then all the people retired except the eleven, and they talked among themselves whom of all the men of the mission they would send to Monterey. Three wanted Fernando, one was in favor of Isidro, two preferred Valentin, and four Juan de Dios; and all the ten concluded that Juan de Dios was the one God desires to go to the comandante of Monterey, and hold himself subject to his orders. And this is to be known by all the people and this paper we all that are here present will sign, affixing thereto a cross because we cannot write; and Juan de Dios will carry it with him. (*Here are the crosses*). Before me, Simon Cota, secretary of the junta." (8)

THE venerable Fr. Vincente Francisco Sarría formerly comisario prefecto of Fernandinos died at Soledad on May 24th, 1835. (9) "Soledad," says Gleeson, (10)"of which Fr. Sarría was pastor was once a flourishing Christian settlement, possessing its hundreds of converts and thousand of cattle. Want had never been known there from the time of its foundation up to the moment of confiscation. Immediately upon the change, however, so great was the plunder and devastation of everything belonging to the mission that the Father who remained at his post with a few of the Indians, was unable to obtain the ordinary necessaries of life; yet reduced as he was to the greatest extremity he would not abandon the remnant of his flock. For thirty years he had labored among them, and now, if necessary, he was ready to die in their behalf. Broken down by years and exhausted by hunger, one Sunday morning in the month of August of the above mentioned year, the holy old man assembled in his little church the few

(8) Bancroft II. 62-624. (9) Ibid. III. 688; Gleeson says with others it was 1838. (10) Gleeson II, 134-135,

converts that remained to him. It was the last time he was to appear before these natives. Hardly had he commenced the holy sacrifice of the Mass when his strength completely failed him; he fell before the altar and expired in the arms of his people, for whom he had so zealously and earnestly labored. Noble and worthy death of a Spanish missionary priest!" (10)

Thus he was the last of the Fernandinos in the north, dying just before the secularization which put an end to the independent Franciscan administration here and elsewhere. As from that time the mission had no resident missionary, Fr. Mercado of San Antonio had charge of its spiritual interests, and made occasional visits from the autumn of 1834. Fr. Mercado declared that this *muerte violenta*, violent death, was due *to escasez de alimentos:* want of food.

---

(10) "Fr. Vincento Francisco Sarría was a Biscayan, born in November 1767 at San Estévan de Echabarris, near Bilboa, at which latter town he became a Franciscan in November 1781. He served at his convent as lector de filosofía for laymen, maestro de estudiantes, and lector de artes de religiosos. He left Cádiz in June 1824, and after four years' service at the college of San Fernando he was sent to California in 1809. His missionary service was at San Carlos in 1809-29, and at Soledad in 1829-1835; that is to say these missions were his headquarters, for he was absent much of the time on official tours. In 1813-19 Fr. Sarría held the office of comisario prefecto of the missions in California, and again in 1825-30, or perhaps a little longer, and he was also president in 1823-25. In the discharge of his official duties he proved himself the worthy successor of Fathers Serra, Lasuen, and Tapis. He wrote several little works, among which was also a curious volume of manuscript sermons in his native Basque. He was a scholarly, dignified, and amiable man; not prone to controversy, yet strong in argument, clear and earnest in the expression of his opinions, devoted to his faith and his Order, strict in observing and enforcing Franciscan rules and conscientious in the performance of every duty; yet liberal in his views on ordinary matters, clear-headed in business affairs, and well liked by all who came in contact with him. As prefect no California friar could have done better, since in the misfortune of his Order he never lost either temper or courage. Declining as a loyal Spaniard to accept republicanism, Fr. Sarría was arrested in 1825 and his exile ordered; but his arrest which lasted about five years was merely nominal, and the order of exile, though never withdrawn and several times renewed, was never enforced. After 1830, old and infirm, but still actively engaged in local missionary duties, he lived quietly at Soledad which he declined to leave in 1834, when the northern missions were given to the Franciscans of Zacatecas, especially as no resident missionary was assigned to this mission." Banc., III, 688-89.

Mission La Soledad.

Bancroft objects to this statement and says: "I do not credit Mercado's charges, or believe that there was an administrator in California who would have maltreated a missionary so widely known and loved." (11) Bancroft elsewhere does not presuppose so much good sense and human feeling in the administrators of other confiscated missions. However, Mofras, an eyewitness, according to Gleeson writes: "We have seen the Rev. Father Gonzalez obliged to sit at the table of the administrator, and to suffer the rudeness of cowherds and majordomos who but a few years before esteemed themselves happy to enter the service of the monks as domestics." Speaking of the mission of San Antonio, the same writer says: "The only religious who still inhabits San Antonio, the Rev. Father Gutierrez, gave us the most hospitable reception; and we saw with indignation that an ancient domestic, who had become administrator of the mission, took advantage of the paralytic state of this ecclesiastic to put him on rations, and even refuse him the actual necessaries of life." (12)

Of the reduced state of the mission of San Luis Obispo he says: "In the building, at present, (1842), in ruins, we found reduced to the greatest misery the oldest Spanish Franciscan of all California, the Rev. Father Ramon Abella, who saw the illustrious Peyrouse in 1787. The mission has suffered such devastation that this poor religious slept on an ox-hide, drank out of a horn, and had only for his food *some morsels of meat dried in the sun!* This venerable Father distributed the little that was sent him among the Indian children, who still inhabit with their families the tottering hovels attached to the mission. Several charitable persons, as well as Father Duran, have offered an asylum to Fr. Abella, but he always refuses and declares that he wishes to die at

(11) Banc., III. 688-690.   (12) Gleeson, II, 132-131.

his post. This worthy man, who has founded several missions in the north, is almost sixty years in the apostleship, but still speaks of going to the conquest of souls, while at the same time in an age so advanced he supports without murmur the humiliation and privation which poverty brings."

THE body of the venerable Fr. Sarría, though he died at Soledad, was taken to San Antonio and there buried in the mission church on the epistle side of the ' presbytery, in the sepulchre nearest the wall, on May 27th. Fr. Ambris was told that years later Fr. Sarría's body was found to be intact. (13)

THERE was but a slight loss in population or in livestock down to 1834, though crops were very small, but later Indians, animals, and property of all kinds rapidly disappeared. The population was about 300 in 1834, but in 1840 it had dwindled down to about 70, with perhaps as many more scattered in the district. Baptisms for the years 1831–34, as far as the records go, numbered 140, rather strangely including more than half adults. Deaths amounted to 150. The debt at the end of 1840, after 6 years of secular rule, was large, and there were left only 45 cattle, 25 horses, and 865 sheep, though the inventory of 1835 had shown an estate valued at $36,000 besides the church property. There was a library at this mission of 51 volumes valued at $186. Secularization was effected in 1835 by Nicolás Alviso, and the successive administrators were José M. Aguila, Salvador Espinosa, and Vincente Cantúa. At the end of 1840 the establishment was on the verge of dissolution. On the 4th of June 1846 Soledad mission was sold to Feliciano Soberanes for $800. (14)

THE statistics for the whole period of the mission existence, 1791-1834, are as follows: Total of baptisms, 2,222, of which 1,235 were Indian adults, 924 Indian

(13) Bancroft III, 689-691. (14) Bancroft, IV, 349 ;352; 661; V, 561.

and 68 children de razon; annual average 50. Total
of marriages, 682, of which 11 were de razon. Total
of deaths, 1,808, of which 1,207 were Indian adults,
574 Indian children, 9 adults and 18 children de gente de razon; an annual average of 40. The largest
Indian population ever reached, 725 was in 1805.
The largest number of cattle possessed by the mission
at any one time was 6,599 in 1831; horses, 1,257 in
1821; mules, 80 in 1807; sheep, 9,500 in 1808; swine,
90 in 1814; all kinds of animals, 16,551 in 1821. The
total product of wheat was 64,254 bushels; barley,
13,056 bushels; corn, 18,240 bushels; beans, 2,260
bushels; and miscellaneous grain, 18,012 bushels. (15)

The "Informes Generales" for 1791-1832 give the
following figures: baptisms, 2,102; marriages, 636;
deaths, 1,679.

CHAPTER XIX.

SAN JOSE.

Mission San Jose Established—Success—Missionaries—Fr. Cueva Retires—Indian Attack—Description Of The Mission By Langsdorff—
New Church Dedicated—State Of The Mission In 1820—Interesting
Items—Statistics—Secularization—Fathers Muro, Quijas, And Gutierrez Retires—Temporal Affairs—Mission San Jose Sold.

According to an order from Mexico, one of the
missions was to be dedicated to St. Joseph, the fos-
ter-father of Our Lord. For this reason the one next
established was placed under his special protection,
and became known as San José. Gov. Borica sent
orders to the commandant of San Francisco to detail

(15) Bancroft III, 69).

a corporal and five men for the mission of San José
to be founded at the Alameda. On June 9th the
troops under Amador, accompanied by Fr. Lasu-
en, started for the spot, where next day a temporary
church, or *enramada*, was erected. The native name
of the site was Oroysom, or Oroyson. On June 11th,
1797, Trinity Sunday, the regular ceremonies of
foundation, blessing the site, raising the cross, Litany of All Saints, Holy Mass, sermon, and Te Deum
were observed as usual by Fr. Lasuen, and the who
festivity concluded with the firing of guns. The
same day all returned to Santa Clara. Five days later
Amador and his men came back to cut timber
in order to construct the necessary buildings. By
the 28th, this work was so far advanced that
the guard could complete it. The same day Fathers Isidoro Barcenilla and Agustin Merino arrived and took charge. The three northern missions
contributed 12 mules, 39 horses, 12 yoke of oxen, 242
sheep, and 60 pigs.

THE first baptism was administered on September
2d by Fr. Catalá. By the end of 1797 there were 33
converts, and in 1800 the number had increased to
286, the baptisms up to that time having been 364,
and the burials 88. Meanwhile the large stock increased to 367, and sheep and goats to 1,600. Crops
in 1800 were about 1,500 bushels, chiefly wheat. The
total for the three years was 3,909 bushels.

Fr. Barcenilla remained at San José till after 1800,
but Fr. Merino was replaced in 1799 by Fr. José Antonio Uría. All three were new-comers, and none remained long in the country. A wooden structure with
grass roof served as a church. (1)

Fr. Barcenilla in April 1802 was succeeded by Fr.
Luis Gil y Taboada until 1804, when the latter's place
was taken by Fr. Pedro de la Cueva, who retired in

---

(1) Bancroft I, 557-558.

November 1806. Fr. José Antonio Uría, who had been stationed here since 1799, also left the mission in 1806. They were succeeded by Fathers Buenaventura Fortuni and Narciso Duran, who were new arrivals from Mexico. (2)

THERE is a vague record that as early as 1802 Fr. Uría and his escort were attacked by the gentiles of the mountains, and that a military force was sent to teach the savages a lesson; but particulars are not known. A subsequent occurrence of the kind is however better recorded. Fr. Cueva having occasion to visit some sick neophytes at a ranchería ten or fifteen miles distant in the eastern hills, was escorted by Ignacio Higuera and two soldiers, besides a few Christian Indians. This was on the 15th of January. Arriving at the ranchería to which his visit was directed, the natives instead of receiving him kindly, discharged a cloud of arrows. Majordomo Ignacio Higuera was killed, Fr. Cueva was struck in the face, one of the soldiers was badly wounded, and three neophytes were killed together with all the horses. The pursuit was checked apparently by the fall of a gentile, and the survivors were enabled to reach the mission. In retaliation Sergeant Peralta made a raid and killed eleven gentiles. (3)

EARLY in May 1806 Langsdorff, a Russian navigator, visited the mission. He gives the following description of Mission San José: "Although it is only eight years since they were begun, the buildings and grounds are already of very considerable extent; the quantity of corn in the granaries far exceeded my expectations. They contained at that time more than 2,000 measures of wheat, and a proportionate quantity of maize, barley, peas, beans, and other grain. The kitchen-

(2) Bancroft II, 131-133. Fr. Pedro de la Cueva, or Cuevas, left Guadalajara on April 23d, 1804, and arrived in California on August 14th. Ill-health, not relieved by a few months' stay at San Diego, compelled him to retire to his college. (3) Banc., II, 34; 138.

Mission San Jose.

garden is extremely well laid out, and kept in very good order; tho soil is everywhere rich and fertile, and yields ample returns. Tho fruit trees are still very young, but their produce is as good as could be expected. A small rivulet runs through the garden, which preserves a constant moisture. Some vineyards have been planted within a few years, which yield excellent wine, sweet, and resembling Malaga. The location of the establishment is admirably chosen, and according to the universal opinion this mission will in a few years be the richest and best in California. The only disadvantage is, that there are no large trees very near. To compensate the disadvantage, there are in the neighborhood of the mission chalk-hills, and excellent brick-earth, so that most of their buildings are of brick. Their stores of corn are much greater than of cattle, consequently the number of oxen slaughtered every week is considerably smaller than at San Francisco, but their consumption of corn and pulse is much greater. The habitations of the Indians are not yet finished, so that at present they live chiefly in straw huts of a conical form."

MEANWHILE work on the mission church was pressed forward, and on April 23d, 1809, Fr. Tapis, superior of the missions, came to bless the new structure. Next day he preached, and Fr. Arroyo de la Cuesta said Mass in the presence of the other Fathers, of several military officers, and of many people from the adjoining pueblo. On the eighth of the following July the new cemetery was blessed with the customary solemnities. (4)

FATHERS Duran and Fortuni baptized more Indians at San José than the missionaries at any other mission, and buried a smaller percentage of their converts than did the Fathers at any other mission ex-

(4) Banc., II, 138-140.

cept San Luis Rey. The mission also took second place in the list as far as population was concerned, which increased from 545 in 1810 to 1,754 in 1820. Sheep raising and agriculture were also prosperous. In January 1811 the dead were removed from the old to the new cemetery. In 1813 there was an expedition after runaways involving a fight on the San Joaquin. (5)

Fr. Buenaventura Fortuni left Mission San José in the autumn of 1825, and from that time Fr. Narciso Duran labored alone. He was also superior of all the missions in 1825–1827. The supplies furnished to the presidio at San Francisco from 1821-1830, except 1827, amounted to $15,125. Tithes and taxes in 1824 amounted to $1,846; in 1828 they still reached $1,167.

In 1827 three adobe rooms were erected for soap making, tanning, and storing of hides. In April 1829, Virmond ordered a bell of 1,000 ℔s, bearing the name of San José Mission. Robinson mentions a large reservoir in the rear, pipes carrying the water to the buildings and gardens, and a fountain with conveniences for bathing and washing in front. In 1822 the lands extended 9 leagues by one to three leagues. (6)

Fr. Duran was succeeded in 1838 by the Zacatecan Fr. José Maria de Jesus Gonzalez Rubio, who remained several years. The mission at this time was probably the most prosperous in California, both before and after secularization. Its highest population of 1,866 souls was reached in 1831, and though the number fell to about 1,400 in 1834, and 580 in 1840, with probably 200 scattered in the district, yet crops were uniformly good, the yield being larger in proportion to the seed sown than elsewhere; and livestock increased steadily to the end. The population down to 1834 decreased to 1,456. There were 860 baptisms during the three years 1830-1834, including 293

(5) Bancroft, II, 375 376.   (6) Bancroft, II, 598-599,

adults in 1881, whilst 893 persons died, and 129 couples were married. Large stock for the same period
increased to 18,710; horses and mules declined to 1,
250; and sheep remained at 18,000 head. Crops a-
mounted to 18,000 bushels each year. In 1835, according to Fr. Gonzalez, the mission had 18,000 cattle,
15,000 sheep, 1,100 horses, and effects valued at $20,
000. Statistics for the whole period of the mission's
existence 1797 to 1834 are as follows: Total of baptisms, 6,737, of which 4,182 were Indian adults; 2,488
Indian children; and 67 children de razon; an annual
average of 177. Marriages, 1,984 of which only four
de razon. Deaths, 5,100, of which 8,524 were Indian
adults; 1,551 Indian children; and four adults and 27
children de razon; an annual average of 184. The
largest number of cattle owned by the mission was
18,000 in 1826; horses, 1,425 in 1834; mules, 100 in
1880; sheep 20,000 in 1826; all kinds of animals 85,
600 in 1826. The total product of wheat amounted to
18,680 bushels; barley, 16,750; corn, 17,200; beans, 8,
790; miscellaneous grains, 8,800 bushels. The "Informes Generales" give the following figures for the period 1797 to December 31st, 1831: Baptisms, 6,637;
marriages, 1,943; deaths, 4,645.

SECULARIZATION was effected in 1836-37, Vallejo
having charge as administrator until April 1840,
when he was succeeded by José Maria Amador. The
inventory made at the time of the transfer showed
a total valuation, not including lands or church property, of $155,000 over and above the debts. (7)

FR. José Maria Gonzalez Rubio left San José in
1842. Fr. Miguel Muro then became the missionary,
but left California about the year 1845.

FR. José Lorenzo Quijas was stationed here in 1843-
44, or at least officiated here during that time, when
he seems to have left the country.

---

7) Bancroft III, 723-725.

Fr. Gutierrez was at San José in 1845 and probably departed for Mexico in the same year. (8)

In 1843 San José, like some of the other missions, was restored to the Franciscans to be administered by them as guardians of the Indians as in former times. Respecting their success there is no definite record. In 1844 they made efforts to get back the live-stock due the mission from private citizens; this brought on trouble with M. G. Vallejo. The dues from Vallejo were 8,000 sheep; from Antonio Buelna, since 1840, one hundred and fifty heifers; from Mariano Castro 110 heifers since 1840; from Juan Alvires 200; from Rafæl Estrada 100; from Guillermo Castro 200 sheep; from Santiago Estrado 100 heifers and 10 bull calves. In 1845 the Fathers asked to be relieved of the care of the temporalities. Mofras gives the Christian Indian population as 400 in 1842, and three years later there may have been 250 still living at or near the mission. (9)

On May 5th, 1846, San José Mission was sold to

(8) Fr. Miguel Muro was a Franciscan of the college of Our Lady of Guadalupe, Zacatecas, who had been a missionary in Texas. Subsequently he served as master of novices at the college in 1834-37, and came to California apparently in 1842, from which time his name appears on the records at San José Mission until May 1845, and at San Francisco in June-October of the same year. Having retired to his college he died of the cholera in 1850. He was a religious of most exemplary life.

Fr. José Lorenzo, Quijas an Indian and probably a native of Ecuador, had been a trader before he became a Franciscan and joined the Zacatecas college. He came with Fr. Diego in 1833, and served at San Francisco in 1833-34, at Solano and San Rafael in 1834-43, and at San José in 1843-44. Bancroft says: "Unfortunately Quijas and two or three other black sheep of the Zacatecan flock were so situated as to come much in contact with foreigners, and this fact did much to discredit all the friars in the opinion of the immigrants. Dr. Sandels found him in 1843 a reformed man at San José, and the same year came his appointment as vice-president of the missions. He disappears from the records in April 1844. A certain Charles Brown claimed to have met him in Mexico in 1857, when he was curate of Ometepec."

Fr. José de Jesus Maria Gutierrez was also one of the Zacatecan Franciscans who came with Fr. Garcia Diego in 1833. He was stationed at San Francisco Solano in 1833-34, at San Francisco or Dolores in 1834-39, at San Antonio in 1840-44, and at San José in August 1844, which is the last record found of him.   Sotomayor 614. Banc. IV, 630-681.

(9) Ibid. IV, 369; 422; 641-682.

Andres Pico and J. B. Alvarado for $12,000 by Governor Pico. The mission had no resident missionary, but was attended by Fr. Real of Santa Clara. (11)

———◆———

CHAPTER XX.

SAN JUAN BAUTISTA.

Instructions To The Guards—Missionary Stations—Founding Of The Mission—The First Missionaries—Missionary Progress—Indian Troubles—Earthquake—Controversy—New Church—Fathers Lopez, Martiarena, And Itturate Retire—Death Of Fr. Delanto—Death Of Fr. Tapis—Biography—Other Missionary Changes—Secularization—Inventory—Statistics—The Mission Sold—Fr. Anzar The Last Missionary.

Governor Borica on May 10th, issued instructions to Corporal Ballesteros and five men who were detailed to act as guard for the new mission to be placed under the patronage of St. John the Baptist. The instructions were similar to those given to the guards of other missions previously founded. It is to be noted, however, that the furnishing of escorts to the Fathers was left more to the corporal's discretion than before; the absence of soldiers at night was declared inexpedient, but not absolutely prohibited. Sending soldiers after fugitive neophytes was, however, still forbidden. These instructions, though prepared especially for this new mission, were ordered published at all the missions.

The site chosen was the southernmost of the two that had been examined, called by the Spaniards for many years past San Benito, but by the natives Popeloutechom, or Popelout. The twenty three ranche-

---

(11) Bapo., V, 301; 096-097,

rías belonging to the mission thereafter were Onexta-
co, Absayruc, Motssum, Trutca, Teboaltac, Xisca, or
Xixcaca, Giguay, Tipisastac, Ausaima, Poytoquix,
Guachurrones, Pagosines or Paycince, Calerdaruc,
Asystarca, Pouxouoma, Suricuama, Tamarox, Thithi-
rii, Uñijaima, Chapana, Mitaldejama, Echautac, and
Yelmus.

As early as June 17th, Corporal Ballesteros had e-
rected a church, missionary-house, granary, and guard
house upon the site chosen, and on June 24th, the
day of the patron saint, Fr. Lasuen, superior of the
missions, assisted by Fathers Catalá and Martiarena,
established the new mission of San Juan Bautista.
The name had been given in the orders of the viceroy. Fathers Manuel Martiarena and Pedro Adriano
Martínez were the first missionaries stationed here;
both were new arrivals of 1794 and 1797 respectively.
The latter served at San Juan Bautista until the end
of 1800, the former left the mission in July 1799, Fr.
Jacinto Lopez taking his place in August 1800.

THE first baptism took place on July 11th, 1797, and
before the end of the year 85 had received the sacrament, and 641 before the end of 1800, whilst 65 died,
and 516 remained as neophytes. Large stock increased
to 728, small stock to 2,080 head, whilst agricultural
products for 1800 amounted to about 2,700 bushels. A
mud-roofed structure was the mission church before
1800. The Ansaimes, or Ansayames, Indians, who
lived in the mountains about twenty-five miles east
of San Juan caused some trouble. In 1798 they are
said to have surrounded the mission by night, but
were forced to retreat by certain prompt measures
of the governor not specified. In November another
band known as the Osos killed eight ranchería Indians, and Sergeant Castro was sent to punish them.
They resisted and a fight occurred, in which Chief
Tatillosti was killed, and another chief and a soldier
were wounded. Two gentiles were captured and

brought in to be educated as interpreters. In 1799 the Ansaimes again assumed a threatening attitude and killed five Moutsoncs, or Mutsuncs, who lived between them and the mission. Acting under instructions from Governor Borica, Castro visited several rancherías, recovered over fifty fugitives, administered a few floggings with some warnings, and brought in a few captives for presidio work. Again in 1800 the Ansaimes killed two Mutsunes at San Benito Creek, burned a house and some wheat fields, and were with difficulty kept from destroying the mission. Sergeant Gabriel Moraga marched with ten men and brought in eighteen captives, including the chiefs of the Ansaime and the Carnadero rancherías.

THERE were shocks of earthquake from the 11th to the 31st of October, 1800, sometimes six in a day, the most severe being on the 18th. The Fathers were so terrified that they spent the nights out of doors. Several cracks appeared in the ground, and of considerable extent and depth on the banks of the Pájaro, and the adobe walls of all the buildings were cracked from top to bottom, and threatened to fall. (1)

DURING the first decade of the nineteenth century there was a controversy at San Juan Bautista about lands. Mariano Castro had gone to Mexico in 1801, and had come back in 1802, with authority to occupy the rancho of La Brea, where he made some improvements. But the Fathers refused to remove their livestock, and sent in a protest to the Fr. Superior, from whom it went to the guardian and the viceroy. After a correspondence lasting several years it was decided that Castro must establish himself elsewhere.

ON June 13th, 1803, the corner-stone was laid for a new mission church. Fr. Viader conducted the ceremonies assisted by the missionaries. On June 3d, 1809, the image of St. John the Baptist was placed on the

(1) Bancroft I, 557-559.

altar in the sacristy, which served for divine worship until the main building could be completed. Fr. Jacinto Lopez labored at the mission until September 1801. when on account of failing health he sailed for Mexico on October 9th. Fr. José Manuel do Martiarena then returned and was stationed here until he left the country in 1804.

Fr. Andrés Delanto succeeded him from August 1804 to September 1808, when he died on the 11th. Fr. Felipe Arroyo de la Cuesta took his place. During all these years Fr. Domingo Santiago de Itúrrate was associate missionary until he retired in 1809. (2)

Fr. Cuesta continued to be the senior missionary but his associate Fr. Ulibarri, who had taken Fr. Itúrrate's place in 1809, was succeeded in January 1815 by Estévan Tapis. Fr. Saenz de Lucío was also here for a time in 1816. The new church was at last finished and dedicated on June 23d, 1812, the Fathers of Santa Clara and San José assisting in the ceremonies.

In 1818 a new altar was completed and consecrated in November. The church measured, it is said, 60x160 feet, was paved with brick, and the ceiling supported by brick arches. The mission was still gaining in neophytes. In cattle it was far in advance of any

---

(2) Fr. Lopez had landed at Monterey on July 23th, 1799. After being stationed at San Antonio for about a year he was transferred to San Juan Bautista.

Fr. Martiarena was born at Renteria, in Guipúzcoa, Spain, in 1754. He became a Franciscan at Zacatecas in 1788, but joined the college of San Fernando in 1791, and arrived in California in 1794. After being stationed at San Antonio from June 1794 to June 1796, he was at Soledad until May 1797, at San Juan Bautista until July 1800, at San Francisco until August 1801, and again at San Juan until August 1804. He officiated at San Gabriel on October 28th, 1804, when it seems he departed for Mexico.

Fr. Andrés Delanto was a native of Miranda de Ebro, Castile, Spain, and came to California in 1804, serving at San Juan Bautista from August of that year continuously until his death.

Fr. Domingo had left the college on February 3d, 1800, and arrived in California August 23d, since which time he labored continuously at this mission until failing health compelled him to ask for retirement. He sailed for Mexico in October 1809. Bancroft II, 7; 133-134.

other mission in the north, having as many as 11,000 head at the close of 1820. (3)

Mission San Juan Bautista.

Fr. Estévan Tapis died in 1825, and was succeeded by Fr. Buenaventura Fortuni in 1825–26; and Fr. Juan Moreno came here at the end of 1830. The mission reached its highest figure of population in 1823 with 1,248 souls, and it was the only one of the old

(3) Bancroft II, 386-387.

establishments, except San Luis Rey, that gained in population from 1820-1830. During the earlier part of this period many gentiles were brought in from the eastern villages. The mission lands in 1822 extended six leagues from east to west and from north to south. (4)

Fr. Felipe Arroyo de la Cuesta remained here till 1832, when he was transferred to San Miguel. Fr. Juan Moreno was at San Juan from 1830-1833, when it seems Fr. José Anzar of the Zacatecas college arrived. The regular statistical reports cease in 1832, when there were 916 Indians on the register. The only subsequent record is to the effect that the number of Indians "emancipated" in 1835 was 68, "presumably heads of families," says Bancroft, possibly representing 250 souls, but probably fewer. The population down to 1834 decreased to about 850.

SECULARIZATION was effected in 1835 by Tiburcio Castro. The inventory at that time showed a valuation of $147,413, including church property, live stock, lands, ranchos, etc. The library contained 182 volumes valued at $501. There were six bells valued at $1,000.

(4) Bancroft II, 622-624. Fr. Tapis was born on August 25th, 1754, at Santa Coloma de Farnes in Catalonia Spain. He received the habit of St. Francis at Gerona on January 27th, 1778. Leaving Cádiz on June 4th, 1786, he came to California in 1790. He was stationed at San Luis Obispo in 1790-93; at Santa Barbara in 1793-1806; at San Carlos in 1807-11; at Purisima in 1811-13; at Santa Inéz in 1813-14; and at San Juan Bautista from January 1815 to November 3d, 1825, the date of his death. At the death of Fr. Lasuen Fr. Tapis was elected president of the California missions in the middle of 1803, and held the position until 1812, having been reelected in 1809. He was also vicar for California to the bishop of Sonora. He received the last sacraments from Fr. Prefec: Sarria, who with Fathers Viader, Fortuni, and Gil was present at his death. The latter buried him on November 4th, in the presbytery on the Gospel side. The superiors bestowed the highest praise in all reports on Fr. Tapis. At the time of his death he was the senior missionary in the California service. He was familiar with several Indian languages, was noted for his habit of studying the individual peculiarities of his neophytes, and fond of teaching boys to read and write. Fr. Gil in the record of his death speaks of him as a truly evangelical man, remarkably prudent in his relations with his fellowmen, "particularly with the superior officers and governors who lived here during the time of his rule; so that all, friars, soldiers civilians, and Indians, loved him."

The mission existed from 1797 to 1834, during which time 4,100 persons were baptized, of whom 1,898 were Indian adults, 2,015 Indian children, and 2 adults and 195 children de razon; an annual average of 108. The total number of marriages was 1,028, of which 58 were de razon. 3,027 deaths occurred, of which 1, 708 were Indian adults, 1,203 Indian children. and 5, adults and 65 children de razon; an annual average of 70. The largest population ever reached, 1,248, was in 1823. The largest number of cattle claimed by the mission was 11,000 in 1820; horses, 1,598 in 1800; mules, 85 in 1805; sheep, 18,000 in 1816; swine, 90 in 1803; and all kinds of animals, 23,789 in 1816. The total product of wheat amounted to 84,638 bushels; barley, 10,830 bushels; corn, 18,400 bushels; beans, 1,871 bushels; and miscellaneous grains, 2,640 bushels. There may have been 80-100 Indians about the mission as late as 1840. (5)

On May 4th, 1846, San Juan Bautista was sold to O. Deleiseques for a debt by Governor Pico. Fr. José Antonio Anzar continued as parish priest at San Juan throughout these years except in the last months of 1845. His name appears as curate on the mission books till 1855, when he probably left California. He seems to have come from Zecatecas a year before the other Zacatecanos, if Bancroft's surmise be correct. (6)

(5) Bancroft III, 858; 691-692; Bancroft, IV, 661.

(6) Ibid. V, 561; Ibid. II, 699. The Informes Generales tell us that from June 24th, 1797, to December 31st, 1831, at San Juan Bautista 3,947 baptisms took place, 983 marriages were blessed, and 2,781 dead buried; and on the last day of December, 1831, the mission possessed 7,070 cattle, 7,017 sheep, and 124 horses.

Fr. Antonio Anzar was in charge of a Sonora mission in 1824. His missionary service was at San Luis Rey in 1832, and at Juan Bautista from 1833, though in 1844 he also had charge of Santa Cruz and San Carlos. In 1843 Fr. Anzar was made president of the Zacatecas Fathers in California.

CHAPTER XXI.

SAN MIGUEL.

BETWEEN San Antonio and San Luis Obispo there was a spot called Las Pozas by the Spaniards, and Vahiá or Vaticá by the natives. "Here" says Fr. Lasuen, "on July 25th, 1797, with the assistance of Fr. Buenaventura Sitjar, and of the troops destined to guard the new establishment, in the presence of a great multitude of gentiles of both sexes and of all ages, whose pleasure and rejoicing exceeded even our expectations, thanks be to God, I blessed the water and the place, and a great cross, which we venerated and raised. Immediately I intoned the Litany of the Saints and after it sang the Mass, during which I preached, and we concluded the ceremony by solemnly singing the Te Deum. May it all be for the greater honor and glory of God, Our Lord. Amen." Thus was founded the mission of San Miguel in honor of "the most glorious prince of the heavenly militia," St. Michael, the Archangel, for which Fathers Sitjar and Antonio de la Concepcion Horra, a new-comer of 1796, were appointed missionaries.

A beginning of missionary work was made by the baptism of 15 children on the day of foundation. At the end of 1800 the number of converts had increased to 885, of whom 53 had died, and 802 were still on the registers as neophytes. The number of horses and cattle was 672, while small animals numbered 1,582 head. The contributions from San Antonio, San Luis Obispo, and Purisima had been 8 mules, 23 horses, 8 yoke of oxen, 128 cattle, and 184 sheep. The crop of 1800 was 1,900 bushels; and the total product of the three years, 8,700 bushels.

Fr. Sit ar left San Miguel and returned to his old mission San Antonio in August 1798. Fr. Juan Martin began a long term of missionary service in September 1797, and Fr. Baltasar Carnicer a short one in May 1799. Fr. Horra, better known by the name of Concepcion, served only about two months, when being declared insane he was sent to Mexico in September. "He is said to have been a very able and worthy friar before he came to California; and in proof of his insanity nothing more serious is recorded than baptizing natives without sufficient preparation, and neglecting to keep a proper register," says Bancroft. It proves, at all events, that the Fathers in California must have been particular about admitting converts into the Church, if one of their number is considered insane for neglecting to instruct the natives before baptism. It is well to bear this in mind while reading Bancroft.

The original mud-roofed wooden church was not replaced by a better until after 1800. (1)

During the first decade of the nineteenth century Fr. Juan Martin continued to be the senior missionary at San Miguel, but Fr. Carnicer left the mission

(1 Banc., I, 559-561. Fr. Antonio de la Concepcion was a Spaniard who had come to California in 1796. His only station was San Miguel. After his return to the college of San Fernando, Mexico, on July 12th, 1799, he secretly made a long report to the viceroy in which he charged the California Fathers with gross mismanagement, with cruelty to the natives, and with inhuman treatment of himself. This matter is treated at some length in the preceding pages. In the mission books of San Miguel this Father's signature appears but once on the death register.

in 1801. Fr. Adriano Martínez succeeded him from
1801 to 1804, when on receiving permission he retired
to Mexico. Fr. Pedro Muñoz during 1804-1807 labored
at San Juan Bautista, and Fr. Juan Cabot succeeded
him for a long term at the beginning of 1807.

In February 1801 Fathers Martin and Carnicer were
attacked with violent pains in the stomach, supposed
to have been the result of poisoning by the Indians.
The two Fathers recovered their health, but Fr.
Pujol, who came down from San Carlos to relieve the
sick missionaries, died from a similar attack as already stated elsewhere in the chapter on Mission San
Antonio. Three Indians in 1802 boasted of having
poisoned the Fathers.

In August 1806 a fire occurred which burned that
portion of the mission buildings which was used for
manufacturing purposes. It destroyed all the implements and raw material, a large quantity of wool,
hides, cloths, and 6,000 bushels of wheat, and besides
damaged a portion of the roof of the church. On August 31st the Fr. Superior of the missions in a circular asked the other missions to contribute for the
relief of the burned mission. (2)

The venerable missionary Fr. Juan Martin remained
at his post during the second decade, and so did
Fr. Juan Cabot until 1819. Fr. Cabot made a trip of
exploration to the valley of the Tulares in 1814, as
narrated in a former chapter. Fr. Vincente Pascual
Oliva succeeded Fr. Cabot in 1819-20, and during 1820-
21 Fr. Tomas Esténega was stationed here.

Fr. Juan Martin continued his labors here until his
death in 1824, but was succeeded by Fr. Juan Cabot.
The mission had but one Father, save in 1821-22,

(2) Bancroft II,149-151. Fr. Adriano Martínez was one of the fi st missionaries of San Juan Bautista, though not personally present a; its foundation on June 21st, 1797, and he served there until the end of 1800, and
then at San Miguel until he sailed for Mexico, where he was chosen
procurator of the college in 1818.

when Fr. Tomás Esténega and after him Fr. Blas Ordaz were here, as was Fr. Uría in 1824. A new church was ready for roofing in 1818. San Miguel reached its largest population with 1076 Indians in 1814.

San Miguel now was but slightly more prosperous than its neighbor San Luis Obispo; its herds and flocks dwindled rapidly, death largely exceeded baptisms, the soil was reported as poor and the pastures limited, though vines flourished and timber was abundant.

ROBINSON describes San Miguel as a poor establishment in 1830. The heat was so great as to be almost insufferable, so that it was jocosely said that the fleas might be seen in the heat of the day gasping for breath on the brick pavements! In 1822 the mission lands were reported as extending 14 leagues north to south, and 34 to 36 leagues east to west. In 1828 the boundaries were the Tulares on the east, 25 leagues; the sea-shore on the west, 12 to 14 leagues; San Luis Obispo lands south, 7 leagues; and San Antonio lands on the north, 7 leagues. (3)

---

(3) Bioc.. II, 354-85; 643-651. Fr. Juan Martin was a native of Spain, having been born at Villastar, Aragon, on January 12th, 1770. After receiving the Franciscan habit in Zaragoza on January 16th, 1787, he studied theology at Teruel. On June 11th, 1793, he sailed from Cádiz, and arrived at San Fernando College in September, and in California early in 1794. He was stationed at San Gabriel from March 1794 to July 1796 as supernumerary, at Purisima until August 1797, when he was transferred to San Miguel and there toiled among the natives until his death on August 29th, 1824, after a painful illness resulting from a dropsical disease of the chest. His remains were buried in the church on August 30th, on the Gospel side of the main altar, by the side of Fr. Ciprés. Fr. Juan Martin may be regarded as the founder of San Miguel to the advancement of whose interests he gave all his energy. He acquired a thorough knowledge of the native language, and was regarded by his superiors as the right man in the right place. Fr. Martin has left a diary of his visit to the gentile Tulares Indians in 1804. In 1818 and again in 1821 he accompanied the Fr. Prefect as secretary on a tour of inspection to the different missions. Fr. Uría, who recorded his death, certified to his exemplary devotion and conformity to the divine will in his last days and hours.

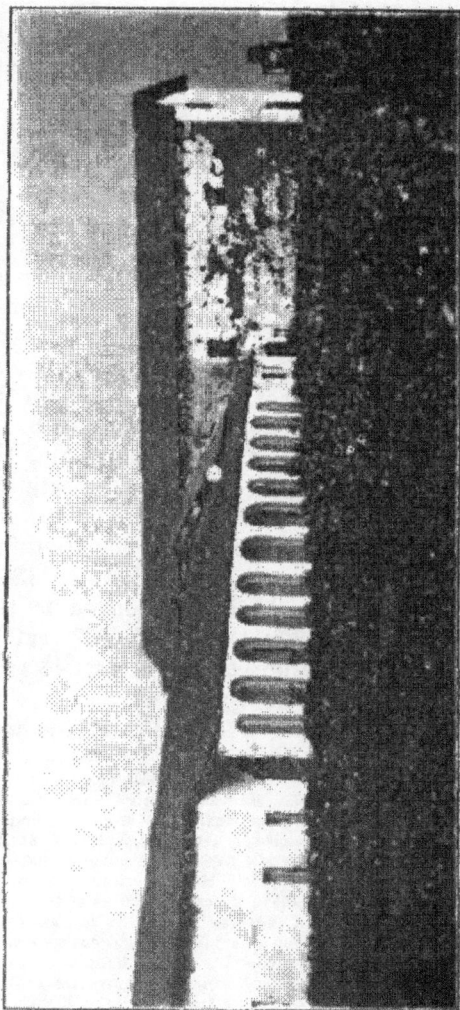

Mission San Miguel.

Fr. Juan Cabot remained at his post until his departure for Mexico in 1885, when he was succeeded by Fr. Juan Moreno until after 1840. Fr. Arroyo de la Cuesta of San Luis spent much of his time here in 1883-85; likewise Fr. Abella in 1839-40.

As early as 1831 Gov. Echeandía's secularization scheme was to be tried at San Miguel. José Castro went to the mission, where he read the decree and made a speech to the assembled neophytes. After listening to the speaker, the Indians expressed a very decided preference for the missionary Father and the old system. The mission was nevertheless confiscated in 1836, Ignacio Coronel acting as comisionado. The inventory on March 1887 showed a valuation, not including church property, of $82,000, which in the middle of 1839 was reduced to $75,000. In 1838 Fr. Moreno complained bitterly of his poverty and the disappearance of the mission property. As late as 1839 the Indians declared to Hartnell, the government inspector, that they wished to have no administrator, but desired to be left with the Father. In 1839 three hundred and sixty one Indians belonged to the mission. At the same time it owned 900 cattle, 249 horses, 3,600 sheep, 80 mules and asses, 46 goats, 44 swine, and 700 bushels of grain (4)

THE statistics for the whole period of the mission's

(4) Banc., III, 307: 683-645.   Fr. Juan Cabot was born at Buñola Isle of Mallorca, in June 1781. He was admitted into the Franciscan Order at Palma in 1796, arrived at Mexico in 1804, and first saw California in 1805. Fr. Juan served at Purisima in 1805-06, at San Miguel in 1807-19, at San Francisco in 1819 to 20, at Soledad in 1821-24, and again at San Miguel from 1824 to 1835. His superiors regarded him as a very zealous missionary. Robinson describes him as a tall, robust man, with the rough frankness of a sailor, colebrated for his good humor and hospitality. Indeed he was known as "el marinero" in contrast with his dignified brother Pedro, "el caballero." In 1814 he made a tour among the gentile tribes of the Tulares, of which the narrative still exists. In 1820-21 he acted as secretary to Fr. Prefect Payeras on his tour of inspection; and in 1826 he refused the oath of allegiance to the Republic of Mexico. According to an article in the San Francisco Bulletin of April 25th, 1864, Fr. Juan Cabot was heard of in Spain by Bishop Amat in 1856, but died a little later.

existence 1797 to 1884, are as follows: Total of baptisms, 2,588, of which 1,285 were those of adult Indians, 1,277 Indian children, and 26 children de razon; an annual average of 67. Total of deaths, 2,038, of which 1,225 were Indian adults, 796 Indian children, and 6 adults and 11 children de razon; an annual average of 58. The largest population ever reached, 1,076, was in 1814. The largest number of cattle owned by the mission at any one time, 10,558, was in 1822; horses, 1,560 in 1822; mules, 140 in 1817; sheep, 14,000 in 1820; goats, 66 in 1884; swine, 245 in 1818; asses, 59 in 1818; all kinds of animals, 24,808 in 1822. The total product of wheat was 72,544 bushels; barley, 9,627 bushels; corn, 6,417 bushels; beans, 646 bushels; and miscellaneous grains, 1,844 bushels. The Informes Generales have the following figures for 1797 to December 81st, 1831: Baptisms, 2,459; deaths, 1,806; marriages, 751. (5)

Fr. Juan Moreno remained in charge of Mission San Miguel until 1842, after which date the establishment was under the spiritual care of the Rev. Miguel Gomez of San Luis Obispo. When Inocente Garcia's administratorship came to an end does not appear. He says that for a long time he did his best to preserve order; but finally reported to Governor Alvarado his inability to control the Indians, and was told to "turn the mission upside down, or to do what he pleased with it," whereupon he gave up the church to the priest in charge, and all property to the Indians. In 1844 the vineyard was restored for the support of the church. In 1845 all property had disappeared, except the buildings, valued at $5,800, which were ordered to be sold at auction. The sale was executed by Governor Pico on July 4th, 1846. P. Rios and Wm. Reed purchased the property, but their title was declared invalid later on by the courts. Many

(5) Bancroft, III, 683-686; Informes Generales, 1831.

of the Indians ran off to the Tulares to join the gentiles, when there were no more cattle to eat. There were about thirty Indians still at the mission in 1841-42. (6)

CHAPTER XXII.

SAN FERNANDO.

"ACHOIS COMIHAVIT"—FOUNDING OF THE MISSION—MISSION SUCCESS—CONTRIBUTIONS—CHURCH BLESSED—FR. PEDRO MUÑOZ RETIRES—DEATHS OF FATHERS LASARO AND LANDAETA—FR. JOSÉ ANTONIO URIA RETIRES—DEATH OF FR. UFRESTI—OTHER MISSIONARIES—EARTHQUAKE—DEATH OF FR. ULIBARRI—FR. IBARRA'S COMPLAINT—MISSION LANDS—DEATH OF FR. PEDRO CABOT—INVENTORY—STATISTICS—FR. BLAS ORDAS MANAGER OF THE PROPERTY—SALE OF THE MISSION—LAST MISSIONARY.

IN order to establish a complete chain of missions from San Diego north, one necessarily had to be placed between San Buenaventura and San Gabriel. A fine rancho, known as Reyes' rancho, and called by the natives "Achois Comihavit," met the approval of the Fathers as a suitable site. Fr. Superior Lasuen had gone down from San Miguel to Santa Barbara, whence he started at the end of August with an escort. On the 8th, of September 1797 assisted by Fr. Francisco Dumetz, and in the presence of the troops and a large number of natives, performed the usual ceremonies, and dedicated the new mission to San Fernando Rey de España, as required by instructions from Mexico. Fr. Francisco Javier Uría became the associate of Fr. Dumetz, and both labored here until after 1800. Ten children were baptized the first

---

(6) Bancroft IV, 630-60); V, 561; 639.

day, and thirteen adults were added to the list early
in October. There were 55 neophytes at the end of
1797, and 310 at the end of 1800, baptisms by that
time having amounted to 352, while 70 deaths occurred. The first marriage took place on October 8th,
1797.

THE number of cattle, mules, and horses was 526;
and that of sheep 600. The products of the soil in
1800 amounted to about 1,000 bushels, and the total
yield for three years was 4,700 bushels. The contributions for this mission, at its foundation, from Santa
Barbara, San Buenaventura, San Gabriel, and San
Juan Capistrano, were 18 mules, 46 horses, 16 yoke
of oxen, 310 cattle, and 508 sheep. (1)

AN adobe church with tile roof was blessed in December 1806. Fr. Dumetz left the mission in April
1802, though he was back for a time in 1804-05. Fr.
Francisco Javier Uría, the other founder of the mission, left the country in 1805; but subsequently re
turned to California, though not to this mission. In
1805 there came Fr. Nicolás Lázaro and Fr. José
Maria Zalvidea; the latter was transferred to San
Gabriel in 1806, while the former died at San Diego
in August 1807.

FATHERS José Antonio Uría and Pedro Muñoz arrived here in 1807. The former retired in November
1808. Fr. Martin de Landaeta succeeded him, but
died in 1816. Meanwhile Fr. José Antonio Urresti had
arrived in 1809, and became the associate of Fr.
Muñoz.

THE neophytes during the first decade of the centu
ry increased threefold, from 310 to 955, whilst deaths
were but little more than half the baptisms. 1,468
persons were baptized, 301 in 1803 being the largest
number in any one year. Seven hundred and ninety-
seven persons died during the same period. In 1804

Mission San Fernando.

there was some controversy about lands; the Fathers protested successfully against the granting of the Camulos Rancho to Francisco Avila. (2)

Fr. Pedro Muñoz left California in 1817, and Fr. Urresti died in 1812. Fr. Urresti was succeeded by Fr. Joaquin Pascual Nuez in 1812-14, and Fr. Vincente Pascual Oliva was stationed here in 1814-15. Fr. Marcos Antonio de Vitoria took Fr. Muñoz place from 1818-20. Fr. Ramon Ulibarri came in January, and Fr. Francisco Gonzalez de Ibarra in October 1820. From 1815-20, it seems but one missionary was stationed at San Fernando.

THE earthquake of December 21st, 1812, did no further damage than to necessitate the introduction of thirty new beams to support the church wall. Before 1818 a new chapel was completed. San Fernando gained slightly in population during the whole period of 1810-20; but reached its highest figure, 1,080, in 1819, and then its decline began. (8)

---

(2) Banc., II, 115-116. Fr. Lázaro, a native of Burgos, Spain, arrived in California on August 31st, 1803, and served at San Fernando from September of that year until June 1807. He went down to San Diego, hoping that a change of climate might benefit his health, but he lived only two months, and died on August 18th. He was buried in the San Diego church.

Fr. José Antonio Uria came to Monterey on July 28th, 1799. He was stationed at San José from August of that year until July 1806; at Santa Cruz in 1806-7; and at San'Fernando until November 1808. In November 1809 he wrote from Mexico that he was in good health and hoped to remain attached to his college.

Fr. Landaeta came to California in 1791, and, after a short sickness at San Luis Obispo, was assigned to San Francisco where he remained until 1795, when sickness compelled him to retire to Mexico. Recovering his health he returned to California in 1800, and again labored at San Francisco until the end of 1807. In January 1808 he was transferred to San Fernando, where he passed to a better life in 1810. (8) Banc., II, 357-358.

(3) Bancroft II, 357-358. Fr. José Antonio Urresti had come to California in August 1804 and was stationed at San Gabriel till September 1806, when he was transfered to Santa Barbara, where he remained until August 1809, after which date he came to San Fernando and labored there among the Indians until his death on January 5th, 1812.

Fr. Pedro Muñoz was born at Puerto de Baños, Estremadura, Spain, on July 19th, 1778, and became a Franciscan on June 10th, 1793. He sailed from Cádis on June 10th 1808, and arrived at the college of San Fernando on September 9th. After coming to California in 1804, he was

Fr. Francisco Gonzalez de Ibarra was stationed here alone, it seems, from 1821, in which year Fr. Ulibarri died.

Fr. Ibarra complained that the soldiers of his guard behaved badly, and caused much ruin by selling liquor and lending horses to the Indians. In 1825 he declared that the presidio was a curse rather than a help to the mission, that the soldiers should go to work and raise grain, and not live on the toil of the Indians, whom they robbed and deceived with talk of liberty while in reality they treated them as slaves. This brought out a sharp reply from Captain Guerra, who advised the fearless Father to modify his tone, or he might suffer from it. The amount of supplies furnished by this mission to the presidio from 1822 to April 1827 was $21,203.

The mission lands at this time extended ten leagues east to west from Tajunga Mountains to Ataguama Mountains; and five leagues north to south from ranchos San Francisco de la Mision and Simí toward San Gabriel and Sanja. (4)

Fr. Ibarra continued his labors at San Fernando alone until the middle of 1835, when he retired for a time to Mexico. His successor was Fr. Pedro Cabot

stationed at San Miguel from October 1804 to July 1807; and at San Fernando till November 1817. He was also at San Francisco temporarily for six months in 1808. Fr. Muñoz made several expeditions into the interior, the most important being that with Lieutenant Moraga in 1806 into the Tulares Valley, of which he left a diary. He retired on account of ill-health.

(4) Bancroft II, 569-570. Fr. Francisco Roman Fernandez de Ullbarri was born February 29th 1773, at All, near Vitoria; Spain. He received the Franciscan habit in 1794 at Victoria, sailed from Cádiz June 20th, 1813, and arrived at San Fernando College on September 9th. Here he worked with some interruption on account of broken health for about five years, when he volunteered for California. He arrived at Monterey on June 22d, 1809. His health was better in the new field, and he was stationed at San Juan Bautista till 1815, at Santa Inéz till 1819. He was at Purisima temporarily in 1818-19, and at San Fernando till 1821. His disease was hemorrhage of the lungs with which he nearly died in February 1821. He was then urged to go to San Gabriel, but refused. He must have changed his mind later for he died and was buried at San Gabriel on June 16th.

from San Antonio, who was statiened here until his death in October 1886. (5)

From this date till August, 1838, there is no mention of a missionary at San Fernando, but Fr. Ibarra may possibly have been here. Then came Fr. Blas Ordaz, who remained during the rest of the decade. Down to 1834 the decrease in neophyte population was less than 100; in live-stock there was no falling off whatever; and the crops were good. At the end of the period, 1840, there were still about 400 Indians in the secularized community. The mission was confiscated early. In October 1834 Antonio del Valle as comisionado took charge of the mission estates by inventory from Fr. Ibarra. San Fernando was to be a parish of the second class with $1,000 salary. Fr. Ibarra delivered to the comisionado $20,000 in hides, tallow, etc., and $5,000 in coin. The inventory in 1835 showed a valuation of $41,714. The church was 40x6 varas or yards, tile-roofed, had a board ceiling, a brick floor, adobe walls, three doors, and seven windows with wooden bars. The sacristy was eight varas square, with one door and window. There were other buildings valued at $15,511; 32,000 vines worth $10,000; 1,000 fruit trees valued at $2,400; a library of 191 volumes worth $417; and credits $5,786. The population from 1830-1834 decreased to 702. There were 89 persons baptized, and 124 burials took place. Large stock remained at 6,000 head, while horses and mules decreased to 520; but sheep still numbered

(5) Banc., III, 645-646. He was the brother of Fr. Juan Cabot, and was born at Buñola, Mallorca, on September 9th, 1777. He was admitted into the Franciscan Order on December 22d, 1796; came to Mexico in 1803; and to California in 1804. His missionary service was at San Antonio in 1804-28; at Soledad in 1828-29; again at San Antonio in 1829-34; and at San Fernando finally in 1835 and 36. Fr. Pedro was known as a dignified, scholarly, courteous man who was known as "El Caballero" in contradistinction to his rougher brother Fr. Juan, called "El Marinero," but he was hardly less popular than his brother. He gave much attention to the language of the neophytes. In 1825-29 he refused to take the oath of allegiance to the republic of Mexico. His remains were interred in the mission cemetery on October 12th by Fr. Ibarra.

8,000 head. The average crop was 1,580 bushels, of which 940 were wheat, 470 corn, and 45 beans.

DURING the whole period of the mission's existence 2,889 persons were baptized, of whom 1,415 were Indian adults, 1,367 Indian children, and 57 children de razon; an annual average of 74. Deaths numbered 2,028, of which 1,036 were Indian adults, 965 Indian children, and 12 adults and 15 children de razon; an annual average of 51. During the same period 848 marriages took place, of which 15 were de razon. The largest number of cattle owned by the mission in one year was 12,800 in 1810; horses, 1,320 in 1822; mules, 840 in 1812; sheep, 7,800 in 1819; goats, 600 in 1816; swine 250 in 1814; and all kinds of animals, 21,745 in 1810. The total product of wheat was 119,000 bushels; barley, 8,070 bushels; corn, 27,750 bushels; and beans, 3,624 bushels. According to the Informes Generales, from 1797 to December 31st, 1831, as many as 2,768 baptisms took place, 1,313 marriages were blessed, and 1,938 deaths occurred.

THE inventory of the property in 1840 showed 4,130 cattle, 2,637 horses, 2,500 sheep, 60 mules, 33 asses, 30 hogs (6)

FR. Blas Ordaz managed the estate after its restoration to the Fathers in 1843. There were probably 800 Indians about the mission at that time. In May 1845 Fr. Ordaz showed that the mission had prospered under his short magement. He had paid off all the debts, and purchased 120 head of live-stock, besides making other improvements. Nevertheless, the mission was taken out of his hands by Gov. Pico and leased to Andrés Pico and Juan Manso in December 1845 at an annual rental of $1,120. (7)

FINALLY, on June 17th, 1846, Governor Pico sold the mission to Eulogio de Célis for $14,000. Celis was bound to support the missionary and provide the ne-

(6) Bancroft III. 645-648.   (7) Bancroft IV. 552; 633.

cessaries for divine worship, and also to give the Indians the use of the lands they occupied during their life-time. Fr. Blas was still here at the time, and he remained until May 1847, the last of the Franciscans. He died at San Gabriel in 1850. (8)

CHAPTER XXIII.

SAN LUIS REY.

EXPLORATION FOR A MISSION SITE—MISSION ESTABLISHED—SUCCESS—FR. PETRI—NEW CHURCH—VARIOUS MISSIONARIES—FATHERS GARCIA AND CARRANZA RETIRE—STATISTICAL—SAN ANTONIO DE PALA—A HOSPITAL—MISSIONARY CHANGES—SURPRISE OF FF. PETRI—PROSPERITY—EXAGGERATION—WHITE POPULATION—FR. PETRI RETIRES—HIS BIOGRAPHY—OTHER MISSIONARIES—STATISTICS—SECULARIZATION—INVENTORY—DEATH OF FR. IBARRA—BIOGRAPHY—LAST MISSIONARY—DEATH OF FR. ZALVIDEA—BIOGRAPHY—SALE OF THE MISSION—MODERN SAN LUIS REY—FREEMASONRY—A NOVITIATE FOR MEXICO—RE-DEDICATION—RECEPTION OF NOVICES—THE COMMUNITY A PRESENT.

IN October 1797 a new exploration was made of the district between San Juan Capistrano and San Diego by Fathers Lasuen and Santiago from San Juan in company of 8 soldiers and five Indians. During December there was a correspondence between Governor Borica and Fr. Superior Lasuen on the subject of the new mission, from which it appears that the large number of docile natives was the chief inducement to found a mission in this region, but that agricultural and other advantages were believed to be lacking.

THE governor issued orders on February 27th, 1798, to the commandant of San Diego, who was to furnish

---

(8) Banc., V, 629. History of the Native Races, p. 675.
The "Our Father" in the language of the Kizh at San Fernando runs thus: "Y yorac yona taray tucúpuma sagoucó motoanian majarmi mom main mono muismi miojor yiact cou r. Panyyogin gimiimorin, majarmi mifoma coyó ogarná yio mamainay mii, yiarmá ogonug y yoná y yo ocaneu coiharnea main ytomo mojag colyamá huermi. Parima.

a guard and to require from the soldiers personal labor in erecting the necessary buildings, without murmuring at site or work, and with implicit obedience to Fr. Lasuen. Nothing seems to have been done, however, until the 13th of June. On that date Fr. Lasuen in the presence of the guard, a few neophytes from San Juan Capistrano and a multitude of gen· tiles, and assisted by Fathers Santiago and Peyri, founded the new mission amid the usual ceremonies, at the spot called by the natives Tacayme, and by the Spaniards in the first expedition of 1769 San Juan Capistrano, or later Capistrano el Viejo. The new mission was placed under the patronage of San Luis, Rey de Francia, to distinguish it from San Luis Obispo. The baptizing of fifty-four children imparted an especial solemnity to the day.

THE mission prospered from the first. In a week Fr. Antonio Peyri, the energetic founder, had seventy-seven baptized children, besides twenty-three catechumens who were under instruction. By the first of July he had six thousand adobes made for the mission buildings. In July he was joined by Fr. José Faura, who was succeded in the autumn of 1800 by Fr. José García. Fr. José Panella, too, was assigned to this mission, and served for a short time in 1798, during the absence of one of the missionaries who had gone to San Juan Capistrano for his health. Fr. Panella made himself disliked, however, and Fr. Lasuen was compelled to recall the other Father, perhaps Fr. Peyri, who was greatly beloved.

IN 1798 two hundred and fourteen persons were baptized, and before the end of 1800 there were 337 neophytes. Since the founding of the mission baptisms numbered 371, and deaths 56. There were 617 horses, mules, and cattle in 1800, besides 1,600 head of sheep; the products of the soil amounted to 2,000 bushels of wheat, 120 bushels barley, and six bushels of maize; the latter was just the amount sown, while eight bushels of beans produced nothing.

FR. Peyri continued to direct San Luis Rey during the first decade of the 19th century. He was very popular; and, being possessed of wonderful administrative abilities and consuming zeal, he reared the grandest adobe edifice that was ever dedicated in Alta California to the glory of God. He completed the structure in 1802. His companion was Fr José García who left California in 1808. Fr. Domingo Carranza succeeded Fr. García, but he, too, retired late in 1810. FR. Tapis now came to San Luis Rey to aid Fr. Peyri for a time.

UNDER these various shepherds the neophyte flock increased from 337 in 1800 to 1,519 in 1810, a larger gain than that of any other mission, with by far the lowest death rate, 28 per cent. In population San Luis Rey was now second only to San Diego, in cattle third on the list; and on a tie with San Gabriel in agriculture; its best crop was exceeded only by that of San Fernando. One thousand four hundred and fifty one persons received baptism during the decade, the highest number in one year, 432, being in 1810. Deaths numbered only 411. Large stock gained from 619 to 10,576; small stock increased from 1,000 to 9,710 head; and horses in 1810 numbered 776. The average yield of grain was 5,250 bushels, though in 1808 as many as 10,875 bushels were raised. (1)

DURING the second decade Fr. Peyri still toiled on,

(1) Banc., I, 562-64; II, 107-108; 'Old Missions" p. 97-98. Fr. Domingo had arrived at Santa Barbara from Mexico on May 7th, 1798, with seven companions. He was then stationed at Santa Cruz from November 1798 till August 1808, when he was transferred to San Luis Rey, and remained there until late in 1810, having served his term and longer. he retired, but on his way to Mexico he fell into the hands of the rebels at San Blas. By them he is said to have been condemned to death, though the sentence was never executed.

Fr. José García had been assigned to California on February 3d, 1800, and arrived at Monterey in August of the same year. His only regular station was San Luis Rey, where he resided from 1800 to 1808 when he was allowed to retire on account of impaired health.

San Antonio at Pala.

but with frequent changes of companions. Fr. Estévan Tapis served in 1811, Fr. Geromino Boscana in
1812-18, Fr. Francisco Suñer in 1814-16, Fr. Ramon
Olbés in 1816-18, and Fr. Jaime Escudé from 1818.
The mission was now by far the most populous in
the province, with a death-rate of only forty-four
per cent of the baptisms and twenty-four per cent of
the total population. In agriculture, but not in live-
stock, except horses, San Luis Rey stood at the head.
In 1817 so many sheep died that the Fathers had to
go north as far as San Juan Bautista for wool to
clothe their neophytes.

In 1810 Fr. Peyri founded a branch establishment
under the invocation of San Antonio at Pala, six
or seven leagues from San Luis Rey. A chapel was
built, and one of the Fathers was generally stationed
there. Within a year or two about a thousand converts were gathered to meet for Christian instruction
and till the soil at Pala. San Luis Rey also had a
hospital where every effort was made to stay the ravages of syphilis and dysentery among the neophytes;
in the hospital was a special chapel and altar. (2)

THE mission was still under the care of its venerable and energetic founder, Fr. Antonio Peyri, during
the whole of the next decade. Fr. Jaime Escudé remained as associate until the end of 1821; Fr. José
Joaquin Jimeno, a new-comer, served from 1827 to
1830; and Fr. José Barona also lived here in retirement in the infirmity of old age after 1827. Peyri
was, unlike most of the Fathers, an enthusiastic
friend of the Mexican republic after it was established, and he took the oath of allegiance. His companions, however, were not disappointed at the proceedings of the new government, but Fr. Peyri was
so surprised and offended at the law of expulsion in
1829 that he tried unsuccessfully to obtain a passport.

(2) Bancroft II, 346-347.

In every element of material prosperity San Luis Rey was now far in advance of any other mission. There is no record that a new church was built, as had been proposed in 1811, but the church and other buildings, the same now standing in ruins to a great extent, were the largest and in some respects the finest in California. San Luis alone of the old missions, except San Juan Bautista, gained in population; baptisms outnumbered the deaths, but it had reached its maxium of 2,869 ncophytes in 1826, and then started on its decline, though herds and flocks had doubled in ten years. Sheep had reached the highest number of 28,600 in 1828, but cattle were still increasing, though the figures have been grossly exaggerated in current newspaper reports. One writer, Taylor, speaks of 80,000 head of cattle, 4,000 horses, and 70,000 sheep! There are many similar exaggerations afloat concerning the old missions and missionaries. The average crop of grain, 12,660 bushels, was nowhere surpassed, though both San Diego and San Gabriel produced larger single crops.

The white population in 1828 was 35. The mission lands in 1822 extended eleven leagues from north to south, and 15 leagues from east to west, besides a rancho 15 leagues off in the northeast. Squirrels, locusts, and crows were very troublesome at times, and the soil rather sterile; but the branch establishment of San Antonio at Pala, seven leagues northeast of San Luis Rey, was still in a flourishing condition. (3)

Fr. Antonio Peyri at the end of 1881 left San Luis Rey, the mission which he had founded and in thirty three years of faithful service had brought to the front rank of the California establishments. He quit the country in company with the exiled Gov. Victoria. Fr. Peyri was unwilling to remain and witness the overthrow of all his plans, and therefore tore himself

(3) Bancroft II, 553-555.

from his beloved mission to return to his mother country. (4)

Fr. José Antonio Anzar, a new comer, succeeded Fr. Peyri in 1832. Fr. Buenaventura Fortuni was stationed at San Luis Rey 1833-36; but for 1837-1839 there is no record, except of Fathers Oliva and Abel-la as visiting missionaries. In July 1839 Fr. Francisco Gonzalez de Ibarra took charge.

San Luis Rey was the only mission that showed a gain in population for 1830-34, and at the end of that period, with 2,844 neophytes on the register, it stood at the head of the list; but also in the number of its live-stock it surpassed all the missions. Baptisms even during this short time amounted to 885, whilst there were 101 marriages, and 824 deaths.

During the existence of the mission, 1798 to 1834, the total number of baptisms was 5,561, of which 3,

(4) Fr. Antonio Peyri was born on January 10th, 1765 or perhaps 1769, at Porera, Catalonia, Spain, and received the habit of St. Francis in the convent at Reus on October 25th, 1787. He sailed from Cádiz on May 8th, 1796 and left the college of San Fernando for California on March 1st, 1796, arriving in July. He was first stationed at San Luis Obispo for two years and in 1798 was one of the founders of San Luis Rey, where, and at the branch establishment of San Antonio de Pala, he labored continuously thereafter. Fr. Peyri was less unfriendly to the Mexican republic than most of the Spanish friars, and he took the required oath in 1826; but in the same year he petitioned the president of Mexico to relieve him of the administration of the mission, In 1820, moreover, he demanded his passports, being as a Spaniard included in the expulsion law of March 20th, and though exemption was offered to him, he insisted, asserting that he was an old man no longer fit for service. He thereupon obtained permission from the Mexican authorities to retire with full payment of the past stipends, amounting to $3,000. Fr. Antonio sailed from San Diego for Mazatlan on his way to Mexico on January 17th, 1832. The tradition is that he had to leave San Luis Rey secretly lest the neophytes should stop him, and that his Indians, 500 strong, hastened to San Diego to prevent his departure, but they arrived only in time to receive his blessing from the receding ship. One of the Indians who aided the departing missionary relates that as his last act Fr. Peyri knelt on the hill and prayed for the mission. He left Mexico in February 1834, and by way of New York and France reached Barcelona in June. Instead of the tranquillity he had expected for his old age, he found only turmoil and strife. It was not even safe to visit his native town. He bitterly regretted having left California, and confessed it was a mistake. He had brought from California two young neophytes, Pablo and Agapito, whom he placed in the Propaganda College at Rome. One of them is said to have become a priest, but nothing definite is known. Bancroft III, 621-622.

580 were those of Indian adults 1,562 Indian children,
and 192 children de gente de razon; an annual average of 151. The total number of marriages was 1,425,
of which 9 were de razon. Deaths numbered 2,859, of
which 1,445 were of Indian adults, 1,367 Indian children, and 12 adults and 85 children de razon. The
largest Indian population at San Luis Rey at any
time 2,869 was in 1826. There were generally from 20
to 50 persons de razon or settlers living at the mission. The largest number of cattle ever possessed by
the mission, 27. 500, was in 1832; largest number of
horses, 2,226 in 1828; mules, 845 in 1828; sheep, 28,
913 in 1828: goats, 1,300 in 1832; swine, 272 in 1819;
and all kinds of animals, 58,767 in 1828. The total
product of wheat amounted to 114,528 bushels; barley, 94,600 bushels; corn, 101,442 bushels; and beans,
10,215 bushels.(5)

SECULARIZATION began here as at San Diego with
Governor Figueroa's experimental "emancipation" in
1833, which resulted in the forming of an Indian
pueblo at Las Flores, with but a small population.
The final confiscation was accomplished in November
1834 by Captian Portilla as comisionado. According
to the accounts rendered by Father Fortuni to Portilla in 1834, the assets were $46,613, and the debts
$14,429. The inventory taken August 22d, 1835,
showed a valuation of $203,737, and a debt of $93,-
000. The church 64x10 varas, or yards, of adobes,
tile-roofed, floor of clay, board ceiling, 9 doors, 18
windows, 4 adjoining rooms, all valued at $30,000,
was included in the total amount, as were also the 6
ranchos valued at $40,437, the most valuable being
Pala, Santa Margarita, and San Jacinto. After the
secularization the decline in Indian population was
more rapid than in wealth, the Indians succeeding

(5) Bancroft III, 621-625. The "Informes Generales" report the following figures for the period 1798 to December 31st, 1831: Baptisms, 5,298; mar-riages, 1,301; deaths, 2,585.

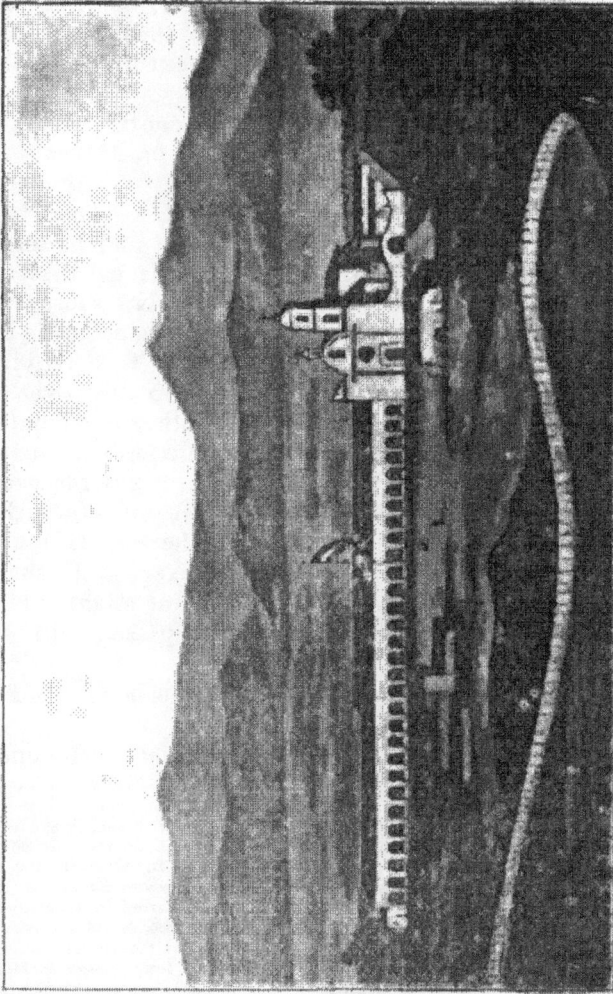

San Luis Rey In Early Days.

in retaining partial control of the mission ranchos of
Santa Margarita, San Antonio de Pala, Santa Isabel,
Temecula, and San Jacinto down to 1840, or perhaps
a little later, In 1840 there were about 1,000 Indians
left at the mission and ranchos. (6)

Fr. Francisco Gonzalez de Ibarra continued to labor at San Luis Rey until his death in 1842 at the
age of sixty years.

AFTER Fr. Ibarra's death Fr. Zalvidea came from
San Juan Capistrano to take his place, and he served
until 1846. The mission had 650 Indians in 1842 and
400 in 1844; but the establishment at Las Flores was
included in both cases. José A. Estudillo acted as majordomo until April 1843, when he was required
under Governor Micheltorena's order to turn over the
property to Fr. Zalvidea; but the Father immediately
put everything in charge of a new majordomo in the
person of Joaquin Ortega, who in turn was succeeded
by Juan M. Marron in July 1845. The inventory then
showed the following property: 279 horses, 20 mules,
61 asses, 196 cattle, 27 yoke of oxen, 700 sheep,
some implements, and other effects of slight value.
Meanwhile all the mission ranchos passed into private ownership. (7)

Fr. Zalvidea, the senior of the little band of Fernandinos, died early in 1846.

MISSION San Luis Rey had no resident missionary

---

(6) Bancroft III, 621-625.
(7) Bancroft IV, 622-624. Fr. Ibarra was a native of Viana, Spain, where
he was born in 1782. He became a Franciscan in the province of Burgos,
and arrived in California by way of Mexico in 1820. After visiting San
Luis Obispo he was stationed at San Fernando, where he served from
1820 to 1835, when he retired to Mexico, but he returned in time to perform the burial service for Fr. Cabot in October 1836. Nothing further is
known of Fr. Ibarra till 1839, from which date he resided at San Luis
Rey until his sudden death in 1842 resulting from apoplexy. Mofras
speaks of the deplorable condition of this Father whom he saw forced to
sit at the administrator's table and listen to the ribaldry of majordomos
and vaqueros who would have thought themselves lucky a few years before to be the Father's servants. He was well liked by the Indians at San
Luis Rey, and was called by them Tequodeuma, indicating a plain, un-
assuming man.

after Fr. Zalvidea's death, except perhaps Fr. Vincente Pascual Oliva for a short time after August. 25th, 1846. The San Luis estate was sold by the governor on May 18th, to José A. Cot and José a Pico for $2,437; but their agent was dispossessed by Gen. Fremont, and they failed to regain possession. Some doubts were expressed, then and later, about genuineness of the sale; but the title was finally rejected on the ground that the governor had no power to sell the missions. A garrison of Mormon soldiers held the place during the greater part of 1847; and from August of that year Captain Hunter as Indian sub-agent for the south took charge of the mission. He was succeeded temporarily by William Williams at the end of 184?. Hunter found a considerable number of Indians remaining about the mission. (8)

---

(8) Bancroft V, 620-623. Fr. José María de Zalvidea was born at Bilbao, Vizcaya, Spain, on March 2d, 1780. He received the habit of St. Francis on December 13th, 1798, and came to the college of San Fernando, Mexico, in September 1804. He arrived in California in August 1805, and was stationed successively at San Fernando in 1805-6, at San Gabriel in 1806-26, at San Juan Capistrano in 1826-42, and at San Luis Rey in 1842-1846. From the first he was regarded by his superiors as one of the best or most zealous of the Fathers, as priest, teacher, and manager of temporalities. Fr. Zalvidea's great field of labor was at San San Gabriel, where he toiled incessantly for twenty years, and with the greatest success, to build up the temporal interests of the mission, but he never thereby neglected spiritual affairs. "He was doubtless in those days a model missionary, says Bancroft, and then and later was regarded by the common people as a saint." He gave much attention to viticulture at San Gabriel, being the first to introduce this industry on a large scale. He wrote a diary of an exploration in 1806, and in 1827 a petition in behalf of the Indians.

In political controversies he took no part; but in 1829 he expressed his willingness to swear allegiance to the Mexican republic so far as was consistent with his state of life. In 1833 he declined a passport to retire, on the ground that there was none to take his place. Fr. Zalvidea was well versed in the native tongue in which he was accustomed to preach at San Gabriel. There is no evidence that he ever had an enemy, or said an unkind word of any man. He refused to quit San Luis Rey, where he believed his services to be needed; but finally it was thought best to remove him to San Juan. A cart was prepared with all possible conveniences, by advice of Fr. Oliva and Apollinaria Lorenzana, who had nursed him for some days. The night before his journey was to be made Fr. Zalvidea died. He was buried in the mission church at the left side of the altar. The date is not known, but it was apparently early in 1846.

Thus ends the history of the most beautiful of all
the California missions, San Luis Rey, as an Indian
mission. It is still in a splendid state of preservation,
but each year stamped its work of destruction upon
it. For over half a century the magnificent structure
has stood mournfully awaiting its inevitable destruction. But behold a friendly hand has at last been
extended in its behalf; and ere long, please God,
San Luis Rey de Francia will be restored to its former beauty, though not to former activity, a living
monument to the noblest band of men that have
graced the pages of modern history. The Indians have
nearly all disappeared; but the sacred edifice has
again be devoted to sacred purposes in our day. (9)

FREEMASONRY, ever the implacable enemy of religious Orders, in which it recognizes its strongest foe,
has made community life in Mexico impossible. Not
contented with having closed up the convents and
monasteries of the first and foremost civilizers of
that land, the anti-Christian sect has determined to
exterminate relgious Orders by forbidding them to
accept recruits to fill up the decimated ranks. There
is a desire for perfection, however, among souls lov-
ing God, and what the liberty-hating Freemason
government of Mexico denies, that the sons of St.
Francis find in the free republic of the United
States. To prevent the Order from dying out in Mexico, the authorities decided to move the novitiate for
the Mexican Fathers to the United States. A house
had been planned for Texas at one time, but finally
San Luis Rey was chosen. Accordingly, through the
intercession of Rt. Rev. Bishop Mora of Los Angeles,

(9) The "Our Father" in the language of the Ketchi about San Luis Rey
is as follows according to Mofras:
"Cham na cham mig tu panga auc onan Moqula cham to gai ha oua che
nag on roina li vi biche ca noc yba heg ga y vi au qui ga to panga.
Cham na cholone mim cha pan pituo mag na jan pohi cala cai gui cha
me halloto gai tom chame, o gui chag cay ne che cal me tus so lli olo
salme alla linoe chame cham cho sivo."

permission was obtained from Rome to establish a novitiate at this mission for the Franciscans of Mexico.

THE old buildings in part have been rendered habitable, and on May 12th, 1893, the ceremonies of re-dedication took place. By ten o'clock fully 300 interested spectators gathered in the church. At that hour Rt. Rev. Francis Mora, Bishop of Monterey and Los Angeles Very Rev. Joaquin Adam, vicar general of the diocese, Very Rev. Louis J. Meier, superior of the Lazarist College, Los Angeles; and Rev. W. L. Dye, secretary to the bishop, entered through the the wide doors of the church. Three wrinkled old Indian women crouched at the doorway, looking wonderingly on the scene that brought back memories of their youth, when the mission was rich and populous.

At the doorway the bishop was received by the community of Franciscans in their somber gray habit who had come from Zacatecas, Mexico, to open a novitiate for their province. These religious were the Very Rev. Father Alba, comissary general of the Franciscan Order in Mexico; Rev. F. Ambrose Malabehar, who was to remain as superior of the covent; Fr. Tiscareno, secretary of the commissioner-general; and Fr. Martínez. The Fathers brought with them as pupils from Zacatecas three Mexican youths, Jesus de la Hos, Manuel Rizo, and Andrés Luerrerow, who all received the habit of St. Francis on that same day, December 12th,

SOLEMN High Mass was celebrated by Very Rev. T. Adam, assisted by Fathers Alba and Dye as deacon and subdecon respectively. Fr. Meier acted as master of ceremonies. After Mass followed the reading of the patent from Rome and the proclamation of the patron saints: San Luis Rey, as patron of the mission church, and Nuestra Señora de Guadalupe, as patroness of the novitiate. "Veni Creator" was then

Corridors Of San Luis Rey.

sung, whereupon the three young pupils of the Fathers knelt before the altar and were invested with the habit of the Franciscan Order. The ceremonies closed with the "Te Deum." Father O'Keefe of Santa Barbara was permitted to stay with the Mexican brethren for some time in order to acquaint them with the manners of the country, and to lend his advice in the reconstruction of the mission.

THE community at the beginning of 1897 was composed as follows: Fr. J. J. O'Keefe, superior; Fr. Raphael Hernandez, master of novices; Fr. Francisco Alvarez; Fr. José Caballero; Fr. Pedro Ocegueda; Fr. Luis Palacios; Fr. B. Aleman; six *fratres clerici*, and four lay-brothers. Fr. Alvarez is now 82 years of age, but very feeble.

CHAPTER XXIV.

SANTA INEZ.

THE MISSION SITE—FOUNDING OF THE MISSION—THE FIRST MISSIONARIES—FR. GUTIERREZ RETIRES—MISSION SUCCESS—EARTHQUAKE—NEW CHURCH—MISSIONARIES—DEATH OF FR. CALZADA—REVOLT—BUILDINGS AND LANDS. DEATHS OF FATHERS VICTORIA AND LA CUESTA—SECULARIZATION—INVENTORY—STATISTICS—DEATH OF FR. MORENO—FOUNDING OF A SEMINARY—SALE OF THE MISSION—THE COLLEGE ABANDONED—THE "OUR FATHER" IN INDIAN.

THE number of missions was increased in 1804 to nineteen by the founding of Santa Inéz. Explorations for a site in this region had begun in 1795 and were completed in 1798 by Father Tapis. The spot selected was called by the natives Alajulapa, or Majalapu, and the order of the viceroy for founding the mission was dated in February 1803. The name San-

t. Inéz, virgin and martyr, Saint Agnes in English, often written Santa Ynez or Ines, seems also to have been selected by Viceroy Iturrigaray. A sergeant and nine men having been assigned as a guard, and duly instructed by the commandant of Santa Barbara, the mission was established with the usual ceremonies on September 17th, 1804, Fr. Tapis preached on the occasion, and was assisted in the ceremonies by Fathers Ciprés, Calzada, and Gutierrez. Commandant Carrillo was present and large numbers of neophytes had come from Santa Barbara and La Purisima, some of them to remain. A beginning of mission work was made by the baptism of twenty-seven children and the enrolling of many catechumens, including three chieftains.

THE first missionaries of Santa Inéz were the Fathers José Antonio Calzada and José Romualdo Gutierrez. The latter left California in 1806. (1)

Fr. Gutierrez was succeeded by Fr. Luis Gil y Taboada. Fr. Gil's place was taken in 1810 by Fr. Francisco Javier de Uría, who had been at the mission as a supernumerary since 1808. By the end of the first year Santa Inéz had 225 neophytes, but over half of them had come already baptized from the adjoining missions.

In 1810 the number was 628; there had been 546 baptisms and 245 deaths. Live-stock in 1810 numbered 3,200 cattle, 420 horses, 61 mules, 11 asses, and 2,800 sheep. Crops varied from 900 bushels in 1807 to 4,500 bushels in 1810. In 1805, and probably later, Santa Inéz had but a poor church, though it was already roofed with tiles. In 1810 as many as 12,508

---

(1) Bancroft II, 27–29. Fr. Gutierrez had come to California probably in 1802, or according to another record, in August 1804. He served at Santa Inés from September 17th, 1804, to July 1806, when he was transferred to San Buenaventura in the hope of benefitting his health; but growing worse he obtained permission to retire, and sailed for San Blas in November.

bs of hemp were shipped to Mexico from Santa Inéz. (2)

THE earthquake of December 21st, 1812, two shocks fifteen minutes apart, brought down a corner of the church at Santa Inéz, destroyed one fourth of the now houses near the church, ruined all the mission roofs, and cracked many walls; but the Fathers did not deem the damage irreparable. In 1813 the little convent was completed, and a granary was built which temporarily served for divine worship; but in 1815 a new church was begun of adobes lined with bricks, which was dedicated on July 4th, 1817.

THE neophyte population reached its highest number of 768 souls in 1816, from which time it steadily declined. On November 10th, 1814, the first baptism of an *isleno*, or Indian from the Island of Lemu, took place; such baptisms were frequent after April 1815.

FR. Uría was in charge of Santa Inéz continuously during this period; but his associate Fr. Antonio Calzada, one of the founders of the mission, died in 1814, and there were several other changes.

FR. Ramon Olbés served here in 1812-14. Fr. Estévan Tapis was at Santa Inéz in 1813-14, Fr. Roman Fernandez de Ullibarri in 1815-19, and Fr. Antonio Catarino Rodriguez, apparently in 1820-21. (3)

FR. Uría continued here until 1824; he had worked

(2) Bancroft, II, 27-29; 180.

(3) Bancroft II, 368-369. Fr. Calzada was born in Florida on November 24th, 1760; but received the habit of St. Francis at the convent of Purísma Concepcion in Habana on February 3d, 1780. He was ordained priest in Mexico on December 18th, 1784, and arrived in California during October 1787. He was first stationed at San Gabriel from 1788 to 1792; then at Purisima until 1804, though absent in Mexico on account of ill health from August 1799 to May 1798. When Santa Inéz was founded he was transferred to the new mission in September 1804, and labored there among the Indians until a stroke of paralysis in 1813 rendered him helpless. A second stroke put an end to his life on December 2kd, 1814. His remains were interred in the church, and on July 4th, 1817, they were transferred to the new church, which had been dedicated that day, and buried outside the presbytery near the railing on the Gospel side.

alone it seems from 1821 to 1828, when Fr. Blas Ordaz arrived. After Fr. Uría's departure, Fr. Blas was alone at the mission.

In the revolt of 1824, which first broke out at this mission on Sunday February 21st, a large part of the buildings is said to have been destroyed; but there is no record of repairs or rebuilding. The soldiers defended themselves and Fr. Uría; but it does not clearly appear that anybody was killed. Early the next day Sergeant Carrillo arrived with a small force, and the hostile Indians seem to have fled to Purisima. Carrillo remained for some time at Santa Inéz, which it appears had not been abandoned.

The buildings in 1829 were similar to those of Santa Barbara. In front was a large brick enclosure used for bathing and washing; to the right were gardens and orchards; to the left were the Indian huts and tiled houses. The mission lands in 1822, between two branch ranges of the sierra, extended 7–9 leagues from north to south, and 5–13 leagues from east to west. From 1822-1827 Santa Inéz furnished $10,767 worth of supplies to the Santa Barbara presidio. (4)

Fr. Blas Ordaz continued his labors at Mission Santa Inéz till 1833, when Fr. José Joaquin Jimeno came from the north. He was assisted by Fr. Marcos Antonio Saizar de Victoria in 1835-36, and Fr. Felipe Arroyo de la Cuesta in 1836-40. Both, Fr. Victoria and Fr. Arroyo, died at this mission. (5)

(4) Bancroft II, 528; 581-582.   (5) Banc., V, 764. Ibid. III. 661-664;
Fr. Vitoria, or Victoria, was a native of the province of Alava, Spain, having been born there in 1760. He became a Franciscan in 1776, and arrived in Mexico in 1804. Reaching California in 1805 he was first stationed at Santa Barbara 1805-1806; then at San Buenaventura from 1806-17, and again 1820-1824; at San Fernando during 1818-20; at Purisima from 1824-1835, and finally at Santa Inéz in 1835-36. H's death occurred on July 25th, 1833. Fr. Victoria was a most virtuous and exemplary man, but always in feeble health, yet beloved by his neophytes.
Fr. Cuesta, who also died at Santa Inéz, was born at the villa of Cubo, Castilla la Vieja, on April 30th, 1780, and was received into the Franciscan Order on August 30, 1796, at Burgos. He sailed from Cádis

THE Indian population decreased from 408 at the end of 1830 to 344 in 1834. At the end of the decade only 180 of the 800 remaining Indians were living in community. The number of baptisms for the three years down to 1834 was 63, but death carried away 109.

THE blight of secularization fell upon the mission in 1836. The inventory taken August 1st, 1836, showed a valuation of $56,487, or $46,180 besides church property, which was valued at about $11,000. The church buildings measured 48½ by 9 varas, had walls of adobe, 4 doors and 8 windows; the sacristy was 9x6 varas with three doors, one window, a tile roof, board ceiling, and a brick floor. The ornaments were valued at $6,231, and the library of 66 volumes at $188.

HARTNEL's inventory of July 1839, mentions 9,720 cattle, 2.180 sheep, 882 horses, 82 mules, 4 asses, 50 hogs, 796 fanegas of grain, 448 arrobas of tallow, 75 arr. lard, 87 hides, 50 arr. wool, 200 arr. $30 worth of soap, etc., and a population of 183 souls. (6)

The whole number of baptisms during the existence

for Mexico on September 21, 1804, and left the college of San Fernando on December 14th, 1807, for California, where he arrived early in 1808. He was successively stationed at San Juan Bautista in 1808-33, at San Miguel in 1833-34, at San Luis Obispo in 1834-35, at Purisima in 1835-36, and at Santa Inés from 1836-40, though it was only at San Juan that his bodily infirmities permitted him to work. His superiors regarded him as a man of great merit, ability, and soul. Since 1813 he suffered almost continually from rheumatism, and he was repeatedly at the point of death. In 1809 he said the first Mass in the now church of Mission San José. In 1826, though maintaining his allegiance to the king of Spain, he took a modified oath to the now government of Mexico. Fr. Arroyo was a scholar and always a student, giving especial attention to the language of the Indians of the San Juan region of which he had already prepared a grammar before 1817. This grammar and the Father's skill in the native idiom are mentioned in Fr. Sarria's report of that year. His Grammar of the Mutsun Language and his Vocabulary or Phrase-book were published by Dr. Shea, New York, in 1861. Robinson describes him as closely confined to his room in study; when tired of reading he would call the children to play before him. Later his legs were paralysed, and he was moved about in a wheeled chair. Fr. Arroyo de la Cuesta died on September 20th, 1840, at the age of 60 years, and his body was buried on the 22d. by Fr. Jimeno in the mission church on the Gospel side near the presbytery.

(6) Arroba — 25 lbs or 32 pints liquid measure.

of the mission, 1804-1834, was 1,372, of which 566 were Indian adults, 757 Indian children, one adult and 48 children de gente de razon; an annual average of 45. The number of marriages was 409, of which 9 were de razon. Deaths amounted to 1,271, of which 730 were Indian adults, 519 Indian children, and three adults and 13 children de razon; an annual average of 42. The largest number of cattle owned by the mission in any one year was 7,300 in 1831; horses, 800 in 1816; mules, 124 in 1822; sheep, 6,000 in 1821; goats, 130 in 1818; swine, 250 in 1816; and all kinds of animals, 12,620 in 1820. The total yield of wheat was 63,250 bushels; barley, 4,024 bushels, corn, 60,850 bushels; and beans, 4,640 bushels. The Informes Generales, or official reports of the Fathers, give the following figures for the period 1804 to December 31st, 1831: Baptisms, 1,836; marriages, 300; and deaths, 1,100.

Fr. Jose Joaquin Jimeno remained in charge of Santa Inés, with Fr. Juan Moreno as associate from 1842, and Fr. Francisco de Jesus Sanchez from 1844. Fr. Juan Moreno died at the end of 1845. (7)

The leading event of the period was the foundation of the "Colegio Seminario de Maria Santisima de Guadalupe de Santa Inéz de Californias" in 1844, as recorded elsewhere. In 1843 the management of the temporalities of the mission was restored to the Fathers. The Indian population in 1845 still amounted to 270 souls, but the estate was rented in December 1845 to José Maria Covarrubias and Joaquin Carrillo

(7) Bancroft IV, 645-647. Fr. Juan Moreno was born on January 27th, 1799, at Montenegro, la Rioja, Old Castile; but became a Franciscan in Mexico. Arriving in California during the year 1827, he was stationed at Santa Barbara until 1829; at Santa Cruz in 1829-30; at San Juan Bautista in 1830-32 at San Miguel in 1833-42; and finally at Santa Inés in 1842-45, during which latter period he also had charge of Purisima, and perhaps lived there a part of the time. Very little is known about him, except that he was a quiet, patient man, well liked by all. He acted as professor in the Santa Inés seminary. His remains were buried on December 28th, 1845.

Mission Santa Inez.

for $580 per year. The mission was finally sold to
the lessees, Cavarrubias and Carrillo, for $7,000 on
June 15th, 1846, but their title later on was declared
invalid. Fr. Joaquin Jimeno continued in charge of
the mission, and was also rector of the ecclesiastical
college, an institution which, with Fr. Sanchez as
vice-rector, still maintained a precarious existence
until 1850, after which date it seems to have been
abandoned, the Fathers withdrawing to Santa Barbara. (8)

CHAPTER XXV.

SAN RAFAEL. (*)

MORTALITY AT SAN FRANCISCO—FOUNDING OF THE MISSION—SAN RAFAEL
A BRANCH OF SAN FRANCISCO—TRANSFER OF INDIANS—EXPLORATIONS—
PROGRESS—STATISTICAL—MISSION LANDS—DEATH OF FR. AMOROS—THE
ZACATECANS—STATISTICAL—FR. MERCADO SLANDERED—SECULARIZATION—
INVENTORY—SALE OF THE MISSION—STATISTICS—THE LORD'S PRAYER IN
INDIAN.

IT was not until 1817 that the missionaries crossed
San Francisco Bay for the purpose of establishing a
permanent mission further north. The mortality at
San Francisco had been frightful for some time; a
panic was almost imminent, when Lieutenant Sola
suggested to the disheartened Father a transfer of

---

(8) Bancroft IV, 645-647; V, 635; 710. The "Our Father," as recited by
the Indians at Santa Inés runs as follows according to Mofras:
"Diós caquicoco upalequen alapa quiae micho opte: paguininigug quique
eccuet upalaca huatahuc itimlashup caneobe alapa. Ulamuhu llabulalisa-
huo. Picsiyug equepe ginsucutanlyug uqulyagmagin, canecheiquique isagin
gucutanagun utiyagmayiyug peux hoyug guie utic lex ulechop santequi-
yug llautechop. Amen Jesus"
(*) The author was unable to obtain an illustration of this mission.

the neophytes across the bay. Some were sent over as an experiment, greatly to the benefit of their health; but at first the Father Superior of the missions, while approving the plan, hesitated about the formal transfer for want of priests, and because of the difficulties of communication. At last, when several neophytes had died on the other side without the sacraments, Fr. Luis Gil y Taboada, late of Purisima, consented to become a supernumerary of San Francisco, and to take charge of the branch establishment. The intention was to found "a kind of rancho with its chapel, baptistry, and cemetery, with the title of San Rafœl Arcángel, in order that this most glorious prince, whose name signifies the healing of God, might care for the bodies and the souls." Sola gives the same reason for the new foundation in his letter of April 3d, 1818 to the viceroy. On December 10th, 1817, Father Sarría wrote to Sola that on Saturday next he would go over with Fr. Duran.

In passing over the bay from San Francisco Fr. Gil was accompanied by Fathers Duran, Abella, and Sarría. On December 14th, Fr. Sarría with the same ceremonies that usually attended the dedication of a regular mission founded the *assistencia* of San Rafœl Arcángel on the spot called by the natives Nanaguani. Though the establishment was at first only a branch of San Francisco, an *assistencia* and not a mission, with a chapel instead of a church, under a supernumerary Father of San Francisco; yet there was no real difference between its management and that of the other missions.

The number of neophytes transferred at first may have been 230, but there is very little evidence on the subject, and subsequent transfers, if any were made either from or to San Rafœl, are not recorded. By the end of 1820 the Indian population had increased to 590. In 1818 an adobe building 87 feet

long, 42 feet wide, and 18 feet high had been errected, divided by partitions into chapel, priest's house,
and all other apartments required, and furnished besides with a corridor of tules. Fr. Gil y Tabonda remained in charge of San Rafæl until the summer of
1810, when he was succeeded by Fr. Juan Amorós.

In May 1818 Fr. President Payeras with Comandante Arguello made a trip by water to San Rafæl.
On his way he made a careful examination of the
surrounding country. From the top of a hill near the
new mission they looked upon the Cañada de los
Olampalies and the Llano de los Petalumas. In his
diary of the trip a small island near San Rafæl is
called Del Oro. A place called Gallinan, two leagues
away, and another called Aranjuez are mentioned.
Petaluma was 12 leagues and Olompali 6 leagues
distant. 38 degrees and 15 minutes was the estimated
latitude of San Rafæl. Fr. Payeras recommended
that a presidio be erected at Bodega and a mission
at Petaluma and Suisun. His opinion of the mission
site was not a favorable one. In his general remarks
on mission sites Fr. Payeras mentions by their present names the Sonoma Creek, the Sacramento, and
the San Joaquin. (1)

San Rafæl, under the care of Fr. Juan Amorós,
was in every respect, save in the item of sheep,
prosperous though not on a very large scale, throughout the decade ending with 1830. Baptisms outnumbered deaths by more than two to one, and the Indian population, notwithstanding the 92 neophytes
sent to Solano, was nearly doubled, reaching its
highest number of 1,140 souls in 1828. It appears
that even a house was built and a beginning made
to convert the Indians in the far north, between Petaluma and Santa Rosa perhaps. The population increased from 590 to 970, though, as was said before,

---

(1) Bancroft II, 429-331..

there were as many as 1,160 Indians at the mission
in 1828. As many as 1,182 baptisms were conferred
during these ten years, the highest number, 228 being in 1824. Deaths numbered 504. Large stock
increased from 504 to 1,548; horses and mules from
104 to 448; but sheep decreased from 2,000 to 1,852.
The average crop was 2,454 bushels, of which 1,165
were wheat; 837, barley; and 219, corn. San Rafael
supplied the San Francisco presidio with $1,811 worth
of goods during 1820-1830.

The lands in 1828 were described as follows: In the
west beyond the the range of hills is an *estero* from
the port of Bodega, called Tamales. The range extends north nine leagues, then the plains of Livan-
tonomé, where the gentiles are being civilized, a
house having been built and lands marked out (Sta
Rose to Petaluma region). Other mission lands are at
ther anchería of Annamus or San Pedro Alcántara in
the corte de Madero, and the Rinconada del Tiburon.
Live-stock feeds northward to the ranchería of Olam-
pali, or Santisimo Rosario. The chief is a Christian
and farmer. Cattle graze in the cañadas of Las Galli-
nas, Arroyo de San José, Novato, Colomache, Echatamal, and Olompali; the horses go farther to Ole-
mochoe, or San Antonio; the stream, dry in summer,
rises in the laguna of Ocolom, or San Antonio, the
lands of which join those of Novato, Colomache, and
Echatamal, "going round the hill." The laguna of
Ocolom seems to belong to the mission, but the natives are warlike. In December 1822 the oath of allegiance to the national congress, the only instance of
the kind recorded in California, was taken by the
Fathers and the neophytes. (2)

Fr. Amorós died at San Rafael in 1832 on July
14th, at three o'clock in the morning, and was buried in the mission church on the 16th by Fr. Fortu-

(2) Bancroft II, 506-597,

ni, who had known him since 1792, and declared him a saint. (3)

After the death of Fr. Amorós, Fr. Esténega of San Francisco was put in charge of San Rafæl until the Zacatecan Fr. José Maria Vasquez del Mercado came in 1833. Fr. Mercado in turn was replaced in 1834 by Fr. José Lorenzo de la Concepcion Quijas, also a Zacatecan Franciscan, who from that year had charge of both San Rafæl and Solano, but he lived at the former place chiefly. Statistics of the last years of this mission are for the most part wanting, but the number of neophytes in 1834 must have been about 500, a decrease of 470 since 1830. In 1840 there were 190 Indians living in the community, with probably 150 more scattered about the district.

Baptisms for the years 1831 and 1832 amounted to 155, including 110 adults in 1831, and 15 in 1832. There are no figures for 1833-84. Deaths for the same two years numbered 66. Large stock increased from 1,548 to something over 2,000; horses and mules decreased from 448 to 372; sheep increased from 1,852 to 8,000. Crops in 1831 amounted to 1,090 bushels; in 1832 to 1,776 bushels.

During 1833 there was considerable trouble between Fr. Mercado and the soldiery. At the instance of Gov. Figueroa Fr. Prefect García Diego suspended Fr. Mercado for an alleged outrage against the Indians, summoned him to Santa Clara, and announced his intention to send him to his college for trial. In

(3) Bancroft II, 596-597. Fr. Juan Amorós was a Catalan, born at Porrera October 10th, 1773. He became a Franciscan at Gerona in 1791 and was ordained in 1797. He reached Mexico in 1803, and arrived in California during the year 1804. He served as a missionary at San Carlos in 1804-19, and at San Rafæl in 1819-32. Fr. Amorós was noted for the zeal with which he undertook every task whether temporal or spiritual. He was a successful business manager, a mechanic of more than ordinary skill, and a kind missionary well liked by his neophytes. He was always in good health, and never could find too much work to do. The tradition is that once when the mission was attacked by savages he crossed the bay of San Francisco on a tule balsa or raft with a woman and several children.

the middle of the next year, Fr. Mercado was freed
from arrest and restored to San Rafael; for the two
Fathers, who had been sent to make an investigation,
learned from fourteen witnesses that the Father had
nothing to do with the outrage. Alf. Vallejo, as usual, showed himself antagonistic to the missionary.

The mission was secularized in 1834, and an inventory taken in September. The pueblo was marked out
in October by Ignacio Martínez, who was probably
the comisionado, and the stock distributed in December. The inventory of September 31st, 1834, showed
the following items: church property, building, $192;
ornaments, etc., $777: library of 75 volumes $108; total 1,077; mission buildings $1,128; garden or orchard
$968; boats, etc., $500; live-stock $4,839; Nicasio ran-
cho $7,250; credits $170; total $18,475; debts $3,448;
balance $15,025.

Hartnell's inventory of September 18th, 1830, gave
a population of 195 Indians at the mission; 474 horses, 20 yoke of oxen, 8 mules, 417 fanegas of grain,
42 hides, 72 deer skins, and 60 arrs. of tallow. The
accounts were in a bad condition as the administrator could neither read nor write. The old Christians
desired their liberty and the distribution of the
property. All complained to Hartnell that scarcely
any land remained to them, and that for two years
no clothing had been distributed. (4)

Fr. Quijas attended San Rafael and all the northern country until 1843, after which date there was
no resident missionary north of San Francisco Bay.
The community was entirely broken up before 1845,
though about 200 Christian Indians may have remained in the district. After the formality of notify-
ing the Indians to reoccupy the mission, its sale at
auction was ordered in October 1845. (5)

On June 8th, 1846, the mission estate was sold to

(4) Banc., III, 324; 346: 715-718.   (5) Banc., IV, 552; 676.

Antonio Suñol and A. M. Pico for $8,000, but the purchasers failed to secure possession, and their titles were later on declared invalid. (6)

During the existence of the mission, or as far as the records are extant, 1817-84, the total number of baptisms was 1,878, of which 1,000 were those of Indian adults, 708 Indian children, and 2 adults and 7 children de razon; an annual average of 103. Deaths amounted to 098, of which 438 were Indian adults, 280 Indian children, and one adult de razon; an annual average of 88. Marriages numbered 548, of which 8 were de razon. The largest Indian population ever reached, 1.140 was in 1828. The largest number of cattle held, if the figures are correct, 2,120 was in 1832; horses, 450 in 1831; sheep, 4,000 in 1822-28; swine, thirty in 1820; and all kinds of animals, 5,508 in 1832. The total product of wheat was 17,005 bushels; barley, 12,830 bushels; maize, 8,657 bushels; beans, 1,360 bushels; and miscellaneous grains, 412 (7) bushels.

(6) Bancroft V, 861. 670.   (7) Bancroft., III, 716. The Informes Generales report 1,708 baptisms, 841 marriages, and 616 deaths for the period 1817 to December 31st, 1851.

The "Our Father" in the language of the Chocoyem spoken in Marin County near Mission Rafael and Eel River is as follows:

"Api maco su lilecoc ma nenas mi nues omal macono all taueuchs oyópa mi taueo chaquenit opú neyatto chaqu·nit opu llietto. Tu maco maye gemun ji naya macono sucuji sulia macono rassocto, chague mat opu ma suli mayaco. Macol yangula ume omutte, ulemi macono omu in·eapo. Nette esa Jesus." Bancroft Hist. Native Races, III.

CHAPTER XXVI.

SAN FRANCISCO SOLANO.

EXPLORATIONS—FOUNDING OF THE MISSION—DISAPPROVAL OF THE SUPERIORS—FR. ALTIMIRA—A COMPROMISE—CHURCH DEDICATED—THE NAME OF THE MISSION—SANTA EULALIA MISSION STATION—THE BUILDINGS—INDUSTRIES—STATISTICAL—CONTRIBUTIONS FROM SAN FRANCISCO—CONVERSIONS—INDIAN TRIBES BELONGING TO THE MISSION—MISSIONARY CHANGES. STATISTICS—THE "OUR FATHER" IN GUILUCO.

Under somewhat singular circumstances a new mission, the twenty-first and last on the list of Franciscan missions, was begun in 1823. For the purpose of finding a suitable site, Fr. José Altimira, accompanied by Francisco Castro and an escort of 20 soldiers, embarked at Francisco on the 25th of June, and spent the night at San Rafœl. Fr. Altimira kept a diary of the trip. Leaving San Rafœl on the 26th, the party travelled five leagues north to Olompali and continued to the head of the creek at the point called Chocuay, where the city of Petaluma now stands. On the 27th the Father and his escort marched over plains and hills, eastward and northeastward, past a small tule lake of 50 by 100 yards, thence a little farther to the large lake of Tolay, thence northeastward to the plain on which is the place called Sonoma. They camped on the stream near the main creek, where a boat arrived the same day from San Francisco. On June 28th, in the afternoon, they crossed over the hills northeastward to the plain, or valley, of Napa, and encamped on the stream, Napa Creek, which the party named San Pedro for the day. On June 20th, the explorers crossed over another range of hills into the plain of the Suisun and camped on the main stream five leagues from Napa, ten leagues from Sonoma, and five leagues southwest of the rancheria of the Hulatos. On July 1st the party went back to Napa and Sonoma, making additioal explorations of the latter valley. On July 2d they went up the valley and over the hills by a more northern route than before, past a tule lake, into the plain of the Petalumas and to the old camping ground on the Arroyo de Lema; and July 3d saw them back by a direct course of two leagues to Sonoma, where after new explorations a site was chosen. On July 4th a cross was blessed and set up on the spot of a former rancheria, and then formally named New San Francisco. A volley of musketry was fired, sacred songs were sung, and Holy Mass was offered up. July 4th might therefore with greater propriety than any other date be celebrated as the anniversary of the foundation, though the place was for a little time abandoned; on the sixth all were back at Old San Francisco.

ONLY the approbation of the Fr. Superior was now wanting. Nothing being heard from Fr. Señan, Fr. Altimira wrote to him again on the subject in very earnest terms, explaining what had been done and on what authority, which was simply the approval of the governor, justifying the proposed measures on the ground that San Francisco was in its last stage, and San Rafael could not subsist alone.

FR. Altimira was advised by Governor Arguello not to wait for his superior's orders, but to make a beginning at once. The Father allowed himself to be persuaded, and started on the 23d of August for Sonoma with an escort of twelve men, including an artilleryman to manage a canon of two pound calibre, and a force of neophyte laborers. They arrived at

New San Francisco on the 25th of August, and at
once began granary, ditch, corral, and other needed structures. There is no record of any formal
ceremony on August 25th, though that is generally
given as the date of foundation. Good progress was
made for a week.

MEANWHILE Fr. Prefect Señan on August 23d, just
before his death, had written to Fr. Sarría on the
subject. He was strongly opposed to the suppression
of so flourishing an establishment as San Rafæl,
which Fr. Altimira advocated, and while he did not
altogether disapprove of the transfer of San Francisco,
he was astounded at the summary and illegal manner in which the secular authorities had disposed of
the subject without consulting the supreme government. On receipt of this communication, Fr. President
Sarría wrote to Fr. Altimira and refused to authorize the change. By this letter of the 31st of August the Father at New San Francisco was interrupted in the work, much to his regret. If Bancroft may
be believed, in a letter to the governor Fr. Altimira
used language not at all commendable. A correspondence followed between Fr. Sarría and Governor Au-
guello. The governor declared that the new establishment would be sustained with its guard under a majordomo, and the Fr. Superior's refusal to authorize
Fr. Altimira to care for its spiritual needs would be
reported to the authorities in Mexico.

Yet positive as was the governor's tone in general,
he declared that he would not insist on the suppression of San Rafæl. It seems that he consented readily enough to a compromise which had been suggested
by the Fr. Prefect. Fr. Altimira also seems to have
approved of the compromise. By the terms of this a-
greement New San Francisco was to remain a mission in regular standing, and Fr. Altimira was appointed its missionary, subject to the decision of the

college; but neither Old San Francisco nor San Rafael was to be suppressed, and Fr. Altimira was to continue associate missionary of the former.

NEOPHYTES were free to go from Old San Francisco to the new establishment, and also from San José and San Rafael, provided they came originally from the Sonoma region. In regard to Indians coming from San Rafael, it was provided that they could return if they wished at any time of the year. New converts might come in from any direction to the mission they preferred, but no force was to be used.

FINALLY on Passion Sunday, April 4th, 1824, the mission church was dedicated in honor of San Francisco Solano, which from this date became the name of the mission to distinguish it from San Francisco de Assisi across the bay. To avoid further confusion the usage arose of calling the missions *Dolores* and *San Solano*, or *Solano*. The church was a somewhat rude structure 24 by 105 feet, built of boards, but well furnished and decorated in the interior; many articles were donated by the Russians.

BEYOND the fact that Fr. Buenaventura Fortuni took Fr. Altimira's place in September 1826, the only information extant respecting the annals of Solano for the rest of the decade, not of a statistical nature, is to the effect that a mission rancho in honor of Santa Eulalia had been established at Suisun before the end of 1824; that a house for the visiting missionary and a corral for horses had been built; and that a neophyte alcalde was in charge of the rancho. In March 1824 the mission already had a granary, e priest's house, and seven houses for the guards, besides the chapel, all of wood. By the end of the year one large adobe house 80 by 120 feet and seven feet high, with tiled roof and corridor, had been completed, and two other structures had been made ready for roofing when an unusually heavy rain destroyed them. A loom had been set up and a begin-

San Francisco Bolano.

ning made of weaving. A garden fenced with willows contained from 150 to 800 fruit trees, and in the vineyard from 1,000 to 8,000 vines were growing. Between 1824 and 1830 cattle increased from 1,100 to 2,000; horses from 400 to 725; and sheep remained at 4,000, though there were as few as 1,500 in 1826. Crops amounted to 1,875 bushels per year on an average, the largest yield being 8,945 in 1826, and the smallest 510 in 1829, when wheat and barley failed completely.

At the end of 1824 the mission had 693 neophytes, of whom 322 had come from San Francisco, 153 from San José, 92 from San Rafæl, and 96 had been baptized at the mission. By 1830, six hundred and fifty Indians had been baptized and 375 buried; but the number of neophytes had reached only 760. At its foundation the mission received from San Francisco 20 yoke of oxen, 25 bulls, 50 cows, 60 horses, and 3,000 sheep, besides some implements. The first baptisms were those of 26 children of both neophyte and gentile parents on April 4th, 1824; then again 13 adult Petalumas were baptized on April 16th; and on the 3d of the following month 28 Ululatos were received into the Church. The first burial was that of a woman on December 26th, 1823, the only death in the year. The last baptism on October 1st, 1839, was numbered 1,494; and the last burial, October 7th, 1830, was numbered 875 in the registers.

The different tribes of Indians that furnished converts, were the Aloquiomi, Atenomac, Conoma, Carquin, Canijolmano, Caymus, Chemoco, Chichoyoni, Chocuyem, Coyayomi, or Joyayomi, Huiluc, Huymen, Lacatiut, Loaquiomi, Linayto or Libayto, Locnoma, Mayacma, Muticulmo, Malaca, Napato, Oleomi, Putto or Putato, Palnomanoc, Paque, Petaluma, Suisun, Satayomi, Soneto, Tolen, Tlayacma, Tamal, Topayte, Ululato, Zaclom, Utinomanoc.

Fr. Fortuni served at San Francisco Solano until 1833, when his place was taken by the Zacatecan Franciscan Fr. José de Jesus Maria Gutierrez, who in turn changed places with Fr. Lorenzo Quijas of San Francisco in March 1834. Fr. Quijas remained in charge of the place throughout the decade, but resided for the most part at San Rafæl. Though the neophyte population, as shown by the reports, decreased from 760 to 650 in 1834, and to 550 by June 4th, 1835, yet there was a gain in live-stock and but slight falling off in crops. Hence the establishment must be regarded as having flourished down to the date of secularization. Mariano G. Vallejo was made comisionado in 1834, and in 1835-36, with Antonio Ortega as majordomo, completed the secularization. Movable property was distributed to the Indians, many of whom retired to their old rancherías.

DURING the years 1831-34, inclusive, a great number of Indians were baptized, as many as 555; the largest number, 232, of whom 109 were adults, were received in 1831. Death carried away 272. Large-stock increased from 2,729 to 6,015 in 1833. There are no figures for 1834. Horses and mules gained from 720 to 1,164; and sheep from 4,000 to 7,114. The average crop amounted to 2,750 bushels, of which 1,414 were wheat; 917, barley; 328, corn; 36, beans; and 39, miscellaneous grains. Perhaps 100 Christian Indians still lived at Sonoma toward the end of 1840, with possibly 500 more in the neighboring districts.

DURING the entire existence of San Francisco Solano as a mission, 1823-35, as many as 1,315 persons were baptized, of whom 641 were Indian adults, 671 Indian children, and three children de razon; an annual average of 101. Marriages down to 1838 numbered 278, of which one was de razon. Death carried off 651 persons, of whom 462 were Indian adults, 187 Indian children, and one child de razon; an annual average of 54. San Francisco Solano enjoyed its largest population, 990 in 1832; its largest number of cattle, 4,849 in 1838; horses 1,148 in 1838; mules, 18 in 1838; sheep, 7,114 in 1833; swine, 80 in 1826-27; and all kinds of animals, 13,193 in 1833. The total product of wheat was 13,450 bushels; barley, 5,970 bushels; corn, 8,270 bushels; beans, 806 bushels; and miscellaneous grain, 640 bushels. After the secularization of Solano the pueblo of Sonoma was founded in 1835. (1)

SAN Francico Solano no longer had any existence as a mission community after 1840, and there is nothing to be said of it during the period beginning with 1840, except that Fr. Quijas occasionally visited the place and, administered to the spiritual wants of the Indians, and perhaps resided here for a time in 1843. There also exists an imperfect list of buildings, utensils, and church property, apparently made in connection with the order of sale in 1845, though in the final order of October this establishment was not named. There were probably 200 Indians residin : at Sonoma or in the vicinity at that time. (2)

On another page the reader will find the official rep rt of the Fathers for the year ending December 31st, 1831. The table shows the date of foundation of each mission, and the whole number of baptisms, marriages, and deaths of each mission from its foundation to December 31st, 1831, besides the number of Indians and live-stock at the close of 1831.

---

(1) Bancroft II, 496-500. "I have in my collection", says Bancroft the original registers of baptisms and burials with the alphabetical index of neophytes, from the beginning down to 1839, three quaint old leather-obtdu nomes, types of similar records at all the missions."

Bancroft III, 719-721. The Informes Generales report the following figures for the period 1823 to December 31st, 1831: Baptisms, 881; marriages, 220; deaths, 480; and the number of Indians at the mission at the close of 1831 was 680.

(2) Banc., IV, 677. The "Our Father" in the Gulluco of San Francisco Solano and Solano County according to Mofras reads as follows:

Allá lgamé mutryocusé mi sahus om mi yahuatall elio usqui etra shou mar tsecall zinm pac onjinta mul zhalige nasoyate chelegua mul snsisoitae tscali zicmatan zchlitiliaa chalehus mosqui pihuatzite ytrima omahua. Emqui Jesus. Banc., Hist. Nat. Races. III, 680.

Fr. Antonio Peyri. *(See page 424)*.

Estado de los Misiones de la Alta California sacado de los informes de sus Misioneros en fin de Diciembre de 1831.

Nombre de las misiones	Su Fundacion (1)	Bautismos (2)	Casamientos (3)	Difuntos (4)	Existentes (5)	Ganado de Mayor (6)	Ganado de Lana (7)	Ganado de Pelo lo. (8)	Ganado de Cerda dl.. (9)	Yeguas y Crias (10)	Caballos Man. (11)	Bestias Mulares (12)
SAN DIEGU.	June 16, 1769.	6,401.	1,707.	4,210.	1,561.	6,223.	17,624.	:24.		931.	240.	132.
SAN LUIS REY.	June 13, 1798.	5,284.	1,391.	3,031.	2,819.	23,003.	25,503.	1,203.	253.	1,503.	603.	253.
SAN JUAN CAPISTRANO.	Nov. 1, 1776.	4,331.	1,110.	3,031.	923.	10,903.	4,931.	51.	40.	303.	91.	31.
SAN GABRIEL.	Sept. 8, 1771.	7,703.	1,577.	5,491.	1,338.	20,533.	13,554.	71.	73.	1,355.	355.	193.
SAN FERNANDO.	Sept. 8, 1797.	2,734.	1,311.	1,328.	811.	6,000.	3,000.			1,000.	213.	61.
SAN BUENAVENTURA.	March 31, 1822.	3,837.	1,094.	3,023.	711.	4,000.	3,103.	31.	4.	161.	143.	61.
SANTA BARBARA.	Dec. 4, 1786.	5,412.	1,457.	3,674.	672.	2,600.	3,703.	37.	63.	303.	213.	191.
SANTA INEZ.	Sept. 17, 1804.	1,373.	530.	1,193.	339.	7,203.	2,230.	33.	63.	140.	183.	112.
PURISIMA CONCEPCION.	Dec. 8, 1787.	3,215.	1,011.	2,557.	434.	10,500.	7,100.		62.	7,30.	270.	180.
SAN LUIS OBISPO.	Sept. 1, 1772.	2,911.	758.	2,213.	203.	2,100.	1,200.		21.	503.	303.	203.
SAN MIGUEL.	July 25, 1797.	2,431.	731.	1,831.	619.	3,762.	8,999.	11.	03.	703.	250.	304.
SAN ANTONIO DE PADUA.	July 14, 1771.	4,432.	1,73'.	3,578.	661.	5,000.	10,000.	53.	63.	703.	250.	80.
N. SENORA DE LA SOLEDAD.	Oct. 9, 1791.	2,102.	631.	1,670.	336.	6,590.	6,353.			003.	170.	98.
SAN CARLOS.	June 3, 1770.	3,703.	1,018.	2,803.	269.	2,000.	4,400.			350.	133.	4.
SAN JUAN BAUTISTA.	June 24, 1797.	3,947.	904.	2,141.	923.	7,070.	7,017.		17.	277.	124.	4.
SANTA CRUZ.	Aug. 28, 1791.	2,424.	520.	1,946.	298.	3,500.	5,603.			803.	140.	82.
SANTA CLARA.	Jan. 18, 1777.	8,473.	2,472.	6,724.	1,184.	9,000.	7,000.			573.	213.	38.
SAN JOSE.	June 11, 1797.	6,637.	1,943.	4,615.	1,996.	12,000.	11,000.		63.	1,000.	303.	40.
N. P. SAN FRANCISCO.	Oct. 9, 1776.	6,823.	2,040.	2,083.	211.	4,203.	3,000.			1,000.	239.	13.
SAN RAFAEL.	Dec. 18, 1817.	1,738.	511.	616.	1,073.	1,200.	2,000.	17.	17.	3,03.	150.	1.
SAN FRANCISCO SOLANO.	Aug. 25, 1821.	881.	223.	439.	903.	2,500.	5,000.	53.	53.	603.	125.	4.
Total.		88,974.	21,672.	61,291.	18,315.	152,900.	133,455.	1,816.	723.	13,533.	4,801.	1,671.

(1) Date of foundation. (2) Baptisms. (3) Marriages. (4) Deaths. (5) Indians on the mission roll. (6) Cattle. (7) Sheep. (8) Goats, etc. (9) Swine. (10) Mares and young. (11) Horses. (12) Mules.

PART III.

MODERN HISTORY.

CHAPTER I.

SANTA BARBARA.

THE modern history of the Franciscans in California dates back to July 15th, 1885, when Old Santa
Barbara Mission was formally incorporated into the
Province of the Sacred Heart of Jesus by the election of Fr. Ferdinand Bergmeier as guardian of the
monastery. To avoid repetitions the reader is referred
to chapters 21 and 22, Part I, and to chapters 14
and 15, Part II, for further particulars. (1)

THERE is little more to put on record regarding the
Santa Barbara community. No parish is connected
with the monastery. The Fathers are occupied in con-
ducting a school for young men that wish to prepare
themselves for the priesthood, in preaching missions
and retreats, and in visiting a few outside stations.
Thus they are in charge of Montecito where in the
past year they administered twenty-one baptisms;
Carpinteria where eight persons were baptized during the same period; and Goleta where only one

---

(1) Some time after the chapters on Santa Barbara had been printed I
obtained a few notes from the "Libro de Difuntos" of this mission. From
these we learn that Fr. José Joaquin Jimeno (see page 200) was born in
the City of Mexico on November 30th, 1804. He made his profession at the
apostolic college of San Fernando in the same city in 1824, and was ordained priest in 1827. He was sent to California in 1823. He died on March
15th, 1856, after a painful sickness lasting six months, and was buried in
one of the vaults under the mission church,

Front and Garden of Santa Barbara Monastery.

baptism took place. Montecito has a church, but at Carpinteria and Goleta Holy Mass is said in private houses.

Fr. Bonaventure Fox died at Santa Barbara monastery on December 2d, 1896, and was buried in the vaults on December 5th. (2) Fr. Aloysius Wiewers fell from a scaffolding on July 14th, 1897. His injuries were such that he had to be annointed on the 18th.

(2) Fr. Bonaventure was a native of Ireland, where he was born at Kilconnel on October 18th 1837. It is not known when he came to America, but he received the Franciscan habit on April 16th, 1857, and made his solemn vows at Santa Barbara on April 18th, 1861. He was ordained priest on December 21st, 1864, and thereafter was stationed at the "Old Mission;" but he also did missionary work among his countrymen and the Mexicans in various parts of the State. In 1879 and 1880 he visited St. Turibius in company with Fr. Ubaldo da Rietti.

Fr. José María de Jesus Alcina, after suffering from a disease of the liver with much resignation for two years, died on August 29th, 1863, and was buried on the 30th in the mission vaults. Fr. Alcina was born at Moya, Villa de Cataluñia, on December 1st, 1831. He was received into the Order at Santa Barbara on July 23d, 1854, and made his profession there on July 30th, 1855. Fr. Alcina was elevated to the priesthood in August 1861. (O'Keefe 31-32; Libro de Difuntos, Santa Barbara.)

In addition to the note on page 262 the Libro de Difuntos tells us that Fr. Gonzales died on November 2d, 1875. After Fr. Antonio Jimeno had left California, in 1859, Fr. Gonzales became superior of the mission and held the office until June 1872, when Fr. Romo was appointed first guardian of the monastery by the Superior General, the Most Rev. Fr. Bernardino.

Fr. Francisco Sanchez, (see page 362) entered the Franciscan Order as deacon in February 1837 at the college of Guadalupe. He made his solemn profession and became priest in the following year. He came to California in 1842. (not in 1833 as stated on page 362, on the authority of Bancroft). While at Santa Barbara Fr. Sanchez held the office of Master of Novices.

On May 15th, 1854, a Communio Suffragiorum Defunctorum was formed between Santa Barbara college and the Dominican Fathers of Benicia, California. The prayers to be said, and the Holy Masses which were to be offered up at the death of a member of either community, are mentioned in the Libro de Difuntos.

In 1872 Fr. Alvarez, now of San Luis Rey, came to Santa Barbara from Guatemala in the fall of 1871. Though not incorporated into the community he remained at the mission until 1874, when he was sent to Pájaro.

In the Catholic Directory of 1878 pages 310 and 477, a Fr. Frederic Schots is mentioned as belonging to the community. Nothing further is known of him.

Fr. Francisco Arbondin (the name is French and is pronounced Arbondan), whose name occurs in a former chapter, studied at Santa Barbara, was professed and ordained there in 1878. He is at present in Guatemala.

CHAPTER II.

PAJARO.

Boys' Orphan Asylum.

THE Franciscan Fathers Francisco Codina and José Sanchez, together with Brother Joseph O'Malley, all of Santa Barbara, took charge of St. Francis's Orphanage for boys at Pájaro near Watsonville on January 7th, 1874. The place or neighborhood had been hallowed by the footsteps of Fathers Crespi and Gomez more than a century before. (1)

WHEN the Fathers arrived at Pájaro the establishment was in debt and sheltered between 50 and 60 boys. The first baptism after that occurred on April 4th, 1874. Fr. Francisco Alvarez, now at San Luis Rey, joined the little community and remained several years down to 1884, when he was recalled to San Fernando college, Mexico, by the Most Rev. Superior General. Fr. Sanchez returned to Santa Barbara in 1870. (2)

AFTER Santa Barbara had been incorporated into the Province of the Sacred Heart, Fr. Victor Aertker was made assistant to Fr. Codina in December 1885; but, at his own request, Fr. Codina was relieved from office, and Fr. Clementin Deymann of the province was appointed rector of the orphanage on July 7th, 1886.

---

(1) See page 48. (2) The Catholic Directory erroneously assigns him to Pájaro as late as 1883.

St. Francis' Orphanage At Pajaro.

He arrived at the asylum on July 24th. Fr. Ondina left the community and probably the country for the Orient about two months after. (3)

IN January 1887 Fr. Victor was transferred to San Francisco, and Fr. José Godiol took his place. As the buildings were found much too small to accommodate the growing number of orphan boys, they were enlarged after some years, and many improvements made to meet the requirements of the age.

THE average number of boys at the institution for the year 1895-1896 was 300. The asylum is situated on a farm of about 200 acres, and now gives shelter to about 140 children between the ages of six and fourteen years. The establishment is partly supported by the State of California.

FR. Herman Wirz of St. Louis was added to the community at Pájaro on October 18th, 1892, and has remained there ever since. Fr. Ubaldo da Rietti was here and at several other houses of the coast for a short time, but never incorporated into the province. When the writer saw him in 1890, Fr. Ubaldo was collecting material for some literary work by permission of the Most Rev. Superior General until recalled to Europe.

IN July 1896 Fr. José Godiol was transferred to the new residence establised at Phoenix, Arizona; but after a few months he returned to Pájaro on account of ill-health.

AT the intermediate chapter of the province, held in St. Louis on July 22d, 1896. Fr. Clementin of the orphanage was appointed commissary provincial for the new commissariat composed of the Franciscan honses on the Pacific coast, not including San Luis Rey which is the novitiate for a Mexican province.

---

(3) Fr. Francisco Codina was a native of Catalonia, Spain. No particulars about this Father could be obtained. He died at Alexandria, Egypt, as a member of the Custody of the Holy Land.

Fr. Clementin Deymann.

The new commissary, however, soon died of Bright's
disease at Phœnix, Arizona, whither he had gone in
hopes of regainning his health. His remains were interred in the vaults of the mission church at Santa
Barbara on December 9th, 1896. (4)

Fr. James Nolte of St. Turibius was appointed to
succeed Fr. Clementin as rector of the asylum; but
soon had to be relieved from duty on account of a
long and serious illness. Fr. Seraphin Lampe of Fruitvale was then put in charge of Pájaro, and holds the
office at this writing, July 1897.

---

(4) Fr. Clementin Deymann was born at Klein Navern, Hanover, Germany,
and came to America in 1863. After completing his classical studies at St.
Joseph's college Teutopolis, Ill., he was received into the Order on December 8th, 1867, and made his solemn vows on December 26th, 1871, at St,
Louis, Mo., where he was also ordained priest on March 19th, 1872. He was
stationed at Teutopolis, Quincy, and Joliet, where he was superior, and
also spiritual director of the mother house of the Franciscan Sisters from
the fall 1873-1882, whon he became superior at Chillicothe, Mo. There he
remained until he was appointed rector of the orphanage at Pájaro. Fr.
Clementin is the author of several devotional works, among which the
most noted are the following translations from the German: 1) The Seraphic Octave. 2) Life of the Venerable Crescentia Hoss. 3) The Seraphic
Manual. 4) Life of St. Francis Solanus. 5) Manual for the Sisterhoods of
the Third Order of St. Francis. Fr. Clementin also wrote many articles of
instruction and history for various weekly papers. In the last year of his
busy life Fr. Clementin was engaged on a life of the Venerable Fr. Margil, apostle of Texas, and he had just completed a sketch of the life of
Fr. Catalá of Santa Clara when death called him to his reward. The latter work, together with many unfinished sketches, are in the possession
of the writer.

CHAPTER III.

SAN FRANCISCO.

St. Boniface', Golden Gate Avenue.

At the request of the Most Rev. Patrick Riordan, Archbishop of San Francisco, Fathers Gerard Becher, Victor Aertker, and Paulinus Tolksdorf took charge of the only German parish in the city of San Francisco on February 16th, 1887. They were accompanied by Brothers Beatus Struewer, Kilian Rothbert, and Onesimus Ehrhardt. These religious came from St. Louis during that year or the year before. They took possession of a house vacated by the Dominican Sisters, and have occupied it ever since.

THE congregation, dedicated to St. Boniface, had been organized for the Germans in 1860, and its first pastor was the Rev. S. Wolf.

The Fathers soon found the church much too small. It was therefore enlarged and took its present shape in the summer of 1887. After some time the Third Order of St. Francis was introduced, and now numbers about 600 members who belong to the various parishes of the city. The Society of Christian Mothers, the Young Men's Society, St. Louis Boys Society, the Sodality for Young Ladies and Girls, and the Confraternity for the Conversion of Sinners are other fruits of the work of the Fathers.

The parish school, the pet child of the Fathers

everywhere, of course received special attention. More teachers were employed among whom was a male teacher for the larger boys. The girls are in charge of the Dominican Sisters.

ANOTHER aim of the Fathers, here as elsewhere, in obedience to the direction of the Holy See, was the introduction of edifying music during divine service. Hence it is not strange that in St. Boniface' church the liturgical regulations of Mother Church are observed.

NOTHING remarkable, nor anything else deserving special mention in a mere historical sketch, occurred at St. Boniface' during these years, and it only remains to enumerate the different religious that were connected with the residence attached to the parish.

FR. Gerard was the superior of the residence and rector of the parish until transferred to Santa Barbara on July 8th, 1891. Fr. Victor meanwhile had gone to St. Turibius Mission in August 1887, and Fr. Eugene Puers took his place. Fr. Paulinus was recalled to St. Louis in the summer of 1887, and Fr Cornelius Schœnwælder replaced him. Fr. Isidor Gey of St. Louis, Mo., was added to the community about the same time.

ON January 20th, 1890, Fr. Zephyrin Engelhardt was transferred from St. Turibius to St. Boniface', to attend Ukiah and the Indian missions of Mendocino County. This he did until the latter part of July, when he was removed to Cleveland, O. He was succeeded at St. Boniface' and in the missions by Fr. Placidus Krekeler of Harbor Springs, Michigan.

THE provincial chapter held at St. Louis on July 8th, 1891, transferred Fr. Gerard to Santa Barbara, and appointed Fr. Paulinus Tolksdorf superior and rector at St. Boniface'; Fr. Eugene Puers was assigned to St. Mary's Memphis, Tenn., where he died a month later on August 8th.

St. Boniface' Church.

AT the same time Fr. Cletus Gierschewski was placed here, whilst Fathers Cornelius and Isidor continued in their positions. (1)

ON August 17th, 1892, Fathers Placidus of St. Boniface' and Gregory Knepper of St. Turibius changed places.

AT the intermediate chapter held December 28th, 1892, Fr. Paulinus was transferred to Chicago, Ills., and Fr. Leo Bruener of Kansas City, Mo., appointed superior and rector of St. Boniface'. Fathers Augustin Henseler of Indianapolis and Seraphin Lampe were assigned to St. Boniface' on the same occasion, whilst Fr. Isidor was called to Chicago.

THE provincial chapter which convened at St. Louis in August 1894 appointed Fr. Leo pastor of the newly organized parish of St. Anthony in the southern part of the city, with Fr. Celtus as assistant. Fr. Maximilian Neuman of Chicago then became rector and superior of St. Boniface'. Fr. Seraphin was chosen superior of the new German parish at Fruitvale, California, and Fr. Augustin Henseler was recalled to the east, whence he returned to Germany. Fr. Titus Hugger of St. Louis was assigned to St. Boniface'; likewise Fr. Pius Nierman of Sacramento.

ON January 1st, 1895, Fr. Gregory was changed to St. Turibius, Ukiah and missions having been surrendered to the archbishop.

AT the intermediate chapter held in St. Louis on

(1) Fr. Eugene Puers was born at Milte, Prussia, on December 25th, 1835. He was received into the Order on May 1st, 1856, and ordained priest on December 25th, 1860. He arrived at Teutopolis, Ills., from Germany in 1861, and was professor in the college until 1871, when he returned to Germany, where he was guardian of the monastery at Werl from 1872 to 1875. When the religious were expelled from Prussia in 1875 he with a number of his brethren went to America, where he was stationed at Teutopolis, Memphis, and Joliet until 1888 when he was assigned to San Boniface. He died of congestion of the brain after an illness lasting only three hours. The remains of Fr. Eugene were interred at Calvary cemetery Memphis, on August 10th.

July 22d. 1896, Fr. Titus was appointed superior
and rector of St. Francis' church Sacramento, California, in place of Fr. Augustin McClory, who was
assigned to St. Boniface'. At the same time Fr.
James Nolte of St. Turibius, and Fr. Vitalis Feldman
of St. Louis, were stationed here. On April 2d, 1897,
the latter went to St. Turibius Mission, and his place
was filled by Fr. Romuald Reinsdorff of St. Louis.

DURING all this years Fr. Cornelius continued here,
except for a short time, when on account of ill-health
he was sent to Los Angeles. From 1890 to 1897 Fr.
Athanasius Gœtte, formerly a missionary in China,
was much of the time at St. Boniface', though generally at St. Joseph's Hospital on account of ill-
health. Early in 1897, having sufficiently recovered,
he returned to China.

ONLY two deaths occured among the religious of St.
Boniface'. Brother Aloysius Nauer died here in February 1890. He had come from Santa Barbara, but
on account of ill-health he was sent to St. Turibius
mission. The change not proving beneficial, Br. Aloysius was sent to St. Joseph's Hospital in charge of
the Franciscan Sisters. There he died of consumption
in the 28th year of his age, and the fifth of his religious profession. His remains were buried at Watsonville.

ON July 3d, 1889, Fr. Gabriel Rieman died at St.
Boniface's convent. The body was taken to the new
Catholic cemetery outside the city on July 6th. (2)

---

(2) Fr. Gabriel Rieman was a native of Wisconsin. He had entered the
Order at Teutopolis in 1882, and was ordained priest at St. Louis on
March 5th, 1887. Soon after he was transferred to Santa Barbara, as even
then his health began to decline. In July 1888 he was removed to St. Turibius, but the change proving ineffectual, he was allowed to remain
for several months at the Mercy Hospital until a few days before his
death. He had reached the 32d year of his age.

CHAPTER IV.

ST. TURIBIUS MISSION.

Mission St. Turibius on the south side of Clear Lake, Lake County, California, two miles north of Kelseyville, was founded for the Indians by the zealous missionary Rev. Luciano Osuna in 1870. In that year the worthy priest bought 160 acres of land, bordering on Clear Lake, from a Mr. O'Brian. The land subsequently passed into the hands of the Most Rev. Archbishop of San Francisco.

Fr. Luciano was a very active man and withal a most pious priest. He was frequently seen in sandals, and in some kind of religious dress unknown to the good Protestants of Lake and Mendocino counties, where scarcely any Catholics could be found in those days. Upon the complaint of some citizens the good missionary was arrested as *non compos mentis*, and brought before the judge for examination. The case appeared somewhat unfavorable for the priest, as he had no friends and no attorney. At last one of the lawyers, a Protestant, was moved to pity and offered to plead the case for Father Luciano. He had read something about the monks in Europe and therefore thought he could assist the priest. The attorney reminded the judge that in Europe in old times there lived men called Benedictines. He had read of them. They were accustomed to go about in just such a garb as Fr. Luciano wore, because that was their rule, and that therefore there was not sufficient reason to consign the priest to the lunatic asylum. This pleading seemed to have made an impression on the worthy judge, for on putting the singularly blunt question to Father Luciano: "Are you crazy?" and receiving the reply: "That is for your honor to decide," the representative of the majesty of the law smilingly let the priest go his way. (1)

REV. Luciano Osuna from July 1870 until November 1870, presumably all over Lake and Mendocino counties, baptized 667 persons, of whom very few were white.

WHEN "Father Luciano," by which name he was known, left St. Turibius, the Franciscan Fathers Bonaventure Fox and Ubaldo da Rietti of Santa Barbara attended the missions in Lake County, from December 1879 until December 1880.

THE Rev. E. D. Geverno had charge until October 5th, 1881, when the Fathers of the Holy Cross of South Bend, Indiana, accepted the mission. Fathers Lauth and Kolopp, together with Brother Clemens, formed the little religious community from October 1881 until October 8th, 1882, when Rev. P. J. Reisdorfer, S. M., succeeded them. He was seconded in his efforts for the Indians by the Rev. William Dempflin, "Father William", as the Indians familiarly called him, a Dominican from Benicia, California. These two priests from October 1882 until March 1883 baptized 271 Indians.

ABOUT this time the Most Rev. J. S. Alemany, O. P., Archbishop of San Francisco, petitioned the Society for the Propagation of the Faith to take charge of Mission St. Turibius. The request was granted, and Revds C. de Romanis and A. Petinelli of the same Society, arrived in October 1883. From

(1) The writer had this story from the lawyer himself. I regret my inability to recall his name, for it should be perpetuated. Whether Fr. Luciano was a member of a religious Order, or not, I could not ascertain.

Indian Sweathouse.

March of that year till their arrival the Rev. William Brenan attended to the spiritual wants of the people.

FATHERS de Romanis and Petinelli remained until August 1887. During these years Fr. William Dempflin, O. P., visited the missions among the Indians and baptized 212 of them.

IN August 1887 the Franciscan Fathers took charge at the request of Most Rev. P. Riordan, Archbishop of San Francisco. Fr. Stanislaus Riemann, till then at Indianapolis, Ind., and Fr. Victor Aertker of San Francisco, together with Brothers Erasmus Beier and Nicolaus Uhrmacher, arrived on August 20th.. They found a small dwelling and a little church used also for a school. The whole was surrounded by a large farm, in one corner of which there was the rancheria of Digger Indians (2) composed of about 100 souls.

IT may interest the reader to know something of a peculiar institution, which is found in every settlement of pagan Indians in northern California. This is the *temescal* (3) or sweathouse. It is usually built near a stream and consists of a hole dug in the ground, roofed over with heavy timber and earth in such a manner as to render it almost air-tight. Entrance is made through a small hole on one side. There is another hole in the top of the structure, directly over the fire-place, which affords free passage

---

(2) DIGGERS is the name applied indiscriminately to the Indians of northern and middle California, and is probably derived from digging roots. Their main reliance is on acorns, roots, grass-seeds, berries and the like. These are eaten both raw and prepared. The acorns are shelled, dried in the sun, and then pounded into a powder with large stones. From this flour a species of coarse bread is made, which is sometimes flavored with various kinds of berries or herbs." Bancroft Hist. Nat. Races, I, 373.

(3) "TEMESCAL is an Aztec word meaning "Casilla como estufa, adonde se bañan y sudan." The word was brought to this region and applied to the native sweathouses by the Franciscan Fathers." Turner, Pacific R. R. Rep. III, 72.

to the smoke. The fire is started in the centre of the temescal; the Indian men, absolutely naked, crawl into the small hole below, and lie or squat around the fire until a state of profuse perspiration sets in, when they rush out and plunge into the water. The writer saw no women or children taking part. Nor does the custom continue when the Indians have been baptized. Thus it is that at every Indian station visited by the Fathers the sweathouse is found in ruins.

As the mission had to support itself, farming and stock raising became an important part of the work assigned to the community. A lay-teacher was employed to conduct the school for twenty Indian children. The Fathers with government aid later on arranged suitable quarters to keep the little ones from the baneful influence of their squalid homes, and placed a lay-brother at the head of the establishment which continues to this day.

THE missions in Lake County still attended by the Fathers are: St. Turibius, Lakeport, Kelseyville, and Lower Lake, at which places there are small churches. Middletown in later years has been added to the list, but Holy Mass is said there in a private house. Except St. Turibius, these stations or white settlements.

MOREOVER the Fathers occasionally visit the Indian rancherías of Sulphur Banks, Upper Lake, Hastings, Scott's Valley, Coyote Valley, and Cash Creek.

MENDOCINO County, east of the Coast Range Mountains, was also attended from St. Turibius until January 20th, 1893. This was an immense district of which Ukiah was the central point. Besides Ukiah 42 miles from St. Turibius, which the Father in charge reached by means of a private conveyance, a rancheria of Digger Indians called Ukiahs, 7 miles south of the county seat, was attended. Here Fr. Victor aided by the Most Rev. Archbishop erected a small church

Mission St. Turibius.

upon a lofty eminence overlooking the valley. A day school was opened there by the writer in 1889, the government paying for tuition. Seven miles south of this rancheria, near Hopland, was another rancheria of Digger Indians who went by the name of Sanél. Here was a small church which was likewise used as a school and conducted by a female teacher under government contract. The building was enlarged early in 1890.

At Hopland Holy Mass was celebrated in a private house, or in the district school building, for the white settlers.

The settlers in Anderson Valley were also visited occasionally and Holy Mass said in a private house.

Late in 1889 a small building was erected at a rancheria of Indians about one mile north of Ukiah, just in front of the Catholic cemetery, with a view of instructing and gaining the Indians who were all pagans. The Archbishop had kindly furnished $200 for that purpose.

Far north, too, in Round Valley, the whites and Indians claimed the attention of the Fathers, so that once the writer was called to administer the sacraments to a dying woman, eighty miles from Ukiah. The trip lasted four days, as the roads were washed out.

Fr. Victor's health began to decline under the hardships, and he was recalled to St. Louis on September 28th, 1888 to be succeeded by Fr. Zephyrin Engelhardt. For a year and a half the latter held the charge, when the Very Rev. Fr. Ferdinand Bergmeier, then provincial, accompanied him on the trip from St. Turibius to Ukiah across the mountains. Thereupon, January 20th, 1890, he was stationed at San Francisco, whence he could reach the Mendocino County missions by rail. This was a graet relief; however, the Mendocino County missions were surrendered to the Most Rev. Archbishop of San Francisco in January 1808.

Fr. Gregory Knepper took Fr. Zephyrin's place at St. Turibius on January 18th, 1890, and remained until August 17th, 1891, when he changed places with Fr. Placidus Krekeler of San Francisco. On January 10th, 1893, Fr. James Nolte of San Francisco was appointed superior in place of Fr. Stanislaus Riemann, who was transferred to Los Angeles. At the same time Fr. Maximilian Klein of St. Louis took the place of Fr. Placidus, who went to Bayfield, Wisconsin.

In the following year, November 20th, Fr. Maximilian succeeded Fr. James who had been assigned to St. Bonifce', at San Francisco. Fr. Athanasius Goette of San Francisco was made assistant and arrived on November 20th, but on account of ill-health he was returned to San Francisco on January 1st, 1805. His place was filled by Fr. Gregory who arrived from San Francisco on January 2d.

On April 1st, 1897, Fr. Gregory was appointed superior, whilst Fr. Maximilian was put in charge of the residence and parish at Fruitvale, California; Fr. Vitalis Feldman of San Francisco became assistant.

During all these years the following lay-brothers were at St. Turibius: Erasmus Beier, Nicolaus Uhrmacher, Leo Buerger, Leander Genoch, Bernard Jurczyk, Arnold Wilms, Irenæus Kraus who is in charge of the school, Pacificus Wojciechowski, Hippolytus Degenhardt, and Placidus Dehm, who has labored in the barn and on the farm from the appearance of the Fathers until now.

At present there are 80 Catholic Indians at St. Turibius; 75 at Sulphur Banks; 30 at Cash Creek; 20 in Coyote Valley; 25 in Scott's Valley; and 20 at Upperlake.

The mission records, from July 1870 to June 1897, contain the following items: Baptisms, 1,500, of which 1,291 where those of Indians; marriages, 245, of which 200 were Indian; and deaths from December 1881 to June 1897 numbered 75, of which 50 were Indian. There are no records of deaths before the period beginning with 1881.

CHAPTER V.

FRUITVALE.

St. Elisabeth's.

Fr. Seraphin Lampe first held service for the Germans of Oakland and vicinity on August 14th, 1892, in "Father King's Hall", corner of Grove and Seventh Streets, Oakland, and thereafter every Sunday and Holyday of Obligation down to October 22d, 1893, when St. Elisabeth's church was dedicated by the Most. Rev. Archbishop of San Francisco. Several Dominican and Jesuit Fathers, Rev. Fr. King, together with Fathers Clementin, Seraphin, and Athanasius assisted on this occasion.

ALL the German-speaking Catholics of Oakland, Fruitvale, Alameda, and Berkeley are supposed to be members of this congregation. A school was soon opened and given in charge of the Sisters of St. Dominic. The average attendance at present is one hundred.

THE first pastor was Fr. Seraphin Lampe; he was assisted by Fr. Stanislaus Riemann. These, togeth-

Very Rev. Kilian Schlœsser.

er with Brother; Nicolaus, Eugene Obert, and Victorni Tillman, formed the community.

In January 1894 Fr. Stanislaus was transferred to Los Angeles, when Fr. Kilian Schloesser of Santa Barbara was assigned to Fruitvale. From December 15th, 1893, to February 15th, 1894, Fr. Provincial Michæl Richardt held the canonical visitation in California, and also visited Fruitvale. Fr. Kilian was absent at Santa Barbara from August 1st, 1894, until September 11th.

Fr. Michæl again visited California from January 11th to March 3d, 1895, and arrived at St. Elisabeth's on January 19th. On December 31st, 1895, Fr. Michæl once more held the visitation at Fruitvale, having just arrived from Tucson, where he had conferred with Bishop Bourgade concerning the acceptance of a parish at Phœnix, Arizona. The parish was accepted, and Fr. Seraphin of Fruitvale appointed rector and superior of the new mission on January 10th, 1896. His place was filled by Fr. Gerard Becher of Santa Barbara.

On September 30th, 1896, Fr. Gerard suffered a stroke of paralysis which disabled him for parish work. He was transferred to St. Anthony's convent, San Francisco, and replaced by Fr. Seraphin of Phœnix for a short time only; for early in 1897 he was appointed rector of the orphanage at Pájaro in place of Fr. James Nolte. Fr. Maximilian Klein of St. Turibius became superior at St. Elisabeth's. Fr. Kilian succeeded Fr. Clementin as commissary of the western houses, but remained at Fruitvale.

— 480 —

St. Elisabeth's Church and Convent.

CHAPTER VI.

SAN FRANCISCO.

St. Anthony's, Army Street.

On July 23d, 1893, it was officially announced in St Boniface' church, that a second German parish would be organized in San Francisco with the approval of the Most Rev. Archbishop and the consent of the Very Rev. Fr. Provincial. The territory comprised was to be the southern part of the city known as "The Mission." Twentieth Street was to be the northern boundary. The patron saint, suggested by the Most Rev. Archbishop himself, was to be St. Anthony of Padua.

A lot was purchased on Army and Folsom Streets, and there church, school, and convent of St. Anthony arose in the course of time. Meanwhile a store-room was rented on Mission Street, and the first Holy Mass said there on November 5th, 1893. Fr. Cletus of St. Boniface' was selected to attend to the incipient congregation temporarily.

On July 15th, 1894, the school was blessed by the Most Rev. Archbishop, and opened with 52 pupils in charge of the Dominican Sisters on July 18th. The average number of children at the present time is 176. The corner-stone for the new church was laid on August 12th, 1894, by the Rev. P. Yorke, chancellor of the archdiocese, as the Most Rev. Archbishop was absent.

THE building, a fine edifice 188 ft. long, was at last dedicated by Most Rev. Patrick Riordan on Sunday March 10th, 1895. His Grace preached the English sermon, and Rev. Father Miller, S. J., of San José addressed the multitude in German. The church is well furnished with vestments, bells, statues, stations, etc., and the music at divine service is strictly according to the regulations of Mother Church, as is becoming to loyal sons of St. Francis.

THERE are several societies connected with the church. The Altar Society began with the organization of the parish under Fr. Cletus on November 5th, 1893. In the course of time the Young Ladies' Sodality, the Third Order of St. Francis, and St. Joseph's Benevolent Society followed.

FROM June 17th, 1894, to January 1st, 1897, there occurred 194 baptisms, twenty marriages, and 58 burials. It is thought that about 1,500 souls belong to St. Anthony's parish at the present time. There are more than 4,000 Holy Communions during the year.

DOWN to the summer of 1895 the Fathers had occupied a little cottage. Ground was broken for a new and more suitable residence on June 5th, and the new structure was blessed on August 2d by Fr. Kilian Schloesser.

THE first pastor appointed to St. Anthony's in 1893 was Fr. Leo Bruener, at the same time rector and superior at St. Boniface'. Fr. Cletus was made assistant and moved into a little cottage, west of the schoolbuilding, with Bro. Nicholaus, at the end of July 1894.

At the provincial chapter, held in St. Louis during August of that year, Fr. Leo was transferred to St. Anthony's as its first resident rector. On November 18th, however, Fr. Cletus went to Minnesota and Fr. Quirinus Stuecker took his place. On November 12th, 1895, Fr. Aloysius Wiewers came from

Santa Barbara and remained until May 22d of the
following year, to undergo medical treatment for his
eyes.

Besides, Brothers Nicholaus, Leander, Dorotheus,
Leo, and Philip assisted the Fathers of St. Anthony's at different times.

———— ◆ ————

CHAPTER VII.

LOS ANGELES.

St. Joseph's.

THE Franciscans were called to Los Angeles in October 1893 by the Rt. Rev. Francis Mora, Bishop of
Monterey and Los Angeles. They were given charge
of St. Joseph's parish, which had been organized for
the German-speaking Catholics by the Rev. Flor.
Bartsch in 1888.

THE Fathers were not wholly strangers to the
place; for as early as August 2d, 1769, the Franciscans Juan Crespi and Francisco Gomez crossed the
north branch of the San Gabriel River, which they
called Rio Porciúncula, where Los Angeles now
stands. From the Franciscan feast of the day the
place was named Nuestra Señora de los Angeles (Our
Lady of the Angeles); hence the name Los Angeles.
However, the town of Los Angeles was not founded
until 1782 by order of Governor Neve. (1)

As the neighboring mission of San Gabriel had
been established long before that date, and as there

---

(1) Bancroft I, 140-143; 340; 344; 319; 400; Life of Fr. Junipero Serra, 35.

were none but Franciscans in the country for many
years later, the spiritual care of Los Angeles fell to
these Fathers. It is not clear when they said the
first Mass there. Bancroft (2) says: "In 1811 authority was obtained for the erection of a new pueblo chapel by the citizens, and the cornerstone was
laid and blessed in August 1814 by Fr. Gil y Taboada of San Gabriel, with the permission of Fr. President Señan."

BEYOND laying the foundation no progress was made
before 1818, since in January of that year Sola ordered that the site be changed in favor of a higher
one near the comisionado's house. At this time the
citizens had subscribed five hundred cattle for the
enterprize, but Sola feared that sufficient funds could
not be realized by selling the cattle, and therefore
proposed to take them and include the cost of the
chapel in the next year's estimate.

In 1819 Fr. Prefect Payeras, through an appeal to
the Fathers, obtained goods for the building fund
worth five-hundred and seventy-five dollars. This sum
with earlier contributions was expended on the
church, and the walls were raised to the window
arches before 1821. Neophytes from San Gabriel and
San Louis Rey did the work at one real a day. Nor
is it certain whether the cornerstone was laid on the
15th or the 19th of August.

MEANWHILE the matter of chapel service was still
an open question. The Fathers of San Gabriel announced their inability of attending to the spiritual welfare of the pueblo and ranchos. Fr. Señan presented the matter in a strong light to the governor,
who in his report of 1818 made an appeal to the
viceroy in behalf of the veterans of the king's service, who had gone to spend their declining years at
Los Angeles, and ought not to be deprived of spirit-

(2) Bancroft II, 351.

ual care. Yet the Angelinos obtained no chaplain.

THE pueblo church was at last finished, perhaps in 1822 or 1823, but certainly not in 1821 as has been represented. In the autumn of 1821 work had been for sometime suspended. The funds had been exhausted, and $2,000 were needed. In this emergency Fr. Payeras made a new and most earnest appeal to the d fferent missions to contribute cattle, laborers, anything, for the completion of the edifice as a monument of missionary zeal in the cause of God and St. Francis. The Fathers seem to have responded liberally. The governor contributed his mite, and even the citizens of Los Angeles seem to have taken a little interest in the matter, so that the church was completed as planned, and was formally dedicated on December 8th, 1822.

IN the beginning of 1821 the municipal authorities sent a petition to the Fr. Prefect that Fr. Gil y Taboada be sent as pastor to Los Angeles; but Fr. Payeras replied that the ill-health of Fr. Gil would render it impossible. (3)

THUS it is plain that by accepting St. Joseph's parish, Los Angeles, the Franciscans were simply returning to an old field cultivated by their brethren eighty and more years before.

THE following Franciscan Fathers have since been stationed at Los Angeles: Victor Aertker, superior, from October 1893; Cornelius Schoenwælder from October 1893 to July 31st, 1894; Stanislaus Riemann from January 1894 to September 3d, 1894; Quirinus Stuecker from September 4th, 1894, to November 9th 1894; Athanasius Gœtte from September 20th, 1894 to November 9th, 1894; Aloysius Wiewers from November 14th, 1894, to December 1895; James Nolte from November 22d, 1894, to August 4th, 1896; and Philibert Hause from July 1896. Brothers Firmus,

(8) Bancroft II, 561-562.

Leo, Heribert, Kilian, Philip, and Ansgar, were also stationed at Los Angeles at various times.

On the arrival of the Fathers fifty-two children attended the school. The average attendance now is about 200; the Sisters of St. Dominic conduct the

St. Joseph's, Los Angeles.

school. The school building was enlarged in 1895. Meanwhile in 1894 the church and residence were enlarged. Whilst this took place a sacrilegious wretch broke into the building, and set fire to the tabernacle. Part of the main altar was destroyed and the church damaged to the extent of $400.

THE parish is composed of about 150 German families. The number of baptisms from October 6th 1893, to April 20th, 1897, was one hundred and ninety-six. There are about 8,000 Holy Communions per annum.

THE Third Order of St. Francis was introduced, and now counts 250 German, Spanish, and English-speaking members. A new church building is contemplated, for which purpose a building association was formed in February 1897. Fr. Servatius Altmicks died here on August 23d, 1890, while on his way from Santa Barbara to Memphis, Tenn.

CHAPTER VIII.

SACRAMENTO.

St. Francis'.

AT the provincial chapter held in St. Louis, Mo., on August 22d, 1894, it was decided to grant the petition of Rt. Rev. Bishop Monogue of Sacramento, and to found a mission at the capital of California. Accordingly Fr. Augustin McClory, till then at Cleveland, Ohio, was ordered to organize a parish. He arrived at Sacramento on October, 16th 1894, and began his work as assistant priest of the Cathedral.

ON Oct. 27th, 1894, the Rt. Rev. Bishop Monogue fixed the limits of the new parish as follows:

WESTERN boundary, 18th Street; eastern boundary, 30th street, with permission to attend the Catholics four or five miles beyond this line, until such time as the Rt. Rev. Bishop might deem it advisable to order otherwise; northern boundary, the river or city lim-

St. Francis' Church and School, Sacramento.

its; southern boundary, three miles north of Freeport until ordered otherwise.

AFTER careful deliberation, warmly supported by the bishop and Fr. Clementin Deymann, a site was a-greed upon which was the half block on K Street, between 25th and 26th streets, 320 feet long and 160 feet wide. The price paid for the lot was $7,000, A house occupied part of the plat, and this was soon converted into a chapel and residence. On January 11th, 1895, Fr. Provincial Michæl, accompanied by Brothers Adrian and Wendelin, arrived at Sacramento, and on the same day the Fathers and Brothers took up their abode in the little cottage. Union Hall on 20th and O Streets was rented, and on Sunday January 20th, 1895, it was used for the first time for divine worship.

BROTHER Adrian now drew the plans for a church and convent, and the contract was let at a cost of $5,126 on February 5th, 1895. Ground was broken on the 7th. The church is a frame structure 34x82 feet, with a cross extension on either side 12x24 feet.

MASS was celebrated in the new church for the first time on Palm Sunday April 7th, 1895. The church was blessed on April 28th, 1896, by the ad-ministrator of the diocese, Very Th. Rev. Grace, now bishop of the diocese, Bishop Monogue having died.

THE new residence was built at the same time, and occupied on May 3d, 1896. It is a two story frame building, 34x50 feet, with a one story addition in the rear for kitchen and dining room.

THE school, which is a frame building containing four large class rooms, was erected in the fall of 1895, and opened on November 5th, 1895.

FR. Augustin, the first superior, was transferred to San Francisco on July 29th, 1896 and Fr. Titus Hug-ger appointed in his place. Fr. Pius Nierman, who had come to Sacramento as assistant when the residence was ready, staid one year, and was then removed to

San Francisco. He returned to Sacramento in July 1896, when Fr. Titus, who had succeeded him, became superior. Brothers Wendelin Hottinger, Leander Genoch, Flavius Czech, Eugene Obert, and Leo Buerger were the other members of the community during these years.

CHAPTER IX.

PHŒNIX.

St. Mary's.

AFTER repeated and urgent requests on the part of Rt. Rev. Bishop Bourgade, Vicar Apostolic of Arizona, the only Catholic congregation in this city was at last accepted by the Very Rev. Fr. Provincial Michael Richardt towards the close of 1895. Fr. Seraphin Lampe of Fruitvale California was appointed superior and rector. He arrived with Fr. José Godiol of Pájaro, California, in January 1896. A few weeks after Fr. Novatus Benzing of St. Louis arrived together with Brothers Ildefons and Robert.

THE congregation, a mixed one of Mexicans and English speaking Catholics, was in a poor condition materially and spiritually, but the Fathers went to work with a will and succeeded in bringing a little life into the people.

As neither church nor dwelling answered the purposes, it was resolved to renovate the old adobe church for the Mexicans, and to erect a new church for the English speaking members, and also to build a brick convent. It is under way now. The old church through Brothers Adrian, Ildefons, and Eugene has assumed a quite different and more agreeable appearance inside and outside.

THE ceiling is vaulted, and two new side altars and other improvements were introduced. Fr. Seraphin was removed to Pájaro in July 1896, and Fr. Novatus made superior. Fr. Severin from St. Louis also was stationed here and arrived August 8th, 1896, in place of Fr. José Godiol, who was returned to California on account of ill-health. Fr. Alban was assigned to Phœnix. To arouse the religious spirit the Fathers labored hard, and invited two Paulist priests from San Francisco, Revds Clark and Doherty, to conduct missions for the people. Thus a mission was preached to non-Catholics at the opera-house from January 17-23, and another for Catholics at the church from the 24-31, which both did much good.

AT Tempe, a Mexican station, 9 miles from Phœnix, which is visited twice a month, one Paulist held a mission for non-Catholics lasting four days. Other places visited by the Franciscans at irregular intervals are Fort Dowell, Mesa, Wickenburg, Santo Domingo, Boquai, and Gila-Bend.

THE bishop also gave the Fathers charge of all the Indians in Maricopa County. These Indians are distributed over three reservations near Phœnix, Tempe, and Gila Bend, but their condition morally and religiously is in a sad way. They are Pímas, Pápagos, and Maricopas, more or less mixed. These tribes have been visited by the Franciscans centuries before, so that here, too, the Fathers are not strangers. Nothing permanent could so far be accomplished. The future may be more successful with the help of charitable people. (1)

(1) Vide "Franciscans in Arizona."

LIST OF FRANCISCANS WHO DIED IN CALIFORNIA FROM 1769 TO 1897.

Date.	Name.	Mission.	Page.
1775.	Luis Jayme,	San Diego,	224.
1782.	Juan Crespi,	San Cárlos,	87.
1784.	Juan Figuer,	San Diego,	233.
1784.	José Antonio de Murguía,	Santa Clara,	327-328.
1784.	Junípero Serra,	San Cárlos,	103-105.
1789.	José Cavaller,	San Luis Obispo.	283.
1793.	Antonio Paterna,	Santa Barbara.	351.
1797.	Julian Lopez,	San Cárlos	253.
1800.	Juan Mariner,	San Diego.	235-236.
1800·	Vincente Fuster,	San Juan Capistrano,	316.
1801.	Francisco Pujol.	San Antonio.	249.
1803.	Fran. Mig. Sanchez,	San Gabriel	270.
1303.	Fermin Fr. Lasuen,	San Cárlos,	134-135.
1804.	Antonio Cruzado,	San Gabriel,	270.
1806.	Vincente Santa Maria,	San Buenaventura,	341.
1807.	Nicolás Lázaro,	San Diego,	412, 414.
1808.	Buenaventura Sitjar,	San Antonio,	262.
1808.	Andrés Dulanto,	San Juan Bautista,	400.
1810.	Marcelino Ciprés	San Luis Obispo,	285.
1811.	Francisco Dumetz,	San Gabriel,	272.
1812.	Pedro Panto,	San Diego,	239.
1812.	Juan Andrés Quintana,	Santa Cruz,	375.
1812.	José Antonio Urresti.	San Fernando	414.
1813.	José do Miguel,	San Gabriel,	272.
1814.	José Antonio Calzada,	Santa Inéz.	434.
1816.	Martin de Landaeta,	San Fernando,	412-414.
1818.	Florencio Ibañez,	La Soledad,	382-383.
1821.	Joaquin Pas'. Nuez,	San Gabriel,	273.
1821.	Juan Ullibarri,	San Fernando,	415.
1823.	José Francisco, Soñaz,	San Buenaventura,	312-13.
1823.	Mariano Payeras,	Purisima Concepcion,	366.
1824.	Antonio Rodriguez,	Purisima Concepcion,	366.
1824.	Juan Martin,	San Miguel,	406-407.
1825.	Estévan Tapis,	San Juan Bautista,	402.
1829.	Antonio Jaime.	Santa Barbara,	357.
1830.	Magin Catalá,	Santa Clara,	331-332.
1830.	Juan Bautista Sancho,	San Antonio,	263.
1831.	Gerómino Boscana,	San Gabriel,	273-74.
1831.	Francisco Suñer,	San Buenaventura,	344.

1831.	José Barona,	San Juan Capistrano,	321.
1833.	José Bern Sanchez.	San Gabriel,	275.
1833.	Luis Gil y Taboada,	San Luis Obispo,	287.
1834.	Francisco Javier Uría,	San Buenaventura,	344.
1835.	Vincente Fr. Sarría,	La Soledad,	385.
1836.	Pedro Cabot,	San Fernando,	416.
1836.	Márcos de Victoria,	Santa Inés,	435.
1838.	Fernando Martin,	San Diego,	241.
1839.	Rafael Moreno,	Santa Clara,	333.
1840.	Buenaventura Fortuny,	San Buenaventura,	344.
1840.	Felipe Arroyo de la Cuesta,	Santa Inés.	435-436.
1842.	Ramon Abella,	Purisima,	333.
1842.	Francisco G. Ibarra,	San Luis Rey,	427.
1845.	Juan Moreno,	Santa Inéz,	437.
1846.	García Diego, Rt. Rev.,	Santa Barbara,	198.
1846.	Narciso Duran,	Santa Barbara,	198-99.
1846.	José Maria Zalvidea,	San Luis Rey,	428.
1847.	Tomás El. Esténega,	San Gabriel,	277.
1848.	Vincente Pascual Oliva,	San Juan Capistrano,	322.
1850.	Blas Ordaz,	San Gabriel,	277.
1856.	José Joaquin Jimeno.	Santa Barbara,	200, 456.
1863.	José Alcina,	Santa Barbara,	458.
1875.	José Gonzalez Rubio,	Santa Barbara,	202.
1876.	Malachias Bannon,	Santa Barbara,	*
1884.	Francisco de Jesus Sanchez,	Santa Barbara,	362, 458.
1889.	Gabriel Rieman,	San Francisco,	468.
1890.	Aloysius Nauer,	San Francisco,	468.
1896.	Ferdinand Bergmeier	Santa Barbara,	207.
1896.	Servatius Altmicks,	Los Angeles,	207.
1896.	Clementin Deymann,	Phoenix, Arizona,	463.
1896.	Bonaventure Fox,	Santa Barbara,	458.
1897.	Francisco Álvarez,	San Luis Rey.	458. **

* According the Tabella Necrologico Sacerdotum Dioecesis Montereyensis,
** Father Alvares died on Saturday July 10th.

GENERAL INDEX.

U. I. O. G, D.

Corrigenda.

Page 8, line 2, read—ecclesiastical.
" 10, " 2, from bottom, omit—to,
" 16 " 7, " " . read—accompanied.
" 17, " 2, " " . read—succeeded.
" 19, note four, read—settlement.
" 20, line 6, from bottom, read—Juan Antonio Rioboo.
" 20, " 5, " " . read—establishment.
" 33, " 2, " " . read—Villuendas, Francisco.
" 43, " 17, " " . read—concluded.
" 66, line 9, from bottom, read—prudence.
" 84, " 8, from bottom, read—returning.
" 99, " 1, " " . read—mournful,
" 101, " 21, read—handkerchief.
" 111, " 2, read—necessary.
" 111, " 8, read—kings.
" 123, " 4, from bottom, read—1797.
" 127, note, read—missionaries.
" 132, " 10, from bottom, read—relations with.
" 138, " 27-28, omit clause—"then it seems stationed
                    at San Jose."
" 141, " 15, from bottom, read—F. J. Uria.
" 165, " 21, read—happened.
" 178, " 11, read—ecclesiastical.
" 191, " 19, read—declares.
" 194, " 18, read—Ambris.
" 200, " 2, read—preparatory.
" 200, " 13, read—announced.
" 203, " 12, read—recruit.
" 208, " 12, read—occurred.
" 207, " 14, read—interim.
" 216, " 10, from bottom, read—each.
" 234, " 13, read—past for part.
" 235, " 2, read—José.
" 254, " 8, read—slab.
" 264, " 4, read—seventy-five.
" 264, note line 2, read—south.
" 273, for note 21, read—3.
" 287, line 3, from bottom, read—dysentery
" 301, note line 11, read—truth.
" 342, " 17, read—Buenaventura.
" 414, " 7, from bottom read—transferred.
" 415, " 10, read—stationed.
" 417, " 9, from bottom, read—management.
" 422, " 22, read—Gerónimo.
" 429, " 21, read—religious.
" 430, " 15, from bottom, read—convent.
" 442, " 18, read—the ranchería.
" 495, " 43, for Arrellano, Fr., read—Arrellano, Rev.